Theology for Pilgrims

Also by Nicholas Lash

His Presence in the World (1968)
Newman on Development (1975)
Voices of Authority (1976)
Theology on Dover Beach (1979)
A Matter of Hope. A Theologian's Reflections on the Thought of Karl Marx (1981)
Theology on the Way to Emmaus (1986)
Easter in Ordinary: Reflections on Human Experience and the Knowledge of God (1988)
Believing Three Ways in One God. A Reading of the Apostles' Creed (1992)
The Beginning and the End of 'Religion' (1996)
Holiness, Speech and Silence (2004)
Seeing in the Dark (2005)

Theology for Pilgrims

Nicholas Lash

University of Notre Dame Press
Notre Dame, Indiana

Published in the United States by
University of Notre Dame Press
Notre Dame, Indiana 46556
www.undpress.nd.edu

Published in Great Britain by
Darton, Longman and Todd Ltd
1 Spencer Court
140-142 Wandsworth High Street
London SW18 4JJ

Library of Congress Cataloging-in-Publication Data

Lash, Nicholas.
Theology for pilgrims / by Nicholas Lash.
    p.   cm.
Includes index.
ISBN-13: 978-0-268-03409-2 (pbk. : alk. paper)
ISBN-10: 0-268-03409-5 (pbk. : alk. paper)
1. Theology. 2. Apologetics. 3. Catholic Church–
                            Doctrines.
    I. Title.
    BT77.L29   2008
    230–dc22   2008005183

Typeset by YHT Ltd, London
Printed and bound in Great Britain by Page Bros, Norwich, Norfolk

Contents

Acknowledgements and Sources

1. Where Does *The God Delusion* Come From?
A revised version of an article that appeared in *New Blackfriars* (September 2007), pp. 507–21.

2. The Impossibility of Atheism
A talk given at Downside Abbey (October 2007) and Oscott College (February 2008).

3. Amongst Strangers and Friends: Thinking of God in our Current Confusion
Previously published in *Finding God in All Things. Essays in Honor of Michael J. Buckley sj*, ed. Michael J. Himes and Stephen J. Pope (New York, Crossroad, 1996), pp. 53–67.

4. Recovering Contingency
Previously published in *Consciousness and Human Identity*, ed. John Cornwell (Oxford, Oxford University Press, 1998), pp. 197–211.

5. Renewed, Dissolved, Remembered: MacKinnon and Metaphysics
Previously published in *In Honour of Fergus Kerr op, on his Seventieth Birthday. Part II, New Blackfriars* (November 2001), pp. 486–98.

6. 'Visio Unica et Ordinata Scientiae'?
Previously published in *Restoring Faith in Reason*, ed. Laurence Paul Hemming and Susan Frank Parsons (London, SCM Press, 2002), pp. 225–37.

7. 'An Immense Darkness' and the Tasks of Theology
Previously published in *God, Truth and Witness: Engaging Stanley Hauerwas*, ed. L. Gregory Jones, Reinhard Hütter, C. Rosalee Velloso Ewell (Grand Rapids, Mich., Brazos Press, 2005), pp. 257–79.

8. Reason, Fools and Rameau's Nephew
Previously published in *New Blackfriars* (September 1995), pp. 368–77.

9. Where Does Holy Teaching Leave Philosophy? Questions on Milbank's Aquinas
Previously published in *Modern Theology* (October 1999), pp. 433–44.

10. Conversation in Context
Previously published in *Between Poetry and Politics: Essays in Honour of Enda McDonagh*, ed. Linda Hogan and Barbara FitzGerald (Dublin, The Columba Press, 2003), pp. 51–66.

11. Sebastiano in Pallara: A Pilgrim's Tale
Previously published in *Jesus Christ Crucified and Risen: Essays in Spirituality and Theology in Honor of Dom Sebastian Moore*, ed. William P. Loewe and Vernon J. Gregson (Collegeville, Minn., Liturgical Press, 1998), pp. 1–12.

12. Fear of the Dark
Previously published in *Modern Theology* (April 2000), pp. 203–14.

13. Travellers' Fare
Previously published in *New Blackfriars* (March 2007), pp. 128–41.

14. The Subversiveness of Catholicity
A revised version of the 1999 Gore Memorial Lecture, delivered in Westminster Abbey, 17 November 1999.

15. Vatican II: Of Happy Memory – and Hope?'
Previously published in *Unfinished Journey: The Church 40 Years after Vatican II: Essays for John Wilkins*, ed. Austen Ivereigh (New York and London, Continuum, 2003), pp. 13–31.

16. What Happened at Vatican II?
Previously published in *The Pastoral Review* (November/December 2005), pp. 15–19; also published as a Catholics for a Changing Church pamphlet.

Introduction

Theologians, like philosophers, dread the question: 'What is it that you people actually *do*?' To come up with an answer that would satisfy oneself, let alone the curious interlocutor, is not easy. 'Reading old books', I used to say to my brother-in-law, a well-respected surgeon, whose hobbies were carpentry and photography but whose library was limited to the half-dozen most up-to-date textbooks in his professional field. Most likely, an answer that might make sense would be intelligible only to someone already halfway persuaded of the value of the enterprise. If you were to think of theology as somehow adding to knowledge in the way that one of the sciences is supposed to do, you would be hard put to show exactly how. Nor does it sound very plausible to claim that theology opens up deeper understanding of human nature in the way that a great novel or a film or a Shakespeare play can do. Much of the most valuable theological work is, of course, just hard slog: scholarly research, palaeographical, exegetical, historical, and so forth, helping in often very small ways to increase our knowledge of what has been done and thought in the past. To the extent that this kind of scholarship documents where we have come from, it will often explain and illuminate where and who we are now. Theological work at a more philosophical level, such as Nicholas Lash has undertaken, is perhaps a bit more like political theory or psychoanalysis, in the sense that it can open up possibilities of emancipation from certain oppressive myths and mystifications that repeatedly gain a grip on people's minds.

The most persistent of these myths, from the philosophical theologian's point of view, is the idea that 'God' is an entity of some kind. What Nicholas Lash has insisted on for decades now is that the theologian's primary function is regulative rather than descriptive. By this he means that the essential and indispensable point of doing theology is to ensure that when we refer to God it is God on whom we set our hearts and not some thing which we mistake for God. Ever since his inaugural lecture in the Norris–Hulse chair at Cambridge in 1978, Nicholas Lash has insisted on theology as 'critical', even endorsing his predecessor Donald MacKinnon's term 'censorial'. Subsequently, in a much more

focused development, he has characterised expounding the doctrine of God as offering a set of 'protocols against idolatry' – a
splendid phrase. The 'critical' dimension of the theologian's task,
as he puts it, 'is to be sought in the direction of the critique of
idolatry', which is to say: 'the stripping away of the veils of self-
assurance by which we seek to protect our faces from exposure to
the mystery of God.' What this means, in particular, is that we have
repeatedly to keep resisting our proclivities to regard God as some
kind of object – whether or not we regard this object as actually
existing. As the first chapter of this book indicates, the picture of
God as some kind of object – non-existent in this case – is taken
for granted in the currently most celebrated attack on religious
belief. Even more instructively, the picture of God as an object of
some kind seems absolutely obvious and beyond contestation to
many of the hundreds of thousands of eager readers of this and
similar ventures in atheistic polemics. The theologian's work is
never done, or evidently even begun.

It is, however, not only self-styled atheists who take for granted
this picture of God as an object of some kind. On Nicholas Lash's
account, atheists are no more prone to this form of idolatry than
the rest of us. Rather, this is why, in another memorable phrase,
he insists that the Christian life is a sort of 'pedagogy': a 'school'
where learning not to refer to God as some kind of thing is one
element in the purification of mind and heart, to which Christians
are called. 'To learn to worship only God, only the holy and
unmasterable mystery that is not the world nor any part of it, is an
unending task', as one of Lash's many formulations runs.

There is, of course, much more to learning to worship the only
true God than seeking emancipation from the grip of the picture
of God as an entity of some kind. Whether by good luck or divine
grace many people may have escaped being captivated by that
picture. Nevertheless, temptations to some form or other of idolatry seem pretty universal. As far as Christians are concerned, the
Bible might even be read as one long, chequered story of how
God weaned the faithful from their desire to worship false gods –
painfully, traumatically, and with much backsliding. More
recently, in our own academic context, there has been interest in
reconnecting theology and spirituality – which is, in effect, to
regard the practice of 'negative theology' as itself a 'spiritual
exercise'.

Here, we may even say, Nicholas Lash keeps returning to the
paradigm case of the theological work of St Thomas Aquinas. In
the prologue to the *Summa Theologiae* Thomas proposes to play his
part in *sacra doctrina*, 'holy teaching', in accordance with a pedagogy, *secundum ordinem disciplinae*, which would be appropriate to
the 'training of beginners', *ad eruditionem incipientium*.

Historically, of course, Thomas was composing a book with the young Dominican friars in mind whom he was teaching: they were 'bored and confused', so he believed, by having no other way of learning but listening to running commentary on Scripture and sitting in on academic disputations. In fact, since he died before completing the work, and left no 'school' of informed and enthusiastic students, we do not know exactly how Thomas intended or expected the *Summa* to be used. He evidently assumed that the training was not mere communication of information about God, in a neutral academic setting. He could not have imagined that possibility. Rather, he seeks to communicate 'the things that belong to the Christian religion' – and we may take it, with Lash, that *christiana religio* means the 'schooling' in liturgy, contemplation, virtue, penance, and so on, which characterised the community of friars among whom Thomas lived.

Historically, it has to be said, Thomas's *Summa Theologiae* took decades, indeed centuries, to make its way, even in the Dominican Order, as its intended pedagogy in the schooling of beginners in the Christian life – if it ever really did. Obviously, proposing that we see the church – the Church? – as a school of contemplation, as Lash suggests, a place where people *learn to learn*, to educate each other in attentiveness to one another, and to educate themselves in attentiveness to the self-disclosure of the hidden God – that seems to go far beyond what Thomas may, perhaps vainly, have hoped for in training the beginners in his care. And yet, granted that, since the proclivity to idolatry is known to be capable of multiple mutations, and perhaps finally ineradicable, the task is never ending – what is more worthwhile for a Christian theologian? In the 'school' in which 'holy teaching' takes place, one of the principal tasks will always be to learn how not to speak of God – how not to picture God. In this respect we are surely all beginners, and, if Lash is right, we always remain so.

Nicholas Lash must have commented on texts on many occasions (as he does so illuminatingly here with regard to Conrad's *Heart of Darkness*). He has certainly zestfully engaged in disputation (as in half the chapters of this book!). The upshot is never boring or confusing. However, he has not ventured on any pedagogical adventure even remotely comparable with the *Summa Theologiae*. More realistically, he has not sought to write up the notes of the many lecture courses that he gave over the years, to constitute his own 'dogmatics'. The intellectual environment in which theology is practised in the United Kingdom is, for whatever reason, not conducive to the production of systematic theologies – any more than, in the English-speaking analytical tradition, philosophical work is likely to issue in comprehensive position statements. The preferred mode of expression is journal-length articles – essays – which may then be gathered, as in this collection. This does not mean, however, that theologians (and philosophers for that matter) do not have distinctive and coherent positions and agendas. Often enough, also, these positions and agendas, recast with originality and flair for current situations, remain in deep continuity with the questions that have preoccupied philosophers and theologians all along, from the earliest times.

In this sense, certainly, Nicholas Lash's essays on the doctrine of God belong to the classical tradition of Catholic Christian theology. He may not be, or wish to be, regarded as a 'Thomist'. There are, anyway, other ways of approaching and organising the data of Christian revelation, as Thomas was well aware when he deliberately chose to consider everything 'in relationship to God', s*ecundum ordinem ad Deum*, or 'in terms of God', *sub ratione Dei*, the phrase that Lash prefers (cf. *Summa Theologiae* Ia, 1, 7). Though accounts of Christian doctrine might be – have been – constructed on the basis of the history of salvation, or by focusing on Christ and the Church, as Thomas reports, his own option is radically theocentric. For Lash, as for Thomas, the focus of 'holy teaching' is not the Bible story or Christ and the Church, let alone religious experience; it is nothing other than the mystery of God and everything in relation to that mystery which is its origin and destiny.

As Lash likes to emphasise, it is 'everything' – 'all things', *omnia* – that are considered in 'holy teaching', since everything is relative to God as origin and end, as source and destiny. One of the theologian's tasks, as he puts it, is to 'seek at the level of reflection, for that *connectedness* which the liturgy enacts and exhibits dramatically' – which is another way in which theological critique of idolatry fits into the wider environment of Christian life as a whole.

Above all, however, Lash keeps returning to Thomas's lapidary announcement at the outset of his most famous exposition of the doctrine of God, to the effect that the question to be considered is 'not so much how God is but *how God is not*' (ST Ia, prologue). The initiation of the beginners that Thomas envisages in the *Summa Theologiae* is a step-by-step consideration of the ways in which God *does not exist* (Ia, 3, prologue): relentlessly denying of God everything that is inappropriate, everything that is characteristic of things in the material world, and, above all, that God belongs to any category of kind, even to the category of substances (article 5). God, in short, is not an object of any kind. Or, to put it differently, we have to revise our concept of 'exists' when we think about God.

As these essays show, Nicholas Lash is interested in many other theological matters. In particular, he raises questions about some current interpretations of the achievement and aftermath of the Second Vatican Council. The centre of his attention is, however, as it always will be for a theologian in the classical tradition of Thomas Aquinas, on the question of God, and that means on the question of how to speak – or rather of how not to speak – of God. What we have to learn, as Lash puts it, is: 'A disciplined sense of unease about what still eludes us, a sense that there *is* something that *does* elude us, the sense that our understanding is inadequate to something we are still only half aware of'.

In this respect, we may conclude that what theologians actually *do*, as Nicholas Lash demonstrates, is to tirelessly, and in his case with wit, understanding and imagination, keep alerting us to the need for 'protocols against idolatry' – against our inveterate tendency to stray after 'strange gods'.

Fergus Kerr

PART ONE

Thinking of God Without Losing Our Way

Chapter 1

Where Does *The God Delusion* Come From?

The puzzling success of a deplorable book

Reviewing *The God Delusion* in *Science*, the distinguished journal of the American Association for the Advancement of Science, Michael Shermer – contributing editor of *Scientific American* and founding editor of *Skeptic* magazine – tells us that the book 'deserves multiple readings, not just as an important work of science, but as a great work of literature'. I find it difficult to decide which of these two descriptions is the more astonishing![1]

On the other hand, an American geneticist who believes Dawkins' earlier book, *The Selfish Gene*, to be 'the best work of popular science ever written', regrets his failure, in *The God Delusion*, 'to engage religious thought in any serious way', and judges 'One reason for the lack of extended argument' in the book to be simply that 'Dawkins doesn't seem very good at it'.[2] Meanwhile, Timothy Jenkins, Dean of Jesus College, Cambridge, an anthropologist and theologian who was once a pupil of Dawkins, says of the book that its author 'sounds like an *autodidact* – a man of considerable intelligence and wide reading, but insufficiently acquainted with the disciplines and histories that lie behind what he has read. He simply believes that the books he agrees with are true, and the books he disagrees with wrong.' 'Although', says Jenkins, Dawkins 'claims to be a scientist (as, indeed, in real life he has been), there is no evidence of a scientific approach nor of scientific habits of mind', 'no notion of evaluating evidence',[3] for example.

Although the central target of Dawkins' unrelenting invective appears to be biblical fundamentalism (an easy sparring partner because Dawkins is simply a fundamentalist in reverse: working with the same picture of religion, the same account of how the

---

1. Michael Shermer, 'Arguing for Atheism', *Science*, vol. 315, 26 January 2007.
2. H. Allen Orr, professor of biology in the University of Rochester, reviewing the book in the *New York Review of Books*, 11 January 2007.
3. Unpublished paper, cited with the author's permission.

Bible is best read – the fundamentalists taking it all to be true, while Dawkins takes it all to be false), he supposes himself to be casting his net a great deal wider. 'I am not attacking any particular version of God or gods. I am attacking God, all gods, anything and everything supernatural, wherever and whenever they have been or will be invented.'[4]

Dawkins makes much of the fact that he is an academic: biologist, Fellow of the Royal Society, at present occupying Oxford's chair in 'the public understanding of science'. Now, it is a fundamental feature of good academic work in *any* field that it is undertaken with a passion for accurate description and disinterested respect for the materials with which one is working. Dawkins, the biologist, seems not to have acquired the mental discipline necessary for work in the humanities and social sciences. One cannot imagine a physicist holding an atomic particle, or a zoologist a yak, with the same sustained contempt and loathing, the same cavalier disregard for accurate description, the same ignorance of the literature, with which Dawkins treats all religious beliefs, ideas and practices. And, in one of the very few places in which a work of theology is mentioned, he devotes three pages to 'Thomas Aquinas's "Proofs"'.[5] What, in fact, we are given is a shoddy misrepresentation of Aquinas' arguments, with no indication of where they might be found, what others have made of them, or what purpose they were constructed to serve.

As Professor Terry Eagleton pointed out, in *The London Review of Books*, 'card-carrying rationalists like Dawkins ... are in one sense the least well-equipped to understand what they castigate, since they don't believe there is anything there ... worth understanding ... The more they detest religion, the more ill-informed their criticisms of it tend to be.'[6]

However, *simply* to counter polemic with polemic does not help to move things on. What I want to do in this essay is, firstly, to indicate in a little more detail some of what I take to be the book's chief weaknesses but then, having done so, try to throw some light on its popularity by setting it in the context of some partly real, partly imagined cultural tensions and conflicts that have been with us for around two hundred years.

4. Richard Dawkins, *The God Delusion* (London, Bantam Press, 2006), p. 36.
5. Ibid., pp. 77–9.
6. Terry Eagleton, 'Lunging, Flailing, Mispunching', *The London Review of Books*, 19 October 2006.

God is not one of the things that there are

Dawkins first formulates what he calls 'the God hypothesis' as the supposition that 'there exists a superhuman, supernatural intelligence who deliberately designed and created the universe and everything in it, including us'.[7] This account is, it seems, to be taken at face value, as a straightforward description of the kind of thing God is. (Perhaps not *quite* straightforward, given the use of the term 'supernatural'. This adjective is used again, and again, and again but is never examined; it does no *work* in his argument and he appears quite ignorant of the history of its usage.)

Central to the book is Dawkins' conviction that belief in God is a matter of supposing there to be, above and beyond the familiar world with all its furniture, one more big and powerful thing. I shall say something about 'belief' later on. For the time being, let us stay with this question of where the concept of God is to be *located* on the map of the things we talk about and the ways in which we talk about them.

According to the geneticist whom I quoted earlier, 'One of the most interesting questions about Dawkins's book is why it was written. Why does Dawkins feel he has anything significant to say about religion and what gives him the sense of authority presumably needed to say it at book length?'[8]

At one point Dawkins asks, almost petulantly: 'Why shouldn't we comment on God, as scientists?'[9] I can think of no reason

---

7. *The God Delusion*, op. cit., p. 31.
8. Orr, loc. cit.
9. *The God Delusion*, op. cit., p. 55. In similar vein, the distinguished physicist Stephen Weinberg has written: 'I find it disturbing that Thomas Nagel in the New Republic dismisses Dawkins as an "amateur philosopher", while Terry Eagleton in the *London Review of Books* sneers at Dawkins for his lack of theological training. Are we to conclude that opinions on matters of philosophy or religion are only to be expressed by experts, not mere scientists or other common folk? It is like saying that only political scientists are justified in expressing views on politics. Eagleton's judgement is particularly inappropriate; it is like saying that no one is entitled to judge the validity of astrology who cannot cast a horoscope' (Stephen Weinberg, reviewing *The God Delusion* in the *TLS*, 17 January 2007).

However, one does not need to be an 'expert' on anything in particular to know that this is a thoroughly bad argument. Casting a horoscope is a practice of some kind, however misguided. Eagleton did not criticise Dawkins for lacking expertise in religious practice – praying, for example. He *did* criticise him for pontificating about Christian theology (which is a vast body of texts and arguments) while being apparently wholly ignorant of it.

whatsoever why a biologist like Dawkins should not comment on the Franco-Prussian War, the paintings of Fra Angelico or the Saudi Arabian penal system. In all such cases, however, if the biologist's comments are to be worth hearing, he needs to do his homework. I doubt if Dawkins would disagree. The question is, then, why does he suppose himself exempt from the necessity of homework when commenting on the question of God?

The answer seems to lie in the curious and repeated insistence that 'God's existence or non-existence is a scientific fact about the universe'; that 'the presence or absence of a creative super-intelligence is unequivocally a scientific question', and so on.[10]

The first thing to be said about this, I think, is that there *are* no 'scientific' facts. There are just *facts*, what is the case. And the unimaginable diversity of things that are the case may be considered in an immense variety of ways, including through the use of those patterns of disciplined investigation which we call 'scientific'. What Dawkins seems to mean is that the existence of God is an *empirical* question.[11] His confidence on the matter rests on his ignorance of the vast and often dauntingly difficult philosophical literature dedicated to considering in what sense this is and is not so. But even if it *were* as self-evident as he supposes that the question of God's existence is an empirical question, why would that fact alone render him competent, as a *biologist*, to comment on it? Biologists are trained to study living organisms. There may, indeed, be people who worship plants or animals and perhaps Richard Dawkins might, as a biologist, help to persuade them of their imprudence, but Jews, and Christians, and Muslims, are not amongst their number!

> Moreover, should someone wish, not merely to 'express views' on politics, but also to denounce, as a bundle of dangerous and irrational nonsense, all political opinions and whatever has been written on political science, then they should first take the elementary precaution of reading the stuff.

10. *The God Delusion*, op. cit., pp. 50, 58–9.
11. 'We haven't yet understood the meaning of the word God if we think that God is something to be found, like an HIV vaccine or aliens in space. Another way of saying the same would be to assert that anything that fits neatly into the world can't possibly be the God who created the world. The search for God is not about reason finding an object of study' (Terrance W. Klein, 'Adventures in Alterity: Wittgenstein, Aliens, Anselm and Aquinas', *New Blackfriars*, January 2007, pp. 73–86; p. 82). Or, as Hegel remarked nearly 200 years ago: 'God does not offer himself for observation' (*Lectures on the Philosophy of Religion*, 1, *Introduction and Concept of Religion*, ed. Peter C. Hodgson [Berkeley, University of California Press, 1984], p. 258).

Belief in God

Where the grammar of the word 'God' is concerned, Dawkins, ignorant of centuries of Jewish, Christian and Islamic reflection on the 'naming' of the holy and utterly transcendent mystery on which the world depends, persists in taking for granted that 'God' is the name of a non-existent thing, a particular, specifiable, fictitious entity.

His understanding of the notion of 'belief in God' (to which I now turn) is as crass and ill-informed as his understanding of what the word 'God' means. He takes it for granted that to 'believe in God' is to be of the opinion that God exists. However, as Saint Augustine pointed out sixteen centuries ago, even the devils know that God exists! One may know quite well that God exists and yet be entirely lacking in the virtue of faith. Dawkins defines faith as 'belief without evidence'.[12] Christianity does not. To believe in God, to have faith in God, as Christianity understands these things, is (to quote Augustine again) 'in believing to love, in believing to delight, in believing to walk towards him, and be incorporated amongst the limbs and members of his body'.[13]

To be a Jew, or a Christian, or a Muslim, is to be a member of a particular *people*: a people whose identity is specified by particular habits of memory and ritual, of understanding and relationship and hope. Dawkins tells the story of a young Afghan who was 'sentenced to death for converting to Christianity'. The story is a tragic commentary on the extent to which the relationships between two traditions, two 'peoples', which should (and sometimes have) understood each other to be 'cousins', have sometimes deteriorated into bitter conflict. Dawkins, however, sees things differently. 'All [the young Afghan] did', he remarks, 'was change his mind. Internally and privately, he changed his mind. He entertained certain *thoughts*.'[14] Not so. He publicly changed his allegiance from one people to another.

Not only does Dawkins suppose 'believing in God' to be a matter of privately entertaining the opinion that a thing called 'God' exists, but he also imagines that those who *are* of this opinion are committed to refusing to think about it. 'Faith', he tells us, '(belief without evidence) is a virtue. The more your beliefs defy

---

12. *The God Delusion*, op. cit., p. 199.
13. See Augustine's *Commentary on John, xxix* (*PL*, xxxv, 1631). The somewhat free translation is my own: see Nicholas Lash, *Believing Three Ways in One God* (London, SCM Press, 1992), p. 20.
14. *The God Delusion*, op. cit., p. 287. For his insistence on the 'private' character of religious belief, see also pp. 289–90.

the evidence, the more virtuous you are.'[15] Instead of providing any *evidence* that religious believers are, characteristically, thus perversely irrational, he ploughs on: 'There are some weird things (such as the Trinity, transubstantiation, incarnation) that we are not *meant* to understand. Don't even *try* to understand one of these, for the attempt might destroy it.'[16] That sentence gives me a strange feeling, as I sit reading it in my study – the walls of which are filled, from top to bottom, with volumes dedicated to attempts at just such understanding. It really is most disquieting that a book so polemically ignorant of the extent to which faith's quest for understanding has, for century after century, been central to the practice and identity of those educational enterprises which we call the great religious traditions of the world, should receive the plaudits that it has.

How to take texts

There is a marvellous passage in one of Cardinal Newman's notebooks that is worth quoting at some length:

> We can only speak of Him, whom we reason about but have not seen, in the terms of our experience. When we reflect on Him and put into words our thoughts about Him, we are forced to transfer to a new meaning ready made words, which primarily belong to objects of time and place. We are aware, while we do so, that they are inadequate. We can only remedy their insufficiency by confessing it. We can do no more than put ourselves on the guard as to our own proceeding, and protest against it, while we do adhere to it. We can only set right one error of expression by another. By this method of antagonism we steady our minds, not so as to reach their object, but to point them in the right direction; as in an algebraical process we might add and subtract in series, approximating little by little, by saying and unsaying, to a positive result.[17]

My question to Richard Dawkins is this: given the *centrality* of this insistence, in Christian thought, for two millennia, on the near-impossibility of speaking appropriately of God, is it ignorance or sheer perversity that leads him wholly to ignore it, and to treat all statements about God as if they were characteristically taken, by

15. Ibid., p. 199.
16. Ibid., p. 200.
17. John Henry Newman, *The Theological Papers of John Henry Newman on Faith and Certainty*, ed. J. D. Holmes (Oxford, Clarendon Press, 1976), p. 102.

their users, as straightforward and literal description? He would, as I see it, have no defence along the lines of: 'I am talking about the religion of ordinary people, not the shifty evasions of theologians', because most Christians are not fundamentalists. They know that they do not comprehend the mystery of God, and that what we say is said in metaphor and parable.

'Of course', says Dawkins at one point, 'irritated theologians will protest that we don't take the book of Genesis literally *any more*. But that is my whole point! We pick and choose which bits of scripture to believe, which bits to write off as allegories.'[18] Notice that 'any more'. Dawkins takes it for granted that Christians have traditionally been fundamentalists, but that as the plausibility of fundamentalist readings of the text has been eroded by the march of reason, 'irritated theologians' protest that they no longer take biblical texts literally. Paradoxically, he has the story almost completely upside down. Patristic and medieval theology worked with a rich, at times almost uncontrollable diversity of 'senses of scripture'. Passages of Scripture gave up their sense only by being read in many different ways. Fundamentalism – in the sense of the privileging of the meaning which a passage, taken out of any context, appears *a priori*, on the surface, to possess – is, as the Old Testament scholar James Barr demonstrated thirty years ago, a by-product of modern rationalism: of the privileging of timeless and direct description, of mathematics over metaphor, prose over poetry.[19]

What I earlier described as Richard Dawkins' 'fundamentalism in reverse' comes through clearly in his curious insistence that the only way to take a biblical text seriously is to 'believe it' literally. To take it allegorically (for example) is to 'write it off'. Somewhere at the back of all this is the myth (the roots of which lie back in ancient Greece) that truth can only be expressed through prosaically direct description, and that all other literary forms are forms of fiction, incapable of expressing truth.

Two more points, still with that passage about 'irritated theologians' in mind. In the first place, what are we to make of the suggestion that there are only two things to do with texts: you either 'write them off' or you 'believe' them? It is, I think, unlikely that someone with so fragile a grasp on the ways in which texts – ancient or modern, religious or secular – are best read should have produced a 'great work of literature'.

In the second place, it is, I suspect, his preoccupation with contemporary American fundamentalism (treated, throughout the book, as more or less paradigmatic of 'religion' across the

18. *The God Delusion*, op. cit., p. 238 (my stress).
19. See James Barr, *Fundamentalism* (London, SCM Press, 1977).

board) which leads him to suppose that decisions *not* to construe
particular passages of Scripture 'literally' are *arbitrary* decisions. As
a result, the question: 'By what criteria do you *decide* which passages are symbolic, which literal?'[20] is taken rhetorically, as if the
absence of appropriate criteria were self-evident. He does not
notice that a good deal of any first-year student of the Bible's time
is spent learning how to distinguish between different 'literary
forms'.

Right and wrong

One of the strangest features of *The God Delusion* is the super-
ficiality of what Dawkins has to say on ethics. It is as if he is not
really *interested* in ethics, perhaps in consequence of the tendency
of Darwinian anthropology to render the notion of human freedom problematic. He is, however, interested in subverting the
belief that, without belief in God, we would behave more badly
than we do: 'Do we really need policing – whether by God or by
each other – in order to stop us from behaving in a selfish and
criminal manner? I dearly want to believe that I do not need such
surveillance – and nor, dear reader, do you.'[21] He is, of course,
insistent that religion does much damage in the world, and that
the religious education of children is a form of child abuse: 'isn't
it always a form of child abuse to label children as possessors of
beliefs that they are too young to have thought about?'[22]
    Dawkins deplores 'the unhealthy preoccupation of early
Christian theologians with sin. They could have devoted their
pages and their sermons to extolling the sky splashed with stars, or
mountains and green forests, seas and dawn choruses. These are
occasionally mentioned, but the Christian focus is overwhelmingly
on sin sin sin sin sin sin sin. What a nasty little preoccupation to
have dominating your life.'[23] Leaving aside the suspicion that
Professor Dawkins has not read very widely in the Fathers of the
Church, the complaint is somewhat curious. How lamentable for
the Fathers to have been preoccupied with the damage done by
human beings to themselves, to others, and to the world of which
we form a part, through egotism, violence and greed; through
warfare, slavery, starvation! What a wiser atheist than Dawkins
might at least agree to be a terrifyingly dark tapestry of
inhumanity, Christians call 'sin', knowing all offences against the
creature to be disobedience to the Creator. And it is especially

20. *The God Delusion*, op. cit., p. 247 (his stress).
21. Ibid., p. 228.
22. Ibid., p. 315.
23. Ibid., p. 252.

paradoxical that Dawkins should deem concern for the dreadful things that human beings do to be a 'nasty little preoccupation' at a time when we are made daily more aware of the perhaps already uncontrollable extent to which our self-indulgent egotism threatens terminally to damage the 'green forests, seas and dawn choruses'.

Complexity and evidence

We have already noticed Dawkins' idiosyncratic description of faith as 'belief without evidence'. And, because there is no evidence for God, he sees no 'good reason to suppose that theology ... is a subject at all'.[24] However, he never, at any point, addresses the fundamental question: what would *count* as evidence for God?

His failure to do so stems partly, I suspect, from the fact that he is not very good at tackling philosophical questions and partly from his unshakeable conviction (to which I have referred already) that the question of God is an empirical question: a question about a real or fictional *thing* or entity of an unusual kind.

This comes across in his handling of an argument of which he seems to be extremely proud: 'I keep saying and will say again, however little we know about God, the one thing we can be sure of is that he would have to be very very complex, and presumably irreducibly so.'[25]

This would, presumably, be the case if God were a material object, a structure with parts, an organism with a very powerful brain, the product of evolutionary processes. Which Richard Dawkins takes for granted that he must be: 'A God capable of continuously monitoring and controlling the individual status of every particle in the universe *cannot* be simple. His existence is going to need a mammoth explanation in its own right.'[26] We seem to be talking about the Wizard of Oz, not the creator of this world and all the worlds there are. Exasperated, Dawkins takes to patronising Professor Keith Ward, who 'seems not to understand what it means to say of something that it is simple'.[27] I suspect, however, that it is Richard Dawkins who has failed to notice that simplicity, like most interesting words, has a wide variety of uses and that when we say that God is simple, we are speaking, as it

24. Ibid., p. 57.
25. Ibid., p. 125.
26. Ibid., p. 149.
27. Ibid., p. 150. For an interesting collection of essays on styles of explanation in the sciences, see John Cornwell (ed.), *Explanations* (Oxford, Oxford University Press, 2004).

were, of a simplicity on the *other* side, not on *this* side, of complexity; a simplicity more like wisdom than like simple-
mindedness.

From religion to science: a story of progress?

Turning from some of the major weaknesses of Dawkins' book to
the larger question of what it is about the climate of the times that
enables so ill-informed and badly argued a tirade to be so widely
welcomed by so many intelligent and educated people, I take as
my text a passage near the end of *The God Delusion* which seems to
me of exceptional importance:

> Religion has at one time or another been thought to fill four
> roles in human life: explanation, exhortation, consolation
> and inspiration. Historically, religion aspired to *explain* our
> own existence and the nature of the universe in which we
> find ourselves. In this role, it is now completely superseded
> by science.[28]

It is the second and third of these three sentences on which I
propose to concentrate: 'Historically, religion aspired to *explain*
our own existence and the nature of the universe in which we find
ourselves. In this role, it is now completely superseded by science.'
I shall do so under three heads: (1) there is no such thing as
'science'; (2) there is no such thing as 'religion'; (3) culture wars
and the paradox of 'progress'.

There is no such thing as 'science'

Martin Rudwick's magnificent study of the emergence of the
modern science of geology at the end of the eighteenth and the
beginning of the nineteenth centuries grew out of the Tarner
Lectures which he delivered in Cambridge in 1996.[29] The first of
those lectures was entitled 'The anglophone heresy of "science"'.

Scientia means knowledge and, in modern culture, 'science' and
its cognates mean the disciplined and critical investigation of
reality. But reality has many different aspects, requiring many
different methods of investigation. In French, or German, or
Italian, the range of *sciences,* or *Wissenschaften,* or *scienze,* will cover
the entire lecture list of a modern university. (There is, in France,
an extremely learned and reputable journal entitled *La Revue des*

28. *The God Delusion*, op. cit., p. 347 (his stress).
29. See Martin S. J. Rudwick, *Bursting the Limits of Time: The Reconstruction
of Geohistory in the Age of Revolution* (Chicago, University of Chicago
Press, 2005).

Sciences Philosophiques et Théologiques.) Only in the English-speaking world do we speak of 'science' in the singular, a habit (or heresy!) which has two unfortunate sets of consequences. On the one hand, it encourages the illusion that there is, roughly speaking, some single set of procedures which qualify as 'scientific'. On the other, it encourages the expectation, where knowledge is concerned, that 'science' is to be favourably contrasted with something else: 'arts' perhaps, or 'letters'.

When C. P. Snow gave the Rede Lecture in Cambridge in 1959, on 'The Two Cultures and the Scientific Revolution', he was expressing an *anxiety* in British culture concerning what many perceived to be 'a profound mutual suspicion and incomprehension' between those he called 'the literary intellectuals' and the natural scientists.[30]

Although the roots of this division can be traced back to the development, in the seventeenth century, of new standards of empirical investigation of the natural world, it is worth bearing in mind that 'the Enlightenment's great intellectual monument', Diderot's *Encyclopédie*, no more represents human knowledge as structured around a division corresponding to what we would now call 'the sciences' and 'the humanities' than had Francis Bacon's *Advancement of Learning* a century earlier (on which the design of the *Encyclopédie* was based).[31]

The construction of this twofold division was a nineteenth-century achievement, and the 'anglophone heresy' seems to have made its first appearance in 1867, in the *Dublin Review*. 'We shall', said W. G. Ward, 'use the word "science" in the sense which Englishmen so commonly give to it; as expressing physical and experimental science, to the exclusion of theological and metaphysical.'[32]

The point is this. Whenever one comes across the concept of 'science', in the singular, being used (as Dawkins does) to support sweeping assertions to the effect that *here*, and here alone, is truth to be obtained, then one is in the presence neither of science, nor of history, but ideology.

There is no such thing as 'religion'

There are, then, sciences galore, but no single enterprise which would count as 'science'. The story of 'religion' is a little different.

---

30. See Stefan Collini, 'Introduction' to C. P. Snow, *The Two Cultures* (Cambridge, Cambridge University Press, 1993), pp. vii–viii.
31. Collini, loc. cit. See below, the tables at end of chapter 8, pp. 132–6.
32. Cited by Collini, op. cit., pp. xi–xii.

In the Middle Ages, *religio* was a virtue, a kind of justice. Justice is the virtue of giving people and things their due. Religion is the virtue of giving God God's due. On this account, there are two ways in which people may fail to be religious. They may fail by treating God as a creature: as some fact or feature of the world, some entity or idea which we might pick over, master or manipulate. (Dawkins is irreligious in this way, treating God, as he does, as a fictional feature of the world.) On the other hand, people may fail to be religious by treating some fact or feature of the world as God: by setting their hearts on, bowing down before, worshipping, themselves, their country, money, sex or 'reason'. (Dawkins is drawn to irreligion in this way as well, through idolisation of evolutionary processes.)

In the fifteenth century, as the Latin word *religio* moved into English, it did so to name communities of men and women whose lives were specifically dedicated to the exercise of the virtue of religion. Thus, what were then called 'the religions of England' we would refer to as religious orders. Then, during the sixteenth and seventeenth centuries, the sense of the word shifted from naming a virtue to naming a set of propositions or beliefs.[33]

A final, fatal shift occurred as an outcome of the struggles usually known as the 'Wars of Religion'. The title is anachronistic, because these were not 'religious' conflicts necessitating the emergence of the State – to keep the peace; 'they were in fact themselves the birthpangs of the State ... for what was at issue in these wars was the very creation of religion as a set of privately held beliefs without direct political relevance'.[34]

In contemporary religious studies there is, notoriously, immense and irresolvable confusion as to what 'religion' might mean. The word now carries a range of meanings all the way from Durkheim's definition: 'the system of symbols by means of which society becomes conscious of itself'[35] to the incoherent, but still widespread, survival of seventeenth-century attempts to 'privatise' the notion.

We are still quite often told that we must keep 'religion' out of

33. See William T. Cavanaugh, ' "A Fire Strong Enough to Consume the House": The Wars of Religion and the Rise of the State', *Modern Theology* (October 1995), pp. 397–420; pp. 403–4. Cavanaugh's remarks on the history of the concept of religion, in this fine essay, draw upon Wilfred Cantwell Smith, *The Meaning and the End of Religion* (New York, Macmillan, 1962).

34. Cavanaugh, art. cit., p. 398.

35. Emile Durkheim, *Suicide: A Study in Sociology*, trans. John A. Spaulding and George Simpson (London, Routledge and Kegan Paul, 1952), p. 312.

'politics', which is interpreted as a requirement to keep private passions and personal beliefs out of the cool rationality of the 'public square'. Setting aside this curiously unreal account of how, in fact, the political process works, consider its incoherence from another angle. We speak of Judaism, Christianity and Islam as 'religions', and yet the history of these three peoples, and of the relationships between them, constitutes a large part of the history of Europe and the Near East (and, in recent centuries, of many other parts of the world as well). And whatever is to be said of those Indian traditions which we usually lump together as 'Hinduism', the Great *Kumbh Mela*, the gathering, every twelve years, of up to thirty million people, for a month, at the confluence of the Ganges and the Yamuna rivers – a gathering so immense that it is clearly visible from space – is a curious expression of the 'private' character of religion.

There are, then, a vast variety of traditions, communities, patterns of behaviour, which may – in a range of often contradictory ways – be said to be 'religions'. But there is certainly no *single* enterprise which would count as 'religion'.

In the light of these remarks, I now return to Richard Dawkins' account of the roles of religion in human life. 'Religion', he says, 'has at one time or another been thought to fill four roles in human life: explanation, exhortation, consolation and inspiration. Historically, religion aspired to *explain* our own existence and the nature of the universe in which we find ourselves. In this role, it is now completely superseded by science.'[36]

Two comments on that. In the first place, notice that Dawkins's list of the roles which religion has been 'thought to fill' entirely fails to mention what is – in the case of the Abrahamic traditions and, I think, in many of the religions of India as well – religion's most fundamental role; namely, the attempted expression, in word and deed, in language, ritual and behaviour, of appropriate *response* to invitations not of our invention.[37]

In the second place, Dawkins sees God as 'a competing explanation for facts about the universe and life. This is certainly how God has been seen by most theologians of past centuries.'[38] Central

---

36. *The God Delusion*, op. cit., p. 347.
37. Thus, for example, David Burrell construes 'Islam' ('submission') as a matter of 'returning everything to the one from whom we received everything' ('personal communication'); quite a good description of Jewish and Christian faith as well.
38. Richard Dawkins, 'A Reply to Poole', *Science and Christian Belief*, vol. 7, no. 1 (1995), pp. 45–50; p. 46. I am grateful to Professor Paul Black for drawing my attention to this exchange between Richard Dawkins and Michael Poole.

though it may be to his polemic, as a scientist, against religion, this contention is, quite simply, wrong.

With the exception of rationalist currents in modern Christianity, Judaism, Christianity and Islam have, by and large *not* attempted to 'explain' either 'our own existence' or 'the nature of the universe'.

The heart of the matter is the doctrine of creation. It is a consequence of the confession that all things are created *ex nihilo*, that to name God as 'Creator' is *not* to offer, at least in any straightforward sense, an 'explanation' of the world's existence. Explanations are stories of causes and effects, and there is no such story which begins with *nothing* (for, as the saying goes, from nothing, nothing follows). 'It is not how things are in the world that is [the mystery]', said Wittgenstein, 'but that it exists.'[39] Dawkins gets very cross with the Astronomer Royal, Martin Rees, for saying something similar: 'The pre-eminent mystery is why anything exists at all. What breathes life into the equations, and actualized them in a real cosmos? Such questions lie beyond science, however: they are the province of philosophers and theologians.'[40] This irritates Dawkins for the rather trivial reason that he cannot bear the idea that theologians might have serious work to do!

It is often said that God is 'the answer' to the question as to why there is anything at all. It is, however, a very *strange* answer, because it does not furnish us with information: it simply *names* the mystery.

Moreover, Jews and Christians and Muslims have always found it important to learn from (for example) Plato and Aristotle, as well as from the Scriptures or the Quran. It was from the philosophers and their 'commentators' that medieval Jews, Christians and Muslims sought to understand the world in which they found themselves. And though some aspects of what they called 'philosophy' transmuted into 'natural philosophy' and hence into what we now call the natural sciences, others did not. In the heat of his polemic against religion, Dawkins not only misattributes to religion explanatory pretensions to which, on the whole, the religions have not laid claim but fails to appreciate that biologists, and others, might be well advised to pay more attention than they sometimes do to problems of philosophy and history.

39. Ludwig Wittgenstein, *Tractatus Logico-Philosophicus*, trans. D. F. Pears and B. F. McGuinness (London, Routledge and Kegan Paul, 1961), 6.44. Wittgenstein has '*das Mystische*'.
40. Martin Rees, *Our Cosmic Habitat* (London, Weidenfeld and Nicolson, 2001), cited from *The God Delusion*, op. cit., pp. 55–6.

Culture wars and the paradox of 'progress'

Chapter Seven of *The God Delusion* is entitled: 'The "Good" Book and the Changing Moral *Zeitgeist*'. Invoking 'a widespread consensus of liberal, enlightened, decent people',[41] Richard Dawkins is serenely confident that, leaving the darkness of religion behind, and notwithstanding 'local and temporary setbacks', the human race progresses steadily into enlightenment and decency: 'the progressive trend is unmistakeable and it will continue'; 'the *Zeitgeist* moves on'.[42]

I have two difficulties with this account. In the first place, emerging from a century which saw more millions slaughtered than during the previous history of the human race, operating as we do an economic system which starves the majority of human beings to feed the avarice of a few whose lifestyle now threatens the very planet with catastrophe, I find it hard to understand how a man as intelligent as Richard Dawkins can sustain such smug and counterfactual Whiggery.

In the second place, Dawkins insists that he speaks as a *scientist* and, specifically, as a Darwinian biologist. This is paradoxical because, as Michael Ruse has argued, 'A worldview that accepts the full implications of Darwinian natural selection has no place for absolute values, including absolute progress ... the causal heart of Darwinian theorizing is against the idea of progress.'[43]

In his study of *The Evolution-Creation Struggle*, Ruse distinguishes Jewish and Christian doctrines of creation from what he calls 'creationism': the worldview of (especially American) biblical fundamentalists. Similarly, he distinguishes the *fact* of evolution, and scientific theories constructed to account for it, from 'evolutionism': the whole 'metaphysical or ideological picture built around or on evolution';[44] such evolutionism, he insists, is 'a religious commitment'.[45]

Richard Dawkins occupies a professorial chair for 'the public understanding of science', an enterprise he deems best forwarded by relentless warfare against religion. However, Michael Ruse seems to me correct in arguing that the struggle between

41. *The God Delusion*, op. cit., p. 286.
42. Ibid., pp. 271, 267.
43. Michael Ruse, *The Evolution-Creation Struggle* (Cambridge, Mass., Harvard University Press, 2005), p. 80. On the cover of Alister and Joanna Collicutt McGrath's lucid rebuttal, *The Dawkins Delusion* (London, SPCK, 2007), Ruse is cited as saying: '*The God Delusion* makes me embarrassed to be an atheist, and the McGraths show why.'
44. Ruse, *The Evolution-Creation Struggle*, op. cit., p. 4.
45. Ibid., p. 275.

'creationists' and 'evolutionists' (of whom, undoubtedly, Professor Dawkins is one) is not a 'simple clash between science and religion but rather between two religions'.[46] The irony of *The God Delusion*, then, is that its author is the high priest of a new religion.

It is nearly fifty years since Snow gave his lecture on 'the two cultures', but when a book as ill-informed and poorly argued as *The God Delusion* can be celebrated in scientific circles as 'an important work of science' and 'a great work of literature', one fears that a price is being paid for the increasingly specialised nature of the astonishing work done in the physical and biological sciences. We measure with astounding accuracy. But good argument is as indispensable to human flourishing as good measurement. As Stefan Collini remarks in his Introduction to a recent edition of Snow's lecture: 'it has not become more obvious since Snow wrote that ... an education in physics or chemistry' (or, I might add, biology) 'is a better preparation for handling the world's problems than an education in history or philosophy'.[47]

46. Ibid., p. 287.
47. Collini, 'Introduction', op. cit., pp. lxix–lxx.

Chapter 2

The Impossibility of Atheism

How to be an atheist

The Inaugural Lecture delivered in Cambridge, in October 2001, by my successor in the Norris–Hulse chair, Denys Turner, was helpfully entitled: 'How to be an atheist'.[1] In order to be an atheist, Turner concluded, all that is necessary 'is to find *that the world is* to be a platitudinously dull fact'.[2] The trouble is, he warned his listeners, that resolutely sustaining this conviction requires 'much hard work, not a little training, and a powerful mental asceticism',[3] because it is dangerously easy to find the fact of the world interesting, even cause for wonder.

The titles of his lecture, and of mine, might give the impression that we move in very different directions. As you will discover, this is far from being the case; I just want to push things one step further than he did. We both agree, on the one hand, that speaking appropriately of God is well-nigh impossible: that almost all the things we say need, correctively, to be unsaid[4] and, on the other hand, that learning to speak appropriately of God is a not unimportant part of what it is to learn to be a creature.

How can it be impossible when there's so much of it around?

I shall return to both those topics in due course. The obvious place to *start*, however, is with the *prima facie* daftness of my title. How *can* atheism be impossible when there is so much of it around?

There is indeed, and most of it takes one of two forms. On the one hand, there is the atheism of those who get on perfectly well without all that stuff. The sophisticated version of this is the

1. Denys Turner, *Faith Seeking* (London, SCM Press, 2002), pp. 4–22.
2. Ibid., p. 22.
3. Loc. cit.
4. There is a marvellous meditation on this in one of Newman's notebooks, in the course of which he says 'We can only set right one error of expression by another'. See above, p. 8.

atheism of those who, like the philosopher John Searle, deny that they are atheists for to admit it might imply that theism was worth the labour of denial. On the other hand, there is the vigorous and noisy atheism (Dawkins-din, we might call it) of those who are convinced that religious belief does so much damage that it must be energetically contested.

The trouble is that *both* these kinds of atheism are intellectually uninteresting, because they take for granted that 'belief in God' is a matter of supposing there to be, over and above the familiar world we know, one more large and powerful fact or thing, for the existence of which there is no evidence whatsoever. Unfortunately, the climate of our times is such that, when any reasonably well-informed Jew, or Christian, or Muslim says that, if *this* is what it is to be an atheist, then the rest of us are atheists as well, we are just not taken seriously.

As the great Jesuit theologian Karl Rahner put it:

> *that* God really does not exist who operates and functions as an individual existent alongside other existents, and who would thus be a member of the larger household of all reality. Anyone in search of such a God is searching for a false God. Both atheism and a more naïve form of theism labour under the same false notion of God, only the former denies it while the latter believes that it can make sense of it.[5]

Is the word 'God' necessary?

According to Karl Rahner, keeping the word 'God' in play, even if only as a question, is part of the very definition of what it is to be a human being. 'The absolute death of the word "God"', he says, 'including even the eradication of its past, would be the signal, no longer heard by anyone, that man himself had died.'[6] By 'the word "God"' he cannot, I think, have meant the *term*, because clearly *Dieu* or *Gott* would do just as well. I like suggesting to people who say, nonsensically, that Muslims 'do not worship the same God' as Christians, that they should visit the still very Catholic country of Malta. The Maltese language is in large part derived from Arabic, and Maltese churches are therefore full of Roman Catholics praising Allah!

In other words, the terms 'God' and 'Allah' are not proper names. Are they, then, *common* names? Do they name a kind, a

5. Karl Rahner, *Foundations of Christian Faith: An Introduction to the Idea of Christianity*, trans. William V. Dych (London, Darton, Longman and Todd, 1978), p. 63.
6. Ibid., p. 49.

class of things? It would seem so, because we say that polytheists are people who worship many gods. And yet, as I indicated earlier, Jews, Christians and Muslims all insist that the object of their worship is not a thing of any kind. God, we say (careful to have a capital 'G' in mind as we say it), is not one of the gods. But that seems a lot of heavy lifting for one little bit of capitalisation to do!

Perhaps what we are trying to say is that the term 'God', as we use it, is not really a *name* at all. What kind of word is it, then, and what kind of work are we asking it to do?

The grammar of 'God'

Take a word with which we usually have less trouble than we do with 'God': the word 'treasure'. A treasure is what is valued, held in high esteem. Notice that, when we say this, we are not implying that the word is the name of a natural kind the members of which, it so happens, are valued. There is no good going into a super-market and asking for five bananas, three rolls of kitchen paper, and four treasures. To call something a treasure tells you nothing about it other than that it is treasured, valued, held in high esteem.

Similarly, a 'god' is what is worshipped, what someone has their heart set on. Once again, when we say this, we are not implying that the word is the name of a natural kind the members of which, it so happens, are worshipped. To call something a 'god' tells you nothing about it other than that it is worshipped.

In the course of modern western history, however, something rather odd happened to the word. Its sense shifted from 'what-we-worship' to become the name of a natural kind (or what some people, ignorant of the history of the term, wrongly call a 'supernatural' kind);[7] a kind of which some people said there were no members (these people called themselves 'atheists') while others insisted that the kind *did* have members (these people called themselves 'theists'); and amongst the theists there were those who maintained that the class had only one member (these were called 'monotheists'), and those who said that it had lots (these were called 'polytheists'). The shift is signalled by the dates when these labels entered the language. The word 'atheist' first appears in English in 1571, and 'atheism' in 1587, whereas,

---

7. The word 'supernatural' describes behaviour over and above the natural capacities of something. I used to tell students that, if they ever came across a rabbit playing Mozart, on the violin, they could be sure that it was acting supernaturally, because rabbits just haven't got it in them to play Mozart. God, alone, cannot act supernaturally, because how could *God* be graced?

perhaps surprisingly, the word 'theist' does not turn up until 1662, to be followed, in 1687, by 'theism'.

In course of time, most sensible, educated people agreed that the class of 'gods' was empty, and modern atheism was born.[8] (There is, incidentally, something distasteful about the ease with which modern western secularists, smugly content to have out-grown the childishness of religious belief, continue to insist that Indians worship many gods.) The point, however, is this. The fact that a culture ceases to take an interest in, or to have good uses for, the word 'god', says nothing whatsoever about what it is that the culture worships, has its heart set on.

Some years ago, the Brazilian Dominican, Frei Betto, friend of Fidel Castro, visited England for the first time.[9] When he was about to leave the country, the editor of the Dominican journal, *New Blackfriars*, asked him to write a guest editorial. He did so and said that, when he arrived in England, everyone told him how *secular* the country had become. But, he said, this is not a *secular* society, it is a *pagan* society. In other words, it just so happens that we do not call the things we worship 'gods'.

In our society the worship of gods, idolatry, is rife, but, at the heart of what it is to be a Jew, a Christian, or a Muslim, is the conviction that non-idolatrous worship is both possible and necessary: the conviction that human beings may worship while yet not worshipping some feature of the world, some idea or entity constituting one item amongst others in the furniture of things, and that thus to worship is, in the last analysis, what it *is* to be a human being.

I shall say more about this later on. For the time being, still staying with the question of the *grammar* of the word 'God', I want briefly to ask: is it a noun or a verb?

'What an extraordinary question! Of course it's a noun!' is, in my experience, most people's immediate reaction. But let's stand back a little, in order to give the question some kind of *context*. Many years ago, J. R. R. Tolkien pointed out to a mutual friend that many basic, fundamental English words which now sound like abstract nouns originally expressed relationship, activity. 'Truth', for example, is the same word as 'troth', a pledge or promise. Let's go back to the beginning, to the burning bush. 'Who shall I tell them sent me?' Moses asks of God. Several English versions give God's answer as 'I am who I am',[10] which has overtones of

8. See Michael J. Buckley, *At the Origins of Modern Atheism* (New Haven, Conn. and London, Yale University Press, 1987).
9. See Frei Betto, *Fidel and Religion* (New York, Simon and Schuster, 1987), the record of 23 hours of conversation between the two men.
10. Exod. 3:14.

'mind your own business' about it and yet, literally if inelegantly, God's answer might be better rendered as 'I shall be that I shall be', which hints at promise, at declaration of that *fidelity* which is perhaps God's central attribute in the Hebrew Scriptures and finds its final expression in the Prologue to the Fourth Gospel: 'full of grace and truth', *charis* and *aletheia* in John's Greek, echoing the Hebrew *hesed* and *emeth*, both words expressing God's generous and absolute reliability, his 'troth', the promise that God is. As the seventeenth-century poet, Angelus Silesius, put it: '*Gott spricht nur immer Ja*': 'God always says only "Yes"'.[11] And, as Michel de Certeau pointed out in a fine discussion of that remark, the full expression in our world of the 'Yes' that God always says and is, is Christ's 'Yes', his obedience unto death. Finally, it is worth bearing in mind that, as the Franciscan Thomas Weinandy puts it, the 'persons of the Trinity are not nouns; they are verbs and the names which designate them – Father, Son and Holy Spirit – designate the acts by which they are defined'.[12]

In a passage in the *Summa* in which Aquinas considers whether the word 'God' names a 'nature' or an 'operation' – whether, in other words, it is better considered as a noun or as a verb, he comes down on the side of noun.[13] But if, as I have been hinting, we would do well to sustain, as he did, the *tension* between substantival and verbal senses of the word, the reason is that whereas, where creatures are concerned, it is always possible to distinguish between their identity and their activity, between who they are and what they do, no such distinction is applicable to God. The holy mystery of God simply *is* the giving, the uttering, the breathing, that God is said to be and do.[14] And, for those unreconstructed souls who prefer the language of scholastic metaphysics to the imagery of Scripture, what else are we saying when we say that God is *actus purus*, 'pure act', if not that, in Him, the distinction between 'is' and 'does' has no application?

11. Silesius, *Cherubinischer Wandersmann*, 2.4, wonderfully discussed in Michel de Certeau, *The Mystic Fable, i: The Sixteenth and Seventeenth Centuries,* trans. Michael B. Smith (Chicago, University of Chicago Press, 1992), p. 175.
12. Thomas G. Weinandy, *Does God Suffer?* (Notre Dame, University of Notre Dame Press, 2000), pp. 45–6; cited in Fergus Kerr, *After Aquinas: Versions of Thomism* (Oxford, Blackwell, 2002), p. 240.
13. Thomas Aquinas, *Summa Theologiae*, Ia, 13.8.
14. See Nicholas Lash, *Holiness, Speech and Silence: Reflections on the Question of God* (Aldershot, Ashgate, 2004), p. 47.

Stage-setting: a tale of four metaphysics

Where have we got to, where this strange little word 'God' is
concerned? We usually use it as a noun, but there is something to
be said for thinking of it as a verb, the name of an activity, a kind
of dance, perhaps. In spite of the capital letter that we use when
speaking of the creator of the world, the word 'God' is not a
proper name. It is, in fact, quite difficult to see in just what sense it
is a *name* at all. This difficulty arises, I now want to suggest,
because learning to name things is a matter of learning where
they 'fit in', what part they play in the general scheme of things,
and God does not play *any* particular part in the scheme of things.
Learning to name something as a 'spoon' or as a 'smile' presupposes familiarity with a whole lot of things to do with eating,
on the one hand, and with human relations on the other. We tend
to forget this. As Wittgenstein put it: it is easy to forget that 'a
great deal of stage-setting in the language is presupposed if the
mere act of naming is to make sense'.[15]

It is easy to identify the 'stage-setting' that is necessary in order
to be able correctly to name some things as spoons and others as
smiles. But what would the 'stage-setting' be for appropriate use of
the word 'God'? According to Karl Rahner, the use of this word,
and this word alone, brings a person 'face to face with the single
whole of reality' and with 'the single whole of [their] own existence'.[16] The context in which God is appropriately named is
nothing less than everything and each of us in absolute dependence on the mystery of our createdness. This, incidentally, is why
the fundamental form of our knowledge of God is adoration,
acknowledgement of our dependence. I shall return to this.

It is said that a taxi-driver once said to T. S. Eliot: 'You're Mr
Eliot, the poet, aren't you?' Eliot agreed that he was, and the
driver went on: 'I get many famous people in my cab. The other
day Bertrand Russell, whom I'm sure you would agree is England's
leading philosopher, got into my cab, and I said to him: "Bertie,"
I said, "what's it all about?", and the git couldn't tell me.' As the
taxi-driver knew, you don't have to be a philosopher to do metaphysics, because everyone works with, or presupposes, *some* sort of
story or account of 'what it's all about'.

Curiously, however, so far as I can see, such accounts fall into
only four kinds, or combinations of these kinds. Think of them as
grouped along two axes. At the North Pole, there is the materialism described by Antony Flew as announcing that 'all there is is,

15. Ludwig Wittgenstein, *Philosophical Investigations*, trans. G. E. M.
    Anscombe (Oxford, Basil Blackwell, 1958), p. 257.
16. Rahner, *Foundations*, op. cit., p. 47.

in the last analysis, stuff; and that whatever is not stuff is non-sense'.[17] At the South Pole, there is thorough-going idealism, for which the philosopher Timothy Sprigge can serve as representa-tive. According to his obituary in the *Guardian*, he held that 'physical qualities by themselves are like the musical score as opposed to the music's heard sound'.[18]

These two types of metaphysics, which we might think of as the metaphysics of mud and music, tell us what there is, but not where it came from nor where it might be heading. They are not stories.

In the far west, however, there are tales of chaos, power and cruelty, of *violence* as the fundamental motor of the world. At this pole we might place either Macbeth or Friedrich Nietzsche. Finally, in the east, where the sun rises, there is a tale of all things coming as pure gift, of the whole story of the world, 'groaning in labour pains until now',[19] as St Paul put it, as birth-pangs of eternal peace. This is the story told by Christianity and rabbinic Judaism. (I say '*rabbinic* Judaism' because, when the first chapter of the Book of Genesis was written, the story was still told, as at the Western pole, as beginning with chaos: that first chapter is a story of God's good *ordering* of the world. It was only with early Chris-tianity, and the Judaism contemporary with it, that primal chaos was banished and, to underline the *absolute* nature of God's giving, all things were said to come from *nothing*.)

Learning to be creatures

Learning to use the word 'God' well, learning to speak appro-priately of God, is a matter of learning that we are creatures, and that all things are created, and created out of nothing. And learning this takes time. In fact, it took the Jewish and then the Christian tradition many centuries. The story of this learning process simply is the history of Jewish and Christian doctrines of God. Moreover, there is a sense in which each generation, and indeed each individual, has to take the time to learn this for themselves; has to grow, or fail to grow, into some understanding of what it means to be, in every fibre of one's being, absolutely dependent on the mystery that we call God.[20]

With the invention of the telescope, Europeans became rapidly aware that the universe was immeasurably more immense than

17. Antony Flew, *An Introduction to Western Philosophy: Ideas and Argument from Plato to Sartre* (London, Thames and Hudson, 1971), p. 45.
18. *The Guardian*, 4 September 2007.
19. Romans 8:22.
20. In this and the following two paragraphs I have adapted some material from Lash, *Holiness, Speech and Silence*, op. cit, pp. 88–90.

they had ever dreamed. '*Le silence éternel de ces espaces infinies m'ef-fraie*'; 'the eternal silence of these infinite spaces *terrifies* me'.[21] That was Blaise Pascal – philosopher, scientist and mathematician – who was born in 1623. Notice that it was not simply the size of the universe which frightened him, but its *silence*. We seem to be alone.

Acceptance of our radical contingency, unnerving in itself, is also acknowledgement of vulnerability, and this is something we are loath to do. And with good reason because, the way things are, mutual dependence between creatures only too often finds expression in structures of slavery and domination. And so, as individuals and as communities, we yearn for independence, for autonomy, for freedom. There is, however, a sense in which the striving for autonomy is the behaviour of the adolescent who has not yet discovered that mature humanity consists neither in servitude nor independence but in mutuality, in reciprocity, in friendship.

Learning to use the word 'God' well is a matter of discovering that our absolute dependence, as creatures, on the mystery of God is the antithesis of servitude, for we have been created to be friends of God and, in that friendship, to find our identity and freedom. Learning to use the word 'God' well is a matter of discovering that everything we have and are is given; that our existence is the finite form of God's self-gift, God's self-communication.

Here, once more, is Karl Rahner, at the beginning of the fourth chapter of his *Foundations of Christian Faith*: 'But now we are coming to the innermost centre of the Christian understanding of existence when we say: Man is the event of a free, unmerited and forgiving, and absolute self-communication of God.'[22] (Apologies for political incorrectness, but 'human beings' would lose the sense of *singleness*, of the solidarity of humankind, and 'humankind' would sound too abstract: think 'Adam', perhaps, the earthling, made from mud.)

Let me paraphrase Rahner's extraordinary assertion. Human existence is what happens when God freely, and forgivingly, communicates Himself. *Himself*. And, moreover, communicates Himself completely, absolutely. I remarked earlier on the importance of remembering that, in God, there is no distinction between identity and operation: between what God *is* and what God *does*. We are expressions of the giving that God is. It is not surprising that one strand in patristic thought should speak of our 'divinisation'.

Notice that what Rahner is doing is subverting our tendency to suppose that divinity and humanity are antithetical: that the more like God we become, the less human we will be. I know many people who suppose themselves to be quite orthodox Christians and yet who do not *really* believe that Jesus Christ is one hundred per cent human – and one hundred per cent divine. To put it very crudely: it is not uncommon, in my experience, to find people who suppose that *part* of Jesus is divine.

In stark contrast with heresies of this kind, Rahner insists that the more divine we are, the more human we become. Saints are more human than sinners, although we often speak as if the opposite were true!

'Man is the event of a free, unmerited and forgiving, and absolute self-communication of God.' In other words, Jesus of Nazareth is the only *completely* human human being there has been. Being God's Word made flesh, he is not *less* human than the rest of us, but more so. And we grow in humanity the more we grow in holiness, the more we grow in God.

Education and idolatry

'*Gott spricht nur immer Ja*': 'God always says only "Yes"'. Let's see what happens when we pass the Prologue to the Fourth Gospel through that filter. 'In the beginning was the "Yes", and the "Yes" was with God, and the "Yes" was God ... And the "Yes" became flesh and dwelt amongst us', thereby enabling our lives, our minds, our voices, to be a sharing in the 'Yes' of God. We are, I said earlier, expressions of the giving that God is. To which we could now add: we are expressions of the 'Yes' God says. All creatures are absolutely dependent, in every fibre of their being, on God's creative utterance, but only human beings can be aware of this, can learn to make of everything they say and do a sharing in God's self-giving.

'God', Hegel once remarked, 'does not offer himself for observation'.[23] He was not denying that we may come to some knowledge, some understanding, of the mystery of God, but insisting that God is not, as it were, available to be inspected at arm's length, picked up with tweezers, dissected, evaluated. In history and in philosophy there is always good academic work to be done on the question of God, work as rigorous and demanding

---

23. G. W. F. Hegel, *Lectures on the Philosophy of Religion*, 1: *Introduction and Concept of Religion*, ed. Peter C. Hodgson (Berkeley, University of California Press, 1984), p. 258.

as in any other field of study, and yet there is a *sense* in which if
such work is not done, at least metaphorically, on one's knees,
with one's shoes off, then it will miss the mark. This is what I had
in mind when I said earlier that the fundamental form of the
knowledge of God is acknowledgement of our dependence, is our
self-giving to the giver that God is, is adoration, 'Yes', 'Amen'.

Most people think that dealing with God is what religion is
about. I have placed the emphasis on life-long learning, and
learning is what people do in schools. I would therefore now
like to say something about the relationship between education
and religion.

For much of Christian history, 'religion' was the name of a
virtue, a virtue which Aquinas discussed under the general heading of 'justice'. To act justly is to render people or things their
due. To act religiously is to give God *God's* due. Acting virtuously,
for Aquinas, is always a bit like walking a tightrope, taking care not
to fall off on either side. Fall off on one side, and you fall into the
vice of superstition, which is the vice of treating some creature as
God – idolatry, magic, fortune-telling are amongst the examples
that he lists. The superstitious person suffers from too much
religion, treating all manner of things as God. Fall off on the other
side, and we exhibit too *little* religion, treating God as a creature,
an object at our disposal – through perjury, sacrilege and simony,
for example.[24]

During the late sixteenth and seventeenth centuries, the
meaning of 'religion' shifted, first from a virtue to a set of propositions and then, in the struggles of the emergent modern
State, to name a domesticated belief system to be manipulated, as
far as possible, 'by the sovereign for the benefit of the State'.[25]
When I called the first of the Teape Lectures which I gave in
several places in India in 1994 'The Beginning and the End of
"Religion" ', it was the end of 'religion' in this specifically modern
sense as the name of just one particular district of our lives, a
district which we may inhabit if we feel so inclined, a largely private pastime of diminishing interest and plausibility, a territory
quite distinct from those we know as 'politics' and 'science' and
'economics' – it was the end of 'religion' in *this* sense to which I
cheerfully looked forward. Subvert this sense of 'religion', and we
might rediscover what the world's great traditions of ritual and
adoration are really all about. We might rediscover why Aquinas
said that the subject-matter of what he called 'holy teaching' is,

24. See Thomas Aquinas, *Summa Theologiae*, IIa, IIae, qq. 81–100.
25. William T. Cavanaugh, ' "A Fire Strong Enough to Consume the
House": The Wars of Religion and the Rise of the State', *Modern
Theology* (October 1995), pp. 397–420; p. 405.

not religion, but the mystery of God and *everything* (*omnia*) in relation to that mystery which is its origin and destiny.[26]

I have laid a lot of emphasis in this lecture on the need for lifelong learning if we are to use the word 'God' well, and so it may not come as a surprise when I tell you that my theme, in those Teape lectures, was that we would do well to think of Judaism, Christianity and Islam, of Buddhism and Vedantic Hinduism, not as 'religions' but as *schools*, schools whose pedagogy, I suggested, 'has the twofold purpose – however differently conceived and executed in the different traditions – of weaning us from our idolatry and purifying our desire'.[27]

Some years ago, I was asked to give a talk to the Higher Education Committee of the Bishops' Conference of England and Wales. I said that the decision of the Church in this country to make primary and secondary education its overall pastoral priority had made good sense at the time that it was taken, a century or more ago. But times have changed. This is now a country in which nearly half the population goes on to some form of higher or further education. But where, and how, are *adult* Catholics taught to pray and taught to think, to make their faith a faith in quest of understanding, a *fides quaerens intellectum*? Where, and how, are adult Catholics taught to read the Scriptures? While in no way underestimating the educational potential of liturgy well celebrated, I do not believe 'at Mass on Sunday' to be an adequate answer to these questions!

In a word, my suggestion was that the time had come for a major strategic rethink of our educational priorities so that we gave more than lip-service to the idea that Catholic Christianity is a school of lifelong learning in the knowledge and the love of God. The suggestion did not go down very well, because I was suspected of trying to undermine our Catholic schools!

It is nearly forty years since, lamenting our apparent inability to think through and realise *institutionally* the achievements of Vatican II, John Coulson spoke of the need 'to educate a new generation into an understanding of our religious language of liturgy and sacrament. Yet it is a language whose grammar can be deeply eroded by a hostile and inhumane environment . . . This is, in the broadest sense a theological task: it is also a responsibility for *adult* (as distinct from primary and secondary) education.' His conclusion leads directly into the next set of issues that I wish to consider: 'A theology that has nothing to say to politics, medicine,

26. See Aquinas, *Summa Theologiae*, Ia, q. 1, art. 7.
27. Nicholas Lash, *The Beginning and the End of 'Religion'* (Cambridge, Cambridge University Press, 1996), p. 21.

or industry, has written a death certificate for the traditions it claims to perpetuate.'[28]

Living without insulation

In August 1967, a great congress took place in Toronto on the theology of renewal.[29] 'Good pope John', said Bernard Lonergan, in his contribution to the proceedings, 'has made "renewal" mean *aggiornamento*, "bringing things up to date".'[30] But if theology needs bringing up to date, he went on, 'it must have fallen behind the times'. When did it do so? He plumped for the year 1680: 'For that, it seems, was the time of the great beginning. Then it was that Herbert Butterfield placed the origins of modern science, then that Paul Hazard placed the beginning of the Enlightenment, then that Yves Congar placed the beginning of dogmatic theology. When science began, when the Enlightenment began, then the theologians began to reassure one another about their certainties.'[31]

The sting, of course, is in the tail. With the dawning of modernity, the pedagogy of inquiry, of the *quaestio*, was supplanted by the pedagogy of the 'thesis', of assertion. We should, I think, take the precision of Lonergan's dating of the sea-change to modernity as a rhetorical flourish. Stephen Toulmin, in an important study of what he calls 'the hidden agenda of modernity', opts for somewhere between 1630 and 1680. But, whenever it happened, *what* happened is no longer in question. What happened in philosophy (including natural philosophy or, as we would now say, physics) was to frame all questions 'in terms that rendered them *independent of context*'.[32] 'The claim', Toulmin remarks later, 'that all truly philosophical problems must be stated in terms independent of any historical situation, and solved by methods equally free of all contextual references, is one of the rationalist claims typical of modern philosophy from 1640 to 1950.'[33]

What was true of modern philosophy was, by and large, true of

---

28. John Coulson, 'Disputed Questions on the Form of the Local Church', *The Christian Priesthood*, ed. Nicholas Lash and Joseph Rhymer (London, Darton, Longman and Todd, 1970), pp. 289–95; p. 294.

29. *Theology of Renewal*, ed. L. K. Shook, 2 vols. (New York, Herder and Herder, 1968).

30. Bernard Lonergan, 'Theology in its New Context', *Theology of Renewal*, vol. i, p. 34.

31. Loc. cit.

32. Stephen Toulmin, *Cosmopolis: The Hidden Agenda of Modernity* (Chicago, University of Chicago Press, 1990), p. 21.

33. Ibid., p. 36.

modern theology as well. The reason why Vatican II's project of *aggiornamento* took the form of *ressourcement* was that 'bringing theology up to date' necessitated abandoning the rationalist pretensions of the 'non-historical orthodoxy' characteristic of neoscholasticism and re-establishing relations with biblical, patristic and medieval Christianity, in all its richness and contingency.

Contingency is, I think, the keyword. Modern rationalism sought escape from the dangerous mortality of particular times and particular places into abstract and eternal truth. It forgot that the Word became flesh, eternity temporal.

It used to be assumed that seventeenth-century philosophy and science were products of prosperity. Toulmin insists that this has now been demonstrated to be nonsense. Mid-seventeenth-century Europe, far from being 'a time of prosperity and reasonableness', now looks, he says, 'like a scene from the Lebanon in the 1980s ... Instead of regarding Modern Science and Philosophy as the products of leisure ... we will do better to turn the received view upside down, and treat them as responses to a contemporary crisis.'[34]

There is, I think, an important truth here concerning fundamentalism, which is, as James Barr demonstrated 30 years ago, an expression of modern rationalism.[35] Fundamentalists often seem to be, and sometimes are, aggressive, but their aggressiveness is not, I think, grounded in confidence but in fear. They are afraid that to contextualise their discourse, and the texts they use, would risk their treasured certainties crumbling into dust.

One of the central themes of P. J. FitzPatrick's marvellous study of the Eucharist (and so much else!), *In Breaking of Bread*[36] concerns the importance of avoiding what he calls the 'insulation' of what, as Christians, we think, and say, and do. His discussion of the topic takes us back, once again, to the seventeenth century. 'In more than one philosophical tradition', he says (a priest of the diocese of Hexham and Newcastle, he taught philosophy for many years at Durham University), 'there has been a turning away from the quest for some ultimate and (to use my own word) insulated certainty, of the sort associated with Descartes.'[37]

'Insulation', he says, 'is put at the service of what is valued, whether this be the eucharistic presence or the status of narratives

---

34. Ibid., pp. 16–17.
35. See James Barr, *Fundamentalism* (London, SCM Press, 1977).
36. P. J. FitzPatrick, *In Breaking of Bread: The Eucharist and Ritual* (Cambridge, Cambridge University Press, 1993). For some reflections of mine on this immensely important work, see below, chapter 13.
37. FitzPatrick, *In Breaking of Bread*, op. cit., p. 297.

in the gospels. It seems to provide them with a fence against awkwardness, and to render them inaccessible to attack. The manoeuvre is a mistake, but it is an understandable one.'[38]

We insulate words and images which we value to keep them safe from corruption from the vagaries of time and circumstance. It does not work. In due time, we end up talking nonsense, not only to the world outside, but also to each other. This is, of course, because there *is* no world 'outside', no world of which our thoughts and words and gestures form no part. 'The Church', says the Dutch theologian, Erik Borgman, 'is not above or outside history, but if it really wants to find the truth and preach it, it should start by recognizing itself in the disciples around the table of the Last Supper: confused and terrified.'[39]

According to Borgman, the greatest achievement of the Constitution *Gaudium et Spes* was its avoidance of atemporal verities, its adoption of a strategy (which partly explains why it was decided to call it a 'pastoral' Constitution) of seeking to avoid all insulation, its insistence that 'the Church takes its shape in and emerges from the world'.[40] Borgman therefore laments the 'renewed attempts' that he detects, during the pontificate of John Paul II, 'at creating the illusion that the Church is perfectly able to pronounce on the present based on eternal principles of unique certainty'.[41]

One small but interesting illustration of this tendency is a (presumably indeliberate) misquotation from Pascal in the encyclical *Fides et Ratio*. Pascal said that 'Just as Jesus Christ went unrecognised among men, so too does truth appear without external difference among common modes of thought. So too does the Eucharist remain among common bread.'[42] The encyclical, however, has, not 'so too does truth', but 'so too, does *his* truth', which says something very different.[43]

---

38. Ibid., pp. 111–12.
39. Erik Borgman, 'The Rediscovery of Truth as a Religious Category: The Enduring Legacy of the Second Vatican Council', *Bulletin ET* (2006), pp. 53–66; p. 63; Borgman is, at this point, paraphrasing a passage from Timothy Radcliffe, 'The Sacramentality of the Word', *Liturgy in a Postmodern World*, ed. K. Pecklers (London, Continuum, 2003), pp. 133–47.
40. Borgman, 'The Rediscovery of Truth', op. cit., p. 55.
41. Loc. cit.
42. '*Comme Jésus-Christ est demeuré inconnu parmi les hommes, ainsi la vérité demeure parmi les opinions communes, sans différence à l'extérieur. Ainsi l'Eucharistie parmi le pain commun*' (Blaise Pascal, *Pensées*, ed. L. Brunschvig, no. 789; ed. L. M. Lafuma, no. 225).
43. The Latin text of the encyclical has '*ita manet veritas ejus*' (13). The mistranslation was not picked up in the most recent English translation, which has 'the truth about him'. See *Restoring Faith in Reason:*

Theological insulation creates the illusion, amongst Christians, that what they have to say is really quite simple and straightforward. There is, for example, a symptomatic *glibness* in most forms of fundamentalism. As I have often said, however, it only seems *easy* to speak of God in the measure that we insulate our religious speech and theological imagination from the endlessly complex and disturbing world in which such speech finds reference.[44]

Moreover, insulation does not work. We may try to keep some words or stories, images or gestures, holy by keeping them, as it were, locked up in the tabernacle. However, this strategy overlooks the fact that, while our *speech* may be holy or unholy, there are no holy or unholy *words*. To give one small example. There is much talk, these days, of 'spirituality', which many people find preferable to 'religion', and Christians say that God is 'spirit'. In the culture at large I rather think that 'spirit', when not used of vodka, is used to mean 'not-matter', the ethereal. Biblical scholars may insist until they are blue in the face that such usages have nothing to do with Scripture, in which spirit is not 'not-matter' but 'not-death': the central metaphors, in Hebrew and in Greek, are those of breath and wind; the breathing that differentiates the living from the dead; the sometimes dangerous unpredictability of wind and storm: the power of God that inbreathes and transforms the world is never under our control. All this is true and exceedingly important, but whatever 'father', 'son' and 'spirit' say to us as we walk down the street they will still say as, entering the church, we make the sign of the Cross.[45] And we should never forget that the same is true of all the words we use, including the word 'God'.

Paradoxically, it is not insulation that will keep the things we value most alive, but having the courage, taking the risk, of what we might call 'total immersion' in the culture. Not passively, of course, or submissively, but energetically, wholeheartedly, salt-of-earthishly, often counter-culturally. Moreover, in the last analysis it is not what we *say* which will keep the tradition alive and render it intelligible, but who and how we *are*, as communities and as individuals. The Word became flesh, and we are called to be that Word's embodiment, a message to the world.

A New Translation of the Encyclical Letter Faith and Reason *of Pope John Paul II, Together with a Commentary and Discussion*, ed. Paul Hemming and Susan Frank Parsons (London, SCM Press, 2002), p. 25.

44. See Nicholas Lash, *Easter in Ordinary: Reflections on Human Experience and the Knowledge of God* (London, SCM Press, 1988), p. 217.
45. See Nicholas Lash, 'On Learning to be Wise', *Priests and People* (October 2001), pp. 355–9.

The impossibility of atheism

If someone is asked: 'Do you believe in God?', and replies 'I do', they may be saying one of two quite different things, because the English expression 'I believe in God' is systematically ambiguous. On the one hand, it may be the expression of an opinion: the opinion that God exists. On the other hand, as used in the Creed, in a public act of worship, it promises that life, and love, and all one's actions, are henceforth set steadfastly on the mystery of God, and hence that we are thereby pledged to work towards that comprehensive healing of the world by which all things are brought into their peace and harmony in God. 'Nicholas Lash, do you take Janet Chalmers to be your lawful wedded wife?' 'I do.' 'Janet Chalmers, do you believe in God, the Father almighty, Creator of heaven and earth?' 'I do.' The grammar of these two declarations is the same.[46]

This situation has come about because, over time, the meaning of 'believe' has undergone a shift similar to that which, as we saw earlier, saw 'truth' emerge from 'troth': a shift from pledge or promise to expression of opinion.[47]

It would seem to follow that if a 'theist' is someone who believes in God, and an 'atheist' someone who does not, then there must be two kinds of 'theism' and two kinds of 'atheism', corresponding to the two senses of belief.

These, I think, are the kind of ambiguities that Karl Rahner had in mind when he said that 'theism can be the mask of a concealed atheism and vice versa, and ... in this sense ultimately no-one can say of himself whether he believes in God or not'.[48] We know what our opinions are, but none of us is so self-transparent as to know quite where, in fact, our hearts are set.

As I remarked at the beginning, the atheism which is the contradictory of the opinion that God exists is both widespread and intellectually uninteresting. It is my impression, however, that most atheists suppose themselves to stand in contradiction to Jewish, Christian and Islamic faith in God. Not only are they mistaken, but atheism in this second sense, as contradictory to faith is, I contend, impossible.

I have argued that one way to the knowledge of God is through

46. See Nicholas Lash, *Believing Three Ways in One God: A Reading of the Apostles' Creed* (London, SCM Press, 1992), p. 18.
47. See Wilfred Cantwell Smith, *Faith and Belief* (Princeton, NJ, Princeton University Press, 1979).
48. Karl Rahner, 'Observations on the Doctrine of God in Catholic Dogmatics', *Theological Investigations*, vol. ix, trans. Graham Harrison (London, Darton, Longman and Todd, 1972), pp. 127–44; p. 140.

recognition and acceptance of our radical contingency, our absolute dependence on the mystery we confess to be Creator of the world. All creatures, I said earlier, are absolutely dependent on God's creative utterance, but only human beings can be aware of this, can learn to make of everything they say and do a sharing in the 'Yes' of God. This sharing we call faith.

The contradictory of faith, in this sense, would be a matter of effectively refusing all such sharing, effectively refusing to have anything whatsoever to do with God. Having nothing whatsoever to do with God would, I suppose, be possible if we had some identity, some basis of existence, *other* than that of being created, and created out of nothing. But we do not. Therefore, effective refusal to have anything whatsoever to do with God can only mean self-destruction, annihilation, return to the *nihil* from which all things came. Catholic tradition maintains the *possibility* of such refusal, the possibility of enacting an effective 'No' to God. But my reading of what this entails would explain why you don't see atheists of the second sort around.

Chapter 3

Amongst Strangers and Friends: Thinking of God in our Current Confusion

The departure lounge in any busy airport is a restless space in which a continuously shifting crowd of strangers mingles, somewhat nervously, against a background of piped music and occasional obscure commands. An uninformed observer might be puzzled by the mix of apparently quite aimless, random movement and co-ordinated group activity: shopping, drinking, the announcement of delays; exchange of tickets, tidying of litter, meeting friends, inspecting luggage, gathering up lost children. Except, however, on rare occasions of comprehensive crisis (a bomb threat, for example) there seems to be no single centre of activity, giving purpose and direction to the whole. Much of what happens in the lounge is admittedly affected, often indirectly, by what goes on in the control tower. But the officials in that high and distant building, misjudging both their power and their grasp of what is going on, may overestimate the limited, though not unimportant, sense in which their work situates them at the 'centre' of the airport's life.

'The problem with atheism is that it is not a problem. It is a situation, an atmosphere, a confused history.'[1] Allegory has its dangers, but to consider contemporary Catholic Christianity as a kind of airport lounge may at least remind us how particular are the standpoints, of experience and expectation, from which each of us engages the confusion that is our common plight.

1. Michael J. Buckley, *At the Origins of Modern Atheism* (New Haven, Conn., Yale University Press, 1987), p. 13. Few scholars in the English-speaking world have done more than Michael Buckley to clarify that 'confused history'. In gratitude for his redoubtable achievement, and in celebration of our friendship, it gives me great pleasure to offer these reflections, an earlier version of which served as one of the preparatory papers for the second Congress of the European Society for Catholic Theology (see the second issue for 1994 of the Society's house journal, *E.T.*, pp. 195–208), which took place in Freising in Germany in August 1995, and in which Mike Buckley took part. The papers reflected the theme of the Congress, which was: 'God – A Stranger in our House?'

If there is, today, a crisis in our thinking about God, the variety of standpoints from which this crisis is experienced and hence described is irreducibly diverse. This diversity does not, itself, constitute the crisis. However, if badly handled and misunderstood, it undoubtedly contributes to its deepening.

To illustrate this, we might set out from the self-evident observation that a crisis in our thinking about God is a crisis about truth. Some people interpret this in epistemic terms, as referring to a crisis of credibility: the culmination of three hundred years' erosion, by the acids of secular modernity, of reasoned belief in God's existence. Others, however, construe it in ethical terms: it is trust in God's reliability and loving-kindness, his unswerving faithfulness, rather than belief in his reality, which is now under the more fundamental threat.

The warrants for both interpretations can, of course, be found in certain features of the account of truth and of God's truthfulness which Christianity inherited and developed from Judaism. Which account comes most readily to mind depends, in part at least, upon the different patterns of experience which differently shape faith's quest for understanding. Thus, in contexts dominated by the preoccupations of 'Enlightened' secularity, questions concerning the existence of a sovereign Creator of the world still stand at centre stage. Elsewhere, however, experience of injustice, slavery, and oppression sets questions about the trustworthiness of God, the reliability of the Redeemer's love, at the forefront of concern.

Thus, on the basis of experiential differences, now this, now that aspect of the mystery gets presented as the norm or centre of the whole. It is as if the history of Christianity were a struggle for supremacy between the three articles of its Creed; a struggle tempting the participants to polemicise into opposition mutually indispensable distinctions lying at the very heart of Christian (which is to say trinitarian) apprehension of the mystery of God.

Thus, for example, in a recent essay on Christianity after Communism, Jozef Tischner distinguished two 'currents' in Catholicism after Vatican II, which he labelled 'catechetical' and 'evangelical'. The former grounds its account of human value in the doctrine of creation, the latter in the doctrine of redemption. So far, it might seem, so good. But Tischner then begins to turn the polemical screw. Where attitudes to the crucifixion are concerned, the catechetical current 'is a breeding-ground for Manichaeism', whereas the other 'places grace in the foreground'. Catholics of the former kind 'are intent on making a show of their convictions', whereas the latter deepen belief in 'the discovery of the heroic dimension of the gospel'. Thus it is, he concludes, that 'we are in an age in which one set of Christians' (most of whom, apparently, inhabit 'the liberal countries of Western Europe') is engaged in a determined struggle for the loosening of Church discipline, while the others (most of whom, one suspects by now, are found in Poland) 'accept persecution and years of imprisonment for faithfulness to the church and her discipline'.[2]

The lesson that I would draw from this is as follows. I entirely accept Father Tischner's contention that intra-ecclesial differences run deep, run, indeed, as he contends, to the heart and centre of the Gospel. As I understand the Creed, however, each of its three articles says something about the *whole* of Christian faith. There are three articles because there are, in God, three persons. If, however, our recognition of the unity of God, and of God's world, is not to be compromised, such understanding as we gain from the standpoint provided by any one of the three articles will require correction from the standpoint of the other two. Thus it is that the very *form* of our confession of faith provides a pattern of restraint upon the range of its misuse.[3] (Hence, after a brief section on the question of God's being, I have grouped the issues I shall comment on under headings evoking each of the articles in turn.)

It follows that while different 'currents' of Catholic thought and action will, indeed, be patterned more closely now to this, now that, article of the Creed, each will require and should expect corrective pressure from other currents, patterned to the other articles. There is thus laid upon all schools and currents in the Church the endless labour of attempting accurately to understand and, in some measure, sympathise with, those whose different experience   differently   shapes   their   action   and   their understanding.

Triumphalisms of every kind, what I earlier described as the 'struggle for supremacy' between particular perceptions of the whole, are, or should be, as alien to the ethos of Catholicism as is liberal relativism. Viewed doctrinally, both are failures to live, and think, and argue within the strenuous requirements of the Creed.

One final comment before concluding these preliminary remarks. It is often suggested that the difficulty experienced these days by so many people in knowing quite what it would be appropriate or sensible to say or think of God is itself evidence of the weakness of belief which characterises contemporary European culture: of the extent to which God has become a stranger in our house. Yet finding speech concerning God unproblematic

2.   See Jozef Tischner, 'Christianity in the Post-Communist Vacuum', *Religion, State and Society*, 20 (1992), pp. 334–5.
3.   See Nicholas Lash, *Believing Three Ways in One God: A Reading of the Apostles' Creed* (London, SCM Press, 1992).

would surely be unreliable evidence of faith. It would seem better to say, with Karl Rahner: 'We are just discovering today that one cannot picture God to oneself in an image that has been carved out of the wood of the world ... this experience is not the genesis of atheism, but the discovery that the world is not God.' Or, as my Cambridge predecessor put it: 'The futility of so much confident speech concerning the ultimate ... is something that only the thrust of a recognizable family of metaphorical expressions can convey.'[4] He had in mind expressions such as 'hiddenness' and 'invisibility', for God's invisibility is not diminished by his appearance in the world, nor his hiddenness cancelled by the utterance in time and place of his eternal Word.

A question of being

The story of the rise and fall of modern deism (or theism, for the two terms were, originally, identical in sense) is the story of a twofold dissociation. It is, first, a tale of the dissociation (between Bacon's day and Diderot's) of memory from argument, of narrative from reason. With the fusion, in the seventeenth century, of the late scholastic passion for univocity and the Renaissance rediscovery of Stoicism's 'nature' (homogeneous in all its parts, an *ens commune* construct of one kind of stuff and of one set of forces) there was born a new ideal for the working of the mind: 'a science that has an unequivocal language with which it speaks and uniform objects of which it speaks.' No time nor patience now for narrative, or poetry, or paradox. Theologians and scientists alike developed a single-minded passion for pure prose.[5]

Secondly, it is a story of the dissociation of things measured from the measuring observer, of objects from subjects, things from thoughts. This twofold dissociation entails, in its turn, a cleavage in the concept of philosophy. On the one hand, philosophy is now transformed into natural philosophy which, in turn, becomes mechanics. On the other, philosophy transmutes into epistemology and consideration of the content of the conscious mind.

4.   Karl Rahner, 'Science as a "Confession"?', *Theological Investigations*, 3, trans. Karl-H. and Boniface Kruger (London, 1967), pp. 390–91 (essay first published in *Wort und Wahrheit*, 9 [1954], pp. 809–19); Donald M. MacKinnon, 'Metaphor in Theology', *Themes in Theology: The Threefold Cord* (Edinburgh, 1987), p. 69 (first published in the *Scottish Journal of Religious Studies*, 1984).
5.   Amos Funkenstein, *Theology and the Scientific Imagination from the Middle Ages to the Seventeenth Century* (Princeton, NJ, Princeton University Press, 1986), p. 41; see p. 72.

On the side of the object, God, the maker of the system of the world and its ultimate explanatory principle, can be quietly disposed of once it is acknowledged that the system needs no such explanation. On the side of the subject, God becomes a useful fiction, symbolic of whatever each one dreams of as the fulfilment of his or her restless striving: money, sex, peace, security, self-importance, power (and atheism, on this side, is little more than the insistence that these things be called by their proper names).

Notwithstanding the best efforts of d'Holbach or Feuerbach or Freud, however, people have not ceased to 'believe in God'. But belief has never been so dangerously ambivalent. Each US dollar bill still bears the message 'In God we trust', but it is difficult to imagine the publication, in any century before our own, of a book entitled: *The God I Want*.[6] And yet we should not, perhaps, exaggerate the novelty of our predicament. Edward Gibbon's eighteenth-century description of the world of ancient Rome has an uncomfortably contemporary ring: 'The various modes of worship ... were all considered by the people, as equally true; by the philosophers, as equally false; by the magistrates, as equally useful.'[7]

Under the impact of this century's appalling suffering, dazzling achievement, and deepening confusion, the paradigms of 'modernity' have slowly lost their grip. If, nevertheless, we find our thinking about God (and human beings and the world) to be in crisis, this is because we do not yet know whether 'postmodern' culture will heal the dualisms and dissociations through the incorporation of modernity into some more nuanced and more comprehensive story, or whether, one-sidedly rejecting the one-sidedness of the age now ending, we shall slide into fresh sectarian conflict, irrationalism, and despair.

Thus, where the Christian doctrine of God is concerned, one of the most striking features of mainstream twentieth-century theology has been the setting aside of modern 'theisms' and the recovery of comprehensively trinitarian consideration of the mystery of God. And yet, this recovery, although now several decades old, is still not mediated, either philosophically into other discourses and disciplines, or pastorally into the general conversations of the culture.

To see this, we need do no more than notice that most of our

---

6.   C. Rycroft et al., *The God I Want* (Indianapolis, Bobbs-Merrill, 1967).
7.   Edward Gibbon, *The History of the Decline and Fall of the Roman Empire*, 6 vols. (London, 1853), vol. 1, chap. 2, p. 36; quoted (from a different edition) by Michael J. Buckley, 'Experience and Culture: A Point of Departure for American Atheism', *Theological Studies*, 50 (1989), p. 458.

contemporaries still find it 'obvious' that atheism is not only possible, but widespread and that, both intellectually and ethically, it has much to commend it. This view might be plausible if being an atheist were a matter of not believing that there exists 'a person without a body' who is 'eternal, free, able to do anything, knows everything' and is 'the proper object of human worship and obedience, the creator and sustainer of the universe.'[8] If, however, by 'God' we mean the mystery, announced in Christ, breathing all things out of nothing into peace, then all things have to do with God in every move and fragment of their being, whether they notice this and suppose it to be so or not. Atheism, if it means deciding not to have anything to do with God, is thus self-contradictory and, if successful, self-destructive.

Playfully, Jean-Luc Marion has asked: 'With respect to Being, does God have to behave like Hamlet?'[9] All human beings have their hearts set somewhere, if only on themselves, and the object of our worship is where our hearts are set. But if Christianity is (like Judaism and Islam) best regarded as a kind of school in which we wean each other from the worship of created things into adoration of the mystery of God alone; if, in other words, the first question to be asked concerning God, and our relationships with God, is not 'to be or not to be?' but what is it that we worship, that we take as God; then this has not yet been communicated widely outside the confines of specialist theology.

A question of contingency

There is still no better summary description of the subject-matter of 'that theology which pertains to holy teaching' than that it treats of God and of 'all things,' *omnia*, in their relationship to God as their beginning and their end, their origin and destiny.[10] But to accept this view of things, and to accept all things as made by God, *ex nihilo*, is to accept contingency: to acknowledge the absolute dependence of all worlds on God. And this we find it

8. This definition of what those who believe in God understand themselves to believe has been offered by a most distinguished and devoutly Christian philosophical theologian: see Richard Swinburne, *The Coherence of Theism* (Oxford, Clarendon Press, 1979), p. 1. For some discussion, see Nicholas Lash, *Easter in Ordinary: Reflections on Human Experience and the Knowledge of God* (London, SCM Press, 1988), pp. 98ff.

9. Jean-Luc Marion, 'Preface to the English Edition', *God without Being: Hors-texte* (Chicago, University of Chicago Press, 1991), p. xx; English trans. of *Dieu sans l'être: Hors-texte* (Paris, 1982).

10. See Thomas Aquinas, *Summa Theologiae*, Ia, q. 1, a. 1, ad 2; q. 1, a. 7. c.

difficult to do, for we are frightened of the dark and nervous of dependence. Such fears are by no means unfounded and, lacking the resources to dispel them, we oscillate between Promethean ambition and nihilist despair.

Among the more surprising runaway bestsellers in recent years, in Britain, has been an essay by one of the leading theoretical physicists of our time: Stephen Hawking's *Brief History of Time*. According to Hawking, a complete explanation of the world, which would include an explanation of why the universe exists, 'would be the ultimate triumph of human reason – for then we would know the mind of God.' An earlier reference to quantum theory's abolition of the necessity for appeal 'to God *or some new law* to set the boundary conditions for space-time' makes clear that Hawking's God is only an explanation of the world.[11] The 'triumph' which he seeks, the knowledge of God's mind, is thereby tinged with pathos, for why should we suppose an explanation to bring peace?

Some scientists, sensing this, give more dangerous expression to their rejection of contingency, dreaming of descendants with 'the advantage of containing no organic material at all', free from 'the biological ball and chain', and thus, at last, capable of becoming 'lords of the universe'.[12] We should not underestimate the influence on our culture of the fear of death, the contempt for the flesh, the terror of contingency, which drives these dreams.

It is, of course, integral to such fantasies to suppose that human beings are not, in the last resort, *animals* at all. Instead of creatures fashioned of flesh, determinate in time and place and circumstance, we suppose ourselves small godlets dropped on earth, 'angels fallen into flesh',[13] mind-things of (potentially) unlimited and unrivalled power. The last two centuries have seen this power unleashed to the irreversible destruction of the fragile wealth and beauty of the world.

Feminists have rightly emphasised the element of *machismo* in this disastrous posturing of 'modern man'. It is with much less justice, however, that ecological movements tend to lay the blame on Jewish and Christian doctrines of creation. The 'dominion'

---

11. Stephen W. Hawking, *A Brief History of Time* (London, Bantam, 1988), pp. 175, 136 (emphasis added).

12. For an excellent discussion of this material, see Mary Midgley's 1990 Gifford Lectures, *Science as Salvation: A Modern Myth and Its Meaning* (London, Routledge, 1992); for the quoted phrases, see pp. 152, 153, 159.

13. Fergus Kerr, *Theology after Wittgenstein* (Oxford, Basil Blackwell, 1986), p. 168, where he discusses the antiquity and power of the Origenist myth.

over other living things which men and women are required to exercise is husbandry, not despotism (see Gen. 1:28). It is the modern world, not ancient Israel, which takes absolute power, unconstrained by circumstance or duty, as paradigm of kingship.

Ask most people what God makes when he creates the world, and they will list the kinds of things which the natural sciences describe: whirling gases, deep seas and rock formations, galaxies and stars. 'Life' may be mentioned, but probably in some rather vague and general way. Almost certainly missing from the list will be such items as rituals and relationships, languages and symbols systems, trade and agriculture. It is as if God did not make the things that human beings do; as if God's self-gift, creative graciousness, were less immediately constitutive of promises and symphonies than of plutonium and silt. Or is it that we think that God made matter, whereas we, like God, are made of 'mind'?

The healing of the deep-laid dissociative dualisms which plague our modern imagination cannot but be a slow, laborious, and costly process. The place to start, it seems to me, is with the recognition that the doctrine of creation out of nothing is not, in itself, good news. It is realism, not cowardice, which makes us frightened of the dark. And it is prudence which makes us suspicious of dependency, for slavery is as familiar a feature of the world as friendship.

The only school in which to learn acceptance of contingency would be one in which we learned, not merely that God makes the world *ex nihilo*, but that the 'nothing' out of which he makes it is the non-necessity, the *gratuité*, of love, and in which, moreover, we also learned that *what* he makes, in love, is harmony and friendship, homecoming and peace. In the Christian scheme of things, these things are discovered, not from the first article of the Creed, the confession of our createdness, considered on its own, but from that first article considered in relation to the second (which speaks of sonship) and the third (which tells us of the Spirit's gift). It is, in other words, only within the pattern provided by the Creed in its entirety that we discover, not only that God makes the world, but that God makes the world parentally, and that the world God makes parentally is the temple of his peace.

This is the kind of school the Church exists to be: a place within the wider culture in which this reading of contingency, of all things' createdness *ex nihilo*, could be, not merely stated, but – in all our common life and labour – even now displayed. Only through such sacramental instantiation of its truth can the doctrine of God's creation of the world become, again, good news.

A question of meaning

That reason's truths are necessary and those of history merely accidental, as Lessing and his contemporaries supposed, is not, itself, a necessary truth, but merely how things seem to people who (as I put it earlier) have dissociated memory from argument, narrative from explanation. Our problem, these days, is rather different. What worries us is not that reason's truths alone seem really true, but rather that, having unmasked 'Reason' as but another idol, another construct of our restless vanity, we mistrust claims to final, comprehensive explanation. Assertions by those who exercise authority that X is absolutely true, or Y a rule without exceptions, are heard less as 'good news' than as *diktat*. Nevertheless, the correlative crumbling of truth into subjectivism, into what 'makes sense for me', is a madness that gives comfort only to the rich and powerful. Thus it is that, speaking and scribbling endless quantities of words, we seem to have forgotten what it would be like to hear some single word, one *logos*, bearing the burden of the meaning of the world, and to hear this word uttered not to our condemnation or oppression but to all things' deliverance, as Gospel, joy.

After Auschwitz and Kolyma, all claims that everything does, in the end, make sense, are suspect. Nor is it, by any means, only God that now seems difficult to understand. Human beings are hardly more intelligible. A certain careless atheism supposes that it is 'religious' truth that has been called in question. But in what 'secular' story would all our killing fields find mention as but unfortunate episodes in an otherwise quite satisfactory tale? In those dark forests, it is the sense not simply of religion but of everything (Aquinas's *omnia* again) that risks unravelling.

It is, perhaps, the very notion of truth 'claimed', 'asserted', that we should set question marks against. 'Claims' are what *I* stake over against *you*, and the gesture of 'assertion', which, in ancient Rome, both set slaves free and bound them into servitude, now connotes my power rather than your liberty. The heart of the matter seems to be that, if there is sense or meaning in the world, it goes before our finding and waits more upon our trust than on our ingenuity. Truth, in the last analysis, is not our achievement, let alone our plaything or our property, but a gift received, a presence recognised.

This was the thesis of a remarkable essay by George Steiner, in which he argued that 'any coherent understanding of what language is and how language performs ... is, in the final analysis, underwritten by the assumption of God's presence.' Many of his readers must have found this statement quite bizarre. He went on to argue that the only way back to recognition of that presence would be through the practice and acknowledgement of what he called 'the core of trust within logic itself, where "logic" is a *Logos*-derivative and construct.' There would be 'no history as we know it, no religion, metaphysics, politics or aesthetics as we have lived them, without an initial act of trust, of confiding', so fundamental as to be constitutive of the relation between word and world.[14] The crisis of our time arises from the fracturing of that relation.

'In the beginning was the Word.' But how might that Word now be heard? How might the world, in all its savagery and darkness, its bewildering and uncontrollable diversity, be given sense as utterance of that constituting Word? The temptation, for the Christian, is to take shortcuts toward the answer. Theology, as the Archbishop of Canterbury reminds us, is 'perennially liable to be seduced by the prospect of bypassing the question of how it *learns* its own language.' Theologies east and west, Catholic and Protestant, conservative and liberal, all tend in one way or another to operate 'with a model of truth as something ultimately separable *in our minds* from the dialectical process of its historical reflection and appropriation.' Under the influence of this model, we grow impatient with 'debate, conflict, ambivalence, polysemy, paradox. And this is at heart an impatience with learning, and with learning about our learning.'[15]

In the previous section I described the Christian life as schooling in contingency. From the standpoint of the present meditation on the meaning of the world, its constitution by the *Logos*, we could call the Church a school of contemplation, a place where people learned to learn, educated each other in attentiveness.

Before the mystery of God, teachableness or docility is contemplation, receptivity: that generous attentiveness of which Mary's '*Fiat*' is the paradigm. Such contemplation, such attentiveness, is patient (and patience connotes suffering); it is 'appropriation of the vulnerability of the self in the midst of the language and transactions of the world.'[16] It is the very form of God's self-utterance in Gethsemane.

There are, it seems to me, three areas in particular in which this

14. George Steiner, *Real Presences: Is There Anything in What We Say?* (London, Faber, 1989), pp. 3, 89. In the 1990 Aquinas Lecture, in Cambridge, I tried to draw out some of the rich theological implications of Steiner's essay: see Nicholas Lash, 'Friday, Saturday, Sunday,' *New Blackfriars*, 71 (March 1990), pp. 109–19.

15. Rowan Williams, 'Trinity and Revelation', *Modern Theology*, 2, no. 3 (1986), pp. 197–8 (second emphasis added).

16. Rowan Williams, 'Theological Integrity', *New Blackfriars*, 72 (1991), p. 148.

theme of the necessity of learning how to learn, of Christian faith as patience and docility, is, at present, of particular importance. The first of these I mentioned earlier, when I suggested that the duty of attempting accurately and generously to understand and represent the words and deeds of those from whom we differ has its roots in the doctrine of God's Trinity. The appropriate character of Christian disagreement is a strictly theological topic, and by no means merely a question of church order or Christian ethics. As such, it is, at present, dangerously neglected.

The other two areas I have in mind would be, on the one hand, the relations between what we loosely call 'Church' and 'world' and, on the other, the relations between Christianity and other religious traditions. The simple point that still needs insisting on is this: the recognition that there is always something to be *learned* – whether from geneticists and sociologists, historians and literary critics, psychologists and philosophers, or from not only Judaism, Islam, Buddhism, and Hinduism, but also from folk religion and even New Age cults – is not a suspect concession to 'liberalism', but a necessary implication of the doctrine that the Word which is, in Jesus Christ, incarnate, is the selfsame Word in the one utterance of which God makes all worlds. It is worth remembering that Aquinas's answer to the question as to whether the diversity of things is due to God was: Yes, because no single creature could give God adequate expression. Not even, by implication, God's own humanity, particular flesh (see Luke 4:18; Isa. 61:1).[17]

To confess that all things (*omnia*) have, in God's self-utterance, their existence, origin, and destiny, is to confess that, in the end, all things make sense. And the sense they make is shown in him whose story – from conception through Calvary to the Father's side – is summarised in the second article of the Creed. That article, however, considered on its own, does not lack ambivalence, for it ends in judgement. This utterance of God, this meaning of the world, this judgement, is good news only if it is forgiveness and not condemnation. And this we learn, not from the second article considered on its own, but only in that gift of life, outpouring of the Spirit, acknowledged in the third.

This, then, is the kind of school the Church exists to be: a place within the wider culture in which contemplativity, attentiveness, openness to truth, all truth, might – even in present darkness, conflict, and confusion – be learned in patient labour waiting on the ending of God's utterance, God's Word of peace.

17. See Aquinas, *Summa Theologiae*, Ia, q. 47, a. 1.

A question of life

In personal relations, distance is a metaphor for lack of interest or affection. We say of people, for example, that they are very 'close' to each other, or that they have grown 'far apart'. The God of modern theism seems very far away: is this an indication of our lack of interest in God, or of God's unconcern for us? Both answers have been given. According to the former, the western world is 'secularised', a place of weak and waning faith, less interested in, or influenced by, religious issues than were previous periods in European history.

Bookshops (at least in Britain) suggest a different story. They may stock few, if any, titles of serious theology or biblical criticism, but they display shelf upon shelf piled high with spirituality, the occult, New Age, Sufism, reincarnation, mysticism, black magic, Tantrism, astrology, and Tarot. If this is 'secularity', its atmosphere is restless, irrational, and superstitious; driven by a poignant and unstructured yearning for something less impersonal and remote ('distance' again!) than the lifeless systems of which academic experts, from quantum physics through to economics, seem to speak.

If our societies are, as is often said, materialist, then this is a materialism obsessed with spirit. And everyone agrees, it seems, that spirit is a good thing. But what does it connote? With what do we contrast it? Spirit is not-matter, not-body, or (in certain New Age and charismatic circles) not-reason. When church leaders are exhorted, or exhort others, to concentrate on 'spiritual' affairs, the implication seems to be that these are matters loftier than, and different from, such down-to-earth concerns as preaching good news to the poor and liberating the oppressed.

It is, moreover, not unknown for even educated Christians to suppose that the distinction drawn, in Romans 8, between flesh and spirit is *more or less* the same as that which we might draw between the body and the mind. So firm the grip in which our imagination is held by the dualisms of modernity that we hardly notice the extent to which, at the heart of Scripture's talk of God as Spirit (and of the world as the effect of, and as affected by, the Spirit that is God) the contrast drawn is between not-life, or lesser life, or life gone wrong, and *life*: true life, real life, God's life and all creation's life in God. Spirit is life outpoured, beyond imagination and control, like wind, the breath of God.

According to the Nicene Creed, the mystery we confess as God is Holy Spirit, life-giving Lord. God gives all life, is intimate to every movement, animates all action, fuels freedom, breaks down barriers, breathes dead bones dancing. This line of thought, generating a sense of all things (*omnia* again) as a kind of organism pulsating to the heartbeat of life-giving Spirit, has some affinity with the gathering recognition – from our economics and our politics to so-called 'chaos theory' in mathematics – that the whole system of the world forms one single, vulnerable, complex web of life.

Of course such thoughts are dangerous: all worthwhile thoughts are. Christianity is not pantheist. We do not worship 'nature' or the world. Life, all life, the life we share, the life that we are called upon to cherish and enhance, true life, eternal life, is *given*, has a whence, a referent. God gives, and what God gives is nothing less than God. But God's God-given life is ever in the movement of the giver's hand, is ever being-given. Christian speech concerning the givenness of God, whom we call grace and life, is speech unceasingly referring the given to the giving. 'Gift', as used of God, attempts to name a relationship of origin.[18]

In other words, where the grammar of Christian discourse is concerned, pantheism is a mistake of the same kind as agnosticism and fundamentalism. It freezes one 'moment' in the movement of our life in God, mistaking what it finds there for a description of divinity. There is nothing that God simply 'is': not silence, speech, or life. But, in the silence that is God, God speaks, and what God speaks is life, in God.

Pantheism distorts the sense of God, but does so neither more nor less than the contraction of the territory to which discourse concerning God refers from all things, *omnia*, to some small margin of our private lives, the supposedly safe Sunday-space we think of as 'religion'.

I have mentioned our deepening recognition of the interdependence of the constituents of the world. But interdependence is not, in itself, good news. The McDonald's sign in every city may be a symptom, not of human solidarity, the dawn of the communion of saints, but rather of the abolition of particularity, diversity, and freedom beneath the wheels of juggernauts beyond accountability and control. We have still good reason to be frightened by voices such as that of Teilhard de Chardin, proclaiming in 1936: 'Fascism opens its arms to the future. Its ambition is to embrace vast wholes in its empire. And in the vigorous organization of which it dreams, it is more anxious than any

---

18. See Aquinas, *Summa Theologiae*, Ia, qq. 37, 38, for some brief discussion of which, see Nicholas Lash, 'Donation' in *Believing Three Ways in One God*, op. cit.

other system to allow for the preservation of the elite (which means the personal and the Spirit).'[19]

To discover the conditions in which the announcement of interdependence would be good news, we must go back to the beginning. If God is life, enlivening Spirit, and if all life, vitality, joy, freedom, are therefore signs and tokens of God's presence, then the right name for God's absence from the world is death. Not mere mortality (for this is, after all, a function of contingency) but deadliness, extinction, the remorseless weight and burden of the world construed as fate.

Individuals still feel guilt. But, notwithstanding our fondness for blaming other nations, other social classes, other groups and 'currents' in society, for our common plight, it is as fate, necessity, rather than as guilt, that we experience the shared and public burden of the world. The gray pervasiveness of our despair (of which disillusion with political process is but one indication) perhaps arises from the recognition that necessity is not, by definition, transmutable into freedom. Whereas, if we were guilty, we might at least cry out for forgiveness.

There is no theory or hypothesis that could transform the world. Despair, however, overlooks a *fact*. The fact is that forgiveness occurs. Friendship and reconciliation may be fragile, but they are facts, and so are peace, and joy, and gentleness.

There is a useful notion in philosophy: that of the 'performative utterance'. Such utterances do not describe, propose, prepare the ground for action; they enact what they announce. Promises are performative. So is God's Word. God speaks: a world exists, a garden flourishes. God speaks: light shines in darkness, prisoners are freed, the dead are raised to life. The outpoured Spirit is what God, speaking, does.

What, on a Christian reading of the world, we learn from the fragile fact of friendship, then, is that we have been forgiven. It is in contrition, in friendship's bonds renewed, that guilt is retrospectively acknowledged. There are, in my opinion, few more succinct summaries of the Gospel than this: We have been made capable of friendship. The 'we' is unrestricted, it refers to everybody, past and present, near and far and, by analogy, to every feature of that web of life of which we form a part. We 'have been' made: the passive voice protects the primacy of grace, the givenness of things. Made 'capable of' friendship, rather than 'made friends', for it is as *duty* that we hear the Word's announcement of the way all things are made and made to be.

19. Pierre Teilhard de Chardin, 'The Salvation of Mankind', *Science and Christ* (New York, Harper and Row, 1968), pp. 140–41; English trans. of *Science et Christ* (Paris, Éditions de Seuil, 1965).

There are no short-cuts to friendship. How could there be, when even God's announcement of the fact, God's self-performing utterance of love, exacts his agony and crucifixion? The 'sponge full of vinegar' given to the dying Christ is an allusion to Psalm 69, which contains the plea: 'Let not the flood sweep over me, or the deep swallow me up' (Mark 15:36; Ps. 69:15 [see 69:21]). It is as if God's utterance, which makes the world, is itself threatened by the chaos that it sets in place as 'nothing'.

A prayer in the Gelasian Sacramentary says of the Holy Spirit that he is himself the forgiveness of all our sins: '*ipse est omnium remissio peccatorum*'.[20] If, in the third article of the Creed, the mystery of God is confessed as given life, communion, friendship, it is in the second article that we acknowledge the price love's utterance, as forgiveness, pays.

This, then, is the kind of school the Church exists to be: a place within the wider culture in which forgiveness is found, in which the godliness of life is celebrated, and in which a foretaste of all things' final friendship even now occurs.

Home or away?

If God is a stranger in our house, then it is quite certain that our house is not our home, for we are made to be at home with God. That we are not yet at home is not, in itself, occasion for surprise. For we are travellers, pilgrim people (hence the image from which this article set out was that of an airline terminal). We are not yet at home. Nevertheless, according to the Gospel, God has already, even now, made himself at home with us, 'pitched his tent' among our dwellings (see John 1:14). Before we take false comfort from the fact that we are still away from home, therefore, we need more carefully to formulate the paradox of our predicament.

If the subject-matter of that theology which pertains to holy teaching is, indeed, the mystery of God and of all things, *omnia*, in their relationship to God, then a crisis in our thinking about God will be a crisis in our thinking about not merely God but everything.

Christian thinking is *fides quaerens intellectum*. Failure to attain that glimmer of understanding of the mystery of God which has, even now, been made accessible to us is, *eo ipso*, misunderstanding of the world of which we form a part. If there is, indeed, a crisis in our thinking about God, then this will show itself, will find expression, in crisis and confusion in our thinking about science

20. *Liber Sacramentorum Romanae Aeclesiae Ordinis Anni Circuli (Sacramentarium Gelasianum)*, ed. L. C. Mohlberg (Rome, Herder, 1968), p. lxxx, no. 639.

and politics, ethics and economics, birth and death and poetry and peace.

And if this crisis has, at present, a distinctive shape, a particular configuration, this distinctiveness consists in the extent to which people – even devout, well-educated Christian people; even priests and bishops (not to mention theologians!) – fail to realise this. If, however, we continue to act, and think, and study, as if relationship with God was mediated by something less than everything, by 'religion' for example, or by the Church alone, if (to turn it round the other way) we continue to behave as if God was one of the particular objects, things, or topics, with which we have to do, then we Christians, who have been called to clarify the darkness, will merely contribute to its deepening.

To recapitulate. Under the heading of 'A Question of Being', I suggested that it is an implication of the trinitarian character of Christian faith that there is no overarching single head, no ultimately privileged descriptive category (neither 'being,' nor 'truth', nor 'love') in terms of which the mystery of God is best considered. In the following sections, I tried to indicate why the Church is to be thought of as a kind of school, within the wider culture, in which the practice and theory of contingency, and sense, and common life, might be learned, and purified, and deepened. This is, perhaps, another way of saying that the Church exists to be a place in which the fact and possibility of friendship among those who had been strangers, of homecoming after exile, might be discovered and displayed.

Chapter 4

Recovering Contingency

At the end of *The Rediscovery of the Mind,* John Searle offered some 'rough guidelines' towards that goal, of which the 'fourth and final' one was that 'we need to rediscover the social character of the mind'.[1] He had already noted, at the midpoint of his argument, that there are two subjects 'crucial to consciousness', about which he had little to say because he 'did not yet understand them well enough': 'temporality' and 'society'.[2] If we take the 'modern' world to mean the world constructed in western Europe and North America in the seventeenth and eighteenth centuries then, notwithstanding the bewildering imprecision with which the epithet 'post-modern' is at present strewn around, it seems to me that, in identifying those two subjects as 'crucial to *consciousness*', Searle showed himself to be, if not post-modern, then at least a most *un*modern kind of thinker.

Much of this chapter will amount to little more than gracenotes to his argument; hints and indications as to why I think he is quite right to point in these directions and as to the effect that moving in them might have on our accounts of who and what we are, and of how we are the kinds of things we take ourselves to be. Before getting under way, however, I have two anecdotes, one general remark, a morsel of polemic, and an explanation.

Did society come first?

Many years ago Lord Longford told an uncle of mine that, in his youth, while still a member of the Conservative Party, he was invited to lunch by Stanley Baldwin. As they strolled in the grounds after their meal, the starry-eyed young politician asked the elder statesman: 'Tell me, sir, is there any one political thinker who has been especially influential in the development of your own thought?' After some reflection, Baldwin replied: 'Yes, there is; there is So-and-so. You see, what I learned from him, and I have

1. John Searle, *The Rediscovery of the Mind* (London, MIT Press, 1992), p. 248.
2. Ibid., p. 127.

never forgotten it, is that, where relations between society and the State are concerned, society comes first. Or was it the other way round?'[3]

It is my impression that, where relations between human individuals and the larger natural and social formations of which they form a part are concerned, much of our current scientific and philosophical thinking is in a disturbingly Baldwinesque condition. We know that we are fragile, interactive products of biology and circumstance, wholly dependent at every level of existence upon the complex webs of causes and effects of which we form a part, and yet, in our discussions about 'human identity', the focus of attention is usually an individual agent as apparently autonomous as any 'early modern man' might have supposed himself to be.

My second (and related) anecdote concerns Geoffrey Lampe, who was Ely Professor of Divinity in Cambridge from 1959 to 1971, and then Regius Professor until 1979. Enormously learned in the writings of the Greek and Latin Fathers, formal or 'grammatical' considerations were quite alien to him. We were close friends, but could never get within earshot of each other on the topic (to which I shall return) of 'subsistent relations' in Trinitarian theology. As his motto in this matter, we could take this sentence from his 1976 Bampton Lectures, *God as Spirit*: 'If there are relations there must be entities that are related.'[4]

My general remark concerns what might properly be called the politics of our topic. Human identity is not simply a natural 'given' in the sense that the identity of a hydrogen atom would appear to be (where by 'given' I mean, at this point, no more than *datum*; although whether, and in what sense, human identity is not merely Latin *datum* but also English 'gift' is a question well worth serious philosophical and theological consideration). Human identity is not simply a natural 'given' because (however unwelcome this claim may be to spirit–matter dualists) the constituents of what we call 'culture' are thereby constituents of human

---

3. Some months after the conference at which this paper was first given, I found myself sitting next to Lord Longford at dinner, and asked him to verify the story. Memory undimmed at 90, he did so with enthusiasm but (as so often happens with historical interpretation) the 'raw' version fits somewhat less neatly to my argument than the 'cooked'. 'So-and-so' was Sir Henry Maine, from whom Baldwin had learned, and had never forgotten, that 'the story of society is a story of evolution from contract to status. Or was it the other way round?'

4. G. W. H. Lampe, *God as Spirit* (Oxford, Clarendon Press, 1977), p. 226.

'nature', and hence of our identity,[5] and culture – the ways we live together, the symbol-systems and the cities that we fashion, the networks of information and control that we construct – is as much a project as it is a given fact.

I say that this remark concerns the politics of our topic because the specification of the project that human being is, is not the prerogative of any particular group of human beings. Hydrogen does not decide what being hydrogen will be. In contrast, determining what human being will be is – however severe the limits within which, in fact, we operate – part of what it means to be a human being. It follows, as the Indian theologian Felix Wilfred remarked recently, that 'Defining the human is not and cannot be the prerogative of one civilization or one people.'[6] (My hope is that this remark may flush out the residual Cartesianism in some of my scientific friends who suppose themselves quite free from the disease!)

Next, a morsel of polemic. As a Catholic theologian with quite conventional views on Christian doctrine, I welcome John Searle's 'biological naturalism' as wholeheartedly as I do Gerald Edelman's attempts to put the mind back into nature.[7] Which may surprise Searle, who curiously supposes that people who believe as I do are likely to be Cartesians suffering from the 'antiscientism that went with traditional dualism, the belief in the immortality of the soul, spiritualism, and so on'.[8] In blissful ignorance, it seems, of the extent to which popular substance-dualist construals of the relationship between the human body and its life, or soul, had for centuries been an embarrassment to mainstream non-dualist Aristotelianism (to say nothing of being incompatible with the Jewish anthropology that the Christian Scriptures breathe), and hence of the extent to which Cartesian dualism is a recent disruptive *innovation* in the history of Christian anthropology, he blithely classifies Cartesianism amongst the 'traditional religious conception[s] of the mind'.[9]

Contrast this muddle with the more plausibly traditional

5. I regret not having yet had an opportunity to read John Searle, *The Construction of Social Reality* (London, Penguin Books, 1995), but am encouraged by the extent to which my remark seems to chime in with his conclusion (see pp. 226–7).
6. Felix Wilfred, *From the Dusty Soil* (Madras, University of Madras, 1995), p. 71.
7. Searle, *Rediscovery*, op. cit., p. 1; Gerald Edelman, *Bright Air, Brilliant Fire: On the Matter of the Mind* (London, Penguin Books, 1992); the title of Edelman's second chapter is 'Putting the Mind Back into Nature'.
8. Searle, *Rediscovery*, op. cit., p. 3.
9. Ibid., p. 4.

conception of the mind that Anthony Kenny once offered in order to indicate 'the magnitude of the Cartesian revolution in philosophy', and to show how dramatically the place where Descartes drew the boundaries of the mind differed from 'where they had been drawn by his predecessors in antiquity and in the Middle Ages, in the tradition going back to Aristotle'. Kenny defined the mind as 'the capacity for behaviour of the complicated and symbolic kinds which constitute the linguistic, social, moral, economic, scientific, cultural, and other characteristic activities of human beings in society'.[10]

Searle's insouciant misdescription of the way that things have stood for most of western cultural history is, it seems, due to the fact that he is one of those people who, in their 'deepest reflections', simply cannot 'take ... seriously' the opinions of people who believe in God; which fact about himself he is modest enough to characterise, at one point, as 'insensitivity'.[11] Here ends the first morsel of polemic.

Finally, to end these scattered introductory remarks, a word of explanation as to why I contributed to the conference of which the volume in which this essay originally appeared is a record. I am a professional theologian and amateur philosopher with an interest in the history of ideas whose scientific education came to a shuddering halt at the age of 17, with the result that I am only able to peer, with fascination, over the shoulders of people such as Searle and Edelman to find out what is going on inside my brain.

With the preliminaries disposed of, there are, in the body of this chapter, three things that I would like to do. First, to offer some reflections on the way that God is 'one', and on the esoteric notion of 'subsistent relations' in divinity. This will enable me indirectly to comment on 'the social character of the mind'. In the second place, it is worth asking how the 'temporal' character of consciousness got lost from view. Here I shall turn for help to Francis Bacon. Finally, I shall try to indicate why what I have called, in the title of my chapter, 'recovering contingency', is crucial to all our efforts to make better sense of who and what, as human beings, we are.

The way that God is one

I hope that the fact that, in this section of my chapter, I am going to talk theology, will not unduly distress those of you who find the enterprise quite uncongenial. Think of what I have to say as

10. Anthony Kenny, *The Metaphysics of Mind* (Oxford, Clarendon Press, 1989), p. 7.
11. See Searle, *Rediscovery*, op. cit., pp. 90–91.

serving the same kind of purpose as those illustrative fictions which philosophers construct when they find thinking about the real world too difficult.

After all, Ludwig Feuerbach was by no means the first to notice that our images of God reflect the forms of our experience. When the people of Israel spoke of God as shepherd or as king, they knew what they were doing (as one can see by noticing that, very often, what they were doing was contrasting God's ways and ours: unlike other judges, God judges justly; unlike other shepherds, God brings back the strayed, strengthens the weak, and so on). If, as Emile Durkheim argued, religion is 'the system of symbols by means of which society becomes conscious of itself',[12] then one way of finding out how human beings understand themselves – what they take to be their nature, identity and purpose – will be by attending to the ways in which they speak about whatever it is that they most cherish, venerate, revere.

It is not uncommon these days for people to discuss whether or not there is 'a God'. In such discussion, godness or divinity is being taken as a nature name, the label for some kind or category of which there may or may not be an instance or some instances. Such speech has little in common with the grammar of the classic forms of mainstream western Christianity (to which, for present purposes, I confine my illustration). God, in this tradition, is not best spoken of as an individual with a nature of some kind, for the One that alone is to be worshipped is beyond all categories, creates and comprehends all kinds.

The conceptual and grammatical resources for giving expression to this recognition (derived from Jewish insistence on the holiness of God) and for sustaining the disciplined negation it requires, were drawn, in part, from Neoplatonism. Christian thinkers, uncomfortable with the priority that the Neoplatonists ascribed to the One, as to the Good, beyond both 'mind' and 'being', may have varied their vantage-point, now laying the emphasis on goodness as the goal and consummation of all things' being and desire, now (as in Aquinas's case) insisting resolutely on the priority of being, but the central thrust was to assert the *identity*, in God, of goodness, unity, and being.[13]

Part of what is at issue here, of course, is the insistence that all things come from one good principle and go to one good end. In

12. Emile Durkheim, *Suicide: A Study in Sociology*, trans. John A. Spaulding and George Simpson (London, Routledge and Kegan Paul, 1952), p. 312.
13. W. J. Hankey, *God in Himself: Aquinas' Doctrine of God as Expounded in the Summa Theologiae* (Oxford, Oxford University Press, 1987), pp. 74–80.

other words, it is as characteristic of Christian cosmology as of Jewish to reject those dualisms for which the world's existence is undying warfare between the darkness and the light, between order and engulfing chaos.

Moreover, lest Neoplatonic metaphors of emanation be too literally construed, Aquinas's ascription of priority to being is at the service of a strategy that sets consideration of the ways in which God does *not* 'exist' at the top of the agenda.[14] Thus, while recognition of contingency may properly awaken wonder, anyone who supposes that they have God in their conceptual or imaginative sights, that they know what God is like (or would be, if there were a God) is not, according to Aquinas, thinking about God at all.

But there is more to it than this. Although it is easy to lose sight of the fact when reading his tersely formal texts, Aquinas is not meditating, abstractly, on divinity or 'godness' but more concretely considering what is to be said of One confessed as Father, Word, and Spirit.[15] Thus, for example, he introduces a discussion of whether God is to be thought of as 'supremely one' by quoting, with approval, a passage from Bernard of Clairvaux in which Bernard passes through eight different kinds of unity – those pertaining, for example, to collections and to organisms, to marriages and to societies – before declaring that 'amongst all the things that rightly are called "one", the summit or high point [*arx*] is occupied by the oneness of the Trinity'.[16]

Rhetoric, yes, but not mere verbal gesturing. The history of Christian theology is the history of attempts to think of one confessed as Father, Word, and Spirit, without collapsing what is thought of into a group of individuals. (If, by the way, we keep in mind the Durkheimian rubric that religion is the system of

14. See Fergus Kerr, 'Aquinas after Marion', *New Blackfriars*, 76, pp. 354–64 (1995). It would be difficult to exaggerate the importance of the fact that Aquinas's entire discussion, in the first part of the *Summa Theologiae*, of God's simplicity, perfection, goodness, immutability, eternity, and even oneness, is announced as a discussion of 'the ways in which God does not exist' (Prologue to the *Summa*, Ia, q. 3).

15. More generally, as David Burrell put it in his study of Ibn-Sina, Maimonides, and Aquinas: 'The unity of God can hardly be apprehended as a purely philosophical assertion. For the phrase itself – 'God is one' – is but shorthand for specific confessions of faith, and our manner of elucidating it should reflect the shape of those confessions' (David B. Burrell, *Knowing the Unknowable God: Ibn-Sina, Maimonides, Aquinas* [Notre Dame, University of Notre Dame Press, 1986], p. 111).

16. See Thomas Aquinas, *Summa Theologiae*, Ia, 14.4, s.c.; Bernard, *De Consideratione*, PL 182, 799.

symbols by means of which society becomes conscious of itself, then we could – impressionistically – interpret what I have just said as implying that, wittingly or unwittingly, the history of Christian theology is the history of attempts to think of given meaning and common life, of message and community, without, on the one hand, divorcing meaning from its ground or, on the other, separating doctrine from life, the ideal from the real.)

'Philip said to him, "Lord, show us the Father, and we shall be satisfied." To which Jesus replies: "Have I been with you so long, and yet you do not know me, Philip? He who has seen me has seen the Father." '[17] Thus it is that the message heard and seen and touched as Jesus of Nazareth, a particular Jew, was said to be one and the same as the message's utterer, as the one called God, Creator, Father. One and the same what? Distinctions were drawn, vocabularies constructed, with varied success. God, it was said, is three 'persons' in one 'nature'. But, even in Augustine, it is (according to Henry Chadwick) 'unclear whether we are being told that the three Persons exist in relation to one another, or whether relation is integral to the notion of Person'.[18]

That last phrase gives us the clue that I want to follow up. Nearly 900 years separate Augustine from Aquinas, in whose hands the doctrine of subsistent relations reached its most thoroughly worked-out expression as a set of protocols with the aid of which we may try to speak of a God who exists as, and only as, the relations that God is. And yet the neatest illustration that I know of how this apparently austere and abstract formal theorem might be 'cashed' may be found in some comments of Augustine's on the Fourth Gospel.

'The Son' (according to that Gospel) 'can do nothing of his own accord, but only what he sees the Father doing.'[19] But what would it mean to say that the Son 'sees' the Father's work? At this point, I want to push a little further a suggestion that Searle makes about conscious subjectivity. According to Searle, 'We cannot get at the reality of consciousness in the way that, using consciousness, we can get at the reality of other phenomena.' The reason for this is that, as he says, 'where conscious subjectivity is concerned, there is no distinction between the observation and the thing observed'.[20] True, but the assumption that, elsewhere in our thinking, the distinction between the 'observation' and the thing 'observed' is always, or even for the

17. John 14:8–9.
18. Henry Chadwick, *Boethius: The Consolations of Music, Logic, Theology, and Philosophy* (Oxford, Clarendon Press, 1981), p. 212.
19. John 5:19.
20. Searle, *Rediscovery*, op. cit., pp. 96–7.

most part, the *kind* of distinction (implying the kind of 'distance') that there is between the eye and an object that we literally 'observe', is quite unwarranted.

In other words, when we say that we 'see' this, that, or the other, what we often mean is that we 'see the *point*' about it, that we understand it. Throughout the Fourth Gospel, 'seeing' is thus used as a metaphor for understanding. And it is this that gives Augustine the clue that he needs: 'The way in which the Son sees the Father is simply by being the Son. For him, being from the Father, that is being born of the Father, is not something different from seeing the Father.' Or, as he put it elsewhere: '*Videndo enim natus est, et nascendo videt*'; 'In seeing he is born, and in being born he sees.'[21]

God's very identity, God's existence, simply *is* 'seeing the point' about Himself, the world, and us. And that relation works both ways: as the seeing of the point, and as the point that is thus seen. And so it is that if, in seeing Jesus, we see the point about him, we have, in seeing it, seen God. Which is what Philip failed to see.

I apologise for dragging you through what may have been, for some, bizarre and unfamiliar material. But I hope that, now, you see the point! Following, once more, my Durkheimian rubric, the suggestion is that a society which thus described – in terms of pure relationship, pure 'donation', without remainder – not merely, we might say, the 'character' of God, but God's very being, God's identity, must surely have had a sense of human identity, of what it is to *be* a human being, profoundly different from one which (like our own) for the most part takes it for granted that, in Geoffrey Lampe's expression, 'if there are relations there must be entities that are related'.[22]

I would, moreover, urge that it is questions of ontology, and not just of ethics, that are at issue here. Of course we are talking about ethics as well, for I take it to be an implication of my earlier reminder that human nature is both *fact* and *project* that the ontology of human being entails some set of ethical proposals or presuppositions.

I earlier described as 'Baldwinesque' our tendency simultaneously to speak as if human individuals were mere epiphenomena – particles of flotsam, or fragments of some vast machine or organism – and agents bearing the burden of autonomy. It would, however, have been just as accurate to describe this inconsistency as 'Thatcherite', because the prophet of a rugged individualism

21. Augustine, *The Trinity*, ed. Edmund Hill (New York, New City Press, 1991), Book ii, 3; *In Joann. Ev.* (CCSL, 36), xxi, 4.
22. Lampe, *God as Spirit*, op. cit., p. 226.

who insisted that 'there is no such thing as society' was no less adamant in her belief that 'you can't buck the market'.

My hunch is that there is no way through these well-known aporia except through the recognition that the two subjects picked out by Searle as 'crucial to consciousness' – namely, temporality and society – are, both historically and conceptually, inextricably interrelated. That being so, and having indicated my conviction that the history of Christian thought may contain neglected resources that might help us in our rediscovery of 'the social character of the mind', I now want to move on and, with a little help from Francis Bacon, suggest when and why it was that the medieval privileging of the relational became, almost literally, unimaginable.

People are stories

According to Searle, 'one of the keys' to the original development of a still widespread world-view that will be baffled by his contention that 'consciousness is just an ordinary biological feature of the world' was 'the exclusion of consciousness from the subject matter of science by Descartes, Galileo, and others in the seventeenth century'.[23] I now want to suggest that it might be useful to put a slightly different spin on the developments that he has in mind by viewing them in terms of what I would call the neutralisation of memory or (if you will pardon the horrid word) the denarratisation of knowledge.

Commenting on Lessing's pronouncement that 'Accidental truths of history can never become the proof of a necessary truth of reason',[24] Karl Barth once said, 'This sentence does not say ... what Fichte later said: "It is only the Metaphysical and on no account the Historical, which makes me blessed." '[25] Nevertheless, that is the direction in which Lessing points. In other words, by 1777 (when Lessing wrote those words) the wedge between 'event' and 'truth' had been so firmly driven home that learned men had quite forgotten that explanations take the form of stories, told by someone, and not by nobody, in one place and not nowhere, in some manner that might have been otherwise.

In 1750, Denis Diderot published his Prospectus for that Bible of French Enlightenment, the *Encyclopédie*. There we see the whole

23. Searle, *Rediscovery*, op. cit., p. 85.
24. G. E. Lessing, 'On the Proof of the Spirit and of Power', in *Lessing's Theological Writings*, selected and introduced by Henry Chadwick (London, Adam and Charles Black, 1956), p. 53.
25. Karl Barth, *Protestant Theology in the Nineteenth Century: Its Background and History* (London, SCM Press, 1972), p. 253.

map of human knowledges (*'connoissances* [sic!] *humaines'*) laid
out in three columns: memory (for history), reason (for philosophy), and imagination (for poetry). Not the least striking thing
about this map, however, is that, with the exception of a slight
adjustment in the location of what Diderot called 'revealed
theology', the entire scheme has been lifted, lock, stock, and
barrel, from Francis Bacon's *Advancement of Learning*, which was
published in 1605, before Descartes, or even Galileo, had made
their mark. It is, therefore, to Bacon's version of the map that I
now turn.[26]

'Any one', said Bacon, 'will easily perceive the justness of this
division that recurs to the origin of our ideas ... it is clearly
manifest that history, poetry, and philosophy flow from the three
distinct fountains of the mind, viz., the memory, the imagination,
and the reason; without any possibility of increasing their number.
For history and experience are one and the same thing; so are
philosophy and the sciences.'[27] The two features of his map to
which I would draw particular attention are, first, the trivial place
occupied by imagination and, second, its comprehensive dissociation of memory from argument, experience from reason.

Under 'imagination', Bacon listed only 'poetry', of three kinds:
'narrative', 'dramatic', and 'parabolic'. With this exclusion of
imagination from the territory of serious enquiry, interest is
thereby abandoned in the cognitive significance of metaphor and
story-telling, of parable, polysemy, and paradox. There is, that is to
say, a striking lack of interest in the concrete forms communication takes between human beings in existing networks of relationship. Bacon's mapping of the mind thus eloquently illustrates
Amos Funkenstein's account of the way in which, at this period,
the fusion of the late-medieval passion for plain speech and single
meanings with the Renaissance rediscovery of Stoic 'nature' – a
world seen as homogenous through and through, made of one
kind of stuff and driven by one set of forces – gave birth to a new
ideal for the working of the human mind: namely, 'a science

26. I have set out a simplified version of Diderot's *Prospectus*, and a
corresponding version of Bacon's, constructed from the table of
contents of his *First Part of the Great Instauration: The Dignity and
Advancement of Learning, in Nine Books*, in *The Physical and Metaphysical
Works of Lord Bacon*, ed. Joseph Devey (London, Henry G. Bohn,
1864), as appendices to chapter 8, below. Whereas Diderot set all
theology, 'natural' and 'revealed', in that part of philosophy known
as the 'Science of God', Bacon included only 'natural theology',
leaving what he called 'sacred or inspired theology' quite outside the
scheme of things to be surveyed from 'the small vessel of human
reason'.
27. Bacon, *Advancement of Learning*, op. cit., book ii, ch. 1.

that has an unequivocal language with which it speaks and uniform objects of which it speaks'.[28]

'For history and experience are one and the same thing; so are philosophy and the sciences', the former being the province of 'memory' and the latter that of 'reason'. History is broken down into 'civil history' – which covers 'memoirs' and 'antiquities', the history of the Church, of prophecy, and of providence – and 'natural history', comprising the story of the heavens, of meteors, of the earth and sea, of monsters, and of the agricultural, manual, and mechanical arts. Philosophy, on the other hand, is reason's study of God, and man – the body and the soul, the arts of conversation, negotiation, and state policy – and of nature: considered either 'speculatively', in physics, or 'practically', in magic and mechanics. Perhaps the most striking thing about this set-up, in which, as I said earlier, memory is set apart from argument, experience from reason, is the reduction of history to data – raw material for the working of the mind.

Items of information 'first strike the sense', said Bacon, 'which is as it were the port or entrance of the understanding'.[29] He seems to be sitting in a kind of capsule, a Tardis perhaps, receiving, through different apertures, raw materials to be processed: reviewed, considered, classified. There is no sense of his being part of a story, or set of stories, which have shaped his world and made things to be the way they are or seem to be; no sense of his being caught up in conversation, part of some larger set of narratives that he must enact, interpret, endorse, or struggle to revise. In other words, as early as 1605 we find Bacon inhabiting a world that is already recognisably 'modern' in that – if not temporality, then at least narratability – a sense of whence and whither, of a story with a plot, is ceasing to be constitutive of human being and of the being of the world. The 'ugly, broad ditch' that Lessing could not cross – between what happens to have happened and what must be true – is, it seems to me, already opening up.[30]

There is no small irony in the recognition that Lessing's ditch should turn out to have been little more than a figment of the modern imagination, because the truths of reason are never quite as necessary as those who formulate them may suppose, and

28. Amos Funkenstein, *Theology and the Scientific Imagination from the Middle Ages to the Seventeenth Century* (Princeton, Princeton University Press, 1986), p. 41. (Which links up with what John Searle was saying: cf. *Rediscovery*, op. cit., p. 20.)
29. Bacon, *Advancement of Learning*, op. cit., book ii, ch. 1.
30. See Lessing, 'On the Proof of the Spirit and of Power', op. cit., p. 55.

historical contingency may bear the meaning of the world and, perhaps, the truth of God. (The nineteenth century, of course, resolved the dilemma in the other direction: not by recovering contingency, but by what Karl Popper called 'historicism', the identification of what happened with what must be so.)

It has taken us too long to learn, again, that there is no neutral vantage-point, no 'nowhere in particular', from which truth may be discerned and the pattern of right action estimated. Narratives take time and, as we learn to find our way between experience and understanding, between what came before and what now lies ahead, it is as constituents of and contributors to a 'story-shaped world' that we proceed.[31] Such formal systems as we may construct, in philosophy or science, are shaped, determined, coloured, by the narrative soil from which they spring.[32]

Because we bear responsibility, individually and socially, for the stories that we tell, the narratives that we enact, the lives that we perform, there is what we might call an autobiographical component to every story that we propose as true. Biographies are stories of lives other than our own, whereas to make the story mine – to claim or to acknowledge that this is what *we* have been up to, what we are doing, where we ought to go – is to render its narration autobiographical. What, with these remarks, I have been trying to do, and I hope that the attempt does not seem too far-fetched, is to indicate connections between the temporal and self-involving character of truthful speech and what Searle calls the 'first person' character of 'the ontology of the mental'.[33]

When did the privileging of the relational become, almost literally, unimaginable? The answer seems to be in the late sixteenth and early seventeenth centuries, when new maps of knowledge not merely (as Searle observes) excluded consciousness from the subject-matter of science but, in their systematic dissociation of memory from argument, of narrative from truth, obscured from view the social, self-involving, tradition-grown or 'conversational' character of the human quest for truth.

31. See Brian Wicker, *The Story-shaped World: Fiction and Metaphysics: Some Variations on a Theme* (London, Athlone Press, 1975).
32. See Nicholas Lash, 'Ideology, Metaphor and Analogy', *Theology on the Way to Emmaus* (London, SCM Press, 1986), pp. 95–119; this essay was first published in Brian Hebblethwaite and Stewart Sutherland (eds.), *The Philosophical Frontiers of Christian Theology* (Cambridge, Cambridge University Press, 1982), pp. 68–94.
33. Searle, *Rediscovery*, op. cit., p. 20.

Recovering contingency

According to Searle, 'the deepest motive for materialism ... is simply a terror of consciousness', and 'the deepest reason for the fear of consciousness is that consciousness has the essentially terrifying feature of subjectivity'.[34] But why should subjectivity be terrifying? In being frightened of it, of what are we afraid? The answer would seem to lie in what Richard Bernstein called 'Cartesian anxiety'. 'Descartes' search for a foundation', said Bernstein, 'is the quest for some fixed point ... [and] the specter that hovers in the background of the journey' undertaken in the *Meditations* is 'not just radical scepticism but the dread of madness and chaos where nothing is fixed'.[35] A dread that Nietzsche also knew.

Here is Stanley Cavell, pushing the anxiety a little further back, behind Descartes, and locating it in the sense of radical solitude, of the absence of reliable relations:

> As long as God exists, I am not alone. And couldn't the other suffer the fate of God? It strikes me that it was out of the terror of this possibility that Luther promoted the individual human voice in the religious life. I wish to understand how the other now bears the weight of God, shows me that I am not alone in the universe.[36]

But why should we suppose that any other, any others, are strong enough, sufficiently reliable, to bear such weight? And so, suspecting any such supposition, any such large-scale trustfulness, to be unwarranted, anxiety is unassuaged.

Against this background, it is not surprising that the interests of modernity should have alternated between reliance on 'objects' – amenable to our control, neutral and unthreatening in their computability – and the retreat to romantic subjectivity, to weekend-worlds of private feeling – that is, of course, for those with the resources to indulge this alternation. (Notwithstanding the resolutely anti-Cartesian character of Searle's programme, it does seem to me that his use of the terms 'objective' and 'subjective' is still too strongly flavoured with subject–object dualism.[37])

Meanwhile, the energy that fuels the fear, that feeds the terror

34. Ibid., p. 55.
35. Richard J. Bernstein, *Beyond Objectivism and Relativism: Science, Hermeneutics, and Praxis* (Oxford, Basil Blackwell, 1983), p. 18.
36. Stanley Cavell, *The Claim of Reason: Wittgenstein, Scepticism, Morality, and Tragedy* (Oxford, Clarendon Press, 1979), p. 470.
37. See, e.g., Searle, *Rediscovery*, op. cit., pp. 20–21.

of our solitude, takes flesh as violence, seeks safety through control. Mary Midgley has often pointed out how even some quite serious scientific works, going all unbuttoned in their final chapter, indulge in fantasies of the control of things by mind, which display a most unscientific dread of death, of flesh, of our contingency.[38] For which reminder that scientists are sinful human beings, she has sometimes been most unfairly charged with being 'anti-science'. Not that the texts she mentions would have come as much of a surprise to Nietzsche, who understood the will to power.

It is time, I think, to go back to the beginning, to the early modern terror of contingency. '*Le silence éternel de ces espaces infinis m'effraie.*'[39] Was it the sheer scale of those spaces or their silence that most terrified Pascal? Insofar as it was the latter, we are brought back to the fear of solitude as the ground of our disquiet. But solitude occurs in context, the context of vast empty spaces through which silent systems turn. We are not simply on our own, it seems, but inexorably, necessarily alone.

'There is', says Searle, 'a sense of panic that comes over a certain type of philosophical sensibility when it recognizes that the project of grounding intentionality and rationality on some pure foundation, on some set of necessary and indubitable truths, is mistaken in principle.'[40] It is as if contingency were more than we can take. However, according to Gordon Michalson, in his study of Lessing, 'contingency is nerve-wracking only for those who have a stake in necessity'.[41] In which case, the recovery of contingency would seem to be, in part, a matter of surrendering that stake.

In 1916, at the age of 27, Ludwig Wittgenstein, during a lull in the fighting on the Russian front, wrote in his notebook: 'The wonderful thing is that the world exists. That there is what there is.'[42] I think it is worth trying to read that note without the background noise created by commentaries on the *Tractatus*; trying to read it, in other words, simply as an expression of wonder at the world's contingency, without invoking the thoroughly misleading category (in this context, and many others) of the 'mystical'.

38. See, e.g., Mary Midgley, *Science as Salvation: A Modern Myth and its Meaning* (London, Routledge, 1992).
39. Blaise Pascal, *Pensées*, 3.206.
40. Searle, *Rediscovery*, op. cit., p. 191.
41. Gordon E. Michalson, *Lessing's 'Ugly Ditch': A Study of Theology and History* (London, Pennsylvania State University Press, 1985), p. 31.
42. Ludwig Wittgenstein, *Notebooks 1914–16*, ed. G. E. M. Anscombe and G. H. von Wright (Oxford, Blackwell, 1961), p. 86; quoted from Fergus Kerr, 'Aquinas after Marion', *New Blackfriars*, 76 (July/August 1995), p. 364.

What is the difference between Wittgenstein's wonder and Pascal's fear? The question is worth asking, if only because no less an authority than G. H. von Wright spoke of a 'trenchant parallelism' between the writings of Pascal and those of Wittgenstein. Con Drury (who mentions this) admitted that there is something in it, but was nevertheless more inclined to emphasise the differences between the two. 'Drury', Wittgenstein once exhorted him, 'never allow yourself to become too familiar with holy things.'[43] The suggestion is that, unlike Pascal, Wittgenstein cannot be suspected of 'fideism', which Drury takes to be a way of avoiding difficulties by too familiar acquaintance with the holy.

Perhaps Wittgenstein's wonder, unlike Pascal's, did not tighten into terror because he had no 'stake in necessity'; did not seek to ground intentionality and rationality 'on some pure foundation'. This, if I follow him, is a good part of the reason why Searle invokes Wittgenstein's authority for his notion of the 'Background' – that sum of 'capacities, abilities, and general know-how that enable[s] our mental states to function'.[44] The important point, for my purpose, being the emphasis upon contingency: 'The Background does not have to be the way it is.'[45]

I spoke earlier of that alternation of subjectivity and a realm of calculated 'objects' with which the modern world has seemed so often stuck. In a recent essay in phenomenology, Jean-Yves Lacoste recast this deadly dialectic in terms of the relations between the earlier and the later Heidegger.[46]

With the Heidegger of *Sein und Zeit*, we find ourselves 'thrown' into a 'world': a worldly world, a *saeculum*, a secularised or disenchanted place. This recognition that we are 'strangers' lacking direction and (as Paul said) 'without God in the world',[47] may be intermittent, but it is as old as Greece and Rome, and much of ancient Judaism and early Christianity. It is, indeed, the keynote of the 'modern' world, but it would be intolerably parochial of us to suppose that we invented it.

The later Heidegger, according to Lacoste, paints a very different picture. We now find ourselves, not wanderers in the world,

43. M. O'C. Drury, 'Some notes on conversations with Wittgenstein', in *Recollections of Wittgenstein*, ed. Rush Rhees (Oxford, Oxford University Press, 1984), p. 94; see pp. 92–3.
44. Searle, *Rediscovery*, op. cit., p. 175. He goes on to say that 'The work of the later Wittgenstein is in large part about the Background' (p. 177).
45. Ibid., p. 177.
46. Jean-Yves Lacoste, 'En marge du monde et de la terre: l'aise', *Revue de Métaphysique et de Morale* (1995), pp. 185–200.
47. Eph. 2:12.

but dwellers in the *earth*, inhabitants of some particular space, some territory (notice *terra* there) whose woods, and springs, and hilltops, are our shrines. We are country-dwellers, peasants, pagans, once again, in tune to voices, forces, vibrancies, to which we owe allegiance and of which we form a part. From Gaia to Glastonbury and Greenpeace, we still inhabit Mother Earth. As with the 'subject–object' version, 'world' and 'earth', secularity and paganism, define each other, demand each other, sustain each other in existence.[48]

If human identity were simply a natural given, a product of its constituents, we might be simply stuck with this dialectic, doomed to oscillate between its poles. But, as I said at the beginning, human nature is as much a project as it is a given fact. Human identity includes the possibility of entertaining possibilities, of taking time together to work out how things are and how they might be made to be.

'Art', said Ernst Bloch, 'is a laboratory and also a feast of implemented possibilities.'[49] He had in mind Goethe's comment on Diderot's 'Essay on Painting': 'the artist, grateful to nature, which also produced him, gives her a second nature in return, but one that is felt and thought and humanly perfected'.[50] Does not art, thus characterised, embrace science and technology, politics and ethics – all the things we do against 'the Background'? And is it not desirable and necessary, integral to *human* 'nature', that we should acknowledge this from time to time and, in so doing, give to contingency the form of celebration? Nor should we exclude the possibility that such celebration may be in praise of God.

48. See Lacoste, 'En marge du monde', op. cit., p. 194.
49. Ernst Bloch, *The Principle of Hope*, vol. 1, trans. Neville Plaice, Stephen Plaice, and Paul Knight (Oxford, Basil Blackwell, 1986), p. 216.
50. Quoted by Bloch, loc. cit.

Chapter 5

Renewed, Dissolved, Remembered: MacKinnon and Metaphysics

An unread review

> I have some longstanding debts: to Donald MacKinnon, who
> introduced me to philosophy at Aberdeen between 1950 and
> 1952; to Cornelius Ernst, who got me to read Wittgenstein,
> together with Aristotle and Thomas Aquinas, at Hawkesyard
> in 1957–60; and to Adolf Darlap, who helped me to under-
> stand Heidegger (much easier than understanding Wittgen-
> stein), in Munich between 1964 and 1965.[1]

Serendipitously, a few days before being invited to contribute to
these celebrations some remarks on that 'longstanding debt' to
Donald MacKinnon, while sorting out some papers I came across
three yellowing pages of typescript. On the top of the final page
was written, in that inimitably energetic and near-illegible hand:
'Done for *Theology* in July 1977, but rejected by the editors as
unsuitable on the inflexible recommendation of Dr James Mark
(reviews editor). DMM.' (This was by no means the only occasion
on which Donald had noted the inflexibility of one to whom he
usually referred as 'the brother of the Commissioner of Metro-
politan Police'.) The spurned offering was a review of Christopher
Stead's *Divine Substance*, which had been published earlier that
year.[2]

'Divine substance': it would be difficult to imagine a topic more
fundamental to that 'controversy between idealism and realism'
which 'lies at the heart of the *Investigations*'; a controversy Fergus'
treatment of which, in the fifth and sixth chapters of *Theology after
Wittgenstein*, and in his contribution to a conference held in
Cambridge, in 1986, in MacKinnon's honour, displays his

1. Fergus Kerr, *Theology after Wittgenstein* (Oxford, Basil Blackwell,
   1986), p. viii.
2. Christopher Stead, *Divine Substance* (Oxford, Oxford University Press,
   1977).

indebtedness, not only to Wittgenstein and Heidegger, but also to MacKinnon.[3]

As my small contribution to these celebrations, therefore, I propose, first, briefly to summarise Fergus' treatment of the controversy in those two texts; secondly, to bring to daylight and to comment on MacKinnon's review and, in the third place, to note a somewhat puzzling disparity in their respective estimations of metaphysical enquiry.

Kerr on the controversy

The fifth chapter of *Theology after Wittgenstein*, 'Suspicions of Idealism', sets out from the 'disconcerting' frequency with which philosophers interpret Wittgenstein's later work as 'an ingenious revival of metaphysical idealism' (Bernard Williams is exhibited as guilty) or, at the very least, as displaying 'idealist inclinations' (the translators of the second volume of Wittgenstein's *Remarks on the Philosophy of Psychology* are in the dock).[4]

In fact, Wittgenstein repudiated 'the realist/idealist dilemma'. His position was that:

> Things do not reveal their properties to us as if we were wholly passive recipients, with no contribution of our own to make. Nor are we absolutely free to impose whatever grid we like upon the raw data of sensation. The colour and number systems belong in the realm of that interplay of nature and culture which is 'the natural history of human beings' (*Philosophical Investigations* 415). There is no getting hold of anything in the world except by a move in the network of practices which is the community to which we belong.[5]

A brief discussion of 'alternative conceptual frameworks' contrasts Wittgenstein's position with Donald Davidson's:

> For Davidson, to think of a conceptual framework is to think of a language; but for Wittgenstein, to think of a language is to think of some activity, such as warning, pleading, reporting and innumerable others ... For Wittgenstein, it is our

3. Kerr, *Theology after Wittgenstein*, op. cit., p. 122; see Fergus Kerr, 'Idealism and Realism: An Old Controversy Dissolved', *Christ, Ethics and Tragedy: Essays in Honour of Donald MacKinnon*, ed. Kenneth Surin (Cambridge, Cambridge University Press, 1989), pp. 15–33. I had been invited to chair the Cambridge conference but, unfortunately, was out of the country at the time.
4. Kerr, *Theology after Wittgenstein*, op. cit., pp. 101, 103; the translators in question were C. G. Luckhardt and M. A. E. Aue.
5. Ibid., pp. 102, 104–5.

bodiliness that founds our being able, in principle, to learn
any natural language on earth ... Paradoxically, it is not our
bodies but our minds that get in the way of our understanding each other.[6]

Wittgenstein sought to trap his reader 'into realizing just how
seductive and compelling the idea is that language rests on
rationality, and human action upon self-consciousness'. The fact
of the matter is, however, that 'Language neither grew on human
beings like hair nor did they sit down and invent it.' Whereas:

the metaphysical tradition entrenches the myth that there
has to be an element of reflection or deliberation in every
respectable human action ... Wittgenstein, with his radical
anti-idealism, keeps reminding us that our action, on the
whole, is an unreflective and instinctive reaction to the
manifold pressures and appeals of the common order to
which one belongs. And the point of reminding us of this
really rather obvious fact, is to persuade us not to be ashamed
of it.[7]

If idealism,

in the philosophical sense, means that ideas are more fundamental than action, or that meanings are all in the head,
then it is hard to imagine a more radically non-idealist way of
thinking than Wittgenstein's ... With his emphasis on action
and life, practice and primitive reactions, Wittgenstein's way
of thinking is as non-idealist as any philosophical reflection
could be. His metaphysics-free vision of human life is radically non-idealist.

Nevertheless, the following chapter, 'Assurances of Realism', seeks
to show that he is 'not an ordinary realist either'.[8]

'The controversy between idealism and realism lies at the heart
of the *Investigations*', not because Wittgenstein thought it important to insist upon his realism, but because 'It is no great exaggeration to say that [his] later work centres upon dissolving this
dilemma', for both the idealist and the realist are in thrall to 'the
myth that speaking, and *a fortiori* thinking and meaning, are,
fundamentally, ostensive definition of physical objects'.[9]

Donald MacKinnon's 1976 presidential address to the Aristotelian Society, entitled 'Idealism and Realism: An Old

6. Ibid., pp. 108–9.
7. Ibid., pp. 114–15.
8. Ibid., pp. 118, 120–21.
9. Ibid., pp. 122–3.

Controversy Renewed', attributed this renewal to Michael Dummett: 'In his recent writings on the philosophy of logic, Michael Dummett has insisted that the dispute between idealism and realism is the central issue of metaphysics.'[10] Fergus Kerr, noting that 'Under Dummett's tutelage, philosophers now regard the controversy as bearing upon certain classes of statements', would, I think, agree, but this agreement carries the sting that the central issues of metaphysics require, in his judgement, not renewal, but dissolution. 'Our *life* has traditionally been regarded as accidental and marginal to the great metaphysical debates about words and things, thought and reality, self and world, and so on', and, 'even in its most modern form', 'the ancient controversy between realists and idealists ... remains entirely within the boundaries of the metaphysical tradition'.[11]

It comes as no great surprise that the concluding section of this chapter is entitled: 'The End of Metaphysics'. Here, Kerr goes so far as to say that 'The metaphysical tradition might even be defined as the age-long refusal to acknowledge the bodiliness of meaning and mind' and, with the last shreds of cautionary qualification discarded: 'The metaphysical tradition just *is* the disavowal of the mundane world of conversation and collaboration in which human life consists.'[12]

The title of Fergus Kerr's paper at the Cambridge conference of 1986, glossing that of MacKinnon's presidential address, succinctly restated his conviction that the ancient controversy required, not 'renewal', but 'dissolution'.

'For years ... sometimes with a certain ferocity, MacKinnon has sought to expose an idealist bias in much modern theology.' That the sense in which this placed him in the 'realist' camp might require somewhat cautious characterisation is suggested by the considerable respect which he showed for Michael Dummett's 'interrogation of realism'.[13] It would seem that, in the 'old controversy', as in its 'renewed' version, something fundamental was at issue which was in danger of being obscured from view by the terms of the debate. Kerr cites Renford Bambrough's version of

10. Donald MacKinnon, 'Idealism and Realism: An Old Controversy Renewed', *Explorations in Theology 5* (London, SCM Press, 1979), p. 138. The following essay in this collection, dating from 1977, was entitled: 'The Conflict between Realism and Idealism: Remarks on the Significance for the Philosophy of Religion of a Classical Philosophical Controversy Recently Renewed'.
11. Kerr, *Theology after Wittgenstein*, op. cit., pp. 135–6.
12. Ibid., pp. 136, 140.
13. Kerr, 'Idealism and Realism: An Old Controversy Dissolved', op. cit., pp. 16, 20.

'Ramsey's maxim: when a dispute between two parties is chronic there must be some false assumption that is common to the two parties, the denial of which will lead to the resolution of the dispute.'[14]

In the present instance, where might that 'false assumption' be sought?

> It was on a Sunday in November 1935, after I had finished Greats at Oxford and was spending a fourth year reading the Honour School of Theology, that one of my former tutors in philosophy, (Mr, now Sir Isaiah Berlin) took me to the Philosophical Society to hear John Wisdom give a paper on Moore and Wittgenstein.

That Sunday evening MacKinnon began to learn a lesson the fruits of which were to remain quite central to his thought, namely:

> the crucial importance of Wittgenstein's contention that we are obsessed by the habit of supposing the meaning of a word to be an object, and in consequence are impatient of the sheer hard work involved in understanding a word or expression, by mastering its role or use.[15]

No one who has been present as often as I have at one of MacKinnon's relentless demolitions of the folly of supposing that 'for every substantive there is a corresponding substance'[16] could be in any doubt as to either the importance or the difficulty of struggling against a philosophical *climate* in which the paradigm of

14. Ibid., p. 21; the reference is to Renford Bambrough, 'Principia Metaphysica', *Philosophy*, 39 (1964), p. 103.
15. Donald MacKinnon, 'John Wisdom's *Paradox and Discovery*', *Borderlands of Theology and Other Essays*, ed. George W. Roberts and Donovan E. Smucker (London, Lutterworth Press, 1968), pp. 222–3; the first clause of the second quotation is cited by Kerr in 'Idealism and Realism: An Old Controversy Dissolved', op. cit., p. 15. In his introductory essay to *Borderlands*, MacKinnon noted that 'in philosophy my chief concern has been with the question of the limits of experience, of intelligible, descriptive discourse, with the kind of questions discussed by Kant as that philosopher is presented in Mr P. F. Strawson's recent book *The Bounds of Sense* and by Professor Wisdom in some of the papers contained in *Paradox and Discovery*' (p. 21).
16. I do not remember any occasion at which MacKinnon pointed out that he was quoting Wittgenstein: 'We are up against one of the great sources of philosophical bewilderment: a substantive makes us look for a thing that corresponds to it' (*The Blue and Brown Books*, p. 1, quoted from Kerr, *Theology after Wittgenstein*, op. cit., p. 145).

human utterance was 'the cat sat on the mat'; a climate in which no one ever asked whose cat it was or where the mat was placed, let alone whether or not 'Fire!' might have been an utterance of equal interest and importance, but only whether we were dealing with what was, in fact, the case, or merely with our impression of it.

Fergus Kerr follows Wittgenstein in characterising a philosophical climate in which it is assumed that, because 'we can think what is not the case', therefore there must be some kind of 'gap between us and the world', as 'metaphysical': 'From the very outset, "Realism", "Idealism", etc., are names which belong to metaphysics. That is, they indicate that their adherents believe they can say something specific about the essence of the world.'[17]

'For Wittgenstein, we might say, it was not a matter of reviving the realist *versus* idealist controversy in the hope of resolving it but rather of recovering a sense of the place of the subject in the world which would render the controversy superfluous.'[18] At which point, Kerr broadens the discussion to notice similarities with Heidegger's attempt 'to put a stop to the whole project of looking for ways to reconcile the subject with the world, mind with reality', and with Charles Taylor's efforts, 'deliberately combining Wittgenstein and Heidegger', to furnish an account of the *self* which is not in thrall to the illusion that human beings are 'detached, observer[s] of the passing scene'.[19]

Perhaps because this essay was a contribution to a Festschrift, delivered in the presence of the one being honoured, Fergus Kerr's essay does not contain any very direct or epigrammatic evaluation of MacKinnon's contribution. But his warm endorsement, in conclusion, of MacKinnon's description of Kant's 'subtle and strenuous effort to have the best of both worlds, to hold together a view which treated learning about the world as a finding, with one that regarded such learning as a constructive act',[20] suggests that, while regretting MacKinnon's continued use of the *terminology* of 'realism' and 'idealism', he does not see this as having fatally undermined the power and importance of his lifelong exploration of the limits of experience.

17. Kerr, 'Idealism and Realism: An Old Controversy Dissolved', op. cit., p. 24; Wittgenstein, *Philosophical Remarks* (Oxford, 1975), p. 86, cited from Kerr, 'Idealism and Realism: An Old Controversy Dissolved', op. cit., p. 23.
18. Kerr, 'Idealism and Realism: An Old Controversy Dissolved', op. cit., p. 24.
19. Ibid., pp. 25, 28.
20. Ibid., p. 31, citing MacKinnon, 'Idealism and Realism: An Old Controversy Renewed', op. cit., p. 138.

Divine substance

After an introductory paragraph expressing his gratitude for 'a
work of first-class importance', MacKinnon's review of *Divine
Substance* heads straight for the heart of the matter:

> The notion of substance is one which has played so central a
> part in traditional Christian theology, and has long been the
> target of such ill-informed criticism that any serious attempt to
> assess its significance and the validity of its employment must
> initially take the shape of the sort of meticulous historical
> inquiry that Professor Stead has undertaken, and only on that
> basis proceed to constructive evaluation. Inevitably, therefore,
> [if] the weight of the first part of his enquiry falls on Aristotle
> this is because he is fully aware both of the extent to which
> both in *Metaphysics Z* and *H*, and in the Categories, Aristotle is
> building on and rigorously criticizing his Platonic inheritance,
> and of the extent to which later exploration of the notion, e.g.
> by the Stoics and Plotinus, proceeded by way of critical
> engagement with Aristotle's table of categories. There are
> issues in which he fails completely to carry conviction [I
> imagine that an edited version would have read: 'fails to carry
> complete conviction'], e.g. in respect of the vexed question of
> the relation between Aristotle's theory of substance, and his
> understanding of individuality. But no one reading what he
> has written on this topic will fail to realise, not only the
> intricacy, but the great importance of the points at issue.

It is not, I think, an exaggeration to say that lifelong wrestling with
that 'vexed question' was at the heart of MacKinnon's philosophical theology, which always found its focus in consideration of the
ὁμοούσιον. In a paper read to a seminar at Cambridge some ten
years before the Stead review was written, MacKinnon, considering the criticism that theologians 'lay upon successive generations
[of Christians] the burden of mastering a particular metaphysical
tradition or a crucial part of it', went on: 'I say metaphysical *tradition*: for it is important to see the doctrine of substance less as a
precisely formulable dogma than as the name of a series of
explorations whose very nature oscillates as they develop.'[21]
According to MacKinnon, 'the central crux of Aristotle's treatment of substance' is to be found in 'the extent to which he
wavers between identifying substance with the individual thing in

21. D. M. MacKinnon, ' "Substance" in Christology – a Cross-bench
    View', *Christ, Faith and History, Cambridge Studies in Christology*, ed.
    S. W. Sykes and J. P. Clayton (Cambridge, Cambridge University
    Press, 1972), pp. 279–300, p. 280.

its concreteness ... and with the form that makes it what it is ... It is as if he cannot make up his mind which of the two best merits being regarded as the nuclear or pivotal realisation of being.'[22] As an 'Appendix on God and Substance in Aristotle' makes clear, similar uncertainty attends attempts to speak of God.

In the very next sentence of that essay on ' "Substance" in Christology', we find a version of his favourite description of metaphysical enquiry; a description which recurs in the review:

> What certainly emerged from a study of the *Metaphysics* is that [Aristotle] believes that 'first philosophy', a very important part of philosophical enquiry, is concerned to give as comprehensive account as possible of such notions as thing, quality, existence, causality, truth, which enter into discourse concerning any subject-matter whatsoever, which indeed seem uniquely pervasive in their exemplification.[23]

The unpublished review continues:

> On page 129 Professor Stead refers to the question whether the categories are concerned with things or with words as 'the one clearly formulated question which we can trace in antiquity'. Here I am sure that his judgement, resting as it does upon extraordinarily impressive scholarship, is unquestionably correct. But I find it impossible not to wish that he had at this point been able to go further, and to explore (with reference to the doctrine of the categories) the relations between the logician, the grammarian, and the metaphysician. He numbers the late Professor G. E. Moore among his philosophical masters, and it is worth noticing that in the very important contribution recently made to the philosophy of logic by [Moore's] literary executor, Dr Casimir Lewy, in his *Meaning and Modality* (CUP 1976), the issues of the relations between words and concepts, sentences and propositions, are regarded as of absolutely central importance. Professor Stead establishes beyond question the impossibility of adequately attacking the problem of substance in abstraction from that of the acceptability of an ontology understood as the attempt to give a comprehensive account of the concepts we find ourselves using in discourse concerning any subject-matter whatsoever, e.g. thing and quality, existence, truth, ground, etc. Clearly verbal and conceptual structures are closely related; but they are distinguishable, and it may be that in order to bring out

22. Ibid., p. 281.
23. Loc. cit.

completely the significance of the issues with which this book
deals for contemporary theology, we need to grapple with the
desperately difficult problem, not simply of word and being,
but of the verbal and the conceptual. It is here, indeed, that
Kant's work, especially in the *Analogies of Experience*, becomes
extremely relevant.

Two comments on the paragraph. In the first place, the reference
to Moore is not unimportant. In his essay on Wisdom's *Paradox
and Discovery*, MacKinnon noted that Wisdom is

> too much in debt to the ruthlessly honest meticulous realism
> of Moore to be bamboozled by the view (encouraged by a
> *superficial* adoption of some of Wittgenstein's styles), that
> religious belief has nothing to do with what is the case. If he
> has learnt the importance of flexibility in understanding
> what we think and say from Wittgenstein, he has also retained
> from Moore a healthy alertness to the depth of the distinc-
> tion between what there is, and what there is not.[24]

In the second place, MacKinnon took his preferred account of
ontology from Peter Geach. Replying, during the 1951 Joint Session of the Aristotelian Society and the Mind Association, to
Quine's paper 'On What There Is', Geach made

> some remarks on Quine's conception of ontological dis-
> agreement. He expresses the hope that people who disagree
> over ontology may find a basis of agreement by 'withdrawing
> to a semantical plane' (p. 35). This hope seems to me illus-
> ory. People with different world-views will still differ when
> they talk about language, which is part of the world.

And he went on: 'Certain concepts, like *existence* and *truth* and
thing and *property*, are used, and cannot but be used, in all rational
discourse whatsoever; and ontology is an attempt to scrutinize our
use of them. To be right or wrong in ontology means being clear
or muddled about such fundamentals.'[25]

24. MacKinnon, 'John Wisdom's *Paradox and Discovery*', op. cit., p. 224.
    Kerr cited the phrase 'the ruthlessly honest meticulous realism of
    Moore' in 'Idealism and Realism: An Old Controversy Dissolved', op.
    cit., p. 15.
25. Peter Geach, 'Symposium: On What There Is', *Freedom, Language, and
    Reality*, Aristotelian Society Supplementary Volume XXV (London,
    Harrison, 1951), pp. 134, 136. Amongst other instances of Mac-
    Kinnon's paraphrases of this passage, see *The Problem of Metaphysics*
    (Cambridge, Cambridge University Press, 1974), p. 96; 'The Relation
    of the Doctrines of the Incarnation and the Trinity', *Themes in
    Theology. The Three-fold Cord: Philosophy, Politics and Theology* (Edin-
    burgh, T. and T. Clark, 1987), pp. 145–67; p. 147.

If I spend time on this point, I do so because fundamentally I am in agreement with what I take to be Professor Stead's positive conclusion, namely that the theologian finds in ontology the means to protect himself against the besetting temptation of an all-embracing subjectivism. What he is trying to say, when he speaks of God, relates to what is the case. For myself, I find it safer to speak of God as 'very ocean of being', or as 'substance', rather than as 'a substance'. While sharing Professor Stead's insistence that Aristotle's theology shall be taken seriously, I am also inclined to give more sympathetic attention than he, to the implications of Gilson's plea that we find Thomas' most significant transformation of that theology in his work on the concept of existence. Yet this may be rightly regarded as a family dispute between two who agree in pleading the importance of the theologian's acceptance of the discipline of ontology. If he accepts this discipline, although his work may sometimes lead him to lose his way in a morass of technicalities, he will be recalled at the same time to an urgent sense that if his work has any significance, it is only as work concerned with what is.

In discussion during a conference in which we both took part, some years ago, John Searle insisted to me that he was not an atheist, because to admit to being an atheist would entail admission that there was an issue here to be denied (or, by some strange group of cultural primitives, affirmed). For those of us for whom the question of God remains as central, and as fundamental, as it has ever been, it is becoming increasingly difficult to know how that question is best expressed, articulated, formulated, in a way that might make it *audible* to those of our contemporaries who share Searle's (historically quite explicable) prejudices and assumptions. Whether or not we deem the polarisation between 'religious experience' (or 'mysticism', or 'spirituality') construed as therapy or gnostic self-improvement, on the one hand and, on the other, the imagined security afforded by varieties of fundamentalism, as a degenerate rehearsal of the 'old controversy', it is not conducive to persuading people that the question of God might be a matter of comprehensive interest, public truth, and common duty.

Whatever one makes of the suggestion that, in ontology, theologians find their best 'protection' against such forms of self-indulgence, it is important to notice the insistence on the '*discipline* of ontology'. MacKinnon had learnt much not only from Aristotle and Kant, from Moore, and Wittgenstein, but also from Aquinas and Karl Barth. He understood, in other words, that the quality of what we *say* is decided by the quality of that disciplined *attentiveness* to 'what is' which, in all circumstances and at whatever cost, precedes, surrounds, and shapes our utterance.

'There is', says Fergus Kerr, 'a sense in which Wittgenstein's work puts an end to metaphysics by inviting us to renew and expand our sense of wonder.'[26] A suggestion which chimes in well with the conclusion to one of MacKinnon's Gifford Lectures: 'Almost we must learn to make the strange into the merely (but emphatically not quite) trivial, in order to approach the unutterable profundities of the familiar, in order to learn to see that familiar anew, as indeed finding at its own level, but not out of its own resources, the means of its transformation.'[27]

> There is a great deal in this book to which there is no space to refer. It may therefore seem churlish to express regret for two omissions. But if I do so, it is because I regard this work as the most important contribution to appear in English for a very long time to the study at the deepest level of the development of Christian doctrine. Although it is wonderfully free of deliberate polemics, by its superb scholarly detachment it shows up the meretricious quality of a great deal of popular writing on this subject. It is for this reason that I must first express a certain regret that Professor Stead has not discussed the relationship between the concepts of substance and event, or found a place for reference to Dr W. E. Johnson's very interesting discussion of the 'continuant' in the third volume of his *Logic*. The second omission is more important.

In spite of which, in ignorance of Johnson's work, I confine my comment to the first. Notwithstanding its brevity, I take this to be an indication that MacKinnon was quite as hostile as Kerr to that forgetfulness of temporality which has been, perhaps, the deepest flaw in so many modern versions of 'the metaphysical tradition', and of the science, and politics, and ethics, in which they found expression.

> Because this work moves at so fundamental a level and deals in so magisterial a way with issues of such importance, one lays it aside almost eager oneself to attempt the necessary sequel, yet aware how little equipped one is in comparison with the author of this book, to attempt it. This sequel would concern itself not with the validity, even the indispensability of the use of such notions as substance in theology, but with the limitations of their yield. If their presence ensures that we

26. Kerr, *Theology after Wittgenstein*, op. cit., p. 141.
27. MacKinnon, *The Problem of Metaphysics*, op. cit., p. 121.

shall not dodge the issue of objective reference, even when
we are concerned to speak of the unfathomable ultimates of
God's self-giving in Christ, it also may put in peril attachment
to the ultimate simplicities that Whitehead claimed towards
the end of *Process and Reality*, were of Galilee rather than
Jerusalem. Yet even as one acknowledges the need openly to
face this peril in a possible sequel, one remembers that
simplicity is itself arguably an ontological concept!

But this review can only end with an expression of gratitude to Professor Stead for a work that is at once a treas-
urehouse of illuminations, and an urgent stimulus to the sort
of resolutely fundamental thinking without which Christian
theology can hardly hope to survive.

The self-correcting pressures of trinitarian thinking were always at
work in MacKinnon's theology, and it is no surprise that, at the
end of a review so highly praising a study of the 'indispensability
of the use of such notions as substance in theology', he should
issue a warning of 'the limitations of their yield', and should do so
in relation to the doctrine of the Cross, of 'the unfathomable
ultimates of God's self-giving in Christ'.

During a session of his seminar in 1972, MacKinnon asked the
(unscripted) question: 'Was there that which Jesus alone could do
under the conditions in which it had to be done which was of such
import for humanity that the risk was justified, the cost well
spent?' In his work, reflection on the tragic was not so much an
alternative to, as the very *form* of, exploration of the metaphysics of
'divine substance'. Near the end of the Giffords he wrote: 'We
have to consider the suggestion that in tragedy we reach a form of
representation that by the very ruthlessness of its interrogation
enables us to project as does no available alternative, our
ultimate questioning.'[28]

What are we to make of metaphysics?

The date: a Friday in the early 1970s. The occasion: a meeting of
Donald MacKinnon's seminar, the 'D' Society. Having been invited to address the Society, Dr Norman Pittenger delivered a
paper on 'A Metaphysics of Love'. It was a warm-hearted enco-
mium of 'process theology', punctuated by contemptuous dismissal of other metaphysical traditions. The chairman held his fire
until a visitor from the United States was rash enough to sing a
similar song. MacKinnon had had enough:

28. Ibid., p. 136.

Whenever I hear someone indulging in that kind of denunciation of classical metaphysical enquiry without any apparent prior comprehension of the issues involved, I am
reminded of an occasion in Oxford, many years ago, when a
distinguished Oxford philosopher (*not* Professor A. J.
Ayer) was indulging in similar denunciation, and Sir Isaiah Berlin
said that *he* was reminded of a man who had not had any
breakfast attempting to vomit; a process as pointless as it is
disgusting.

It was, of course, quite inexcusable; an example of what I once
described as MacKinnon's sometimes self-indulgent talent for
denunciation.[29] But it was quite unforgettable, and it was (I must
admit) enormous fun.

I am not, of course, for one moment suggesting that Fergus
Kerr's hostility to metaphysics would have been likely to provoke a
similar outburst. Whatever Fergus' *assessment* of the metaphysical
tradition, he is as closely and comprehensively familiar with it as
anyone I know. And yet, for me at least, a puzzle remains. For all
the contrasts of style and temperament, there are deep con-
sonances between the two men's philosophical interests and
theological concerns. In the one case, however, these interests
and concerns find expression in comprehensive disavowal of the
metaphysical; in the other, in energetic and sometimes belligerent
insistence on its indispensability.

While both speak about 'the metaphysical *tradition*', my
impression is that Kerr would be less likely to characterise that
tradition as 'a series of explorations' than as a set of 'commitments' that do most damage when they are, as they too often are,
'ignored or denied'.[30] I would find no difficulty in acknowledging
that, historically, both versions of the metaphysical have been at
work, endlessly and variously intertwining – shaping, for good and
ill, the ways in which we think and work – but to suppose that
Western metaphysics can be reduced to *either* strand (as Kerr's
definitions would have us do) would seem itself to be an exercise,
if not in just the kind of metaphysics which he deplores, then at
least of an otherwise uncharacteristic apriorism.

Where the 'old controversy' is concerned, it is surely clear that
MacKinnon, like Wittgenstein, was simultaneously 'radically non-
idealist' and 'not an ordinary realist either'.[31] Earlier, I quoted

---

29. See my obituary of Donald MacKinnon in *The Guardian*, 5 March
    1994.
30. MacKinnon, '"Substance" in Christology', op. cit., p. 280; Kerr,
    Theology after Wittgenstein, op. cit., p. 187.
31. Kerr, *Theology after Wittgenstein*, op. cit., pp. 118, 120; see note 8 above.

Fergus Kerr's assertion that 'the metaphysical tradition just *is* the disavowal of the mundane world of conversation and collaboration in which human life consists'.[32] No one who knew Mac-Kinnon well would, I think, suspect him of such disavowal. As George Steiner put it, in an address in Cambridge after Donald's death: he was 'immersed in history, in historicity. He insisted on grounding theology and metaphysics in concrete material history ... He found it difficult to take seriously a body of philosophic thought that was innocent of the daily papers.'[33] And Rowan Williams, who spoke of 'his fear of any metaphysic that traded in the reconciliation of what could and should not be reconciled', moved to the heart of MacKinnon's theological concern:

> After 30 minutes [of a lecture], you were devastatingly aware that you needed to become more, not less, worried by evil as a theologian; that most available 'solutions' were sophisticated ways of helping you to be untruthful about the reality of suffering; and that if the Christian vision had anything to contribute, it might be, not a consolatory word, but a recognition that tragedy was inbuilt into a contingent world. Not even Jesus' choices could be unshadowed: the triumph of the cross is the shipwreck of Judas and the beginning of the pathologies of anti-Semitism. Donald would not allow you to evade the particular, and his hostility to grand schemes that 'answered' the problem of evil has much to do with this.[34]

Fergus Kerr's work, like Donald MacKinnon's, consistently refuses to evade the particular, and is admirably and strenuously critical of the forces at work in our society which encourage and shape us in the direction of such evasion. So far, then, I do not think that my remarks amount to more than a request that, in his continued engagement in this struggle, he discriminates rather more than heretofore in his characterisation of the 'metaphysical tradition', even if both Wittgenstein and Heidegger may have failed to do so!

There is, however, one last question that I would like to raise. Let us suppose that we had more or less succeeded in achieving the profound social, cultural and intellectual transformations that would be required if we were, in practice, effectively to 'dissolve' the 'old controversy' once and for all. Let us suppose, in other words, that we had, we might say, 'come to our senses', and laid

32. Ibid., p. 140; see note 12 above.
33. George Steiner, 'Tribute to Donald MacKinnon', *Theology* (January/ February 1995), pp. 2–9; pp. 2–3.
34. Rowan Williams, obituary of Donald MacKinnon, *The Tablet*, 12 March 1994.

the ghost of our dissociation from the world of which we form a part.

What, in these happy circumstances, would be the *forms* which the question of God – which is, amongst other things, a question about contingency, and change, and hope – might appropriately take? As we took up again, in whatever fresh figure, the exploration of the 'names' of God, would not that exploration be such as to continue to require consideration of issues which would be (in Donald MacKinnon's sense, though not in Fergus Kerr's) 'ontological', 'metaphysical'? After all, Fergus Kerr himself, 'lifting' a phrase of Donald MacKinnon's, has said that 'we need many more practitioners of *the philosophy of theology*'.[35] Would we not, for example, need to continue to give painstaking consideration to questions concerning the 'grammar' of the word 'god' itself, and of the language of 'existence' in relation to the mystery of God? There are, of course, no short cuts in such enquiries:

> by remarking that theology is grammar, [Wittgenstein] is reminding us that it is only by listening to what we say about God (and what has been said for many generations), and to how what is said about God ties in with what we say and do in innumerable other connections, that we have any chance of understanding what we mean when we speak of God.[36]

Nevertheless, is it really only the 'adherents' of misplaced loyalties known as 'realism' and 'idealism' who 'believe that they are saying something specific about the essence of the world'?[37] Is this not *also* in some sense true of those who confess themselves disciples of the crucified and risen one?

In wishing Fergus every happiness on his seventieth birthday, and in gratitude for all that he has done so far, I hope that he may spend the next few years helping us to continue to address questions such as these.

---

35. Kerr, *Theology after Wittgenstein*, op. cit., p. 171, paraphrasing MacKinnon, *Explorations in Theology 5*, op. cit., p. 147.
36. Kerr, *Theology after Wittgenstein*, op. cit., pp. 147–8.
37. Wittgenstein, *Philosophical Remarks*, op. cit., p. 86, cited from Kerr, 'Idealism and realism: an old controversy dissolved', op. cit., p. 23; see above at note 17.

PART TWO

Road-signs: Theology and Other Things We Say

Chapter 6

'Visio Unica et Ordinata Scientiae'?

'Concepts Have Dates': a Parable

In the late 1840s, the establishment in the University of Cambridge of honours examinations in the Moral Sciences (comprising moral philosophy, political economy, modern history and law) and the Natural Sciences (comprising anatomy, physiology, chemistry, botany and geology) was resisted chiefly on the grounds that 'undergraduates would be diverted from the serious pursuit of mathematics if by acquiring an ordinary degree they could indulge a bent for the natural or the moral sciences'.[1] (Some surprising absences from that list of natural sciences are explained by the fact that astronomy, geometry and 'natural and experimental philosophy' – roughly: physics – were deemed branches of mathematics.) There exist in Cambridge, to this day, a 'Moral Sciences Club', consisting exclusively of philosophers, and a 'Philosophical Society', established in 1819, to which only natural scientists are admitted.

These local eccentricities may serve as a reminder that, as Bernard Lonergan remarked to my uncle Sebastian Moore, on the occasion of their first meeting: 'Concepts have dates.' This is no less true of the concepts of 'philosophy', or 'science', or 'reason', than it is of any other. My aim in this essay is twofold: first, to argue that the notion of the history of philosophy largely presumed in the Encyclical *Fides et ratio*, and in the commentaries on it that I have seen, is, in important respects, insufficiently historical and, secondly and in consequence, that the contributions which theologians and philosophers can hope to make to overcoming what the Pope calls 'an increasing fragmentation of knowledge' are immeasurably more modest than he seems, in this Encyclical, to suppose.

---

1. D. A. Winstanley, *Early Victorian Cambridge* (Cambridge, Cambridge University Press, 1955), p. 211.

In what sense of 'philosophy' is philosophy so important?

Confronted as we are by 'an increasing fragmentation of knowledge', and a widespread loss of nerve in the capacity of human beings to understand themselves and the world in which they live, John Paul II wrote *Fides et ratio* in order 'to reaffirm the intense interest the Church has in philosophy', to reiterate that 'the Church is utterly persuaded that faith and reason "contribute to each other" ', and because 'It is often the case that only in the discipline of philosophy do we find mutual understanding and dialogue with those who do not share our faith', an understanding 'all the more important' if we are effectively to address 'the pressing questions which face humanity – [such as] ecology, peace and the co-existence of different races and cultures'.[2]

Against the background of my experience of more than 30 years' participation, as a theologian with philosophical interests, in the bewilderingly varied range of conversations which constitutes the life of a modern university, I confess to being unconvinced that the climate in which such conversations operate, in which we learn things from each other, and more or less fruitfully agree and disagree, could, for the most part, be described as pertaining to or derived from 'the discipline of philosophy'. It is, at least, worth noting that, if 'philosophical' is the appropriate description of the ground on which we meet, its appropriateness would remain unrecognised by many, perhaps most, of the participants in serious conversation concerning 'the pressing questions facing humanity'.

Twenty years ago, the philosopher Edward Craig gave a series of radio talks 'directed to an audience supposedly puzzled by the relationship between philosophy, the subject currently practised, taught and studied in most universities of the English-speaking world, and what I called "Philosophies", those sweeping maps of reality which the traditional philosopher figure of the popular intellectual image used to provide for our guidance in thought and behaviour.'[3]

Perhaps one of the reasons why it is quite difficult to identify the sense, or senses, of 'philosophy' with which the Pope is working is that he seeks admirably to sustain the connection between philosophy in the somewhat diffuse sense of the rendering explicit of implicit world-views, grand narratives and 'sweeping maps of reality', and philosophy in the sense of a craft

2. *Fides et ratio*, §§ 81, 63, 100 (citing Vatican I's Constitution *Dei Filius*), 104.
3. Edward Craig, *The Mind of God and the Works of Man* (Oxford, Clarendon Press, 1987), p. 1.

or 'discipline' sufficiently specific for it to make sense to appoint 'Professors of Philosophy' alongside professors of earth sciences, comparative law, molecular biology and ancient Chinese literature.

The same connection was invoked in a fascinating exchange, occasioned by the Encyclical, between the Austrian philosopher Clemens Sedmak and the English theologian Philip Endean. Sedmak produced a vigorous and provocative account of the relations between philosophy and Magisterium. He defended four theses: that a normative understanding of philosophy has characterised Christian faith from the beginning; that 'the Catholic magisterium has repeatedly established criteria for what it calls a *sana philosophia*'; that magisterial texts cannot be formulated without implicit philosophical assumptions; and that philosophy has a special role, recognised by the Magisterium, in interdisciplinary work.[4]

In a measured and beautifully crafted response, Endean showed that, at least where the English-speaking world is concerned, there are no grounds for the suspicion, voiced by Sedmak (and perhaps underlying the Pope's lament that 'to a large extent ... modern philosophy ... gives a wide berth to the metaphysical search for man's ultimate questions in order to concentrate attention upon matters which are of particular and localised interest and are perhaps even merely formal'), that some Catholic philosophers turn to the analytic tradition as a way of gaining emancipation from magisterial control.[5] Acknowledging that Sedmak had important points to make 'about magisterial authority and philosophy', Endean regretted that he undermined an important case by arguing it 'in a one-sided and insufficiently nuanced fashion'. Sedmak, he said, is being 'inexact when he identifies his target as "Oxford", as analytic philosophy as such; his real concern is with an anti-realism, a relativism, and a loss of belief in metaphysics, that are by no means universal among analytic philosophers'.[6]

In an eirenic and constructive reply, Sedmak generously acknowledged that his earlier contribution bore signs 'of the rigidity of youth and reveals a certain immaturity', urged that 'The concept of philosophy is ... an ongoing task rather than an

---

4. Clemens Sedmak, 'Rom, Athen und Oxford: Katholisches Lehramt und Philosophie', European Society for Catholic Theology, *Bulletin ET*, 10 (1999), pp. 139–48. I have cited the English translation of his second thesis from Endean's reply, p. 41.
5. *Fides et ratio*, § 61.
6. Philip Endean, 'Philosophy and the Magisterium: A Contribution from "Oxford"', *Bulletin ET*, 11 (2000), pp. 39–54, p. 51.

achievable definition', and offered the following description of philosophical knowledge: it 'does not produce encyclopedic or empirical knowledge ... and it does not produce symbolic or religious knowledge ... The "Unique Selling Proposition" of philosophy is the generation of categorical or grammatical knowledge ... The main tool of philosophy is the distinction.'[7] That description of philosophy's task is not far from Aristotle's notion of ontology, as expressed by Peter Geach: 'Certain concepts, like existence and truth and thing and property, are used, and cannot but be used, in all rational discourse whatsoever; and ontology is an attempt to scrutinize our use of them.'[8] Aristotle may have called this 'first philosophy', and later writers may have named it 'metaphysics', because it is treated by him in a volume of that name; it remains, however, but one 'branch' of a considerably larger 'tree' known, until quite recently, as 'philosophy' or 'science'.

The question that I now want to put to the Encylical is this: when Pope John Paul II speaks of 'philosophy', is it the tree, or is it the branch, that he has principally in mind?

Dramatis personae

Papal encyclicals are written according to well-established literary conventions, one of which is to populate the text with dramatic personifications of key themes and concepts: the style is one which might not unreasonably be called 'baroque'. In the present case, characters called 'Faith' and 'Reason' begin as limbs, but soon take on a life of their own: 'Faith and reason seem to be like two wings by which the human spirit is raised up toward the contemplation of truth'; a little later: 'reason itself, intent upon investigating man from one angle only ... seems to have forgotten that the same man is always invited to progress toward a truth which transcends himself'.[9] Notice that, according to this convention, it is 'reason', not human beings, that has 'forgotten'.

Even though such rhetorical devices may not mislead people

7. Clemens Sedmak, ' "How Many Idiots?" ': The Idea of the Catholic Magisterium and its Relation to Philosophy', in *Bulletin ET*, 11 (2000), pp. 132–51, esp. p. 138.

8. Peter Geach, 'Symposium: On What There Is', in *Freedom, Language and Reality*, Aristotelian Society Supplementary Volume XXV (London, Harrison, 1951), p. 136. This description was much loved, and used, by my Cambridge predecessor, Donald MacKinnon: see, for example, D. M. MacKinnon, *Themes in Theology. The Threefold Cord: Essays in Philosophy, Politics and Theology* (Edinburgh, T. & T. Clark, 1987), p. 147.

9. *Fides et ratio*, Preface, § 5.

trained to read these texts (and although, near the end, the Pope addresses 'theologians', 'philosophers' and 'scientists',[10] the Encyclical's primary audience is 'the bishops of the Catholic Church'), they do make it dangerously easy to imagine that 'faith' and 'reason', 'theology', 'philosophy' and 'science' are, as it were, the names of individuals which, although they have a history (about which the Encyclical has quite a lot to say), nevertheless retain, through that history, a more or less constant identity through all the adventures that they undergo.

Laurence Hemming, noting that 'One of the criticisms advanced in Anglophone reception of this Encyclical has been that it to a certain extent hypostatises "reason" and "faith" ', defends the Encyclical on the grounds that, when well read, its insistence that it is 'the human person as such' that is 'the "place" of truth' safeguards us 'from hypostasising either faith or reason'.[11] I have no doubt that, philosophically, Hemming is correct. My criticism is stylistic: as any student of rhetoric from St Augustine onwards should be well aware, the forms of what we say shape understanding and imagination against the grain of good intentions.

What I have called the 'baroque' tradition shaping the rhetoric of *Fides et ratio* has its origins in early modern thought, certain habits of which, it seems to me, tend to obscure the Encyclical's admirable central thrust and argument. By rhetorically attributing to certain concepts a stability of identity which only individuals enjoy, we generate conceptual confusion and mis-narrate these concepts' history. I now propose briefly to amplify and illustrate this twofold charge.

The tangled roots of 'faith and reason'

'Despite the fact that more than a hundred years have passed since the appearance of Leo XIII's encyclical *Aeterni Patris*', says the Pope, in the opening paragraph of the Encyclical's conclusion:

> we think it imperative to insist more clearly on the close link between faith and philosophy ... we have judged it both appropriate and necessary to underline the importance of philosophy for the understanding of faith, as well as the limits philosophy faces when it forgets or denies the truths of revelation. The Church is utterly persuaded that faith and

10. *Fides et ratio*, see §§ 105–6.
11. Laurence Paul Hemming, 'Unreasonable Faith', *New Blackfriars*, 81 (2000), pp. 389–400, esp. pp. 389 and 398.

reason 'contribute to each other'; since both at the same time exercise a critical and purifying critique, while also providing a stimulus for further inquiry and deeper understanding.[12]

Does not the drift of that paragraph, taken in conjunction with the title of the Encyclical, give the impression that there are, as it were, two camps: one populated by 'faith', 'revelation' and (implicitly) 'theology', the other by 'reason' and 'philosophy', even if the thrust of the Encyclical's argument is to urge their mutual indispensability?

It is not, I think, the distinction between 'theology' and 'philosophy' that is the problem although, even here, to draw that distinction too rigidly would seem prematurely to exclude the possibility of a philosophical theology that was as philosophically rigorous as it was theologically devout. One might do better to distinguish, as Anselm did, between *monologion* and *proslogion* – between thoughts thought in apparent, or attempted, or provisional autonomy, and thoughts thought, in principle, and in intention, on one's knees before the crucifix, responsive to the silent mystery of God.

Nor is it the fluidity of the connotations of 'philosophy' (a fluidity admittedly in tension with the tendency, when considering the history of philosophy, unduly to harden the contours of the concept) that, in itself, necessarily causes the confusion – for reasons that I indicated earlier, when I mentioned the work of Edward Craig. Sometimes, philosophy is a 'gift' or task; sometimes it is that which assists the construction of 'a logical coherence of assertions ... distinguished by a firm body of teachings'; sometimes it is instinct in us all: 'man is naturally a philosopher'.[13]

It is the eponymous team captains, 'Faith' and 'Reason', that are the problem, because the roots of the indispensable distinction between 'proslogue' and 'monologue', thus drawn, lie deep in that disjunction between 'believing' and 'reasoning' which is at the very heart of Enlightenment rationalism. The confusions which this generates, for the consideration of that cluster of absolutely fundamental problems with which the Encyclical is concerned, are twofold.

On the one hand, notwithstanding the widespread recognition that, except as a tactical device, any such disjunction is entirely fictional, because all good reasoning expresses and proceeds from prior commitments and beliefs, and relies, at every step along the way, on believing – albeit cautiously and not uncritically – the

---

12. *Fides et ratio*, § 100 (citing *Dei Filius*).
13. *Fides et ratio*, §§ 3–4, 64.

testimony of others engaged in this and similar collaborative enterprises, it is still possible to hear distinguished persons say (as I heard Professor Lewis Wolpert say on BBC Radio not very long ago) that science proceeds by reason and religion by faith.

On the other hand, it is perfectly clear that the 'faith' of which the Pope speaks is not belief in general, or habits of believing, but Christian faith in God: that credence *in Deum* which Augustine memorably characterised as: 'in believing to love, in believing to delight, in believing to walk towards him, and be incorporated amongst the limbs or members of his body'.[14] But surely that which is to be contradistinguished from such believing, such 'faith', is not 'reason' but sin, the creature's refusal to be a creature, refusal to exist in obedient and absolute dependence upon the mystery of God?

I am suggesting, in other words, that the Pope would have served his purposes more effectively and straightforwardly if, instead of urging that mutual suspicion between 'faith' and 'reason' be replaced by trust and co-operation, he had deployed the rich resources that are available, both theological and philosophical, to subvert the foundations on which the endlessly misleading early modern disjunction between faith and reason was established.

Of what is the history of 'philosophy' the history?

Before making some remarks about the history of the 'tree', a few words concerning that 'branch' of philosophy known as metaphysics or ontology. John Paul II is deeply disturbed by 'the lack of trust in reason itself displayed to a large extent by modern philosophy itself, in that it gives a wide berth to the metaphysical search for man's ultimate questions'; and he emphasises 'the need of a *truly metaphysical* philosophy of nature, able to go beyond empirical evidence in such a way that, seeking the truth, it arrives at something absolute, ultimate and grounded'.

The Pope insists that he is not speaking of 'metaphysics as about some particular school or historical tradition'.[15] Nevertheless, the emphasis on ultimacy, absoluteness and transcendence, suggests that the concept of metaphysics with which, in fact, he works possesses a high degree of specificity.

Commenting on this section of the Encyclical, Francis Selman

---

14. My somewhat free translation from *'quid est ergo credere in eum? Credendo amare, credendo diligere, credendo in eum ire, et eius membris incorporari'*. Augustine, *Commentary on John*, in *Patrologia Latina* 35, col. 1631.

15. *Fides et ratio*, §§ 61 (cf. 55), 83.

says that 'When we go *beyond* physics, we come to *meta*physics ... physics leads to metaphysics as we have to go *beyond* physics to answer some of its questions.'[16]

At first sight, all these metaphors of spatial distance, of 'transcending' and 'going beyond', may appear quite harmless. It is, for example, true that, in order profitably to consider questions such as: 'What, then, does or does not count as a "thing"? Is gravity a thing, is grace, and is the human mind?',[17] it is useful to have considered, in as much detailed specificity as possible, a very great variety of different kinds of thing. In this sense, metaphysical enquiry undoubtedly 'comes second', spreads its wings at dusk, 'goes beyond' particular enquiries.

And yet, in early modern thought (including, of course, the neo-scholasticism which was an aspect of it) such spatial metaphors often played a much more substantial and questionable part. To put it very crudely: in the traditions that I have in mind, it sometimes seems as if concepts such as 'existence', 'being', and 'substance' denote a layer of reality lying deeper than, 'beyond', the familiar world of our experience. And, near the heart of these strange habits of imagination is the belief that God is to be sought at the most 'absolute' and 'ultimate' layer of all, 'beyond' the world.

But such a god, the god of early modern theism or deism (we should never forget that these two terms, when first coined, were, for some time, interchangeable in sense), has little in common with that incomprehensible and holy mystery which spoke through the prophets, took flesh in Jesus, and has – in the outpouring of the Spirit – come closer to us than our own most private thoughts. To say this is not to opt for 'Jerusalem' rather than for 'Athens'; it is merely to suggest that bad metaphysics makes a poor partner for theology. To take up again Peter Geach's account of Aristotle's metaphysics, it would seem very strange to say that 'existence and truth and thing and property' do not pertain to the reality of the everyday, familiar world, but only to some mysterious other territory that lies 'beyond'.

There are affinities between medieval distinctions of 'material' and 'formal' modes of predication, Kantian distinctions between the 'categorical' and the 'transcendental', and Wittgenstein's distinction between 'empirical' and 'grammatical' investigations.

16. Francis Selman, 'The Recovery of Metaphysics', *New Blackfriars*, 81 (2000), pp. 376–88, esp. pp. 378f. (The first two stresses are Selman's, the third is mine.)
17. Cf. Nicholas Lash, *'On What Kinds of Things There Are'*, *The Beginning and End of 'Religion'* (Cambridge, Cambridge University Press, 1996), pp. 93–111, esp. p. 96.

The tendency of much early modern thought to substitute for such distinctions a distinction between two levels or layers of reality (a tendency exemplified in the disastrous shift in the grammar of the 'supernatural') has little to commend it.

Now let me turn to the larger question: of what is the 'history of philosophy' the history? In one sense, of course (and it is a sense which the Encyclical acknowledges), it is simply the history of the human quest for wisdom, a history which therefore includes, but is by no means exhausted by, the history of the sciences, much of the history of religion and ethics and theology, as well as the history of what we might now call 'philosophy'. There are, however, a number of passages in which it seems as if, for the Pope, the focal sense of 'philosophy' is, and has always been, the enterprise in which those whom we would now call 'philosophers' have been engaged.

Thus, for example, to say that 'Among the ancients the study of natural sciences was not divorced from philosophical knowledge' seems, historically, a curious way of putting it. Similarly, when speaking of the need for philosophy to 'rediscover its *fullness of wisdom*', the Pope says that this will give 'philosophy a useful spur to conform to its proper nature'. (The last six words are my translation of '*ut suae ipsius naturae accommodetur*', which the translation used in the volume in which this essay originally appeared renders, somewhat obscurely, as 'to bring itself into its own genius'.)[18] But in what sense of 'philosophy' does philosophy have a 'nature', let alone a 'proper' nature?

'Saint Albert the Great and Saint Thomas ... were the first learned men to admit the necessary autonomy that philosophy and the sciences needed, so that each should depend upon arguments belonging to their own sphere.'[19] But is this not anachronistically to read back into the thirteenth century distinctions between 'philosophy' and 'science' which were (as my opening parable indicates) only laboriously worked out during the nineteenth century?

'It should', says the Pope, 'also not be forgotten that in our modern culture the place of philosophy has been transformed. Rather than as wisdom and universal knowledge, it has been reduced to a position of one among many in the fields of knowledge. Indeed in some ways it has been consigned to a quite marginal role.'[20] But what is the 'it' which has been thus 'reduced'? We could hardly reply 'philosophy', for that would beg the question! After all, it would be equally correct to say that, in

---

18. *Fides et ratio*, §§ 19, 81 (my stress).
19. Ibid., § 45.
20. Ibid., § 47.

point of terminology, 'science' has gradually been 'reduced' (especially in the English-speaking world) from 'universal knowledge' to only a few of the many fields of human knowing. But, although labelling only some branches of knowledge 'sciences' does have disadvantages, these do not include depriving the other branches of appropriate criteria of rigorous procedure and hence, on another account of what 'science' means, of their scientificity.

Insisting that 'the discipline of philosophy has great importance, which must not be removed from any programme of theological studies or the training of students in seminaries', John Paul II says that the Fifth Lateran Council's confirmation (in 1517) of the decision that 'before the study of the theological *curriculum* begins, a period of time must be allotted to the special study of philosophy', had 'its roots in the experience of the Middle Ages'.[21] But surely the Council was simply stipulating that students for the priesthood, before they entered into the study of theology, should have received a good general education?

'Under the shade of wisdom'

My concern about the Pope's tendency to restrict the range of reference of what 'reason' does to that branch of serious enquiry and ordered knowledge which we now call 'philosophy' is that he risks inadvertently understating the scale and gravity of the challenge which confronts us.

Writing in *New Blackfriars* after the death of Elizabeth Anscombe, Fergus Kerr said: 'She will be remembered for her resistance to the utilitarianism which now almost completely dominates our culture (consequentialism, as she renamed it).'[22] It is against this dominance of consequentialism, and other diseases of our reasoning, that John Paul II makes his plea for the need for philosophy to rediscover 'its *fullness of wisdom*' (although 'its sapiential breadth' might perhaps be an inelegant but more accurate translation of '*sapientialem amplitudinem*', because what he is surely driving at is the need to recognise that cleverness and erudition are simply not enough).[23] And yet, in my experience, although our universities are now infected, from outside, by the view that their purpose is to make the country rich, it is not amongst academics, and certainly not amongst academic philosophers, that the homelands of consequentialism are to be found,

21. Ibid., § 62.
22. Fergus Kerr, 'Comment: A Great Philosopher', *New Blackfriars*, 82 (2001), pp. 54–5, esp. p. 55.
23. *Fides et ratio*, § 81.

but in the broader commanding heights of our pagan and individualist late-capitalist culture.

That, I think, is the first thing that needs to be said. But the second (and I do not suppose that the Pope would disagree with this) would be that it is by no means only, or even primarily, amongst philosophers that the need to recover a sense of the sapiential is so urgent, but across the whole sweep of what Newman called 'the circle of the sciences'. And it is here, it seems to me, that the Pope's concentration on 'philosophy' may be misleading.

In an address to university teachers, on 9 September 2000, Pope John Paul II said that they 'must make universities "cultural laboratories" in which theology, philosophy, human sciences and natural sciences may engage in constructive dialogue'.[24] That is a noble ambition and an urgent need, but it would be difficult to overestimate the obstacles that stand in the way of its achievement.

'We therefore wholeheartedly declare ourselves convinced', says the Pope, 'that man can reach a single, ordered vision of knowledge.'[25] This declaration seems to me central to the concerns of the Encyclical, but it is not easy to interpret or assess. On the one hand, I take John Paul II to be declaring that the world – the whole of God's creation, from the beginning to the end, in all the vastness of its temporal reach and complexity of structure, and not withstanding the bewildering diversity of human cultures and traditions – is one in such a sense as to entail the unity of truth. To put it in terms of contemporary philosophical discussion: the Pope is, I take it, rejecting the notion of wholly incommensurable conceptual frameworks; the notion that there are or might be languages which are such as to be, in principle, incapable of being translated into one another.[26] Notwithstanding the immense difficulty which participants in different cultures and traditions, or different academic schools and styles and disciplines, regularly experience in reaching common understanding, to insist, in this sense, on the unity of truth is to insist that failure to reach such understanding is not, in principle, inevitable.

On the other hand, it does not follow from the oneness of the world, and the unity of truth, thus understood, that there is or could be some one true story of the world in the sense of a unified and unifying comprehensively explanatory 'theory of everything'.

24. Quoted from *Osservatore Romano* (English or Italian edition, 13 September 2000), p. 2.
25. *Fides et ratio*, § 85.
26. See Fergus Kerr's discussion of Donald Davidson and Wittgenstein in *Theology After Wittgenstein* (Oxford, Blackwell, 1986), pp. 105–9.

There are two reasons why the currently fashionable quest (in certain scientific circles) for such imperial explanation is to be resisted. In the first place, as the American lawyer, Joseph Vining, has argued in a powerful critique of total theories: 'there is a deep connection between totalitarian social and political thought ... and total theories of the nature of the world', because both total theories and totalitarianism reduce the human person to the status of an 'instance'.[27] In the second place, the imperialist project is unfeasible because, as Karl-Otto Apel saw, 'the fact that a natural science requires the existence of a linguistic community of communication as an a priori for its own existence cannot be grasped scientifically but must be understood hermeneutically'; an observation convergent upon the Nobel Prize-winning neuro-scientist Gerald Edelman's claim that it follows, from what we now know about the processes of the human brain, about the 'recursive symbolic properties of language', and about the historical irreversibility of specific 'symbolic and artistic realisations in society and culture', that 'there can be no fully reducible description of human knowledge'.[28]

In the passage from which I set out, the Pope speaks, however, not of humanity reaching a single *explanation* of the world, but a 'single, ordered *vision* of knowledge'.[29] What kind of 'vision' does he have in mind? We should not, I think, exclude the possibility that the attainment, by the whole of humankind, of such a 'vision', is better understood as an expression of eschatological hope, of the goal of our ceaseless cognitive striving, than as historical expectation.

But in what forms might this vision find interim, provisional expression? Two related possibilities come to mind: on one hand, the dramatic or symbolic forms that we associate with liturgy and public ritual; on the other, Christianity and Judaism are by no means the only cultural traditions to draw upon narrative, parabolic and (in a non-pejorative sense) mythic expressions of such a goal and vision.

The invocation of such general, cultural considerations clearly does not go nearly far enough to meet the urgency of the Pope's

---

27. See Joseph Vining's inaugural lecture to the Erasmus Institute at the University of Notre Dame, 'On the Future of Total Theory: Science, Antiscience and Human Candor' (private publication for the Erasmus Institute, 1999), p. 6.

28. Kurt Müller-Vollmer, 'Introduction' in Kurt Müller-Vollmer (ed.), *The Hermeneutics Reader* (New York, Continuum, 1985), p. 44; Gerald M. Edelman, *Bright Air, Brilliant Fire: On the Matter of Mind* (London, Penguin Press, 1992), p. 177.

29. *Fides et ratio*, § 85 (my stress).

insistence that 'the interior unity of modern man is severely frustrated by the fragmentation of human knowledge'.[30] And yet, to be brutally frank, the nearer we come to the 'academic coalface', the less realistic seems his plea that universities should be so transformed as to become ' "cultural laboratories" in which theology, philosophy, human sciences and natural sciences ... engage in constructive dialogue'.[31]

Having begun with one Cambridge parable, I will end with another. For over 30 years, I have been a member of a dining club, the 'Triangle Club', which we created in order to promote the kind of dialogue which *Fides et ratio* sees as 'all the more important' in our day.[32] The members of the Triangle (the three corners being: philosophy, theology, the sciences) meet once a term and one of their number, or a guest, reads a paper. I have learnt much, over the years, from our meetings. And one of the things that I have learnt is that the numbers of scholars and scientists able and willing, for a variety of reasons, to engage, in a sustained way, in such conversations, are so minute as to have almost no impact whatsoever on the broader culture of a university. There is no disputing the desirability of the 'dialogue' for which the Pope pleads. But where are the educational, political, religious, economic and cultural pressures which might facilitate its promotion, and the radical transformation of institutions and attitudes (to say nothing of budgets and timetables!) which this would require? And yet, unless some movement is made in this direction, the attainment of the kind of common understanding necessary if we are fruitfully to address 'the pressing questions which face humanity' seems ever more elusive.[33]

30. Ibid., § 85.
31. See above, n. 24.
32. *Fides et ratio*, § 104.
33. Ibid., § 104.

Chapter 7

'An Immense Darkness' and the Tasks of Theology

Prologue

Before the fourteenth century, Christians believed that, with Christ's coming, the daylight of eternity had dawned, conquering the darkness of the times before. (Admittedly, this confident periodisation was counterpointed by the recognition, celebrated every Christmas and at every Easter Vigil, that the dispelling of the darkness in which we always live and suffer by the daylight of Christ's coming is ever fresh, astonishing, expected yet miraculous pure gift.)

But it was Petrarch, whom the present displeased, and who would have much preferred to live in ancient Rome, who first 'reversed the traditional Christian distinction between "ages of darkness" and "ages of light".' I wonder whether Joseph Conrad knew that it was, above all, in his epic *Africa* that Petrarch took 'darkness' as symbol not of primitive beginning but of subsequent decline?[1]

The confusion of religion and the disappearance of God

In his magisterial study of *Conrad in the Nineteenth Century*, Ian Watt took 'one of the ideological lessons of *Heart of Darkness*' to be that 'nothing is more dangerous than man's delusions of autonomy and omnipotence'. 'In *Heart of Darkness*', he said, 'Conrad affirmed the need, as Camus put it, "in order to be a man, to refuse to be a God".'[2]

This seems to me exactly right in its implication that theological issues are central to Conrad's story. And yet, so far as I can see, this

1. Louis Dupré, *Passage to Modernity: An Essay in the Hermeneutics of Nature and Culture* (New Haven and London, Yale University Press, 1993), p. 148. Dupré drew upon Theodore Mommsen, 'Petrarch's Conception of the Dark Ages,' *Speculum*, 17 (1942), pp. 226–42.
2. Ian Watt, *Conrad in the Nineteenth Century* (London, Chatto and Windus, 1980), p. 168, citing Albert Camus, *L'homme revolté*.

possibility is rarely even *mentioned*, let alone seriously considered, in the literature.[3] The novel has been variously described as an adventure story, as political – anywhere from first courageous indictment of the savage rapacity of imperialism in Leopold II's Congo to 'bloody racist' – as psychological, or existential, or as 'a symbolic presentation of moral and ideological problems'; even as metaphysical, in the somewhat vague and gestural sense of being about 'the nature of mankind'. But almost never are its central themes construed as theological.[4]

3. One text may count as a partial, rare exception: Stanley Renner, 'Kurtz, Christ, and the Darkness of *Heart of Darkness*', *Renascence*, 28, no. 2 (Winter, 1976), pp. 95–104. Renner explores 'the parallelism between Kurtz and Christ'. Reading Kurtz as a parable of 'the historical Jesus stripped of what Conrad called "the Bethlehem legend"' (p. 101), he interprets the lie to the Intended as exemplifying the 'reserve' with which those who have seen through the illusions of religious belief protect the simple faithful from the truth they are not strong enough to bear. Renner described this theme as 'one of the few underdeveloped areas in the voluminous scholarship surrounding *Heart of Darkness*' (p. 95). He found only one previous treatment of the theme: William Leigh Godshalk, 'Kurtz as Diabolical Christ', *Discourse*, 12, no. 1 (Winter 1969), pp. 100–107.

4. This possibility is not even mentioned in a special issue of *Conradiana* devoted to discussion of different ways in which *Heart of Darkness* had been, and might be, taught in the classroom: see *Conradiana*, 24, no. 3 (1992).
    Conrad himself tended to present it as 'a story of the Congo', as 'experience pushed a little (and only a little) beyond the actual facts of the case' (from a letter of 22 July 1906, and a note of 1917, cited from Joseph Conrad, *Heart of Darkness. An Authoritative Text; Backgrounds and Sources, Criticism*, ed. Robert Kimbrough, 3rd edn [New York and London, W. W. Norton, 1988], pp. 199, 197). (Henceforward, the text of *Heart of Darkness* from this edition will be cited as *HD*, and other material as *Norton*.) Ian Watt called the novel 'an early expression of what was to become a worldwide revulsion from the horrors of Leopold's exploitation of the Congo' (*Conrad in the Nineteenth Century*, op. cit., p. 139); according to Ross Murfin, Thomas Moser took it to be 'a work critical of racist European imperialism' (Joseph Conrad, *Heart of Darkness*, ed. Ross C. Murfin, *Case Studies in Contemporary Criticism*, 2nd edn [Boston, Bedford Books of St Martin's Press, 1996], p. 104, commenting on Thomas Moser, *Joseph Conrad: Achievement and Decline* [Cambridge, Mass., Harvard University Press, 1957]); 'bloody racist' was Chinua Achebe's famous verdict in the original version of his 1975 Chancellor's Lecture at the University of Massachusetts, later amended to 'thoroughgoing racist' (see *Norton*, pp. 251, 257; Peter J. Rabinowitz, 'Reader Response, Reader Responsibility: *Heart of Darkness* and the Politics of Displacement', in Murfin, *Case Studies*, op. cit., p. 131). According to Albert Guerard, Marlow 'is

According to Garrett Stewart, Marlow himself, who is portrayed, at the beginning and the end, as adopting 'the pose of a meditating Buddha', and thereby 'resembl[ing] an idol',[5] 'partially incarnates that idolatry masquerading as an almost religious truth ... which is the monitory center of his tale'.[6] It is the 'almost' that is interesting. To put it with misleading brevity: my hunch is that the failure to read the story theologically is due, at least in part, to the assumption that the subject-matter of theology is religion, rather than all things whatsoever in relation to the mystery of God, their origin and end.[7] Moreover, notwithstanding the profusion of religious imagery in *Heart of Darkness*, from the 'pilgrims' to 'inconceivable ceremonies of some devilish initiation',[8] it would seem very odd to classify it as a 'religious' novel: *Loss and Gain* in Africa, perhaps! Accordingly, before turning to the text, some

recounting a spiritual voyage of self-discovery' (Albert J. Guerard, *Conrad the Novelist* [Cambridge, Mass., Harvard University Press, 1958)], p. 39), whereas Frederick Crews read the story as an expression of the Oedipus complex (see Frederick Crews, *Out of My System: Psychoanalysis, Ideology, and Critical Method* [Oxford, Oxford University Press, 1975], discussed, with other psychological readings of the text, by Murfin in *Case Studies*, op. cit., pp. 106–8). For soberly critical comments on the contributions of Guerard and Crews, see Ian Watt, *Conrad in the Nineteenth Century*, op. cit., pp. 238–40. Michael Levenson made the interesting suggestion that Conrad shifted his aim in the course of writing, from the primarily political focus of the first section to the primarily psychological of the third (see Michael Levenson, 'The Value of Facts in the *Heart of Darkness*', *Nineteenth-Century Fiction*, 40 [1985], pp. 261–80, reprinted in *Norton*, pp. 391–405). In his edition of Conrad's *Congo Diary and Other Uncollected Pieces* (New York, Doubleday, 1978), Zdzislaw Najder warned that using the *Diary* as an aid to reading *Heart of Darkness* 'may distract us from seeing what it essentially is: not a relation about places and events, but a symbolic presentation of moral and ideological problems' (cited from *Norton*, p. 156). On what he calls 'Nature of Man' interpretations, see Peter J. Rabinowitz, in Murfin, *Case Studies*, op. cit., pp. 137–8.

5. *HD*, pp. 76 (cf. p. 10), p. 7.

6. Garrett Stewart, 'Lying as Dying in *Heart of Darkness*', *PMLA*, 95 (1980), pp. 319–31; cited from *Norton*, p. 370. John Lester curiously describes Marlow's final pose as 'a reminder of the misguided idolatry revealed in Marlow's story' (John Lester, *Conrad and Religion* [Basingstoke, Macmillan, 1988], p. 63), as if there were versions of idolatry on offer that were *not* misguided.

7. See Thomas Aquinas, *Summa Theologiae*, Ia, 1, 7.

8. *HD*, p. 49; the 'faithless pilgrims' make their first appearance on p. 26.

brief remarks about the confusion of 'religion' and the disappearance of God would seem to be in order.[9]

In 1996, surveying the methodological confusion attending the study of religion, especially in the United States, with warring schools and tendencies often having little more in common than antagonism to theology, Professor Catherine Bell of Santa Clara University remarked: 'That we construct "religion" and "science" is not the main problem; that we forget that we have constructed them in our own image – that is a problem.'[10] I take that to be, in part, a warning against the dangerous illusion that 'religion' and 'society' are the names of natural kinds.

'Words matter', as John Bossy remarked in his 1981 Inaugural Lecture in the University of York, and 'without a sense of their history they become manipulable in the cause of obfuscation'.[11] Religion, in its modern sense, as a 'social institution' with its own constitutive 'beliefs and practices'[12] (which will, of course, vary from one 'religion' to another), was invented, or constructed, in the seventeenth century, in the interests of political control.[13] As an example of the kind of obfuscation that Bossy had in mind, I offer Samuel Preus' definition of 'explanation' in matters of religion: 'the proposal of alternatives to the explanations that the *religious* offer for religion'.[14]

For much of the twentieth century, Weberian views of religion as in irreversible decline before the rising tide of 'rationality'

9. For two very different attempts, on my part, to show how this confusion went and to suggest how it might be unscrambled, see: my review, in the *Journal of Theological Studies*, n. s. 37 (1986), pp. 654–62, of *Nineteenth Century Religious Thought in the West*, ed. Ninian Smart, John Clayton, Patrick Sherry and Steven T. Katz, 3 vols. (Cambridge, Cambridge University Press, 1985), and my 1986 Richard Lectures in the University of Virginia: Nicholas Lash, *Easter in Ordinary. Reflections on Human Experience and the Knowledge of God* (Charlottesville, Va., University Press of Virginia, 1988).

10. Catherine Bell, 'Modernism and Postmodernism in the Study of Religion', *Religious Studies Review*, 22 (1996), pp. 179–90 (p. 188).

11. John Bossy, 'Some Elementary Forms of Durkheim', *Past and Present*, 95 (1982), pp. 3–18 (p. 17).

12. Robert Towler, *The Need for Certainty. A Sociological Study of Conventional Religion* (London, Routledge and Kegan Paul, 1984), pp. 2, 5.

13. See William T. Cavanaugh, ' "A Fire Strong Enough to Consume the House": The Wars of Religion and the rise of the State', *Modern Theology*, 11 (1995), pp. 397–420.

14. J. Samuel Preus, *Explaining Religion: Criticism and Theory from Bodin to Freud* (New Haven, Yale University Press, 1987), p. xx; cited from Bell, 'Modernism and Postmodernism in the Study of Religion', art. cit., p. 181.

(whether this erosion be seen as matter for celebration or lament) existed in tension with Durkheimian accounts according to which 'something eternal in religion': namely, worship and faith, is destined to outlast the replacement of 'religious thought' by the 'scientific thought' that is its 'more perfected form'.[15]

According to Robert Towler, however, Thomas Luckmann's *The Invisible Religion*, first published in 1963, was 'the last major contribution to the sociology of religion to use the word "religion" to denote beliefs and ideas with no super-empirical or supernatural reference, as Durkheim had done'.[16]

For most of Jewish and Christian history, 'gods' have been what people worshipped. That is to say: the grammar of the word 'god' is similar to that of 'treasure'. A treasure is what you value; a god is what you worship. Only in the seventeenth century did the term 'god' become, instead, the name of a natural kind: a kind of which (some people thought) there were no instances or, at least, no instances that could not be shown to be, in fact, instances of some other kind. Then, once it had been shown that the class of 'gods' was empty, the word 'god' had no further use (except, of course, by anthropologists patronising cultures deemed less adult than their own). Hence what Michael Buckley called 'the massive shadow that Nietzsche and Newman watched descending upon Europe' in the nineteenth century; the shadow of God's eclipse, or disappearance.[17]

The world's great traditions of devotion and reflection, discipline and worship, memory and hope, are best understood not as 'religions', in the modern sense, but as *schools*: schools 'whose pedagogy has the twofold purpose – however differently conceived and executed in the different traditions – of weaning us from our idolatry and purifying our desire. All human beings have their hearts set somewhere, hold something sacred, worship at some shrine.'[18] Insofar as what we worship is some fact or feature

15. Emile Durkheim, *The Elementary Forms of the Religious Life*, translated and with an introduction by Karen E. Fields (New York, The Free Press, 1995), pp. 432, 431.
16. Towler, *The Need for Certainty*, op. cit., p. 3. Unfortunately, Towler, as is customary these days, uses the term 'supernatural' in the degenerate modern sense of entities and forces 'outside' what we take to be the 'natural' world. One bizarre consequence of this shift is to make it commonplace to speak of God as 'a supernatural being'. Bizarre because it used to be supposed that *only* God could *not* act supernaturally, for what grace could elevate or heal God's nature?
17. Michael J. Buckley, *At the Origins of Modern Atheism* (New Haven, Conn., Yale University Press, 1987), p. 322.
18. Nicholas Lash, *The Beginning and the End of 'Religion'* (Cambridge, Cambridge University Press, 1996), p. 21.

of the world, some object or ideal, commodity or dream or theory, nation, place or thing (and most of us include ourselves amongst the things we worship), then we are idolaters. To learn to worship only God, only the holy and unmasterable mystery that is not the world nor any part of it, is an unending task.

Sacredness, for Durkheim, is a quality acquired by objects when they are 'set apart and forbidden' by some social group.[19] Thus, although his account goes with the grain of modern usage in denying to religion independent cognitive capacity, it goes against the grain in its admirable emphasis upon the *relational* character of the 'holy' or the 'sacred': of what were once called 'gods'.

Durkheim was born in 1858, the year after Joseph Conrad. *Heart of Darkness*, I propose to argue, is 'about idolatry' in a sense that the author of the *Elementary Forms* might have appreciated. And, insofar as it is about idolatry, its concerns are (on my understanding of the tasks of theology) theological, notwithstanding the fact that neither Durkheim nor Conrad were, in any conventional sense, 'religious believers'.

Those who made the shift, during the nineteenth century, from talk of 'God' to talk of 'the Absolute', supposed themselves to be changing the subject. But God's disappearance did not mark the end of worship. Ceasing to call the object of one's worship 'God' does not stop the worship being worship (and hence, by definition, the worship of *some* 'god'), nor reflection on it being still theology, even if theology that supposes itself not to be theology is likely to be bad theology.[20] (There is far more theology around these days than most people appreciate, even if most of it is rather odd. This essay is offered in gratitude for Stanley Hauerwas' friendship, and in celebration of his work, in the belief that my understanding of what does and does not count as good – and bad – theology goes 'with the grain' of his.)

'In the older Durkheimian tradition', says Towler, 'there are those who have continued to identify such things as communism,

---

19. Durkheim's famous definition, at the end of the first chapter of the *Elementary Forms*, was: 'A religion is a unified system of beliefs and practices relative to sacred things, that is to say, things set apart and forbidden – beliefs and practices which unite into one single moral community called a Church, all those who adhere to them' (p. 44).

20. 'I hope to make it apparent that "scientific" social theories are themselves theologies or anti-theologies in disguise' (John Milbank, *Theology and Social Theory: Beyond Secular Reason* [Oxford, Basil Blackwell, 1990], p. 3). See also Fergus Kerr, *Immortal Longings: Versions of Transcending Humanity* (London, SPCK, 1997).

psychoanalysis and humanism as surrogate religion.'[21] But, whatever the conventions of current sociological orthodoxy, there are – where the grammar of 'god' is concerned – good reasons for continuing to prefer an account, closer to Durkheim's, according to which the rituals of the Soviet state, or American veneration of the flag, are, as forms of public worship, no more 'surrogate' than devotion to the Blessed Sacrament or the cult of Kali in Calcutta.

John Lester, in his study of *Conrad and Religion*, says that there are, in a '*figurative* sense, several deities clamouring for worship' in Conrad's tale.[22] But this is arbitrarily to suppose that 'gods' are not what people worship but only what (some) people *call* 'gods'. As I read *Heart of Darkness*, however, the theme of worship that is so central to the story has to do with *real*, not 'figurative', worship and, in that sense, treats of real, not 'surrogate' religion.

Echoes of Scripture

In 1970, deploring the extent to which 'a whole school of criticism has succeeded in emptying *The Heart of Darkness* of its social and historical content ... through the endless reduction of deliberately created realities to analogues, symbolic circumstances, abstract situations', Raymond Williams insisted that 'there is all the difference in the world between discovering a general truth in a particular situation and making an abstract truth out of a contingent situation'.[23] Similarly, Peter Rabinowitz complains of the way in which what he calls 'the Rule of Abstract Displacement', according to which 'good literature is always treated as if it were about something else' than it appears to be, 'has almost completely colonized writing about Conrad's novel'.[24]

In arguing that *Heart of Darkness* is about idolatry, then, I am not denying that it is 'about' the Belgian Congo, or the perils of fanaticism, or the devastation wrought by our rapacious egotism. It is about all these things – as aspects and instances of idolatry.

21. Towler, *The Need for Certainty*, op. cit., p. 4, where the notion of 'surrogacy' is taken from Roland Robertson, *The Sociological Interpretation of Religion* (Oxford, Blackwell, 1970). Robertson employs it in pursuit of a strategy which 'tends strongly towards the exclusivist type of definitional approach' (p. 39).
22. Lester, *Conrad and Religion*, op. cit., p. 169 (my stress).
23. Raymond Williams, *The English Novel from Dickens to Lawrence* (St Albans, Paladin, 1974), pp. 118–19.
24. Rabinowitz, 'Reader Response', pp. 139, 141. And Ian Watt describes 'The modern critical tendency to decompose literary works into a series of more or less cryptic references to a system of non-literal unifying meanings' as 'a misguided response to a very real problem' (*Conrad in the Nineteenth Century*, op. cit., p. 195).

The point is plain enough: Kurtz is really worshipped, and so is ivory; both Kurtz and ivory are gods.

In much of the literature, however, the issue is obscured by thick mists of confusion generated by modern notions of 'religion'. I have in mind, for instance, John Lester's reference to 'the secular use of religious terminology in the novels', or Dwight Purdy's assertion that 'in Conrad theophany is secularized'.[25]

Matters are further complicated by the increasing extent to which the critics are becoming biblically illiterate. Yet *Heart of Darkness* is heavy with echoes of the Bible, not because Conrad was a Christian, but because he was a Pole who, in order to steep himself in English idioms and imaginative resources, 'read and reread the King James Bible with great care'.[26]

It may be useful, therefore, before addressing the central issue of the place of worship in *Heart of Darkness* – which I propose to do with reference to: the interruptions to Marlow's story, the theme of speech and silence, and Kurtz's death – if I briefly indicate some of the biblical allusions that are too often overlooked.

Marlow's journey begins with his visit to 'the Company's offices' in 'a city that always makes me think of a whited sepulchre'.[27] (And it is to this 'sepulchral city' that, after Kurtz's death, he will return.)[28] The allusion to Matthew 23 sets off two associated trails that run right through the story: on the one hand, hypocrisy and 'hollowness', the whitewashed tombs of imperial adventure and, on the other, the bleached dead bones, of men and elephants, that are its purpose and the price that's paid.[29]

---

25. Lester, *Conrad and Religion*, op. cit., p. 171; Dwight H. Purdy, *Joseph Conrad's Bible* (Norman, University of Oklahoma Press, 1984), p. 19.
26. Purdy, *Conrad's Bible*, op. cit., p. 8. Although nominally a Catholic, Conrad was not, apparently, familiar with the Douay version (see Purdy, pp. 145–6).
27. *HD*, p. 13.
28. *HD*, p. 70.
29. On hypocrisy and hollowness, consider, for example: the chief accountant's 'appearance was certainly that of a hairdresser's dummy, but in the great demoralisation of the land he kept up his appearance. That's backbone. His starched collars and got-up shirt-fronts were achievements of character' (*HD*, p. 21); 'Once when various tropical diseases had laid low almost every "agent" in the station [the Manager] was heard to say, "Men who come out here should have no entrails." He sealed the utterance with that smile of his as though it had been a door opening into a darkness he had in his keeping' (*HD*, p. 25); 'I let [the brickmaker] run on, this papier-mâché Mephistopheles, and it seemed to me that if I tried I could poke my forefinger through him and would find nothing inside but a little loose dirt, maybe' (*HD*, p. 29); 'the whisper' of 'the wilderness

On arrival at the Central Station, Marlow meets the Manager and a foppish fellow, a 'young aristocrat' with 'a forked little beard':

> The business entrusted to this fellow was the making of bricks – so I had been informed; but there wasn't a fragment of a brick anywhere in the station, and he had been there more than a year – waiting. It seemed he could not make bricks without something, I don't know what – straw maybe.[30]

This light allusion to the savagery and sadism of slavery, to Pharaoh and his taskmasters,[31] is quite lost on Richard Adams, who makes no reference to it, while, in another *Penguin* edition, Robert Hampson adds a solemn one-word note: 'Proverbial'.[32]

In addition to the many such allusions to particular passages of Scripture, there are a number of places in which religious imagery and terminology are clustered to particular effect. Here, to give just one example, is Marlow, early on, wondering what he will find up river, in the heart of darkness:

> What was in there? I could see a little ivory coming out from there and I had heard Mr Kurtz was in there. I had heard enough about it too – God knows! Yet somehow it didn't bring any image with it – no more than if I had been told an angel or a fiend was in there.[33]

Finally, and of particular importance, there are passages that require what I can only call a *christological* reading of Kurtz (even if, as I shall suggest when considering his death, it is an inverse or parodied Christology). 'I seemed', says Marlow, early in the journey up river, 'to see Kurtz for the first time ... *setting his face* towards the depth of the wilderness, towards his empty and

---

... echoed loudly within [Kurtz] because he was hollow at the core' (*HD*, pp. 57–8; a thought that comes to Marlow while he is looking, through his spyglass, at one of the hollow skulls that decorate the posts round 'the long decaying building' that was Kurtz's bungalow).

30. *HD*, pp. 26–7.
31. See Exodus 5.
32. See Richard Adams, *Joseph Conrad: Heart of Darkness*, Penguin Critical Studies (London, Penguin Books, 1991); Joseph Conrad, *Heart of Darkness with The Congo Diary*, edited with an introduction and notes by Robert Hampson (London, Penguin Books, 1995), p. 134. At the other extreme, Dwight Purdy suggests that 'we can revise Marlow's line [that 'All Europe contributed to the making of Kurtz', *HD*, p. 50] to say that everyone in Exodus contributes to the making of Kurtz' (Purdy, *Conrad's Bible*, op. cit., p. 69).
33. *HD*, p. 29.

desolate station ... His name, you understand, had not been pronounced once. He was: "that man".'[34] *Ecce homo!*

When the dying Kurtz has been brought on board the steamer, 'I heard Kurtz's deep voice behind the curtain: "Save me – save the ivory, you mean. Don't tell me! Save *me*! Why, I've had to save you. You are interrupting my plans now ... Never mind. I'll carry my ideas out yet – I will return."'[35]

It is several pages later that Marlow recounts the struggle he had had with Kurtz, before he succeeded in bringing him to the boat:

> I had to deal with a being to whom I could not appeal in the name of anything high or low ... There was nothing above or below him – and I knew it ... Soul! If anybody had ever struggled with a soul I am the man. And I wasn't arguing with a lunatic either. Believe me or not, his intelligence was perfectly clear ... But his soul was mad ... No eloquence could have been so withering to one's belief in mankind as his final burst of sincerity ... when I had him at last stretched on the couch, I wiped my forehead while my legs shook under me as though I had carried half a ton on my back down that hill. And yet ... he was not much heavier than a child.[36]

Interrupting the story

At the beginning and the end of *Heart of Darkness*, Marlow, as I have already mentioned, is described as 'adopting the pose of a meditating Buddha' and thereby resembling 'an idol'.[37] Much has been written about Conrad's interest in Buddhism and on the theme of Marlow's journey leading, if not to enlightenment, at least towards self-knowledge.[38] (It is worth noticing that, just before he finally meets Kurtz, Marlow – who has made it clear to Kurtz's Russian admirer that he wants to hear no more about the rituals of which his master was the object – remarks: 'I

34. *HD*, p. 34 (my stress); cf. Luke 9:51; John 19:5. I do not think it is too fanciful to see, in the arrival of the 'devoted band' that 'called itself the Eldorado Exploring Expedition', 'each section headed by a donkey carrying a white man in new clothes and tan shoes bowing from that elevation right and left to the impressed pilgrims' (*HD*, p. 32), a parody of Palm Sunday.
35. *HD*, p. 61.
36. *HD*, pp. 65–6. Purdy sees in that 'struggle' an echo of Genesis 32, and Adams describes the end of the passage as 'a grotesque parody of the St Christopher story' (*Heart of Darkness*, op. cit., p. 82).
37. *HD*, pp. 76–7.
38. See Lester, *Conrad and Religion*, op. cit., pp. 59–67.

suppose it did not occur to him that Mr Kurtz was no idol of mine.'[39])

Thus it is that, appearing as 'a Buddha preaching in European clothes and without a lotus-flower', Marlow prefaces his tale with a contrast between the colonisation of Britain by ancient Rome: 'just robbery with violence, aggravated murder on a great scale, and men going at it blind – as is very proper for those who tackle a darkness', and contemporary British imperialism: 'What redeems it is the idea only. An idea at the back of it, not a sentimental pretence but an idea; and an unselfish belief in the idea – something you can set up, and bow down before, and offer a sacrifice to.'[40]

With that, the stage is set and, as the frame narrator puts it: 'we knew we were fated, before the ebb began to run, to hear about one of Marlow's inconclusive experiences'.[41] There are, however, several interruptions to his tale, interruptions which constitute 'one of the most noticeable formal characteristics of Conrad's narrative', and which have the effect of preventing the reader from simply continuing to go with the flow of the story, alerting him to 'something that resists narrativization'; what Brook Thomas calls 'the glimpse of the truth we have forgotten to ask'.[42] The point that I want to emphasise, however, is that each of these interruptions – at least three of which express some tension or resistance on the part of Marlow's listeners – is prefaced by what one might call an intensification of theological allusion.

The first of these interruptions occurs shortly after the first mention of Kurtz, identified by the brickmaker as 'The chief of the Inner Station', which tells Marlow virtually nothing![43] While

39. *HD*, pp. 58.
40. *HD*, p. 10. There is a disappointing and misleading discussion of this passage, with too little close reading of the text, in Patrick Brantlinger, '*Heart of Darkness:* Anti-Imperialism, Racism, or Impressionism?', in Murfin, *Case Studies*, op. cit., pp. 284–5. With the qualification that I indicated earlier (see above, p.100), Garrett Stewart is nearer the mark: 'Idealism degrades itself to idol worship, as we know from the perverse exultation and adoration of Kurtz in the jungle, his ascent to godhead ... In line with the imagery of adoration, Marlow himself is twice described in the prologue as an inscrutable effigy ... His own person partially incarnates that idolatry masquerading as an almost religious truth ... which is the monitory center of his tale' (cited from *Norton*, p. 370).
41. *HD*, p. 11.
42. Brook Thomas, 'Preserving and Keeping Order by Killing Time in *Heart of Darkness*', in Murfin, *Case Studies*, op. cit., pp. 250–51.
43. *HD*, p. 28. '"Much obliged", I said laughing. "And you are the brickmaker of the Central Station. Everyone knows that"' (loc. cit.).

'the great river ... flowed broadly by without a murmur ... the man jabbered on about himself. I wondered whether the stillness on the face of the immensity looking at us were meant as an appeal or a menace. What were we who had strayed in here? Could we handle that dumb thing, or would it handle us?'[44]

Marlow cannot, at this stage, *envisage* Kurtz: 'He was just a word for me. I did not see the man in the name any more than you do. Do you see him? Do you see the story? Do you see anything? It seems to me I am trying to tell you a dream.' Shortly after which Marlow was 'silent for a while'. Then: ' "No, it is impossible ... We live, as we dream – alone ...".'. He paused again as if reflecting, then added: "Of course in this you fellows see more than I could then. You see me, whom you know ...".' But, of course, they don't because: 'It had become so pitch dark that we listeners could hardly see one another. For a long time already he, sitting apart, had been no more to us than a voice.'[45]

Lest anyone suspect that to find this passage rich in Johannine paradox of sight and blindness is to read too much into it, Conrad drives home the Gospel overtones by evoking Gethsemane in this darkness in which Marlow is set 'apart': 'There was not a word from anybody', says the frame narrator; 'The others might have been asleep, but I was awake.'[46]

Introduced by the contrast between the stillness of the forest and the brickmaker's 'jabbering', this whole passage is also the first full statement of the central theme of speech and silence on which I shall comment in more detail later on. Here, the ironies, as we would expect from Conrad, are multiple. Kurtz, whom at this stage he cannot visualise, who is 'just a *word* for me', will, when Marlow *does* come closer to him and to understanding his significance, be 'little more than a *voice*'.[47]

A few pages later, Marlow, in his mind's eye, 'seemed to see Kurtz for the first time ... setting his face towards the depth of the wilderness'.[48] There follows another detailed description of the dark, 'impenetrable' stillness of the forest, 'ominous' in its patience, 'inscrutable' in its intention. After a while, Marlow almost ceases to notice this stillness, being preoccupied with more mundane matters concerning the navigation of the shallow river, picking a course between 'hidden banks' and 'sudden stones'. In such circumstances, he says:

44. *HD*, p. 29.
45. *HD*, pp. 29–30.
46. *HD*, p. 30; cf. John 9; Matt. 26:36–46.
47. *HD*, pp. 29, 48 (my emphases).
48. *HD*, p. 34 (see note 34, above).

'reality ... fades. The inner truth is hidden – luckily, luckily. But I felt it all the same; I felt often its mysterious stillness watching me at my monkey tricks, just as it watches you fellows performing on your respective tight-ropes for – what is it? half a crown a tumble ...'

'Try to be civil, Marlow', growled a voice, and I knew [says the frame narrator] there was at least one listener awake besides myself.[49]

Even the City and the Stock Exchange, it seems, are silently attended by something like divine judgement.

There follows a passage in which Marlow is confronted by the energy and sheer *otherness* of black Africa:

a glimpse ... of peaked grass-roofs, a burst of yells, a whirl of black limbs, a mass of hands clapping ... The steamer toiled along slowly on the edge of a black and incomprehensible frenzy. The prehistoric man was cursing us, praying to us, welcoming us – who could tell? We were cut off from the comprehension of our surroundings.[50]

By now, the reader is becoming familiar with the fact that Marlow regularly misreads, or fails to read, what is going on. The steamer's journey into Africa is a journey through retrospectively parted veils of misconstrual.

Now, no sooner has he accounted for his incomprehension by the fact that 'we were travelling in the night of first ages, of those ages that are gone', than, with 'truth stripped of its cloak of time', some recognition of the common humanity that he shares with the strange figures on the bank begins to dawn on him. This is too much for his listeners (and, perhaps, for many of the readers of *Blackwood's Magazine*): 'Who's that grunting? You wonder I didn't go ashore for a howl and a dance? Well, no – I didn't. Fine sentiments, you say? Fine sentiments be hanged! I had no time.'[51]

An attack on the steamer, originally attributed by Marlow to unprovoked aggression (in due course, he discovers that the Africans were trying to save Kurtz from being 'saved' by him)[52] results in the death of his African helmsman. 'And by the way', says Marlow to one of the 'pilgrims' who brings a message from the Manager, 'I suppose Mr Kurtz is dead as well by this time.'[53] There follows an extraordinary passage, the theological richness

---

49. *HD*, pp. 35–6.
50. *HD*, p. 37.
51. *HD*, pp. 37–8.
52. 'Save *me!* Why, I've had to save you', says Kurtz (*HD*, p. 61). 'They don't want him to go', explained the Russian (*HD*, p. 54).
53. *HD*, p. 47.

of which I shall indicate later on, in which Marlow mourns the
fact that:

> 'Now I will never hear him ... I will never hear that chap
> speak after all – and my sorrow had a startling extravagance
> of emotion ... [as if he had] missed my destiny in life ... Why
> do you sigh in this beastly way, somebody? Absurd? Well,
> absurd ... Here, give me some tobacco.' There was a pause of
> profound stillness, then a match flared, and Marlow's lean
> face appeared worn, hollow ... 'Absurd!' he cried. 'This is the
> worst of trying to tell ... Here you all are each moored with
> two good addresses like a hulk with two anchors, a butcher
> round one corner, a policeman round another ... And you
> say, Absurd!'[54]

Finally, if I am justified in insisting on the extent to which interruptions to the narrative signal passages of heightened theological
significance, then we would surely expect some such interruption
after Kurtz's death – the climax of all the main threads to
the story.[55]

However, Cedric Watts, who notes that 'twice previously, Marlow's narrative had been interrupted by sceptical, disgruntled
sounds from his audience', thereby establishing a critical distance
between Marlow's voice and Conrad's, denies that there is, at this
point, 'a further sceptical interruption from Marlow's hearers'
and takes this to be an indication that 'Marlow's confusion is
largely shared by Conrad'.[56]

I am not so sure. After Kurtz's death, Marlow falls ill, apparently delirious:

---

54. *HD*, p. 48.
55. '*All* the main threads' may be a little too strong; some critics would
defer the climax until Marlow's lie to 'the Intended': his inability to
confront her with the truth of Kurtz's last words. ' "Repeat them",
she murmured in a heart-broken tone. "I want – I want – something
– something – to – to live with." I was on the point of crying at her,
"Don't you hear them." The dusk was repeating them in a persistent
whisper all around us, in a whisper that seemed to swell menacingly
like the first whisper of a rising wind. "The horror! The horror!"
"His last word – to live with", she insisted. "Don't you understand I
loved him – I loved him – I loved him." I pulled myself together and
spoke slowly. "The last word he pronounced was – your name" ' (*HD*,
p. 75).
56. Cedric Watts, *A Preface to Conrad*, 2nd edn (London and New York,
Longman, 1993), p. 137.

The voice was gone. What else had there been? But I am of course aware that next day the pilgrims buried something in a muddy hole. And then they very nearly buried me. However, as you see, I did not go to join Kurtz there and then. I did not. I remained to dream the nightmare out to the end and to show my loyalty to Kurtz once more.[57]

However discreetly, that 'as you see' establishes some distance between Marlow and his audience (and Conrad's readership), *enough* distance, perhaps, to invite us to clarify the confusion in which he remains.

Silence and speech

'What the study of literature does, particularly that of nineteenth-century literature', according to John Coulson, 'is to reveal the *form* of the questions which *should* have concerned theologians', but which (with the exception of Newman) for the most part 'did not'.[58] The 'form' that Coulson had in mind is nowhere better expressed than in a passage from an unpublished notebook on 'faith and certainty' – a passage which Coulson set as the epigraph for his study of *Religion and Imagination* – in which Newman says that, because 'We can only speak of Him ... in the terms of our experience', therefore '*We can only set right one error of expression by another. By this method of antagonism we steady our minds,* not so as to reach their object, but to point them in the right direction ... *by saying and unsaying, to a positive result*'.[59]

What Newman was doing was recovering, for the nineteenth century, the recognition – central to the Christian imagination from the fifth century to the fifteenth – that 'a theological language subjected to the *twin* pressures of affirmation and negation' works in permanent tension between what Denys Turner calls 'its

---

57. *HD*, p. 69. Marlow's final reference is to the lie to 'the Intended': see above, note 55.

58. John Coulson, *Religion and Imagination: 'In aid of a grammar of assent'* (Oxford, Clarendon Press, 1981), p. 4.

59. *The Theological Papers of John Henry Newman on Faith and Certainty*, partly prepared for publication by Hugo M. de Achaval; selected and edited by J. Derek Holmes; with a note of introduction by Charles Stephen Dessain (Oxford, Clarendon Press, 1976), p. 102. The passage is dated 1 December 1863; the italicised words in the quotation are those that Coulson took as epigraph: cf. Coulson, *Religion and Imagination*, op. cit., p. ii.

wordiness and its astringency ... its desire to speak and its knowledge of when to stop'.[60]

A great deal, perhaps too much, has been written on the endlessly subversive patterns of paradox woven by Conrad on the theme of light and darkness, black and white, ivory and evil. Far less attention has been paid to the no less central theme of speech and silence: the silence of the African forest and the 'wordiness' of Kurtz. I know no better route towards appreciation of the theological density and richness of *Heart of Darkness* than through reading Conrad's treatment of this theme in terms of Newman's 'method of antagonism'.

F. R. Leavis was notoriously scornful of Conrad's application of 'the same adjectival insistence upon inexpressible and incomprehensible mystery' to 'the evocation of human profundity and spiritual horrors'. Had he been more attentive to the role played, in larger contexts of discourse and imagination, by negation and 'unsaying', he might not have so pompously concluded that Conrad 'is intent on making a virtue out of not knowing what he means'.[61]

As Marlow sets off on the two-week trek towards the Central Station, there is 'a great silence around and above'. On arrival, he finds the white men wandering

> here and there with their absurd long staves in their hands like a lot of faithless pilgrims bewitched inside a rotten fence. The word 'ivory' rang in the air, was whispered, was sighed. You would think they were praying to it. A taint of imbecile rapacity blew through it all like a whiff from some corpse ... And outside, the silent wilderness surrounding this cleared speck on the earth struck me as something great and invincible, like evil or truth.[62]

Cedric Watts has referred to 'the "demonisation" of the jungle in *Heart of Darkness*'.[63] But this will not do: the 'silent wilderness' is not demonic; it is *inscrutable*. 'Evil' or 'truth'? We cannot tell; it will not deliver up its sense: 'the silence of the land went home to

60. Denys Turner, *The Darkness of God: Negativity in Christian Mysticism* (Cambridge, Cambridge University Press, 1995), pp. 22 (his emphasis), 21. For indications that Newman *knew* what he was doing, see, e.g., Coulson, *Religion and Imagination*, op. cit., p. 64.
61. F. R. Leavis, *The Great Tradition: George Eliot, Henry James, Joseph Conrad* (1948; reprinted London, Penguin Books, 1972), pp. 204, 207.
62. *HD*, pp. 23, 26.
63. Watts, *A Preface to Conrad*, op. cit., pp. 63–4.

one's very heart – its mystery, its greatness, the amazing reality of its concealed life'.[64]

Marlow is at pains to emphasise that the 'great silence' of the 'impenetrable forest', the 'stillness' which confronts the brick-maker and the Manager 'with its ominous patience', 'did not in the least resemble a peace. It was the stillness of an implacable force brooding over an inscrutable intention.'[65] As I hinted earlier, the threat with which the silent wilderness is pregnant is the threat of *judgement*. Hence Marlow's heightening sense (of which, as an Englishman, he is somewhat ashamed: 'You know the foolish notions that come to one sometimes') that, from this dark stillness, with its 'air of hidden knowledge, of patient expectation, of unapproachable silence', will come speech:[66]

> You should have heard [Kurtz] say, 'My ivory'. Oh, yes, I heard him. 'My Intended, my ivory, my station, my river, my ....' Everything belonged to him. It made me hold my breath in expectation of hearing the wilderness burst into a prodigious peal of laughter that would shake the fixed stars in their places.[67]

Contrast this passage (which occurs in the lengthy description of Kurtz's character that Marlow inserts into the narrative at the moment of the helmsman's death) with that which follows the Russian's account of Kurtz's influence upon him:

> 'We talked of everything', he said quite transported at the recollection ... I looked around, and I don't know why, but I assure you that never, never before did this land, this river, this jungle, the very arch of this blazing sky appear to me so hopeless and so dark, so impenetrable to human thought, so pitiless to human weakness.[68]

Thus the tension that drives the story forward, the tension between 'unsaying' and 'saying', lies between the impenetrable, perhaps doom-laden 'astringency' of the forest's silence and the 'wordiness' of Kurtz's egotism.

As I mentioned earlier, when Marlow sets off from the Central Station, he still has only the haziest idea of who Kurtz is: 'at the time ... He was just a word for me' (and he himself, as darkness

64. *HD*, p. 28.
65. *HD*, pp. 35–6.
66. *HD*, pp. 35, 56.
67. *HD*, p. 49.
68. *HD*, p. 55.

now falls upon the Thames, becomes 'no more ... than a voice' to his audience aboard the *Nellie*).[69]

On the occasion of the helmsman's death, Marlow, whose unexplained but 'dominant thought' is that Kurtz himself is also dead, makes

> the strange discovery that I had never imagined him as doing, you know, but as discoursing. I didn't say to myself, 'Now I will never see him', or 'Now I will never shake him by the hand', but, 'Now I will never hear him'. The man presented himself as a voice.[70]

And, although the impression that Kurtz is already dead proves mistaken – at least in the sense that Marlow finds him *physically* alive – yet, he adds a little later, 'I was right, too. A voice. He was very little more than a voice.'[71]

In the beginning was the word: 'Going up that river was like travelling back to the earliest beginnings of the world ... An empty stream, a great silence.'[72] But, at the heart of this still darkness, a voice resounds, a word is uttered. It was Kurtz's 'eloquence' which gave him the power to elicit adoration from the Africans: ' "Kurtz got the tribe to follow him, did he?" I suggested. [The Russian] fidgeted a little. "They adored him," he said.'[73] After Kurtz's death, Marlow will read his draft report to the International Society for the Suppression of Savage Customs, in the opening paragraph of which Kurtz explained that 'we whites, from the point of view of development we had arrived at, "must necessarily appear to them [savages] in the nature of supernatural beings – we approach them with the might as of a deity." ' Marlow found Kurtz's 'peroration ... magnificent ... It gave me the notion of an exotic Immensity ruled by an august Benevolence. It made me tingle with enthusiasm. This was the unbounded power of eloquence – of words – of burning noble words.' Then he came to the note 'at the foot of the last page, scrawled evidently much later in an unsteady hand ... "Exterminate all the brutes!" ' [74]

---

69. *HD*, pp. 29–30.
70. *HD*, pp. 47–8. As Ian Watt says: 'Even at this stage Kurtz's power is a verbal one' (Watt, *Conrad in the Nineteenth Century*, op. cit., p. 230).
71. *HD*, p. 48.
72. *HD*, p. 35. A comparison between this passage and the studied ambiguity of the passages, in the 'frame' of the story, considering the darkness of the Thames (cf. *HD*, pp. 7–10, 76) leaves the reader uncertain as to whether this is a journey 'back' because Africans are 'primitive', or because Kurtz is 'that man' (*HD*, p. 34), Adam, losing paradise.
73. *HD*, p. 56.
74. *HD*, pp. 50–51.

Until almost the last moment of his life, the power of Kurtz's eloquence is undimmed. Borne towards the steamer on a stretcher, he is still 'A voice! a voice! It was grave, profound, vibrating, while the man did not seem capable of a whisper ... No eloquence could have been so withering to one's belief in mankind as his final burst of sincerity.' Even as the 'brown current ran swiftly out of the heart of darkness bearing us down towards the sea ... Kurtz discoursed. A voice! a voice! It rang deep to the very last.'[75] When, at last, 'The voice was gone', Marlow reflects that, finding himself so close to death a little later, 'I found with humiliation that probably I would have nothing to say. This is the reason why I affirm that Kurtz was a remarkable man. He had something to say. He said it.'[76]

'Heaven and earth shall pass away, but my words will not pass away.' Back in the 'sepulchral city', Kurtz's 'Intended' unintentionally nudges Marlow towards the lie with which his story ends: ' "It is impossible that all this should be lost ... Something must remain. His words at least have not died." "His words will remain," I said.'[77]

Cries and whispers

'He was very little more than a voice.' But the voice of Kurtz, into whose making 'all Europe contributed', is, as it were, the vortex of all the voices in the darkness of the world:

> And I heard – him – it – this voice – other voices – all of them were so little more than voices – and the memory of that time itself lingers around me, impalpable, like a dying vibration of one immense jabber, silly, atrocious, sordid, savage, or simply mean without any kind of sense.[78]

This is, of course, remembering with hindsight. At the time, the voice was so *strong* that 'the man did not seem capable of a whisper'. And yet, it is exactly in that form that Kurtz's darkest utterance comes forth: 'He cried in a whisper at some image, at some vision – he cried out twice, a cry that was no more than a breath: "The horror! The horror!" ' And this expiring whisper echoes 'the whisper [which] had proved irresistibly fascinating', with which the silent wilderness had 'whispered things about himself which he did not know'.[79]

75. *HD*, pp. 60, 65–6, 67.
76. *HD*, p. 69.
77. Matt. 24:35; *HD*, pp. 70, 74–5.
78. *HD*, pp. 48, 50, 48–9.
79. *HD*, pp. 60, 68, 57.

Moreover, just as Kurtz's voice was remembered as the centre of the 'dying vibration of one immense jabber', so the 'low voice' of the Intended 'seemed to have the accompaniment of all the other sounds full of mystery, desolation, and sorrow I had ever heard ... the whisper of a voice speaking from beyond the threshold of an eternal darkness'. And finally, at the moment of the Lie, this dark 'whisper ... seemed to swell menacingly like the first whisper of a rising wind. "The horror! The horror!"' [80]

'Some commentators', says Cedric Watts, find Kurtz's last words 'affirmative, others find them nihilistic, others find them obscure'.[81] It is, of course, possible to find them all of these, a view the plausibility of which is strengthened by the lengths to which Conrad goes to emphasise Marlow's own uncertainty as to how these last words are best read.[82]

One thing, at least, is clear, and that is the care with which Conrad presents Kurtz's death as an inversion of the death of Christ.[83] Here is Matthew's Gospel:

> Now from the sixth hour there was darkness over all the land unto the ninth hour. And about the ninth hour Jesus cried with a loud voice, '*Eli, Eli, lama sabachthani?*', that is to say, 'My God, my God, why hast thou forsaken me?' ... Jesus, when he had cried again with a loud voice, yielded up the

80. *HD*, pp. 48, 74–5.
81. Watts, *A Preface to Conrad*, op. cit., p. 136.
82. 'Marlow suggests the following meanings for "The horror! The horror!"': (1) Kurtz condemns as horrible his corrupt actions, and this "judgement upon the adventures of his soul" is "an affirmation, a moral victory". (2) Kurtz deems hateful but also *desirable* the temptations to which he had succumbed: the whisper has "the strange commingling of desire and hate", and therefore is not a moral victory after all, it seems. (3) Kurtz deems horrible the inner natures of all humans: "no eloquence could have been so withering to one's belief in mankind as his final burst of sincerity", when his stare "penetrate[d] all the hearts that beat in the darkness". (4) Kurtz deems horrible the whole universe: "that wide and immense stare embracing, condemning, loathing all the universe ... 'The horror!'"' (Watts, *A Preface to Conrad*, op. cit., p. 136; cf. *HD*, pp. 70, 69, 65–6, 72).
83. According to John Lester, 'To regard Jim as archetypal Christ or Kurtz as diabolic Christ is, in many ways, to cease regarding them as individual characters' (Lester, *Conrad and Religion*, op. cit., p. xxiii). But any theologian knows that Christology goes off the rails when it loses sight of the fact that 'the Christ' is a particular Jewish individual. Indeed, the sustaining of the tension between these two acknowledgements could almost be said to be constitutive of competent Christology.

ghost. And behold the veil of the temple was rent in twain, from the top to the bottom; and the earth did quake, and the rocks rent.[84]

Notice five features: darkness, the voice, the repeated cry – seemingly of despair – the rending of the veil and expiration of the spirit, surrender of the breath of God:[85]

> One evening coming in with a candle I was startled to hear him say a little tremulously, 'I am lying here in the dark waiting for death.' The light was within a foot of his eyes. I forced myself to murmur, 'Oh, nonsense!' and stood over him as if transfixed. Anything approaching the change that came over his features I have never seen before and hope never to see again ... It was as though a veil had been rent. I saw on that ivory face the expression of sombre pride, of ruthless power, of craven terror – of an intense and hopeless despair ... He cried in a whisper at some image, at some vision, he cried out twice, a cry that was no more than a breath: 'The horror! The horror!'[86]

The place of restraint

The centurion in Matthew's Gospel, who 'feared greatly', says: 'Truly this was the Son of God.'[87] At the heart of Christianity is the recognition that the crucifixion was a kind of victory – which is, in fact, what Marlow proclaims the death of Kurtz to be.[88] But victory for what? According to one critic: 'the great moral centre of *Heart of Darkness*' consists in Kurtz's ability, 'without external religious sanctions of any sort', to judge himself condemned.[89] If this be victory, for Kurtz or humankind, what would defeat be like?

At the opposite extreme, there are critics who see Kurtz as 'fellow-artist', with his creator, 'of that nihilism that Conrad ...

84. Matt. 27:45–46, 50–51.
85. Most of the critics miss some or all of these allusions. Dwight Purdy, whose suggestion that the passage also carries overtones of Genesis 15 I find ingenious but not persuasive, misses only the reference to the breathing of the spirit: see Purdy, *Conrad's Bible*, op. cit., pp. 47, 105.
86. *HD*, p. 68.
87. Matt. 27:54.
88. His dying cry is said to be 'an affirmation, a moral victory paid for by innumerable defeats, by abominable terrors, by abominable satisfactions. But it was a victory' (*HD*, p. 70).
89. Juliet McLaughlan, 'The "Value" and "Significance" of *Heart of Darkness*', *Conradiana*, 15 (1983), pp. 3–21; cited from *Norton*, pp. 383, 382.

found so attractive'.[90] 'Attractive' surely misdescribes the kind of drawing-power exercised by the darkness with which the failure of the Promethean project may confront us. 'Marlow', says Ian Watt, 'is horrified, and so, just before his end, is Kurtz, to understand what happens to a man who discovers his existential freedom under circumstances which enable him to pervert the ultimate direction of nineteenth-century thought: not the disappearance but the replacement of God.'[91]

In the end, however, 'neither Conrad nor Marlow' find darkness 'irresistible'.[92] And the source of their resistance lies in what Conrad calls 'restraint'. Against an individualist Romanticism which had established 'the ideal of absolute liberation from religious, social, and ethical norms', Conrad – Polish aristocrat and English gentleman – grounded his ethic in 'the Victorian trinity of work, duty, and restraint'.[93]

On the journey up river, Marlow, knowing how much easier it is 'to face bereavement, dishonour, and the perdition of one's soul – than this kind of prolonged hunger', is amazed at the restraint displayed by the starving African crew, outnumbering the whites by thirty to five: 'Restraint! I would just as soon have expected restraint from a hyena prowling amongst the corpses of a battlefield. But there was the fact facing me ... like a ripple on an unfathomable enigma.'[94]

In contrast, it is lack of restraint which brings about the helmsman's death: 'Poor fool! If he had only left that shutter alone. He had no restraint, no restraint – just like Kurtz.' In circumstances lacking the external restraints of what we think of as 'civilisation', the wilderness 'found [Kurtz] out early'. Lack of restraint 'in the gratification of his various lusts' caused his downfall.[95] Lacking restraint, he made himself the worshipped centre of the world and, in so doing, disclosed the sub-human animality of post-Darwinian nightmare.[96]

Human beings, in order to be human, must refuse to be divine, to be objects of other people's worship (or their own!). If Conrad

90. Brantlinger, '*Heart of Darkness* ...', op. cit., p. 295. A little earlier, he says: 'For Conrad, Kurtz's heroism consists in staring into an abyss of nihilism so total that the issues of imperialism and racism pale into insignificance' (p. 293).

91. Watt, *Conrad in the Nineteenth Century*, op. cit., p. 166.

92. Ibid., p. 253.

93. Ibid., pp. 228, 167.

94. *HD*, p. 43.

95. *HD*, pp. 51, 57.

96. See E. N. Dorall, 'Conrad and Coppola: Different Centres of Darkness', *Southeast Asian Review of English*, 1 (1980), pp. 19–27; in *Norton*, p. 305; cf. Watt, *Conrad in the Nineteenth Century*, op. cit., p. 227.

was not alone in seeing this, he was unusual in clear-sighted recognition of the idolatrous character of Leopold II's African adventure.

But, if we may not be worshipped, may we worship? Or is all worship, at its heart, idolatrous? Partly for temperamental reasons, and partly because of the narrow range of options available to him in the 1890s, so far as the 'grammar' of the concept of God is concerned,[97] Conrad was undoubtedly drawn towards the latter view.

'He had the faith – don't you see – he had the faith', says the journalist to whom, back in the 'sepulchral city', Marlow hands over Kurtz's report: 'He could get himself to believe anything – anything. He would have been a splendid leader of an extreme party.'[98]

Conrad rejected as 'distasteful' the Catholic Christianity in which he was brought up, partly because he found ritual uncongenial and 'the absurd oriental fable from which it starts irritates me', and partly on account of what Cedric Watts called 'an Augustan distaste for fanaticism'.[99]

And yet, the power of *Heart of Darkness* arises, in part, from the unspoken recognition that Conrad has so little to put in place of the idolatry that he deplored. Only the cannibals display the 'restraint' which, for Conrad as for his contemporaries, epitomised the virtues of the English gentleman,[100] and the 'efficiency' which he supposed the saving grace of *British* imperialism makes only marginal appearance.[101] Moreover, the passage in which Marlow insists that it is efficiency which 'redeems' and 'saves *us*' describes even this ideal as idolatry: 'something

97. For a brief view of these options, see my review of *Nineteenth Century Religious Thought in the West*, mentioned above in note 9.

98. *HD*, p. 71.

99. Joseph Conrad, *Letters from Conrad, 1895 to 1924*, ed. Edward Garnett (London, Nonesuch Press, 1928), p. 265; cited from Watts, *A Preface to Conrad*, op. cit., p. 48.

100. 'Restraint' was 'the key defining quality of that increasingly vague figure – the English gentleman' (the late Professor Tony Tanner, personal communication). It is impossible not to be reminded of Newman's brilliantly ironic portrayal, sketched nearly half a century earlier, of 'the ethical character, which the cultivated intellect will form, apart from religious principle' (John Henry Newman, *The Idea of a University*, ed. with an introduction by I. T. Ker [Oxford, Clarendon Press, 1976], pp. 180–81).

101. 'What saves us is efficiency' (*HD*, p. 10). It is Marlow, the only Englishman in his story, who knows that rivets are what was 'really wanted', to get the steamer under way again, and who is exasperated by the *in*efficiency of the failure to provide them (see *HD*, p. 30).

you can set up, and bow down before, and offer a sacrifice to'.[102]

Human beings, in order to be human, must refuse to be divine. Yet all the forms of this refusal seem threatened by their subversion as idolatry. '"We have lost the first of the ebb," said the Director suddenly.' *All* rivers seem 'to lead into the heart of an immense darkness'.[103] Nowhere, perhaps, did Conrad more prophetically articulate the crisis of western culture as the nineteenth century ended than in his inability to consider the possibility that, in the twofold struggle against self-divinisation and idolatry, human beings might, through disciplined acceptance of contingency, once again learn what it is to be a *creature* and, in that discovery, find forms of worship that are not idolatrous. The tasks of theology, as I understand them, are set at the service of such education.

'The burden of my argument in this last lecture, and the overarching ambition of all my lectures, is to show that Christian practice and theology are neither self-referential nor self-justifying.'[104] The nightmare of modernity was the fear that, unless 'we' ordered things, they would fall apart, be meaningless. The terror of postmodernism lies in the recognition that the quest for meaning is a waste of time. The duty of the reasonable remnant is to insist, against both hubris and despair, that 'we' do not have either the first word or the last, and that in this discovery may be found our given peace.

Epilogue: in search of bones

'The Accountant had brought out already a box of dominoes and was toying architecturally with the bones.'[105] It is, of course, in search of venerated bones that pilgrims journey. Nor should we forget that 'bones and ivory were for centuries mistakenly believed to be the same substance'.[106] 'The word "ivory" rang in the air ... You would think' that they, who wandered 'like a lot of faithless pilgrims', were 'praying to it'.[107]

'Ivory! I should think so. Heaps of it, stacks of it. The old mud shanty was bursting with it', bursting with what Kurtz called 'My ivory'. In the same passage, Marlow describes the emergence of

102. *HD*, p. 10.
103. *HD*, p. 76.
104. Stanley Hauerwas, *With the Grain of the Universe* (Grand Rapids and London, Brazos Press, 2001, and SCM Press, 2002), p. 207.
105. *HD*, p. 7.
106. Adams, *Heart of Darkness*, op. cit., p. 8.
107. *HD*, p. 26; on 'ivory', see pp. 29, 33, 36, 44, 55.

Kurtz, when at last they reach the Inner Station, as the disinterment of a corpse: 'You should have heard the disinterred body of Mr Kurtz saying, "My Intended" ... and the lofty frontal bone of Mr Kurtz! ... The wilderness had patted him on the head, and behold, it was like a ball – an ivory ball.'[108] It is as a venerated relic, then, that Kurtz appears. The dying Kurtz, borne towards the steamer, resembles 'an animated image of death carved out of old ivory'. And, as Kurtz dies, Marlow sees 'on that ivory face ... intense and hopeless despair'.[109]

Thomas à Becket, Mr Kurtz, the elephants of Africa: variations woven, with Conrad's mastery of irony, on the theme of pilgrimage in quest of ivory, of dead white bones, the venerated skeletons of forms of faith. The final twist to Conrad's story, beyond authorial control, has his bones, like Becket's, laid to rest in Canterbury,[110] thereby opening up fresh dangerous possibilities of pilgrimage.

108. *HD*, p. 49.
109. *HD*, pp. 59, 68.
110. After a Requiem celebrated (as, some decades later, would be those of my father- and mother-in-law) in the Catholic church of St Thomas of Canterbury. See Watts, *A Preface to Conrad*, op. cit., p. 38.

Chapter 8

Reason, Fools and Rameau's Nephew

In the autumn of 1993, I found myself called upon to give the concluding address to a conference in Stockholm – jointly sponsored by the Royal Dramatic Theatre of Sweden, the Royal Institute of Technology, and the Swedish Centre for Working Life – entitled: 'Skill and Technology: on Diderot, Education and the Third Culture'. One focus of the conference was Diderot's Dialogue, *Rameau's Nephew*, my appreciation of which has, I hope, been properly enhanced as a result of having sat through not only a dramatisation of it in German but also an operatic version, by a Finnish composer, with a Swedish libretto.

Nobody knows for sure whether or not Denis Diderot had a conversation with Jean-François Rameau, nephew of the composer, in the Café de la Régence in Paris, in April 1761. Nor does it matter. Diderot certainly wrote the first draft of the Dialogue in that year, reworking it in 1773, 1778 and 1782, the year before he died. The history of this short text (less than 70 pages in the Flammarion edition) is so extraordinary that one almost suspects Diderot himself of having somehow arranged it.

Although it has been described as 'the very centre of his writing'[1] and has provoked a still-burgeoning library of commentary and interpretation, the Dialogue was never published or referred to by Diderot in his lifetime, and it first saw the light of day in a German translation, done by an admiring Goethe from a French manuscript which he had been lent by Schiller, who seems to have obtained it from a German officer in St Petersburg. Goethe's translation appeared in 1805.

It exerted considerable influence on Hegel's *Phenomenology of Spirit* (the first of the two passages on which I shall comment later in this chapter seems, for example, to have helped shape the dialectic of lordship and bondage) and it first appeared in French in a translation back from Goethe's German – Diderot's own carefully prepared manuscript only being discovered, quite by chance, in a second-hand bookshop in Paris, in 1891. (In 1865, incidentally, Karl Marx told his daughter that Diderot was his

---

1. Peter France, *Diderot* (Oxford University Press, 1983), p. 75.

favourite prose writer and, in 1869, he sent a copy of *Rameau's Nephew* to Engels.)[2]

Rameau's Nephew is a conversation between two characters: 'Moi', a *philosophe*, a sober spokesman for Enlightenment virtues and values, a person of endless curiosity but somewhat conventional imagination, and 'Lui', the nephew, a more or less professional sycophant, hanger-on, procurer, resident buffoon in the household of M. Bertin – which was a centre of opposition to Diderot and the Encyclopaedists. (Perhaps we should say that Lui *had* been resident buffoon in the Bertin *ménage* because, as we discover in the course of the conversation, he has recently been thrown out after insulting – which is to say, obscenely speaking the truth to – a priest, a fellow-guest at Bertin's table.)

Lui, the individualist, the amoralist, the anarchist, in restless quest of recognition as a 'genius', while despising the disruptive egotism characteristic of genius in its conventional forms, is a musician of real, if modest, talent. And yet, he *is* a genius, not only as a social parasite but also – as Diderot's text displays far more eloquently than any utterance could do – as a mime artist, a conjurer of wordless evocations not only of the social world but of the natural, unreasoning world as well.

From a literary point of view, these mimes are heart and centre of the text (and, incidentally, the best reason why dramatisations of the Dialogue are doomed to failure). Interrupting, unavoidably, the dialogue form, they are described, by Moi, in passages of such brilliance as to set question-marks against the exactness of any *philosophe*'s scientific ordering of things – for does not Lui depict the world, in wordless gesture, more accurately and eloquently than any fruit of all Moi's erudition could do? – and yet, it is Moi's pen that sets down in words this physical description. We shall return to this.

'Moi' and 'Lui' are usually translated 'I' and 'He'. I prefer to render them as 'Me' and 'He' (or 'Him'), which seems at least to hint at something other than complete identity between the author of the text and *each* of his two acting subjects. This is important, because it is a great mistake to suppose that 'Me' is simply Diderot and 'He' just someone else, an other. It is not for nothing that the *philosophe* comes across, not unsympathetically, but somewhat drably, while all the colour and panache, vitality and danger, emanate from He. Yet, lest we turn sentimental, and grow too fond of this amoral and subversive layabout, the dialogue ends with He's chilling description of how he put his wife out 'on the game'. And we know, reading this, as Diderot knew when he

---

2. See P. N. Furbank, *Diderot: A Critical Biography* (London, Secker and Warburg, 1992), p. 467.

wrote it, that the real-life Rameau's wife died, in childbirth, in the early summer of 1761.

So much for preliminaries. *Rameau's Nephew* raises, to my mind, two distinct, but by no means unconnected, sets of issues. The first concerns the connotations of 'reason': of rationality, knowledge, wisdom, and related notions. For the second we might formulate the principle: in order to ascertain what is of most interest, theologically, in the work of the great atheists of the eighteenth and nineteenth centuries, pay little or no attention to what they have to say about 'religion'. Concentrate, instead, on what they have to say about the things which matter to them most, and on the way in which they say it.[3]

At least in academic circles, we speak more easily, these days, of 'reason', and of 'rationality', than we do of 'wisdom'. Not that we have lost all sense of connection between these two clusters of ideas. People may reason well or badly but, when we describe someone's behaviour as 'unreasonable', or 'irrational', we are usually implying something more like folly than a weak grasp upon the rules of inference.

With what, in different contexts, then, do we contrast 'reason'? With whimsy, perhaps, or feeling; with faith, quite often, and, on occasion, with insanity. (The concatenated associations are, or should be, quite disturbing.)

'It is clearly manifest that history, poetry, and philosophy flow from the three distinct fountains of the mind, viz., the memory, the imagination, and the reason; without any possibility of increasing their number. For history and experience are one and the same thing; so are philosophy and the sciences.'[4] Bacon's *Advancement of Learning* was first published in 1605. Although we still tend, as Bacon did, sharply to distinguish 'science' from 'history', and 'experience' from 'philosophy', our reasons for doing so are rather different from his. They no longer, for example, rest upon an assumed disjunction between memory and argument (not, at least, if we have learnt anything from what is known as 'hermeneutics').

Bacon's world, the world of early Stuart England, is very different from that, a century and a half later, of the Encyclopaedists' Paris.

---

3. I tried to keep this principle in mind, some years ago, when writing a book about Karl Marx. See Nicholas Lash, *A Matter of Hope: A Theologian's Reflections on the Thought of Karl Marx* (London, Darton, Longman and Todd, 1981).

4. Francis Bacon, 'First Part of the Great Instauration. The Dignity and Advancement of Learning, in Nine Books', book ii, ch. i, in Joseph Devey (ed.), *The Physical and Metaphysical Works of Lord Bacon* (London, Henry G. Bohn, 1864), p. 78.

Yet one of the surprising things about Diderot's Prospectus for the Encyclopaedia (published in 1750) is the extent to which he took over – lock, stock, and almost barrel – Bacon's scheme of things.

(To show this I have, in Table A, set out the elements of Bacon's table of Contents on the pattern of Diderot's *Système Figuré des Conoissances* [sic!] *Humaines*, which appears as Table B. One difference between them, as Furbank remarks, is that whereas Bacon excluded what we might call *sacra doctrina* from his scheme, Diderot incorporated *all* of theology within 'philosophy', the field of 'reason'.)[5]

The sustained dissociation, in both schemes, of argument from memory, of 'reason' from 'experience', sets reason's quest, the quest for ordering and ordered sanity or wisdom, freewheeling in the void. Reason, order, the enlightened mind, thus senses itself vulnerable to *dis*order, chaos, madness. There may have been, in Diderot, an effervescent optimism, a boundless sense of possibility; but if, as seems to be agreed, there was no room for the tragic vision in his scheme of things, neither do we find there the kind of smugness, the cocky self-assurance, that some other forms of 'rationalism' exhibit.

Thus, if one of the things that I would emphasise is the apparently spontaneous and untroubled way in which the Baconian disjunction of argument from memory, of 'reason' from 'experience', is carried forward into the very heart of French Enlightenment, another would be the recognition, in Diderot's case if not in that of his contemporaries, of the consequent *vulnerability* of 'reason'.

It is, moreover, worth remarking that, notwithstanding Diderot's strategic differentiation between reason, memory and imagination, he is almost Wittgensteinian in his insistence on the *diversity* of reason, on the many different guises reason has. Thus, with characteristic disregard for the apparent inconsistency, his identification of reason with but one of what Bacon called 'the three distinct fountains of the mind' exists in counterpoint to a more general sense of reason as specifying that which differentiates human from non-human nature, while yet doing so in such a manner as to suggest, ironically, that truly human, truly reasonable, human reason is really very rare.

'Haven't you noticed', he wrote to a friend in 1773, 'that the diversity of that prerogative, which we call "reason", is so great that, on its own, it corresponds to the full range of animal

---

5. See Furbank, *Diderot*, op. cit., p. 37. I have greatly simplified Diderot's scheme, which is reproduced in full on Furbank, p. 77.

instincts?'[6] And he runs through a list: the human wolf, the human tiger, human fox; the pike, devouring everything; the snake, self-coiled in a hundred ways; the bear, the crow, and so on. Nothing, he says, is more rare than the man who is simply human through and through: '*Rien de plus rare qu'un homme qui soit homme de toute pièce.*'[7]

The King's Fool

HIM: There is no better part to play, with the great ones of this world, than that of fool. There once used to be an official King's Fool, but there has never been an official King's Wise Man. I'm Bertin's fool, and fool to many others: yours, perhaps, at this moment; or, perhaps, you're mine. A really wise person wouldn't have a fool. So anyone who has a fool isn't wise; and, if he isn't wise, he's a fool; and, perhaps, if he's a king, his own fool's fool.[8]

On this, the first of two brief passages that I have chosen to illustrate my reading of the Dialogue, there are four things to be said. In the first place, there are advantages, in these matters, in working with a text first written in a foreign tongue. It keeps us on our toes. Thus, for example, 'fool' is a sound enough translation of '*fou*'. But how different would be the sense if, instead, we rendered '*fou*' as 'clown', or 'jester', 'idiot', or 'madman' (from many points of view, equally plausible translations)?

Secondly, notice that the *sense* of 'wisdom' (and hence, of 'reason', of 'philosophy', and of much else besides) is, as it were, counter-defined, delimited, or called in question, by the sense of folly or unreason rather than the other way round.

At the beginning of the Dialogue, this is not yet clear: 'Come

6. See Jean-Claude Bonnet (ed.), *Diderot. Le Neveu de Rameau* (Paris, Flammarion, 1983), p. 163.
7. Loc. cit.
8. I have risked my own translation of the passage, because Leonard Tancock's, in the Penguin Classics edition, has 'jester' for 'fool', which loses the implicit contrast between folly and reason. See Denis Diderot, *Rameau's Nephew and d'Alembert's Dream*, trans. Leonard Tancock (London, Penguin, 1966), p. 83.
    '*LUI: Il n'y a point de meilleur rôle auprès des grands que celui de fou. Longtemps il y a eu le fou du roi en titre; en aucun, il n'y a eu en titre le sage du roi. Moi je suis le fou de Bertin et de beaucoup d'autres, le vôtre peut-être dans ce moment; ou peut-être vous, le mien. Celui qui serait sage n'aurait point de fou. Celui donc qui a un fou n'est pas sage; s'il n'est pas sage, il est fou; et peut-être, fût-il roi, le fou de son fou*' (Bonnet, *Diderot*, op. cit., p. 91).

rain or shine, my custom is to go for a stroll in the Palais-Royal every afternoon at about five ... I hold discussions with myself on politics, love, taste or philosophy, and let my thoughts wander in complete abandon, leaving them free to follow the first wise or foolish idea that comes along.'[9] Almost the first hint of danger comes when the nephew exclaims: 'You know, of course, that I am an ignoramus, a fool, a lunatic, rude, lazy ... an out and out shirker, a rogue, a gormandizer.'[10]

How should we decode this seeming self-abnegation? The nephew knows (it seems) that he is a fool. But, knowing that, he's wise. And what of us? The question must be asked, because the phrase: 'yours, perhaps, at this moment; or, perhaps, you're mine' is one of a handful of places in the Dialogue in which the reader is alerted to the uneasy recognition that it is *me*, the reader – and not a character *called* 'Me' – who is being addressed!

In the third place, it is worth noting the line of reading that runs, through Hegel and Marx, to Michel Foucault. Foucault devoted the Preface to the Third Part of his *History of Madness* to a discussion of *Rameau's Nephew*. His comment on our text: 'and so unreason becomes reason's reason – at least insofar as reason only knows itself as possession'[11] reminds us of the young Marx: 'Private property has made us so stupid and one-sided that an object is only *ours* when we have it.'[12]

Finally, notice that there is at least a hint (even though we are reading Diderot) that the 'fool' performs, if not messianic, then at least prophetic functions. Thus, at the beginning of the Dialogue, the nephew is introduced as one of those eccentrics, on the margins of society, who, when 'one of them appears in a company of people he is the speck of yeast that leavens the whole [*c'est un grain de levain qui fermente*] and restores to each of us a portion of his natural individuality. He stirs people up and gives them a shaking, makes them take sides, brings out the truth, shows who are really good and unmasks the villains. It is then that the [man of good sense] listens and sorts people out.'[13]

9. Tancock, op. cit., p. 33.
10. Ibid., p. 45.
11. Michel Foucault, *Folie et Déraison: Histoire de la Folie à l'Age Classique* (Paris, Plon, 1961), p. 417.
12. Karl Marx, 'Economic and Philosophical Manuscripts', *Early Writings*, introd. Lucio Colletti, trans. Rodney Livingstone and Gregor Benton (London, Penguin, 1975), p. 351. See Lash, *A Matter of Hope*, op. cit., p. 89.
13. *Rameau's Nephew*, p. 40. I have rendered '*l'homme de bon sens*' (Bonnet, p. 47) as 'man of good sense' in preference to Tancock's 'wise man' (p. 35).

Foucault's comment on this passage, with its echo of 1 Corinthians 5:6, is that folly, unwisdom, unreason, is thus charged with making truth's way in the world. Of course, the wise ones of this world, insofar as they discern the truth that folly speaks, have their own way of neutralising it. As He says (and Foucault picks this up): 'If we' (outsiders, layabouts, the unrespectable) 'say something good it is just by accident, like lunatics or visionaries.'[14]

The sound of silence

But you would have gone off into roars of laughter at the way he mimicked the various instruments. With cheeks puffed out and a hoarse, dark tone he did the horns and bassoons, a bright, nasal tone for the oboes, quickening his voice with incredible agility for the stringed instruments to which he tried to get the closest approximation; he whistled the recorders and cooed the flutes, shouting, singing and throwing himself about like a mad thing: a one-man show featuring dancers, male and female, singers of both sexes, a whole orchestra, a complete opera-house, dividing himself into twenty different stage parts, tearing up and down, stopping, like one possessed, with flashing eyes and foaming mouth. The weather was terribly hot, and the sweat running down the furrows of his brow and cheeks mingled with the powder from his hair and ran in streaks down the top of his coat. What didn't he do? He wept, laughed, sighed, his gaze was tender, soft or furious: a woman swooning with grief, a poor wretch abandoned in the depth of his despair, a temple rising into view, birds falling silent at eventide, waters murmuring in a cool, solitary place or tumbling in torrents down the mountain side, a thunderstorm, a hurricane, the shrieks of the dying mingling with the howling of the tempest and the crash of thunder; night with its shadows, darkness and silence, for even silence itself can be depicted in sound.[15]

14. *Rameau's Nephew*, p. 40. '*Si nous disons quelque chose de bien, c'est comme des fous, ou des inspirés; par hasard*' (Bonnet, p. 52). The text used by Foucault, interestingly, has '*philosophes*' for '*inspirés*' (see Foucault, *Folie et Déraison*, op. cit., p. 419).

15. *Rameau's Nephew*, pp. 103–4. The literary quality of the passage is so central to the argument that I give the French text of the closing lines: '*Que ne lui vis-je pas faire? Il pleurait, il riait, il soupirait; il regardait, ou attendri, ou tranquille, ou furieux; c'était une femme qui se pâme de douleur; c'était un malheureux livré à tout son désespoir; un temple qui s'élève; des oiseaux qui se taisent au soleil couchant; des eaux ou qui murmurent dans un lieu solitaire et frais, ou qui descendent en torrent du haut des montagnes; un orage; une tempête, la plainte de ceux qui vont périr, mêlée au sifflement des vents, au fracas du tonnerre; c'était la nuit, avec ses*

I know at least one distinguished *diderotien* who considers this the most beautiful passage in the Dialogue. Perhaps, therefore, the less heavy-footed comment it receives from me, the better. There are just two features of it to which I would draw attention.

In the first place, as I indicated earlier, the paradox of Diderot's brilliant *literary* rendering, through this description, of He's *wordless* evocations of the world, goes to the heart of the philosophy of this most anti-Cartesian of spokesmen for 'Enlightenment'.[16] The paradox is pushed as far as it will go: Diderot writes so brilliantly that, reading his text, we think we can imagine what is being described, but how, might one suppose, did He succeed in giving *physical* expression to birdsong ceasing at the setting sun, to temples rising into view, and so on?

In the second place, what *kind* of 'night' is it, 'with its shadows, darkness and silence', that can be depicted in this fool's pantomime? Can we *name* the silence which the fool, in his antic wisdom, *shows*? There are, of course, many different ways in which such questions might be answered. But any answer worth our serious consideration would surely stand just as far from glib, supposedly quite clear and 'rational' apologies for what the early modern world decided to call 'theism' as it would from the easy, careless, tap-room atheism in which (like our contemporaries) so many of Diderot's friends and colleagues tended to indulge.

Foucault was, like Diderot, I think, a *serious* atheist. Commenting on the darkness of that 'night with its shadows', he speaks of the 'vertigo' of reason's self-unravelling, in which the truth of the world is only sustained as the interior of an absolute void, the absence of all shape and meaning.[17]

Rameau's Nephew ends enigmatically. He is off to the opera:

'What's on?'

'Something of Dauvergne's. There are some quite nice things in his music; the pity of it is that he wasn't the first to write them. There are always some of the dead who plague the living. Can't be helped ... Good-bye, Mr Philosopher. Isn't it true that I am always the same?'

'Alas, yes, unfortunately.'

ténèbres; c'était l'ombre et le silence; car le silence même se peint par des sons' (Bonnet, p. 110).

16. According to Foucault, *Rameau's Nephew* offers us, '*au milieu du xviiie siècle, et bien avant que ne soit totalement entendue la parole de Descartes, une leçon bien plus anticartésienne que tout Locke, tout Voltaire ou tout Hume*' (*Folie et Déraison*, op. cit., p. 421).

17. '*Ce vertige, où la vérité du monde ne se maintient qu'à l'intérieur d'un vide absolu*' (Foucault, *Folie et Déraison*, op. cit., p. 423).

'So long as I have that misfortune for another forty years! He laughs best who laughs last.'[18]

The nephew's parting laughter, as Foucault heard it, is not hilarity, but a kind of cry. Unreason remains, ironically, solitary: its suffering is the sadness of a hunger whose depths cannot be plumbed.[19] Foucault, it seems to me, rightly picks up the difference between the laughter at the end, the laughter into darkness, and the 'roars of laughter' which the mime initially provoked. And, in that difference, in the contrast of those cries, the pantomime, fool's genius, lacking all complacency, has something of the character of a *De Profundis*.

18. *Rameau's Nephew*, p. 125; '*Rira bien qui rira le dernier*' (Bonnet, p. 130).
19. '*Le délire reste ironiquement seul: la souffrance de la faim reste insondable douleur*' (Foucault, *Folie et Déraison*, op. cit., p. 424).

Table A

LEARNING

Faculty	Branch	Division	Subdivision	Category	Details
Memory	HISTORY	Civil	Ecclesiastical		General History of the Church · History of Prophecy · History of Providence
			Civil		Memoirs · Antiquities · Perfect History
			Generations		H. of the Heavens · History of Meteors · H. of Earth and Sea · H. of Massive or Collective Bodies · History of Species
		Natural	Praeter-generations		Monsters
			Arts		Agricultural · Manual · Mechanical
Reason	PHILOSOPHY	God	Natural Theology		
		Natural (Speculative)	Metaphysics		of Final Causes · of Form
			Physics (Efficient Causes & Matter)		Sciences of the Principles of Things · Sciences of the Structure of Things · Sciences of the Variety of Things
		Natural (Practical)	Magic (Experimental Philosophy)		
			Mechanics		
		Man	Human		Body (Medicinal, Cosmetic, Athletic & Voluptuary Arts) · Soul (Inspired Essence, & Sensible or Produced Soul)
			Civil		Art of Conversation · Art of Negotiation · Art of State Policy
Imagination	POETRY				Narrative · Dramatic · Parabolic

Anyone will easily perceive the justness of this division that recurs to the origin of our ideas. Individuals first strike the sense, which is as it were the port or entrance of the understanding. Then the understanding ruminates upon these images or impressions received from the sense, either simply reviewing them, or wantonly counterfeiting and imitating them, or forming them into certain classes by composition or separation. Thus it is clearly manifest that history, poetry, and philosophy flow from the three distinct fountains of the mind, viz., the memory, the imagination, and the reason; without any possibility of increasing their number. For history and experience are one and the same thing; so are philosophy and the sciences.

Nor does divine learning require any other division; for though revelation and sense may differ both in matter and manner, yet the spirit of man and its cells are the same; and in this case receive, as it were, different liquors through different conduits. Theology, therefore, consists – 1. of sacred history; 2. parable, or divine poesy; and 3. of holy doctrine or precept, as its fixed philosophy. As for prophecy, which seems a part redundant, it is no more than a species of history; divine history having this prerogative over human, that the narration may precede, as well as succeed the fact.

Bacon, Advancement of Learning (1605),
Book II, Chapter 1

Having now, excellent king, with our small bark of knowledge, sailed over and surrounded the globe of the sciences, as well the old world as the new (let posterity judge with what success), we should pay our vows and conclude; did there not still remain another part to be viewed; viz., sacred or inspired theology. But if we were disposed to survey it, we must quit the small vessel of human reason, and put ourselves on board the ship of the Church, which alone possesses the divine needle for justly shaping the course. Nor will the stars of philosophy, that have hitherto principally lent their light, be of farther service to us; and, therefore, it were not improper to be silent, also, upon this subject, as well as upon that of government. For which reason, we will omit the just distribution of it, and only contribute ... a few particulars in the way of good wishes ... We shall, therefore, only propose three appendages of theology; treating not of the matter already formed, or to be formed by divinity, but only of the manner of forming it ...

For if we should believe only such things as are agreeable to our reason, we assent to the matter, and not to the author:

which is no more than we do to a suspected witness ... And, therefore, the more absurd and incredible any divine mystery is, the greater honour we do to God in believing it; and so much the more noble the victory faith ...

Let us, therefore, conclude, that sacred theology must be drawn from the word and oracles of God; not from the light of nature, or the dictates of reason.

Bacon, *Advancement of Learning* (1605), Book IX

Table B
Système Figuré des Connoissances Humaines

ENTENDEMENT

Memoire — Raison — Imagination

HISTOIRE (Memoire)

- **Sacrée / Ecclésiastique**
- **Civile**
  - Histoire Civile
  - Histoire Litt. — Mémoires / Antiquités / Histoire Complète
- **Naturelle**
  - Uniformité de la nature
    - Histoire céleste
    - Histoire des Météores
    - de la terre de la mer
    - des minéraux
    - des végétaux
    - des animaux
    - des éléments
  - Ecarts de la nature
    - Prodiges célestes
    - Météores Prodigieux
    - Prodiges sur la terre et la mer
    - Minéraux monstrueux
    - Végétaux monstrueux
    - Animaux monstrueux
    - Prodiges des éléments
  - Usages de la nature
    - Arts
    - Métiers
    - Manufactures

PHILOSOPHIE (Raison)

- Métaphysique générale ou ontologie
- **Science de Dieu**
  - Théologie Naturelle
  - Théologie Révélée
  - Science des esprits bien et malfaisants
- **Science de l'homme**
  - Pneumatologie ou science de l'âme
  - Logique
    - Art de penser
    - Art de retenir
    - Art de Communiquer
  - Morale
    - Générale
    - Particulière
- **Science de la nature**
  - Métaphysique des corps ou physique générale
  - Mathématiques
    - Pures
    - Mixtes
    - Physicomathématique
  - Physique particulière
    - Zoologie
    - Astronomie physique
    - Météorologie
    - Cosmologie
    - Botanique
    - Minéralogie
    - Chimie

POESIE (Imagination)

- **Narrative**
  - Poème épique
  - Madrigal
  - Roman
- **Dramatique**
  - Tragédie
  - Comédie
  - Opéra
  - Pastorales
- **Parabolique**
  - Allégories

For the vast field that Diderot and d'Alembert were to deal with, a

'tree of knowledge' based, like Buffon's, upon *things* (i.e. upon the *objects* of knowledge) seemed to them totally impracticable; thus they opted instead, as Francis Bacon before them, for a system based upon human faculties (that is to say, on the *sources* of knowledge). Of these faculties, *memory*, *reason* and *imagination* were to be regarded as the most fundamental, and to them would correspond the three great branches of knowledge, History, Philosophy and Poetry, with their various subdivisions – the whole ramification being eventually set out in Diderot's *Prospectus* in the form of an elaborate chart or 'Illustrated System of Human Knowledge'. The 'tree' adopted was fairly close to Bacon's in *The Advancement of Learning*, but differed from it, significantly, in treating revealed religion as a mere branch of 'philosophy'.

Furbank, Diderot, pp. 36–7

Chapter 9

Where Does Holy Teaching Leave Philosophy?
Questions on Milbank's Aquinas

In this short paper, I am going to be rude about John Milbank.[1] I enter, however, a twofold plea in mitigation. First: in the time available, the only way to avoid being steamrolled by John's energetically erudite polemic seemed to be to attempt a countervailing pugnacity. In the second place, the disagreements that I want to register are set in a much vaster context of agreement and respect.

I propose, as territory of discussion, the first two essays in *The Word Made Strange*.[2] From each, I take one passage that can serve as marker for our conversation. From 'A Critique of the Theology of Right', I take: 'Against Burrell one must say that ... any use of evaluative perfection-terms, *already* assumes a metaphysics of participation, such that grammar here grounds itself in theology, not theology in grammar.'[3] From 'Only Theology Overcomes Metaphysics', I take: for Aquinas, 'the domain of metaphysics is not simply subordinate to, but completely *evacuated* by theology, for metaphysics refers its subject matter – "Being" – wholesale to a first principle, God, which is the subject of another, higher science, namely God's own, only accessible to us via revelation. This is *not* a matter of mere causal referral, but of the entire being of *ens commune* and its comprehensibility. And here we have reached the absolute crux of this matter, and the turning point in the destiny of the West.'[4]

The issues are, in part, historical: I think John Milbank has Aquinas wrong both on analogy and on the relations between

---

1. This paper was originally read to the 'D Society' in Cambridge, in November 1997, to mark the twentieth year of my chairmanship of that venerable seminar.
2. John Milbank, 'A Critique of the Theology of Right', 'Only Theology Overcomes Metaphysics', in *The Word Made Strange: Theology, Language, Culture* (Oxford, Blackwell, 1997), pp. 7–35, 36–52.
3. Milbank, *The Word Made Strange*, op. cit., p. 16.
4. Ibid., p. 44.

theology and metaphysics. They are also, however, in part contemporary: whereas, according to him, being 'uncertain as to
where today to locate true Christian practice ... the theologian
feels almost that the entire ecclesial task falls on his own head',[5] I
see no reason for any such burdensome pretension on the theologian's part; and whereas, according to him, theology, 'if it wishes
to think again God's love, and think creation as the manifestation
of that love, then it must entirely evacuate philosophy, which is
metaphysics, leaving it nothing ... to either do or see, which is not
– manifestly, I judge – malicious',[6] I shall suggest that this view,
which we may call 'the theocratic tendency', has little to commend
it as a contribution to the common quest for wisdom and the
healing of the world.

What might 'metaphysics' mean?

A preliminary difficulty concerns the historicality of the concept
of 'metaphysics'. By this I mean that whereas, on some occasions,
Milbank uses the term with quite specific connotations as to
context and, hence, to sense, on others it is used as if its sense
were more or less historically invariant. For example, he gives a
quite precise account of that 'new science of *ontology* which
emerged in the seventeenth century, and which coincided with
Suarez's use for the first time of "metaphysics" to name a systematic discipline',[7] and he reminds us that Heidegger's reading
of 'the entire philosophical tradition and the Christian appropriation of philosophy as the history of metaphysics or onto-
theology' often amounted to 'reading it through neo-scholastic
spectacles'.[8] In contrast, the peroration of the essay, with its
exhortation to the theologian entirely to 'evacuate philosophy,
which is metaphysics', seems (for lack of any indication to the
contrary) to apply, indiscriminately, to 'metaphysics' as understood by Plato or Aristotle, Aquinas or Scotus, Kant or Heidegger.
All these 'malicious' enterprises, apparently, it is the duty of
theology to 'overcome'.

Peter Geach, replying, during the 1951 Joint Session of the

5. Ibid., p. 1.
6. Ibid., p. 50.
7. Ibid., p. 40.
8. Ibid., p. 41. Not only would it be a little hard on Heidegger to blame
   him for this tendency, inasmuch as a great deal of the historical work
   – by Bouillard, and Chenu, and Lonergan, and countless others –
   which undermined the foundations of baroque 'Thomism' was only
   published late in his career, but ironically, I shall later be charging
   Milbank himself with vestigial neo-scholasticism.

Aristotelian Society and the Mind Association, to Quine's paper 'On What There Is', made

> some remarks on Quine's conception of ontological dis-
> agreement. He expresses the hope that people who disagree
> over ontology may find a basis of agreement by 'withdrawing
> to a semantical plane' (p. 35). This hope seems to me illu-
> sory. People with different world-views will still differ when
> they talk about language, which is part of the world.[9]

And he went on:

> Certain concepts, like *existence* and *truth* and *thing* and
> *property*, are used, and cannot but be used, in all rational
> discourse whatsoever; and ontology is an attempt to scruti-
> nize our use of them. To be right or wrong in ontology
> means being clear or muddled about such fundamentals.[10]

Donald MacKinnon, who was fond of quoting (or slightly mis-
quoting) that passage, described it as being faithful 'to the tradition classically formulated in Aristotle's *Metaphysics*'.[11] Let us
suppose MacKinnon and Geach to be correct, not only about
Aristotle, but about Aquinas (for they both understood the latter's
understanding of 'metaphysics' to be, at least in this respect,
straightforwardly Aristotelian). It follows, I suggest, in the first
place, that their account opens the door to consideration of
metaphysical enquiry as being 'grammatical' in a sense now
commonly associated with Wittgenstein and, in the second, that
there is no *prima facie* reason for deeming the territory of metaphysics to have been 'completely evacuated' by theology or, to be
more exact, by what Aquinas called '*theologia quae ad sacram doctrinam pertinet*': that theology which pertains to holy teaching.[12]

Analogy and grammar

In the first essay of *The Word Made Strange*, John Milbank criticises
'many recent treatments of analogy' for their 'post-critical confinement of analogy to "our use of language", detached from

9. Peter Geach, 'Symposium: On What There Is', *Freedom, Language, and
   Reality*, Aristotelian Society Supplementary Volume XXV (London,
   Harrison, 1951), p. 134.
10. Ibid., p. 136.
11. D. M. MacKinnon, 'The Relation of the Doctrines of the Incarnation
   and the Trinity', in *Creation, Christ and Culture: Studies in Honour of T.
   F. Torrance*, ed. R. W. A. McKinney (Edinburgh, T. & T. Clark, 1976),
   pp. 93–4.
12. *Summa Theologiae*, Ia, 1, 1 ad 2.

questions of participation in Being'.[13] A few pages later, we are told that 'For Aquinas the possibility of analogy is grounded in this reality of participation in Being and goodness. Analogy is not, as he conceived it, primarily a linguistic doctrine.'[14]

Only one of the 'many' treatments is identified: Herbert McCabe's appendix on 'analogy' to his edition of Questions 12 and 13 of the *Prima Pars*. That succinct and accurate little text begins: 'In the opinion of the present translator too much has been made of St Thomas's alleged teaching on analogy. For him, analogy is not a way of getting to know about God, nor is it a theory of the structure of the universe, it is a comment on our use of certain words.'[15]

Baroque scholasticism tidied up Aquinas's occasional and unsystematic remarks about analogical predication and inflated the results into a structure of metaphysical doctrine eventually labelled, in the manuals, 'the analogy of being'. Such usage, however, was not Aquinas's, and mere assertion will not make it so. It is not the malign influence of Kant, but the excellence of twentieth-century medieval scholarship, that has enabled us to discover the gulf which separates Aquinas from (for example) Suarez or Cajetan.[16]

13. Milbank, *The Word Made Strange*, op. cit., p. 9.
14. Ibid., p. 15.
15. Herbert McCabe, in Thomas Aquinas, *Summa Theologiae*, vol. 3: *Knowing and Naming God* (Ia. 12–13), ed. Herbert McCabe (Cambridge, Blackfriars, 1964), p. 106; referred to in Milbank, *The Word Made Strange*, op. cit., p. 32. Milbank almost certainly also had in mind the endorsement of McCabe's judgement by David Burrell, who opened a chapter on 'Analogical Predication' with the remark: 'Aquinas is perhaps best known for his theory of analogy. On closer inspection it turns out that he never had one' (David B. Burrell, *Aquinas: God and Action* [London, Routledge and Kegan Paul, 1989], p. 55) and may have remembered that I have, from time to time, agreed with them both: see Nicholas Lash, 'Ideology, Metaphor and Analogy', in *The Philosophical Frontiers of Christian Theology: Essays Presented to D. M. MacKinnon*, ed. Brian Hebblethwaite and Stewart Sutherland (Cambridge, Cambridge University Press, 1982), pp. 68–94; reprinted in *Theology on the Way to Emmaus* (London, SCM Press, 1986), pp. 95–119.
16. 'Thomas speaks of an *analogia nominum* (analogy of names or terms) and thus an analogy of the names of God, and not yet of an *analogia entis* (analogy of being), a concept which Cajetan introduces only in the sixteenth century and which acquired its status as a principle only in our own century through the work of E. Przywara' (Walter Kasper, *The God of Jesus Christ*, trans. Matthew J. O'Connell [London, SCM Press, 1984], p. 97).
    Elsewhere, in criticism of *The God of Jesus Christ*, Milbank says:

Aquinas's remarks on analogical predication are, in a quite straightforward sense, 'grammatical'. If John Milbank is reluctant to take my word for this, or Herbert McCabe's, I refer him to a splendidly accurate and lucid recent account of Aquinas's treatment of the ' "analogical" status' of certain terms used in the naming of God. This account is to be found on p. 393 of a fascinating paper, in *The Heythrop Journal*, on 'The History of the One God', the author of which is a certain John Milbank.[17] According to the essay in *The Word Made Strange*, however, David Burrell muddies the waters with 'his notion of a "grammatical" approach to the unknown beyond the known, which is a conversion of Lonergan's transcendentalism into linguistic terms'.[18] As I

'Human thought is allowed a pre-theological, Scotist-Heideggerian apprehension of a sheerly categorical *esse*' (Milbank, 'The Second Difference', *The Word Made Strange*, op. cit., p. 175). On which, two comments. First, the reader turning to one of the two passages in Kasper explicitly adduced as warrants for this charge may be surprised to find him insisting: 'God, therefore, can be known only through God' (Kasper, *God of Jesus Christ*, op. cit., p. 113). In the second place, *if* Milbank means that the very notion of 'sheerly categorical *esse*' is incoherent, because *esse* is an infinitive, then, although I think he is largely wrong about Kasper, he is probably right about that entire conceptualist tradition initiated by Scotus. My suspicion, however, is that, in keeping with the very tradition that he deplores, he is himself interpreting 'being' in dangerously substantival terms.

It may be worth mentioning that whereas Kasper seemed confident that it was Cajetan who introduced the notion of *analogia entis* (while giving no reference to its occurrence in Cajetan's writings), according to Henri Bouillard (to whose work, surprisingly, Kasper made no reference): '*le terme d'*analogia entis *ne figure pas chez saint Thomas. On le retrouve en revanche chez Saurez, qui, s'il ne l'a pas créé, l'a du moins vulgarisé. A notre connaissance, Cajetan ne l'emploie pas non plus*' (Henri Bouillard, *Karl Barth: Parole de Dieu et Existence Humaine*, vol. 2 [Aubier, Editions Montaigne, Collection *Théologie*, 39, 1957], p. 199), citing two instances of the expression in the *Disputationes Metaphysicae*.

So far as the central issue on this point between John Milbank and myself is concerned, it is encouraging to find Bouillard insisting, in 1957, that '*Chez saint Thomas, l'analogie qualifie l'*usage *de certain concepts* [or, as McCabe had it, 'our use of certain words'] ... *Chez Cajetan et Suarez, elle est une propriété du concept lui-même*' (loc. cit., his stress).

17. See John Milbank, 'History of the One God', *Heythrop Journal*, xxxviii (1997), pp. 371–400.
18. Milbank, *The Word Made Strange*, op. cit., p. 13. The gestural vagueness of the epithet puts Milbank in company with a great deal of loose talk about 'transcendentalism' in contemporary theology. Even

read Burrell, however, there is no question of grammatical alertness serving as voyage of discovery, as a device for 'straddling the boundary of the sublime'.[19] It is, more modestly, a matter of scrutinising our use of certain concepts (to use Geach's terminology). The aim of Milbank's essay is to indicate 'how pervasive' are the 'transcendentalist presuppositions' of modern theology.[20] In Burrell's case, as in McCabe's, however, Milbank, like a bent detective, has planted the dangerous substances which he then triumphantly discovers.

To illustrate this, let us follow up the references to Lonergan. In a later essay, Milbank announces that 'Bernard Lonergan's understanding of the Thomist *Verbum* is misleading' inasmuch as he 'at once *reduces* Aquinas to Aristotle (for whom the intellectual act *was* purely intransitive) ... and makes him anticipate post-Kantian transcendentalism'.[21] The attached note simply reads: 'See Bernard Lonergan, *Verbum: Word and Idea in Aquinas* (Notre Dame, Indiana, 1967) and S.T.I.Q. 27, 1 ad 2, 3'.[22]

This cavalier disdain for evidence makes it difficult to understand, let alone assess, the three sentences which Milbank deems sufficient to dispose of Lonergan's nuanced account of Aquinas's developing understanding of 'utterance', human and divine, through 300 pages of close analysis of primary texts (the *index locorum* alone runs to 24 pages). I have a suspicion that he overlooked Lonergan's reference to 'Kant, whose critique was not of pure reason but of the human mind as conceived by Scotus'.[23] Be

Douglas Hall, who, in an earnest but somewhat flat-footed study, attempts to group twentieth-century interpreters of Aquinas into three types: 'participationist, transcendental, and analogical' (Douglas C. Hall, *The Trinity: An Analysis of St Thomas Aquinas; 'Expositio' of the 'De Trinitate' of Boethius* [Leiden: E. J. Brill, 1992], p. 3), concedes that there really is no 'transcendental school', and that Lonergan and Rahner are as different from each other as each of them is differently critical of Kant (see p. 6). Incidentally, the phrase 'which is a conversion ... linguistic terms' is not to be found in the earlier version of this essay: see John Milbank, ' "Between Purgation and Illumination": A Critique of the Theology of Right', in *Christ, Ethics and Tragedy: Essays in Honour of Donald MacKinnon*, ed. Kenneth Surin (Cambridge, Cambridge University Press, 1989), p. 169; I do not regard its addition as an improvement.

19. Milbank, *The Word Made Strange*, op. cit., p. 13.
20. Ibid., p. 7.
21. Ibid., p. 93.
22. Ibid., p. 114.
23. Bernard J. Lonergan, *Verbum: Word and Idea in Aquinas*, ed. David B. Burrell (London, Darton, Longman and Todd, 1968), p. 25. A lengthy footnote documents this charge with reference to a series of

that as it may, let us follow up his other reference: to Question 27 of the *Prima Pars*.

According to Lonergan, 'it seems clear that the movement of Thomist thought is definitely away from conceiving the divine processions as productions'.[24] Article 1 of Question 27 is one of the texts cited in evidence. The article considers '*utrum sit processio in divinis?*' The second objection answers in the negative, on the grounds that 'whatever proceeds is diverse from its source', whereas '*in Deo non est aliqua diversitas, sed summa simplicitas*'. Aquinas's reply is that, when we say that there is 'proceeding' in God, we are speaking of something more like 'having an idea', than like moving something around or heating it (examples in which 'proceeding' *is* a kind of 'production'). The kind of 'proceeding' that is the thinking of a thought is immanent to the thinker. The more perfect the thought, the greater its identity with (or non-diversity from) the thinker. And, since the divine understanding is the very pinnacle of perfection, '*necesse est quod verbum divinum sit perfecte unum cum eo a quo procedit absque omni diversitate*'.[25] As Lonergan puts it, summarising a passage in the body of the article: 'the errors of Arius and Sabellius are reduced to the mistake of conceiving the divine processions in terms of agent and effect'.[26] Thomas Aquinas was not an Arian, which is what Milbank, with his insistence that the intellectual act is transitive, appears to be.

'Ontology is an attempt to scrutinize our use of ... certain concepts, like *existence* and *truth* and *thing* and *property.*'[27] This is not a 'confinement' of ontology, or metaphysics, to ' "our use of language", detached from questions of participation in Being',[28] but the reappropriation of an ancient tradition which understood the distinction between 'formal' and 'material' discourse; a distinction which has some affinity (I put it no more strongly) with that drawn, by Wittgenstein, between 'grammatical' and 'material' uses of language.

Baroque scholasticism lost sight of this distinction and, as a result, got into the dreadful habit (to put it very crudely) of talking about 'being', with or without a capital initial, as if it were an entity of some kind. Whatever the conventions, in German or

texts from Scotus, Cajetan, and others. (It is worth remembering that Lonergan's study of *Verbum* was first published, between 1946 and 1949, as a series of five articles in *Theological Studies.*)

24. Ibid., p. 197.
25. *Summa Theologiae*, I, q. 27, 1, ad 2.
26. Lonergan, *Verbum*, op. cit., p. 197.
27. See reference in n. 9.
28. Milbank, *The Word Made Strange*, op. cit., p. 9.

in French, there is, in my opinion, much to be said, where English is concerned, in favour of trying to avoid the term 'being' and, so far as possible, translating *esse* as 'existence' and *ens* as 'reality'. After all, *ens commune*, about which volumes of misleading pretentious nonsense have been written, means neither more nor less than 'reality in general'. But nobody supposes 'reality in general' to name some mysterious, 'metaphysical' kind of stuff, lurking behind, or hidden within, the people and the things with which we have to deal. I am, therefore, grateful to Thomas Gilby, in his translation of the first article of the *Summa* (to which I shall return a little later on), for rendering '*Sed de omnibus partibus entis tractatur in philosophicis disciplinis, etiam de Deo*' as: 'Yet the philosophical sciences deal with all parts of reality, even with God.'[29]

To conclude this section of my remarks, I come back to the first of the two marker-passages from which I set out. 'Grammar here grounds itself in theology, not theology in grammar.'[30] If, by 'theology' is meant, not any and every kind of speech concerning God, but 'that theology which pertains to holy teaching', then: of course! Milbank, however, supposes this to be said 'Against Burrell'. But where on earth, in all his writings, does David Burrell state, or imply, that theology is *grounded* in grammar? Theology is 'grounded' in prayer, and praise, and work, and suffering; in the gift of the Sprit and the grace of discipleship; in all that rich, conflictual terrain which Milbank discounts because he supposes Christianity only to exist, these days, in theory.[31] But some of the things we think, upon this ground, are, nonetheless, 'grammatical' in character; that is to say, they function as 'rules' rather than 'descriptions'.[32]

The dangerous tendency of Cardinal Milbank

I have already indicated my regret at the vagueness of many of Milbank's key assertions, and his failure to furnish them with appropriate warrants. Like Cardinal Ratzinger, rather than risk

29. Thomas Aquinas, *Summa Theologiae*, vol. 1: *Christian Theology* (Ia. 1), ed. Thomas Gilby (Cambridge, Blackfriars, 1964), pp. 5–6, 7.
30. Milbank, *The Word Made Strange*, op. cit., p. 16.
31. See Milbank, *The Word Made Strange*, op. cit., p. 1, para. 1.
32. 'In emphasizing the fluidity of the grammatical/material distinction, [Wittgenstein] was drawing attention to the fact that concept-formation – and thus the establishing of rules for what it does and does not make sense to say ... is something that is always linked with a custom, a practice' (Ray Monk, *Wittgenstein: The Duty of Genius* [London, Jonathan Cape, 1990], p. 468).

examination of the evidence, he prefers thunderous denunciation from a safe distance. Two examples must suffice.

'This is not at all to say – following interpreters like Rahner and Metz – that Aquinas builds on an anthropological foundation. On the contrary', his is a 'wholly theological anthropology', according to which 'human beings are only properly known within our imitation of God'.[33] No texts by either Metz or Rahner are offered in support of this extraordinary claim. One wonders what Milbank makes of what Rahner calls 'the innermost centre of the Christian understanding of existence', namely, that 'Man is the event of a free, unmerited and forgiving, and absolute self-communication of God'.[34] In other words, Jesus Christ is the only fully human human being that there is. It would be difficult for an anthropology to be *more* theological than that!

But my favourite example of Cardinal Milbank in full cry is: 'There are, then, genuine grounds of suspicion of the Scott Holland/Forsyth/MacKinnon (metaphysically Butlerian–Kantian) tendency...'![35]

Aquinas on metaphysics

It is time to turn to the second of my marker-passages, 'the absolute crux of the matter', the claim that, for Aquinas, 'the domain of metaphysics is not simply subordinate to, but completely *evacuated* by theology'.[36] The note provided in support of this contention reads: 'Thomas Aquinas, *In Metaphysica*, Prologue'.[37] This reference is really quite astonishing.

Although the labelling is unusual, and no indication is given as to edition, or date or place of publication, I take it to be a reference to the *Proemium* to Thomas's commentary on Aristotle's *Metaphysics*, a brief text (less than two pages in Cathala's edition)

---

33. Ibid., p. 15.
34. Karl Rahner, *Foundations of Christian Faith: An Introduction to the Idea of Christianity*, trans. William V. Dych (London, Darton, Longman and Todd, 1978), p. 116. For an even more succinct formulation: 'When God wills to be non-divine, the human person comes to be' (Rahner, 'On the Theology of the Incarnation', *Theological Investigations, Vol. IV*, trans. Kevin Smyth [London, Darton, Longman and Todd, 1966], p. 116, following the amended translation suggested by George Vandervelde, 'The Grammar of Grace', *Theological Studies*, 49 [1988], p. 450).
35. Milbank, *The Word Made Strange*, op. cit., p. 23.
36. Ibid., p. 44.
37. Ibid., p. 51.

probably written in 1269, three years after the first question of the *Prima Pars* (with which I shall compare it).[38]

The argument of this little text runs as follows. Since all disciplines are directed to one end: namely, human happiness ('*beatitudo*'), there must be one which rules the rest, which one will rightly be called 'wisdom', because it falls to the wise to direct others ('*Nam sapientis est alios ordinare*'). (This last phrase, a quotation from the *Metaphysics*, is one which, in the first Question of the *Prima Pars*, Aquinas weaves into his nuanced account of the relationship between the wisdom that is acquired through study and the wisdom that is a gift of the Holy Spirit.)[39]

This governing '*scientia*', dealing with whatever is maximally intelligible ('*maxime intelligibilia*'), will be the most luminous and comprehensive in its understanding (a paraphrase for '*maxime intellectualis*'). 'Intelligibility', however, can be taken in three ways: in relation to the knowledge of causes, in relation to universal principles (such as reality, unity and multiplicity, possibility and actuality – '*Quae quidem sunt ens, et ea quae consequuntur ens, ut unum et multa, potentia et actus*'), and to whatever can be considered independently of matter, such as number ('*sicut mathematica*'), or can exist thus independently, such as God and minds ('*sicut Deus et intelligentiae*').

This threefold consideration is, however, the business not of three disciplines but one, because we are talking about three aspects of the consideration of reality in general (our old friend '*ens commune*'), but this one discipline will have three names: in relation to causes, we call it 'first philosophy' ('*prima philosophia*'); in relation to reality in general, we call it 'metaphysics' ('*metaphysica*'); in relation to pure mind, we call it 'divinity' or 'theology' ('*scientia divina sive theologia*').

The first thing to be said about this laconic little text is that, unsurprisingly (since it is introducing a commentary on Aristotle's *Metaphysics*), it makes no mention of God's revelation. But the

---

38. See M.-R. Cathala (ed.), Thomas Aquinas, *In Duodecim Metaphysicorum Aristotelis Expositio* (Turin and Rome, Marietti, 1964), pp. 1–2; for dates, see James A. Weisheipl, *Friar Thomas d'Aquino: His Life, Thought, and Works* (Oxford, Basil Blackwell, 1975), pp. 361, 379. Amongst the commentaries on this little text, I have found helpful James S. Doig, *Aquinas on Metaphysics: A Historico-Doctrinal Study of the Commentary on the Metaphysics* (The Hague, Martinus Nijhoff, 1972) and John F. Wippel, *Metaphysical Themes in Thomas Aquinas* (Washington, DC, Catholic University of America Press, 1984); see also Wippel's essay, 'Metaphysics', in Norman Kretzman and Eleonore Stump (eds.), *The Cambridge Companion to Aquinas* (Cambridge, Cambridge University Press, 1993), pp. 85–127.

39. *Summa Theologiae*, Ia, 1, 6.

second would be that, although it is written by a Christian theologian with a very high view of the surpassing excellence of Christian teaching, it does not give the impression of supposing that, *post Christum*, there is nothing for metaphysics either to do or see that is not malicious.

But the third point I would want to make is that I am genuinely baffled by John Milbank's reference to this text. There are plenty of places in his writings in which St Thomas *does* contrast the scope and function of theology and philosophy, but this is not one of them.

On one key issue, the *Proemium* is so succinct as to be misleading. If the subject-matter of metaphysics is reality in general and if, from one point of view, it may be called 'theology', because it considers those things that exist altogether independently of matter, such as God and minds, does it follow that 'reality in general', '*ens commune*', embraces not only creatures but also their Creator? The short answer is 'No', but we would have to turn to other texts to find the answer given.[40] God, according to Aquinas, is neither the subject of metaphysics, nor is he included under its subject, except indirectly, as the unknown first cause or principle of reality in general.[41]

God is not what metaphysics is about. In contrast, the subject-matter of 'that theology which pertains to holy teaching' *is*: God himself and all things in relation to God their origin and destiny.[42] I should have thought that the first Question of the *Prima Pars* would have suited John Milbank's purposes much better than the *Proemium* to the Commentary on the *Metaphysics*.

Water into wine

Thomas Aquinas was, 'by vocation, training, and self-understanding an ordained teacher of an inherited theology'.[43] His decision 'to write as a theologian when he wrote in his own voice

---

40. 'In ST IaIIae.66.5, ad 4, Aquinas writes that *ens commune* is the proper effect of the highest cause, God. This precludes including God under *ens commune*, for he would then cause himself. Aquinas explicitly refuses to include God under *esse commune* in his Commentary on the *Divine Names*. See In DDN 5.2.660' (Wippel, 'Metaphysics', op. cit., p. 117).

41. See Wippel, 'Metaphysics', op. cit., p. 86; Doig, *Aquinas on Metaphysics*, op. cit., pp. 376–381.

42. '*Omnia autem tractantur in sacra doctrina sub ratione Dei, vel quia sunt ipse Deus vel quia habent ordinem at Deum ut ad principium et finem. Unde sequitur quod Deus vere si subjectum hujus scientiae*' (*Summa Theologiae*, Ia, 1, 7, c).

43. Mark D. Jordan, 'Theology and Philosophy', in *The Cambridge Companion*, p. 232.

was chiefly the result of his view that no Christian should be satisfied to speak only as a philosopher'.[44] Philosophy, as Aquinas understood it, was a hierarchy of bodies of knowledge and a pattern of teaching embodied in communities of study, in philosophical 'schools'. He had the greatest respect for such schools – whether pagan, Jewish, or Islamic – and learned a great deal from their work. But he was in no doubt that Christian schools drew far more deeply from far richer springs.

The question that he asks, in the very first article of the *Summa Theologiae*, is whether any teaching is needed *apart* from, *over and above*, the teaching of philosophy: '*utrum sit necessarium* praeter *philosophicas disciplinas aliam doctrinam haberi*'? And his answer, of course, is not only 'Yes', but that the character of the teaching given to us by God's gift for our healing ('*salus*') is such that the theology which pertains to holy teaching differs in kind from that theology, that naming of God, which occurs in philosophy: '*Unde theologia quae ad sacram doctrinam pertinet differt secundum genus ab illa theologia quae pars philosophiae ponitur*'.[45]

'Over and above' ('*praeter*'); 'differs in kind' ('*differt secundum genus*'). Such language suggests a very different view of the matter from John Milbank's insistence that 'the domain of metaphysics is ... completely *evacuated* by theology'; so completely, indeed, that, if metaphysics still attempts to stay in business, it can only do so 'maliciously'.[46]

In his commentary on Aristotle's *Ethics*, St Thomas, following a tradition of Stoic origin, classifies the sciences, or 'parts of philosophy', into: natural philosophy (which includes metaphysics, because 'reality in general' is an aspect of the world as we find it), rational philosophy (logic, semantic theory, and so on), moral philosophy and the mechanical arts.[47]

We draw these maps very differently today but when, in my introductory remarks, I (maliciously!) referred to John Milbank's 'theocratic tendency', I had in mind his silence as to where and how, with metaphysics once 'overcome', the map of those 'parts of philosophy' which we now call the arts and sciences, is to be drawn, and what we might suppose the appropriate relationships to be between its elements and the practice of Christian theology. To put it very simply: in the conquest of metaphysics, how *much* of the work of the modern university is 'overcome' and its 'domain

44. Ibid., p. 233.
45. *Summa Theologiae*, Ia, 1, 1 ad 2.
46. Milbank, *The Word Made Strange*, op. cit., p. 44; see p. 50.
47. See Thomas Aquinas, *In Decem Libros Ethicorum Aristotelis ad Nicomachum Expositio*, ed. R. M. Spiazzi (Turin, Marietti, 1964), Lectio 1, 1–2 (p. 3).

... completely evacuated'? I cannot see how anyone could find this question unimportant or uninteresting, or suppose its answers to be obvious.[18]

48. In the course of an argument with Leonardo Boff, in *Theology and Social Theory* (Oxford, Basil Blackwell, 1990), Milbank announces that '*all* knowledge implies faith in God for Aquinas' (p. 248, his stress).

This statement seems so preposterous that one turns eagerly to the notes in order to discover what warrants are offered on its behalf. Three passages are indicated. The first from the commentary on Boethius's *De Trinitate*, is a straightforward exposition of the necessary place that '*fides*' occupies between '*opinio*' and '*scientia*'. Of the other two, from the first Question of the *Prima Pars*, the second is simply a general reference to the discussion, in article 6, of the senses in which 'holy teaching' may be said to be 'wisdom'.

The first, however, is to the reply to the second objection to article 5. That article asks whether holy teaching is of greater 'dignity', stands higher in the scheme of things, than other branches of knowledge: '*utrum sacra doctrina sit dignior aliis scientiis?*' The second objection argues that lower disciplines draw upon higher ones, as music (for example) draws upon mathematics. And since holy teaching draws on philosophical disciplines (Jerome is quoted as an expert witness) it is therefore of lower standing ('*inferior*') than they are. The reply to this objection characteristically exploits an ambiguity in the notion of one activity drawing upon (literally: 'accepting something from', '*accipere ... aliquid*') another. Aquinas points out that, from the fact that architects 'draw upon' the skills of tradesmen, and statesmen those of soldiers, it does not follow that architecture is inferior to carpentry, or statesmanship to archery. In 'drawing upon' other disciplines, holy teaching treats those 'other disciplines as subcontractors, footsoldiers, captives, slaves' (Eugene F. Rogers, *Thomas Aquinas and Karl Barth: Sacred Doctrine and the Natural Knowledge of God* [London, University of Notre Dame Press, 1995], p. 50). Milbank's Aquinas, however, apparently supposes every bricklayer's apprentice to share the architect's apprehension of the project and every foot-soldier to be a member of the General Staff.

A proper examination of Milbank's curious claim would require careful differentiation between a range of 'knowledge' words, especially between '*scire*' and '*cognoscere*': see Rogers, *Thomas Aquinas and Karl Barth*, op. cit., pp. 116–17, where Rogers makes good use of what he calls 'Preller's rule'. According to Victor Preller, ' "*scire*" is never used [by Aquinas] in connection with cognition of God through natural reason: the word is "*cognoscere*" ' (Rogers, op. cit., p. 36, citing Victor Preller, *Divine Science and the Science of God: A Reformulation of Thomas Aquinas* [Princeton, NJ, Princeton University Press, 1967], p. 32).

'Aquinas', according to Milbank, 'never allowed that any other science was autonomous in relation to theology' (*The Word Made Strange*, op. cit., p. 247). This is most misleading. When work in some other science (history, say, or philology) is undertaken on behalf of

St Thomas would, I think, have agreed with John Milbank that 'a Christian theology done well ought to speak more and better things about matters of concern to philosophy than the philosophers themselves can say'.[49] The snag is, of course, that doing theology 'well', as Aquinas understood these things, requires not only erudition and intelligence, but also that holiness and wisdom without which the excellence of 'holy teaching' cannot be displayed.

Aquinas's own preferred image for the relationship between theology and philosophy was drawn, not from the battlefield, but from the wedding-feast at Cana. 'Those who use philosophical texts in holy teaching, by setting them at the service of faith, do not mix water with wine, but turn water into wine.'[50] The wine poured out for the feast is, indeed, incomparably more excellent than the water it once was but, this side of the kingdom, alongside celebration there is still some washing-up to do.

holy teaching, then there is a sense in which its 'autonomy' is, by such service, circumscribed. But nothing, either in Aquinas's theory, or in his practice, whether in Paris or elsewhere, supplies John Milbank with the warrants for his belligerently hegemonic account of the relations between holy teaching and other intellectual practices.

Milbank believes that, for Aquinas, '*all* knowledge implies faith in God'. On Aquinas' account, as I understand it, what is required, in order for knowledge to be knowledge, is that it be knowledge of some feature of God's creation; *not* that it necessarily be known or confessed to be such (see John I. Jenkins, *Knowledge and Faith in Thomas Aquinas* [Cambridge, Cambridge University Press, 1997], p. 122).

49. Jordan, 'Theology and Philosophy', op. cit., p. 248.
50. '*Unde illi, qui utuntur philosophicis documentis in sacra doctrina redigendo in obsequium fidei, non miscent aquam vino, sed aquam convertunt in vinum*' (Thomas Aquinas, *Expositio super Librum Boethii de Trinitate*, ed. Bruno Decker [Leiden, E. J. Brill, 1955], 2.3, ad 5 [p. 96]). The objection to which he is replying had suggested, citing Isaiah 1:22, that the use of philosophy *diluted* holy teaching. The translation is my own, because that given by Mark Jordan ('Theology and Philosophy', op. cit., p. 235) seems somewhat misleading, and (see p. 249) he incorrectly gives the reference as 2.4, ad 5.

(Eugene Rogers makes suggestive use of the Cana image in differentiating Aquinas's treatment in the *Contra Gentes* from that in the *Summa Theologiae*: see Rogers, *Aquinas and Barth*, op. cit., p. 158.)

PART THREE

Road-works: Theology and Other Things We Do

Chapter 10

Conversation in Context

Bekan, Sydney and St Anselm

The undertaker from Galway, having adjourned 'to a pub in downtown Ballyhaunis for a jar or two of grief therapy ... gleans the story of the Canon and brings it back to Galway with glosses. "This Canon, ye see, came down from Maynooth and was all about theology. Then he brought down these theologians to talk, but the people didn't turn up to hear them, d'ye see. They didn't want it. Why would they? Theology in Mayo?" '[1]

Things being the way they are, the undertaker had a point. And yet, as one of 'these theologians', I have the fondest memories of what we called 'the Bekan Council', presided over by 'this Canon', J. G. McGarry, by then the parish priest of Ballyhaunis, and by Enda McDonagh's mother.

From the west of Ireland to the east of New South Wales and, to be more specific, to the Catholic Institute in Sydney. A few years ago, Cardinal Martini of Milan, staying with the Archbishop of Sydney, expressed a wish to visit the Institute. As they are being shown round the library, Cardinal Martini is delighted to see that the Institute subscribes to his favourite French journal of New Testament studies. 'What are your favourites?' he asks his host. 'Oh, in my job', Cardinal Clancy is said to have replied, 'I don't get time to read books.' Or, as the undertaker might have said: 'They didn't want it. Why would they? Theology in Archbishop's House?'

I have been asked to reflect on the relationships between theology and the life of the Church. The cardinal from Sydney and the undertaker from Galway speak (I suspect) for the vast majority of Catholics – bishops, priests and laypeople – in taking

---

1. The story is told by Ned Crosby, 'Inferiority or Good News?', *Faith and the Hungry Grass: A Mayo Book of Theology*, ed. Enda McDonagh (Dublin, The Columba Press, 1990), pp. 114–21, 115–16.

for granted that no relationships of general, direct and practical importance, exist.[2]

We might well ask who is to blame for this, wondering why bishops and priests show little interest in theology and whether it is true and, if so, why, that 'Lay people in general feel ignored by theologians and excluded from the world of theology'[3] but, for present purposes, I would prefer to try to break up a little of the ground of habits of imagination that we too easily take for granted, digging around the edges of what we take 'theology' and 'Church' to mean. The best place to start, though this may well seem paradoxical, is with the relationship between them.

There is, of course, nothing we can say, or do, or suffer, that does not spring from, is not, in some measure, shaped by, the times and places and relationships that have made us who and what we are. Nevertheless, although it may take two to tango, there are some things that we can do more or less on our own. Thinking, or weeping, for example.

Setting down one's thoughts on paper is a kind of speaking and, in this sense, not all our speaking takes the form, directly and straightforwardly, of conversation. And so, St Anselm, more than 900 years ago, could name a little tract that he had written: 'monologue', or 'soliloquy'. And although much philosophy takes the form of conversation (usually as energetic and often acerbic disagreement), philosophers may, from time to time, soliloquise, write monologues.

Most of what we say or think, however, is said and thought, not only in context, but in company, as we react to circumstances and events, and respond to what others have already said and asked of us. Later in this essay I shall argue not only that the fundamental form of speech is conversation, and that serious speech is speech in which the speaker acknowledges responsibility for uttering, for giving voice to, some aspect of the world of which we are the 'speaking part', but also that the fundamental form of

2. During the many years in which I sat on successive versions of the Theology Committee of the episcopal conference of England and Wales, the conference never sought our views on God or justice, on death or science or suffering. In the first five turbulent years after Vatican II, our opinion was sought three times: once to commission a statement on christology, once to ascertain our views on the appropriate age for confirmation, and once to ask whether there were theological objections to lay people receiving communion more than once a day (see Nicholas Lash, 'English Catholic Theology', *The Month* [October 1975], pp. 286–9).

3. Nuala Bourke, 'Lay Theology: The Search for a Living God', *Survival or Salvation: A Second Mayo Book of Theology*, ed. Enda McDonagh, (Dublin, The Columba Press, 1994), pp. 141–8, 146.

conversation is, in fact, contemplativity, attentive prayerfulness, recognition that all things come into being through the Word that God's own self is said to be.

Which is why, a year after writing the little tract that he had called *Monologion*, St Anselm wrote another, in which passages of prayer – of Anselm's conversation with the silent mystery of God – are seamlessly interwoven with passages of strenuous and demanding argument, as Anselm struggles, in this silence, for some understanding: 'Let me seek you in desiring you; let me desire you in seeking you.' In this tract, Anselm only speaks of God in speaking to him. Which is why he calls this tract *Proslogion*, 'address', 'an allocution'.[4]

The *Monologion*, we might say, is the work of a philosopher; the *Proslogion* of a theologian. Two hundred years later, Thomas Aquinas was to say that the subject-matter of what he called 'holy teaching' is the mystery of God and 'all things', '*omnia*', absolutely everything, in its relationship to God, its origin and destiny.[5]

Geologists study rocks, historians what human beings said and did, astronomers the movement of the stars. The theologian, in contrast, has no particular piece of turf to call her own: she studies whatever it is that she has made her own particular interest in its relationship to God, its origin and destiny. And she can only do this well in the measure that her enquiry is rooted and grounded in contemplativity, in wondering relation to the mystery of God.

In a nutshell: the Church is the community of those who know the fundamental forms of human speech to be conversation grounded in response to that one Word in whom all things come to be. And theology is the vastly varied forms of language in which this knowledge finds expression and through which it seeks some understanding.

Globalisation and the gathering of God

Modern western culture has transformed the world far more dramatically, and irreversibly, than any previous episode in human history. In medicine and astronomy, in physics, in engineering and in economics, human beings have achieved breathtaking advances in their knowledge and control of the things and forces of which the world is made.

4. *Saint Anselm's Proslogion*, translated with introduction and commentary by M. J. Charlesworth (Oxford, Clarendon Press, 1965), ch. i, p. 114 ('*Quarem te desiderando, desiderem quaerendo*'), Prologue, p. 104 ('*Quod ut aptius fieret, illud quidem* Monologion, *id est soliloquium, istud vero* Proslogion, *id est alloquium, nominavi*').
5. See Thomas Aquinas, *Summa Theologiae*, Ia, q. 1, art. 7, c.

Increasing information and technical skill have not, of course, been matched by deepening wisdom or by growth in virtue. During the century just ended, we put our new-found power to use in slaughtering and enslaving million upon million of women, children, and men. And today, things are so organised by us as to enable a minority to live in luxury far beyond our needs while most of us are driven further and further into abject poverty, and our rape of natural resources threatens to tip into terminal imbalance the mechanisms which have, for billions of years, kept planet earth alive.[6]

During the eighteenth century, 'the Cartesian division of matter from mind, causes from reasons, and nature from humanity ... ceased to be of concern to natural philosophers alone ... [and] played a major role in social and political thought as well.'[7] The tragically ambivalent achievements of modernity have been driven by the bizarre conviction that something known as 'mind' or 'reason' is, or can make itself to be, the master of the world.

Ironically, of course, it did not dawn on those who constructed the worldview of modernity – devout Catholics such as Descartes, Lessius, and Mersenne – that their understanding of the kinds of things that human beings are, of the rest of the world, and of the relationships between them, was breaking quite new ground, at best in tension with, at worst quite contradictory to, the mainstream Christian and Jewish traditions on which they drew.[8] (An irony compounded, these days, by the widespread and mistaken belief that something very like Cartesian dualism has been 'traditional' in Christianity.)[9]

Briefly to illustrate: consider the 'soul', and the use made of the biblical injunction to 'Be fruitful and multiply, and fill the earth and *subdue* it.'[10] To sidle up to 'soul', let us begin with 'mind'. Are 'mind' and 'matter' best understood as two different things or entities? This is a question much discussed these days by scientists and philosophers. For what it is worth, my own view is that 'mind' is not well thought of as a 'thing'. This does not mean that I do not think that we have minds, can think and speak, make plans, and so on. It simply means that what it is to 'have a mind' is, I

---

6. On that last point, see Kenneth J. Hsu, 'The Mortality of the Planet', *Is the World Ending?*, ed. Sean Freyne and Nicholas Lash (Concilium, 1988/4), pp. 63–73.

7. Stephen Toulmin, *Cosmopolis: The Hidden Agenda of Modernity* (Chicago, University of Chicago Press, 1992), p. 107.

8. See Michael J. Buckley, *At the Origins of Modern Atheism* (New Haven, Yale University Press, 1987).

9. See my remark about the philosopher John Searle (above, p. 54).

10. Gen. 1:28 (my stress).

suggest, best understood (in the tradition going back to Aristotle) as a matter of having 'the capacity for behaviour of the complicated and symbolic kinds which constitute the linguistic, social, moral, economic, scientific, cultural, and other characteristic activities of human beings in society'.[11]

Think, then, of your mind, not as a 'thing' stuck somewhere in your head, but as your *ability* to do the kinds of things that human beings, distinctively and characteristically, do: they make plans, tell stories, dream dreams, and construct elaborate systems of organisation and behaviour. And then try to think in a similar way about the distinction between the 'body' and the 'soul'. In a similar way, but not identically. The distinction is similar because to speak of human beings as 'souls' is to speak of their capacity to do the kinds of things that human beings, distinctively and characteristically, do. However, talk of 'mind' stops there, whereas when we talk of ourselves as 'souls' (at least in Christian speech) we go further: we recognise our creatureliness, acknowledge that everything that we are and have is *gift*; that we are 'gift-things' given the capacity and duty to return the gift we are in praise and celebration.

If this was how we thought about our minds and souls, we would be less inclined to succumb to the illusion that we somehow stand outside and apart from the world of which we form a part, the world into whose webs of time and place we are, as all things are, in everything we say and do and suffer, tightly woven. If this was how we thought about our minds and souls, we would be less inclined to read the biblical injunction to 'subdue the earth' as licence for exercise of power unchecked by solidarity with, and duty towards, the rest of the created world. The creator God of the book of Genesis is a king, who appoints a viceroy to rule as God would rule, expending infinite care on every creature; a king (to pick up the complementary metaphor from chapter 2), who 'plants a garden', in which he places a gardener. Gardeners may tame the wilderness, but they do not pillage and destroy, understanding as they do their duties towards and interdependence with, the plants and animals they tend.

By now, the reader is entitled to some explanation as to why some elementary observations on what might be meant by 'Church' should be approached from the vast and seemingly eccentric distance of a handful of polemical generalisations about the damage done by modern dualism. The answer would go something like this. The Church is a people, an assembly of men

11. Anthony Kenny, *The Metaphysics of Mind* (Oxford, Clarendon Press, 1989), p. 7.

and women. Therefore, we will not think sensibly about the Church unless we think sensibly about the kinds of things that human beings are. Moreover, human beings are creatures, constituents of the world of which they form a part. Therefore, we will not think sensibly about human beings unless we think sensibly about the world which God creates.[12] It follows, I suggest, that, in order to think sensibly about the Church, the best place to begin would be by saying something sensible about the world, and this apparently straightforward project has been made much more difficult by modernity's illusion that human beings, or at least their minds, do not form part of the natural world, part of the bodies that they are; that 'mind', or 'reason', or 'the soul', do not form part of nature, part of what (in fact) there is.[13]

Enda McDonagh, if I understand him, is thinking in a similar direction when he says: 'Without some basic trust in the earth and its fruits, human life would be impossible ... Trust in the earth grounds human beings' trust in one another and ultimately their trust in God.'[14] Human beings – bodies, minds, and souls – form part of nature, part of what there is. Human beings are made to be the gardeners of the world. What gardeners do is cultivate, and 'culture' is the general term for all the ways in which we cultivate the world. And yet, too often, culture has, in modern times, 'been defined too narrowly' as if it referred exclusively to things like music, dance, or literature. In contrast, Donal Dorr reminds us, 'the old culture included agriculture, horticulture, and aquaculture'.[15]

Dissociate us – through misconstrual of 'mind', or 'soul', or 'culture' – from the earth-facts that we are, from the 'nature' of which we form a part, and we begin to wreak incalculable damage upon the bodies which we have forgotten that we are, and upon the earth of which we cease to see ourselves as being a part. Ethna

---

12. For those readers who prefer to have these things clothed in academic dignity, I am suggesting that our ecclesiology is shaped by whatever anthropology we simply take for granted, and that our anthropology, in turn, is shaped by whatever ontology we simply take for granted.

13. There are suggestive similarities between the way in which we often talk about 'nature' – as if it were something 'over there', outside us – and the way in which many people in England still talk about Europe.

14. Enda McDonagh, 'Shall We Hope?', *Survival or Salvation?*, op. cit., pp. 248–55, 252.

15. Donal Dorr, 'Exile and Return', *Faith and the Hungry Grass*, op. cit., pp. 66–81, 70.

Viney speaks with dramatic accuracy of Mayo's mountains when she says that 'Their salvation is necessary for our survival.'[16]

The founding fathers of modernity – Descartes and Galileo and their contemporaries – sought systematically to exclude the human mind from 'the subject-matter of science'.[17] This separation of consciousness from nature, of speech and thought from what we speak and think about, sustained the illusion that we can speak the truth from nowhere in particular, that 'reason' springs from no particular soil, knows no particular place or time.

Learning to put our minds back into our bodies is a matter of learning to put ourselves back into particular times and places, a matter of learning to acknowledge the interdependence of everyone and everything, including the interdependence between the things that human beings are and do and undergo and the operation of all the other forces and features which constitute the world.

All the talk these days of 'globalisation' is, perhaps, an incipient recognition of this interdependence of everything. 'One thing', however, 'which has thus far escaped globalisation is our collective ability to act globally.'[18] In other words, the most urgent challenge that confronts the human race today is the requirement to imagine and construct a global *politics* which can contain and counter the destructive violence unleashed by the unchecked operation of a global market.[19] What shape such a politics will take, we do not know. We have not been here before. It seems to me, however, that at least as important as the construction of appropriate *institutions* will be the development of what one might call a genuinely global *imagination*; a sense of solidarity with the whole of humankind – past, present and future. In the development of such a global imagination, Christianity undoubtedly has a part to play – not merely because it has been around for a long time and continues to shape the identity of very many people, but also on account of its self-constituting narrative, or what we usually call the doctrine of the Church, to which I shall turn directly in a moment.

Is there not, however, a tension between the demand that we learn to develop a global imagination, that we learn to speak and act in recognition of the interdependence of everything, and my

16. Ethna Viney, 'Saving All Our Holy Mountains', *Survival or Salvation?*, op. cit., pp. 29–42, 30.
17. John Searle, *The Rediscovery of Mind* (London, MIT Press, 1992), p. 85.
18. Zygmunt Bauman, 'Whatever Happened to Compassion?', *The Moral Universe*, ed. Tom Bentley and Daniel Stedman Jones (London, Demos, 2001), pp. 51–6, 53.
19. See Nicholas Boyle, *Who Are We Now? Christian Humanism and the Global Market from Hegel to Heaney* (Edinburgh, T. & T. Clark, 1998).

insistence that truth is only discerned and uttered and enacted in particular places, and at particular times? No, because the 'universal' is not the antithesis of the 'particular', but its form and context.

Thus, for example, Mary Robinson has said that local (and hence particular) community is 'both a focus and a sign' of wider (and, I would add, in principle, of universal) community.[20] 'Universality' that is not rooted in the richness of particulars is illusory, and very dangerous, being itself no more than some inflated and disguised particularity. This is, perhaps, what Padraig Flynn means when he says that: 'all truth is specific, never general'.[21] Hence Enda McDonagh's insistence on the need for 'the localisation of theology ... as counter-balance to the rush to universalisation in commerce, of course, but also in politics and in culture'.[22]

Contemporary opposition to globalisation is grounded in the well-founded fear that, the way the world is at present constituted, innumerable fragile and vulnerable particulars – particular people, particular cultures, particular communities – are being flattened and obliterated by the steamrolling activity of what are, in fact, merely other and vastly more powerful particulars (economic and political) whose particularity is disguised by the illusions of necessity: 'You can't buck the market', as Margaret Thatcher once remarked.

The development of a genuinely global imagination, and of genuinely global institutions, requires the recognition that: 'The social and political watchword ... is not dependence or independence but *interdependence*', and that 'interdependence is a reciprocal process involving mutual rights and obligations between the members' of the human race.[23] Which is where the doctrine of the Church comes in.

What do we mean by 'church'? The word itself may not seem particularly helpful: 'church', 'kirk', '*Kirche*', come from the late Greek word '*kuriakon*', 'the Lord's house'. Unless, however, we are well attuned to biblical imagery of the living 'temple', 'Lord's house' might mislead us into supposing that we were speaking of a building, rather than a people.

'*Ecclesia*' is more useful: the Latin transcription of a Greek word (with, in classical Greek, no religious uses or connotations) for an assembly of citizens. The Septuagint sensibly chose this word to

20. See Mary Robinson, 'Preface', *Survival or Salvation?*, op. cit., p. 7.
21. Padraig Flynn, 'Context and Continuum: Europe and Mayo', *Survival or Salvation?*, op. cit., pp. 216–23, 219.
22. McDonagh, 'Introduction: Between Westport and Asia Minor', *Faith and the Hungry Grass*, op. cit., pp. 7–13, 7.
23. Enda McDonagh, 'Shall We Hope?', op. cit., p. 251 (my stress).

render the Hebrew '*kahal*', which signified the assembly of God's chosen people.

'Church', then, is an assembly, a gathering, a people summoned, called together for some task, some common purpose. This people is, of course, the human race: called, *ex nihilo*, into common life, communion, in the life of God. It is, as *Lumen Gentium* puts it, the gathering, by God's reconciling grace, of all the just 'from Abel, the just one, to the last of the elect'; of which gathering, eschatological assembly, that which we usually call 'the Church' subsists as 'a kind of sacrament' or symbolic enactment.[24]

More concretely, as article 26 of the Constitution puts it: 'This church of Christ is truly present in all legitimate local [gatherings] of the faithful ... united with their pastors.'[25] Each celebration of the eucharist, each diocese, is not a fragment or small part of some vast multinational corporation: it is the universal, Catholic, 'global' Church in its entire particular existence, in this time and in this place.

But, of course, the universal Church, God's gathering of humankind, will – in each particular place and time – be a community of limited experience and resources; of only so much holiness, and scholarship, and wisdom; a fragile group of sinful men and women in continual need of strengthening and enrichment, of education and correction, from all those – of every age and race and culture – with whom it exists in communion. In other words, the process of interdependence – of 'communion', solidarity, '*koinonia*' – is as fundamental to the identity and flourishing of Christianity as we have already seen it to be in social and political affairs in general. (Nor is this, of course, in any way surprising; it is merely an illustration of a principle I indicated earlier: that we will not think sensibly about the Church unless we think sensibly about the kinds of things that human beings are. Each and every account of what we mean by 'Church' has social and political presuppositions and implications.)

Article 4 of *Lumen Gentium* speaks, in imagery as ancient as Ezekiel, of the Church as the dwelling-place or temple of 'the Spirit of life, a fountain of water springing up to life eternal'.[26] This gathering into peace of humankind is what God does. It is pure gift.

---

24. Dogmatic Constitution '*Lumen Gentium*', art. 2 (quoting a homily of Gregory the Great); see art. 1.

25. *Lumen Gentium*, art. 26. '*Congregationes*', in the Council's Latin, is usually rendered 'congregations' but, in 'church-speak', we are sometimes in danger of forgetting that congregations are gatherings!

26. *Lumen Gentium*, art. 4. Which brings us back to 'Church' as 'Lord's house'.

Historically, and sociologically, there is not, of course, the slightest doubt that the entire 'symbol-system' that is Christianity – this vast and ancient network of stories and associations, of images and rituals and enactments, confused, argumentative, conflictual – is something that human beings have done, to both their glory and their shame.

Nevertheless, the truth of this acknowledgement is not undermined by the deeper recognition that, in the last resort, everything we are and have is gift; that (to invoke St Anselm) our best and truest speech is not 'monologue', our solitary utterance, but rather 'proslogue': address, response, to each other, and to the holy mystery whose world-making Word it is which moves us to respond. Hence my initial characterisation of the Church as the community of those who know the fundamental forms of human speech to be conversation grounded in response to that one Word in whom all things come to be. Which brings us to theology.

The possibility of conversation

Or should do, if theology is, as I suggested earlier, the vastly varied forms of language in which such knowledge finds expression and through which it seeks some understanding. Yet ours, it seems, is a community in which almost everyone, from the undertaker to the cardinal, assumes theology not to be their business. This can only mean either that we have a strange view of theology, or that we have a rather curious attitude towards the Gospel's truth. If it is true, then surely it is – interesting? And, if it is interesting, then is it not worth talking about, and thinking about, and making some attempt to understand? And what are the innumerable and endless exercises of our attempts to understand – from the questions of the child to the adult's cry of agony before the darkness of the world; from the meticulous explorations of the scholar to the poet's refreshment of narrative and imagery worn too smooth with casual use – what is all this vast and endless labour but the work of Catholic theology, the conversation of a community concerned to make its speech conformable with the music of God's eternal Word?

If these are not, for the vast majority of Catholics, the connotations of 'theology', then this may be, in part, because of the extent to which confession of the Gospel's truth has become dissociated from the sense that Christian life consists in the unending labour of making this truth ours. It would, I think, be difficult to overestimate the challenge which the healing of such dissociation poses to the speech and practice, ritual and imagination of the Church.

The one who 'suffered under Pontius Pilate' is said to be the 'utterance' of God, God's Word. Or, to be a little more exact, that man is said to be the appearance in our human history of the Word through whom all things come into being. Everything there is is grounded in God's utterance: *a fortiori*, it is that utterance which grounds the possibility of every human utterance, and hence of the possibility of common conversation between the fractured and disputatious peoples of the world; that utterance which underlies the possibility of fostering the global imagination which we so desperately need. This, at any rate, is the suggestion that I now want to unpack a little.

To talk of 'conversation' is to talk of language and (so deep-laid are the scars of dualism) this may mislead us into supposing that the recognition of our common humanity is something which first happens, as it were, 'inside our heads': that 'recognition' is a mental act. And yet, when strange tribes meet, it is each other's physical behaviour which they watch, to which they react. The recognition that the stranger is a fellow human being entails an element of mutual vulnerability, a requirement that a kind of trust be mutually offered – and accepted, or betrayed. (We might consider the history of the handshake as a parable of this.) In other words: underlying the conviction that global conversation may be possible is an openness to the sharing of a common human life which is, in turn, grounded in an acknowledgement of mutual vulnerability, a common trust.

Human beings are creation's 'speaking part'. We are the things that can, and must, articulate the drift and sense of things. 'Can', maybe, but how come 'must': where does a sense of obligation enter in? We are, as George Steiner put it, 'at liberty to say anything',[27] but whereas the frivolous nihilisms of post-modernity construe such liberty as licence (the tone is usually petulant: 'I can say what I want'), the liberty to say anything is better understood as the burden of our responsibility to attempt to speak the truth in an almost unbearably dark and complex, almost (it seems, at times) illegible, and hence unutterable, world.

Steiner is highly critical of the Wittgenstein of the *Tractatus* – a text which ends, notoriously: 'Whereof one cannot speak, thereon one must remain silent.' 'For the *Tractatus*, the truly "human" being ... is he who keeps silent before the essential.'[28] Such insistence on keeping silent before the essential, now so pervasive in our society, may wear the masks of modesty or 'mysticism' to disguise our abdication of responsibility. We 'keep silent' before

27. George Steiner, *Real Presences: Is There Anything?* in *What We Say* (London, Faber and Faber, 1989), p. 53.
28. Ibid., p. 103.

God, and truth, and justice. We 'hold our peace', and, in the silence, millions starve and die.

Many people still suppose that, with the God whose utterance grounds all human speech forgotten, and with silence kept about the things that really matter, we might settle for some modest, homespun humanism, some comfortable common sense. That is not, in fact, how things work out. Increasingly, in place of serious conversation, cacophony takes the form of a dangerous and unlovely combination of, on the one hand, strident and destructive *monologues* – the cultural, political, scientific and religious fundamentalisms which drown out courtesy and attentiveness on every side – and, on the other, what Steiner calls '*kitsch* ideologies'.[29]

To be human is to be able to speak, to say 'Yes' or 'No': to be able to *respond* to places, times, and people – and, perhaps, to God. Steiner handles, with impressive honesty, the difficulty (in our supposedly 'post-religious' culture) of giving intelligible expression to the recognition that the possibility of *speech* – of attending to and responding to each other – is grounded in the possibility of *prayer* – of attending to and responding to the silence of God's Word. He puts it this way: 'The embarrassment we feel in bearing witness to the poetic, to the entrance into our lives of the mystery of otherness in art and in music, is of a metaphysical-religious kind.' If that seems to be making rather heavy weather of it, do not forget that the 'witness' he is bearing is borne by one who would not, I think, easily classify himself as a believer. He goes on: 'What I need to state plainly here is both the prevailing convention of avoidance, and my personal incapacity, both intellectual and expressive, to overcome it adequately ... Yet the attempt at testimony must be made and the ridicule incurred. For what else are we talking about?'[30]

If, then, there is a sense in which the fundamental form of speech is prayer, response, our words' acknowledgement that all things come into being through the Word that is with God in the beginning, the Word that God's own self is said to be, of what kind of prayer are we speaking? Of praise, for example, gratitude for all gifts given, or of petition, acknowledgement of need?

I remember, many years ago, having an animated debate about this with the late, great Herbert McCabe. I was arguing for praise, or gratitude, and Herbert for petition. Over the years, I have come to realise that the question was not well posed, the alternatives unreal. What is at issue is the creature's relation to the Creator, a relation which only human beings, the speaking part of things,

29. Ibid., p. 230.
30. Ibid., p. 178.

can voice. That relation is one of radical contingency, of absolute dependence. Of ourselves we are, quite literally, nothing. This might suggest that the fundamental form of speech, of the 'voicing' of this relationship, should indeed (as McCabe insisted) be that of petition, because we are in need of absolutely everything. The creature is absolutely beholden to the Creator.

And yet, there is something wrong here. We do not need to *ask* for our existence. It is already given. It is as constituted creatures with an identity, a history, that we express, articulate, give voice to, our creaturely condition. If McCabe was not quite right, however, it does not follow that I had the better argument, and that it would be more accurate to say that the fundamental form of prayer is gratitude for what we have been given. Why not? Because the language of gratitude and praise does not, in itself, sufficiently express the continued absoluteness of contingency, of our dependence on the mystery of God. Moreover, neither answer, neither 'praise' nor 'petition', makes mention of the connection between our relationship to God and our relations with each other, and yet the latter are, of course, the expression of the former (as the twenty-fifth chapter of St Matthew's Gospel spells out at some length).

The fundamental form of speech is prayer. What kind of prayer? We could do worse than call it 'contemplation', as defined by Rowan Williams: 'Contemplation,' he says, 'is a deeper appropriation of the vulnerability of the self in the midst of the language and transactions of the world.'[31] The notion of 'vulnerability' neatly combines recognition of contingency, of the creature's absolute dependence on the mystery of God, with the point that I made earlier to the effect that the possibility of global conversation is grounded in openness to the sharing of a common human life which is, in turn, grounded in acknowledgement of mutual vulnerability, of common trust. To be human is to be able to speak. But to be able to speak is to be 'answerable', 'responsible', to and for each other and to the mystery of God.

Hospitality and conversation: the road to Emmaus

The darkness of the world is beyond all explanation. Which is why we speak about the 'mystery' of evil. We too often forget, however, that goodness is a mystery as well; that kindness, generosity, the 'giftness' of reality, is also beyond all explanation. 'Religious thought and practice make narrative images of the rendezvous of

---

31. Rowan Williams, 'Theological Integrity', *New Blackfriars*, 72 (1991), p. 148.

the human psyche with absolute otherness, with the strangeness of evil or the deeper strangeness of grace.'[32]

I like that: 'the deeper strangeness of grace'. The one example of such a 'rendezvous' which Steiner mentions is the meeting on the road to Emmaus. There is, I believe, an immensely important lesson to be learnt from the emphasis which all the Gospels place upon the difficulty of recognising the risen Christ. What does God look like? The figure hanging on the crucifix. But to recognise this figure as the human face of God is to recognise the risen Christ.

As the disciples walked the 'seven miles' towards Emmaus, they were 'talking with each other about all these things that had happened'.[33] A lot of talking, but they did not know what to say (a familiar state of affairs, in theology and elsewhere). The stranger who joins them on the road does not change the facts. 'Jesus of Nazareth who was a prophet mighty in deed and word before God and all the people' (as they tell the stranger – a typical piece of Christian behaviour: telling God who he is!); Jesus of Nazareth remains, as they say, 'condemned to death and crucified'.[34]

What the stranger does, as he takes them back through the history of Israel, and the Scriptures which they thought they knew so well, is to give them an entirely new sense of what has been going on. 'Were not our hearts burning within us?' they say later, as they gradually begin to see the point; begin, we might say, to speak a new language.

At the end of the road, the context is one of hospitality: they invite the stranger in. He is the guest; they are his hosts. At least, this would have been so, in the old language. What they discover, when they are at table, is that it is they, in fact, who are the guests, recipients of hospitality; and that it is he who is the host.

And then, at last, 'they recognised him; and he vanished from their sight'.[35] That last phrase is, perhaps, misleading, because the one who 'vanished' was the kind of man you meet along the road: one in the figure of a human being bounded, as all human beings are, by mortality. What they 'recognised', as they began to see the point, was his new presence as the bread he broke, the life he shared, at this beginning of that new conversation which is, for all eternity, uninterruptible.

32. Steiner, *Real Presences*, op. cit., p. 147.
33. Luke 24:13–14.
34. Luke 24:19–20.
35. Luke 24:31.

Chapter 11

Sebastiano in Pallara: A Pilgrim's Tale

It is not reason that is against us, but imagination.[1]

Pilgrimage

Many roads meet at places of pilgrimage. People come from different directions, with different agendas, different dreams, different histories. And, therefore, however familiar the places that they come to, however much-visited, well-studied, and researched, not only does each traveller find something fresh there but, in their quest and their discovery, each contributes to the wealth that others, after them, will quarry.

Like all holy places, places of pilgrimage are microcosmic. What is to be found there is not less than everything: ourselves, our heart's rest, homecoming in God. But everything this side of death is found in figure, in symbol, enigmatically, and its construal needs patient, disciplined attentiveness.

This essay is about a window, the south transept window of Notre Dame de Chartres. For Holy Week of 1991, my wife and I made pilgrimage to Chartres. Chartres, to which, outside Jerusalem and Rome, few centres of Christian pilgrimage can stand comparison. Chartres, of which, in his fine study of Charles Peguy (whose poems we took with us at Easter), Alan Ecclestone said: 'all human work ends here, so that in time to come men will no doubt do it differently but not better, will speak as clearly in their different tongues, but not say more than this.'[2]

1. John Henry Newman, *The Letters and Diaries of John Henry Newman*, vol. xxx, ed. Charles Stephen Dessain and Thomas Gornall (Oxford, Clarendon Press, 1976), p. 159. Newman was writing, on 7 December 1882, on the supposed conflict between science and theology, to W. S. Lilly (1840–1919). Lilly, a scholar of Peterhouse, Cambridge, became a Catholic in 1869, and served (from 1862 until 1872) in the Madras Civil Service, as also did Sebastian Moore's father, my grandfather, who on 21 November 1897, arrived in Madras to take up the post of Assistant Collector and Magistrate.
2. Alan Ecclestone, *A Staircase for Silence* (London, Darton, Longman and Todd, 1977), p. 64.

Communication

'. . . but not say more than this.' For nearly half a century, Sebastian Moore has *worked* a language in which to communicate, directly, straight from the heart *and* head, what he once called 'the basic grammar of religion, God, you, and your neighbour.'[3] I say 'communicate,' not popularise. Popularisation is a notion to be shunned, for it too easily conjures up images of experts dispensing, with benign but condescending smile, rough crumbs from their rich table to the *populus*, the peasants at their door. But (as Sebastian and I have tried, in different ways, to say for years) in the matter of the knowledge of God, there are no experts, no privileged group of people 'in the know,' no Fellows of the Royal Society.

Popularisation is easy; you just leave out the really interesting bits. Communication, on the other hand, the integral and complete utterance of what must be said – the preaching of the Gospel – is (of ourselves) impossible; it summons all integrity and craftsmanship to fashion artifacts that echo the logic of God's incarnation; it gives God's bewildering brilliance fresh particular flesh – in just this pattern, these images, these ordered words.

Many roads meet at places of pilgrimage. In trying to 'read' this window that I offer as a parable of theology well done, of good communication, I shall approach it from three different directions and with three different companions. First, with the help of St Thomas Aquinas, I shall ask what it was they saw who saw the risen Christ. The answer that is given in the window to this question opens up a puzzle, a detective story, a search for the relationship between ideas and images or (to be more exact) between the teaching in the schools of Chartres and the frescoes in the apse of an ancient church in Rome. Being neither an art historian nor a medievalist nor an expert on Aquinas, I shall unavoidably and unashamedly exhibit the amateurishness that is the condition of us all.

Seeing is believing

To preach the Gospel is to proclaim Christ's resurrection. The Eastern churches' Easter greeting says it all: 'Christ is risen. He is risen indeed.' That is all there is to say. It can be said, completely said, in just three words (or even one: on Easter night, the first-sung 'Alleluia' says it all). But, in order to help us hear the message and see the point, it also needs continual exposition and

---

3. Sebastian Moore, *No Exit* (London, Darton, Longman and Todd, 1968), p. 14.

elaboration, often at great length and in great detail and in an endless variety of ways. Part of the theologian's duty is to try to spell it out. Karl Barth did this, for instance, in *Church Dogmatics*. But, as he would have been the first to acknowledge, those fat black volumes do 'not say more than this': Christ is risen.

Christ is risen. Those who say this bear witness to it. 'The Lord has risen indeed, and has appeared to Simon!' Simon, therefore, is an eyewitness, which is just as well because, as everybody knows, there is no testimony to touch that of the eyewitness: seeing is believing (as Thomas the apostle might have said). Luke does not tell us how Simon recognised the risen Lord when he appeared to him. On the other hand, he tells us in great detail how Cleopas and his companion at first were sad and foolish and slow of heart, but then their hearts began to burn as they listened to the Scriptures being interpreted to them, 'beginning with Moses and all the prophets', until, at last, at table, with bread blessed and broken and distributed, 'their eyes were opened and they recognised him.' That makes them eyewitnesses, too, like Simon. The extraordinary thing is that, in the very act of recognition, Jesus disappears: 'their eyes were opened and they recognised him; and he vanished out of their sight.'[4] Do they, then, no longer see him? Might it not be better to say: they came to see that the understanding at which they arrived along the way, culminating in the breaking of bread, *was* what it now was to 'see Jesus'?

I am trying to nudge the notion of 'seeing the risen Christ' into the company of such notions as 'seeing the point'. To some readers this will sound suspiciously 'subjective'. There is, I fear, no easy exorcism of the unimaginative and destructive dualisms according to which the only options open to us are either dreaming or gaping, either withdrawal into private fantasy or falling victim to brute fact. Yet, in their waking hours, sane people know that there is a difference between seeing the point and failing to do so, and that, in this difference, objectivity lies. And Christians, though not at all immune from the epistemological diseases plaguing our culture, at least have excellent medicine to hand in the endless subtlety and care with which the evangelists weave their tapestries of irony and allusion concerning faith and sight and light and darkness, sin and knowledge and unseeing.

Saint Thomas was born in 1224, the same year in which (almost certainly) the finishing touches were put to our window at Chartres. In 1273, a few months before his death the following year, he constructed a Question for the Third Part of the *Summa* concerning the 'manifestation' of Christ's resurrection. It is, as it were, half a diptych; an earlier Question considered the

4. Luke 24:34, 27, 31.

'manifestation' of Christ's birth.[5] Coming and going, Christmas and Easter: twin aspects of the single mystery we have been shown, two facets of the visibility of what faith sees in Jesus.

In each Question, the opening article considered whether his birth (or resurrection) should have been shown to all and sundry, and finds good reasons why it was not so. The second article of Question 36 then asks whether the birth of Christ should have been shown to anyone (and article 3 considers whether those to whom it was in fact shown – Mary and Joseph, shepherds and magi, Simeon and Anna – were well chosen). The reader who supposes this to be, at least in Mary's case, a silly question, has not seen the point. The point is not that Mary needed to be shown her son but that, without it being shown to her, she could not possibly, in seeing him, have seen the Lord's anointed. And, if nobody had known whose birth this was, no witness could be given and no faith born, for faith (St Thomas reminds us, quoting Romans 10) comes by hearing.

In Question 55, the second article does not ask whether the resurrection should have been shown to anyone but, rather more pointedly, whether it would have been fitting for the disciples to see Christ rise (*'utrum fuisset conveniens, quod discipuli viderent Christum resurgere'*). After all, it was their duty and their destiny to bear witness to the resurrection, and the best testimony, St Thomas agrees, is that of the eyewitness. The argument seems sound enough. How, we wonder, will Aquinas wriggle out of it since, as every schoolchild knows (and, in case we have forgotten, he himself reminds us in the *sed contra*), *nobody* saw Christ rise.

Oh, but they did! 'The apostles were indeed able to bear eye-witness testimony to Christ's resurrection because with sharp-sighted faith they saw Christ risen living whom they knew dead: as we are brought through faith's hearing to what the blessed see, so those who first heard it from angels were brought to see *Christ rising*.'[6] It is an astonishing passage, and the key to it, I think, is the

5. See *Summa Theologiae*, IIIa, qq. 36, 55.
6. (My emphasis.) The passage is so important that, to my rough translation, I add the Latin of the Marrietti edition: '*Apostoli potuerunt testificari Christi resurrectionem etiam de visu: quia Christum post resurrectionem viventem oculata fide viderunt, quem mortum sciverant: sed sicut ad visionem beatam pervenitur per auditum fidei; ita ad visionem Christi resurgentis pervenerunt homines per ea, quae prius ab angelis audierunt.*' The translator in the current Dominican edition presumably saw what Aquinas had written but, failing to see the point, could not believe his eyes. That, at any rate, is one explanation of his bizarre rendering: 'The Apostles were also able to offer eyewitness testimony to Christ's resurrection; for they saw with their own eyes the one in whom they believed, Christ alive whom they knew to have died. But

echo, once again, of Romans 10, 'faith comes by hearing.' The angels proclaimed the message, broke the news, told them not to seek the living among the dead. They saw the point and, seeing it, they saw the dead one rise. The argument is so succinct that, had we not already met it, in extended narrative form in Luke 24, we might suspect some sleight of hand.

In a retreat preached to his brethren at Downside (for the text of which I am most grateful to him), Sebastian Moore insisted that Christ's resurrection is 'known by the awakening of the heart alone'. Only an entirely false and unsustainable dichotomy of knowledge and love can prevent us from seeing (!) that such awakening is, as the Fourth Gospel tirelessly insists, a turning from blindness to sight, from darkness to daylight. We talk, readily enough, about 'blind' faith. St Thomas was working with its contrary, with what he calls *fides oculata*. What a pity that we lost that good word 'oculate', which the Oxford Dictionary has as 'observant' or 'sharpsighted'. There is nothing *less* blind than the awakened heart, the living faith, in the light of which the risen Christ is visible. And this transition, this awakening, this *metanoia*, this 'coming to see the point about Jesus', just *is* what it is for faith's new eyes to see Christ rise.

The Mauclerc Window

Everything, we said earlier, is found, this side of death, in figure, in symbol, enigmatically. It must be so, because to see the risen Christ is to see our unknown future, all creation's healing and fresh flourishing in God. Revelation, says Rowan Williams, is 'essentially to do with what is generative in our experience – events or transactions in our language that break existing frameworks and initiate new possibilities of life.'[7] But, of course, the possibilities that are thus initiated can only (being new) be indicated metaphorically, sketched in figures drawn from the familiar.

There is a helpful note inserted by some scribe into the First Book of Samuel: 'Formerly in Israel, when a man went to inquire of God, he said: "Come, let us go to the seer"; for he who is now

since men attain the beatific vision through that hearing which pertains to faith, so too they ultimately attained the vision of Christ risen from the dead only through the message they had first heard from angels' (*Summa Theologiae*, vol. 55, *The Resurrection of the Lord* [IIIa, 53–9], trans. and intro. C. Thomas Moore OP [London, Blackfriars and Eyre and Spottiswoode, 1976]), p. 43.

7. Rowan Williams, 'Trinity and Revelation', *Modern Theology*, 2:3 (1986), p. 199.

called a prophet was formerly called a seer.'[8] And what do seers see? They see the point, the wood for the trees, the heart of the matter; get some fresh glimpse, shaped by their particular circumstance, of where things are going, of the sense and direction of things as seen from the standpoint of God's 'over-sight' or providence. In other words, to see the risen Christ is to see what seers have always seen, 'beginning with Moses and all the prophets', brought into sharp and final focus at the point at which, *sub Pontio Pilato*, the true light that enlightens everyone illuminates, unconquerably, all the darkness of the world.

We come, at last, to Chartres, and reach our window. Of your charity, pray for Pierre Mauclerc, Count of Dreux and Duke of Brittany, who gave this window. In case you forget him, he and his wife and children, John and Yolande, kneel, on either side of their coat of arms, at the foot of the five tall lancets set beneath the rose. In the central lancet, as in so many places in this vast building dedicated to her assumption, Mary, crowned, holds her child. Flanking them, the tall, strong figures of Jeremiah, Isaiah, Ezekiel, and Daniel, the four great seers of Israel, giants among those who proclaimed, in figure, the promise Mary bore.

The prophets are bearing on their shoulders four smaller figures, recorders of the news of Easter: Luke, Matthew, John, and Mark. All eyes turn upwards. What is the vision which, from their respective vantage points, they see? Above the lancets is the great rose itself, a shining mandala, in the centre of which is 'one seated on the throne. And he who sat there appeared like jasper and carnelian, and round the throne was a rainbow that looked like an emerald.' In this case, actually, the throne is emerald and he who sits there holds one hand in blessing and, in the other, the cup of the new covenant. In the next circle, four pairs of censing angels and Ezekiel's four living creatures, symbols, now, of the evangelists. Then, in two further circles, 'twenty-four elders, clad in white garments, with golden crowns upon their heads' (interspersed, it must be said, with twelve small quatrefoils bearing the arms of Dreux and Brittany).[9]

Stand beneath this south, sun-flooded window and you may see, today, as any visitor to Chartres for more than seven centuries may have seen, just what the Gospel writers saw: the resolution, heart and centre of the world, jewel-shining, the throne of God, the new Jerusalem, the risen one, our promised peace.

Iconographically, the rose itself, for all the splendour of its execution, is quite conventional; its theme is often found in French south-facing roses. It is the lancets, intriguingly

8. 1 Sam. 9:9.
9. See Rev. 4:2–4; Ezek. 1.

juxtaposing prophets and evangelists, that are exceptional and that will occupy our attention for the rest of this paper. What I most want to emphasise at this point, however (although it will, I hope, become even more obvious as we proceed), is the extraordinary theological richness and sophistication of this 'text'. This is no work of 'popularisation' and yet it is *accessible*, in the twentieth century as in the thirteenth, to anyone who is brought to see Christ rising, the Christ who 'interpreted to them in all the scriptures the things concerning himself'.[10] Faith comes by hearing: to read this window with sharp-sighted faith is to trust the awakening of the whole familiar dark world into the light of God.

Dwarfs and giants

The puzzle or detective story that I mentioned earlier concerns the sense of a proverb and the relationship between that proverb and this window. The proverb became something of a slogan in the history of science (even Isaac Newton used it), expressing confidence in intellectual progress while yet modestly acknowledging the debt each generation owes to those who went before. 'The dwarf sees further than the giant, when he has the giant's shoulders to mount on.'[11] That is how Coleridge put it, and he took it from Burton's *Anatomy*. Burton, in turn, had taken it from a commentary, produced in Salamanca in 1574, by the Spanish Franciscan Diego de Estella, on the verse in Luke: 'I tell you that many prophets and kings desired to see what you see, and did not see it, and to hear what you hear, and did not hear it.'[12]

According to Raymond Klibansky, in an article that we shall consider in more detail later on, 'the painter [of our window] can hardly have intended to call St John a dwarf in comparison to Ezekiel.'[13] I have no reason to suppose that Diego de Estella had

10. Luke 24:27.
11. Samuel Taylor Coleridge, '*The Friend* (1818). Volume II. Section the First, Essay VIII', *The Collected Works of Samuel Taylor Coleridge: The Friend, i*, ed. Barbara E. Rooke (London, Routledge and Kegan Paul, 1969), p. 249. Newton, aged 33, writing to Robert Hooke, his senior by 7 years, on 5 February 1676: 'If I have seen further it is by standing on the shoulders of Giants.' His biographer points out that there is, in fact, an undertone of contempt in Newton's application to Hooke of what he calls a 'time worn image frequently cited in the literary quarrels of the ancients and the moderns in connection with the idea of progress' (Frank E. Manuel, *A Portrait of Isaac Newton* [Cambridge, Mass., Harvard University Press, 1968], pp. 144–5).
12. Luke 10:24.
13. Raymond Klibansky, 'Standing on the Shoulders of Giants', *Isis*, 26 (1936), p. 148.

ever been to Chartres. His use of the proverb in his commentary, however, does at least suggest that Klibansky's dismissal of the possibility that it could find application in the relations between prophets and evangelists overshoots the mark.

In the window, the shock of the suggestion that, for all their privileged vantage point, the evangelists in some sense are pygmies, little people, when measured against the stature of the major prophets, is visually softened by the juxtaposition of the four pairs of seers with the mother and child in their midst. God's Word incarnate, after all, is not demeaned by resting, child-sized, in the bent arm of the tall figure of his mother, 'daughter of Sion'.

All this, so far, is speculation, skirmishing. The next thing we must do is try to trace the proverb to its source and ascertain its meaning. This time we start at Chartres, with John of Salisbury, who was bishop there from 1176 to 1180: 'Bernard of Chartres used to say that we are like dwarfs on the shoulders of giants, so that we can see more than they, and things at greater distance, not by virtue of any sharpness of sight on our part, or any physical distinction, but because we are carried high and raised up by their giant size.' That all seems clear enough, and Klibansky, in 1936, was confident that 'the simile of the dwarfs is an original one and was invented by Bernard himself.'[14]

We might have left it there, but for the fact (one of the fascinations of this story is the number of different threads that need to be connected) that, according to one commentator on medieval Jewish science, 'The simile of the pigmy apparently was first employed by Zedekiah Anav, citing an ancient sage.' According to the French translation from the Hebrew, which Jeauneau helpfully provides, Zedekiah Ben Abraham Anav, a thirteenth-century Italian talmudist who lived in Rome, attributed the saying to Isaiah of Trani. Confusingly, there seem to have been two 'ancient sages' of this name, but this need not disturb us, since the elder of the

14. '*Dicebat Bernardus Carnotensis nos esse quasi nanos, gigantium humeris insidentes, ut possimus plura eis et remotiora videre, non utique proprii visus acumine, aut eminentia corporis, sed quia in altum subvehimur et extollimur magnitudine gigantea*' (John of Salisbury, *Metalogicus*, book iii, ch. 4 [Migne, *PL* 199, col. 900]); Klibansky, art. cit., p. 148. In this same passage, however, Klibansky disputed Delaporte's claim that the window is connected with Bernard's saying on the grounds that 'Bernard dies before the actual building of the cathedral began, and ... the window in question belongs to a relatively late stage of the construction.' See Yves Delaporte, *Les Vitraux de la Cathédrale de Chartres* (Paris, 1926), p. 432.

two was only born in the late twelfth century.[15] So we are back to Chartres, where Bernard was chancellor of the schools from 1119 to 1126. The proverb may, in fact, antedate Bernard himself by a few years if, as has recently been suggested, it can now be traced to Ivo of Chartres, who was bishop there from 1090 to 1116, from whom it was mediated to the painters of the window by Gilbert de la Porrée (1076–1154), colleague of Bernard and teacher of John of Salisbury.

Whatever the exact date of the proverb's first expression, it was undoubtedly in use in the schools of Chartres in the twelfth century. Unless we have some idea of its likely meaning in that place, at that time, we cannot estimate the ease or difficulty of its application, in the early thirteenth century, to the relations between prophets and evangelists.

According to Foster Guyer (who made no mention of the window) the proverb expresses 'a belief in the general advance of humanity accompanied by a feeling of natural inferiority'. This is in keeping with what seems to have been the accepted view of historians of ideas in the 1930s: namely, that the notion of intellectual 'progress' (Klibansky uses the word) first found expression, however tentatively, in the schools of Chartres. Recent studies have been more cautious. Brian Stock, for example, says that Bernard of Chartres' own age 'was a continuation of the classical world in faithfully reproducing its concepts, styles, and cultural ideals. But Bernard was prepared to grant that in other respects it had perhaps surpassed even the ancients.' Within the framework suggested by the metaphor of dwarf and giant, 'the classical debate on myth and science, which had really begun with Aristotle's critique of Plato's *Timaeus*, was reopened in a new context.'[16] But Stock, it must be noticed, still assumes that the proverb gives lapidary expression to a *Weltanschauung*, a general understanding of the philosophy of history.

It was precisely this reading of the proverb that Jeauneau, with daunting erudition, contested, insisting that what was at issue, in the debates of the period, was solely the sense in which it is possible, in the world of 'arts' or 'letters,' to 'do better' than those

15. S. W. Baron, *Social and Religious History of the Jews*, vol. viii (New York, Columbia University Press, 1958), p. 347. Baron cites the full proverb in his text (p. 140). See E. Jeauneau, ' *"Nani gigantum humeris insidentes"*: Essai d'interprétation de Bernard de Chartres', *Vivarium*, 5 (1967), pp. 79–99.

16. Foster E. Guyer, 'Dwarf on Giant's Shoulders', *Modern Language Notes*, xlv (June 1930), p. 399; Klibansky, art. cit., p. 148; Brian Stock, *Myth and Science in the Twelfth Century: A Study of Bernard Silvester* (Princeton, 1972), pp. 6–7.

who had gone before. It was, from first to last, a matter of what counted as good speech, good writing: of striving to *say it better.*[17] What none of the commentators seem to have observed is that, seen in this light, the proverb is admirably fitted to express the reciprocal relationship between the Testaments.

Thus, on the one hand, there is that which, from the standpoint of Christian belief, was unseen by the prophets but which the apostles saw. And if 'the answer given in revelation clarifies the question a man asks',[18] might we not construe the history of witness borne by prophet and evangelist in terms of the attempt to 'say it better' in response to God's ever more exactly uttered Word? On the other hand, we forget at our peril that the gospels are, from first to last, interpretations of the Jewish Scriptures. To read them otherwise (and it matters not whether the style of our forgetfulness is 'liberal' or 'literalist' in character) is, in effect, to clamber down from the shoulders of the prophets. But, if we do climb down, one thing is certain: the risen Christ will disappear from view.

My first conclusion, then, is that, so far as the sense of the saying is concerned, there is no good reason to suppose that it did not serve as inspiration for our window. There is, however, another ground on which this claim has been contested.

The road from Rome

According to no less an authority than Emile Mâle, the inspiration for the window is not to be sought, as people once supposed, in the schools of Chartres, but further back in time and far away: in the Rome of the late tenth century. It is here, therefore, that our pilgrimage to Chartres begins again. In the apse of the church of San Sebastiano in Pallara, on the Palatine, there is a double frieze. In the upper part, the elders of the Book of Revelation, on bended knee, offer to God their golden crowns. Beneath, a line of vigorous old bearded men bear on their shoulders younger men, with haloes, who hold up their hands to heaven.[19] There seem to

17. See Jeauneau, art. cit., p. 98.
18. Karl Rahner, 'The Foundations of Belief Today', *Theological Investigations*, xvi, trans. David Morland (London, Darton, Longman and Todd, 1979), p. 9.
19. See Emile Mâle, '*Etudes sur les Eglises Romaines: L'Empereur Otto III à Rome et les Eglises du Xe Siècle*', *Revue des Deux Mondes*, xli (1937), pp. 70–71. The passage is repeated in Mâle, *Rome et Ses Vieilles Eglises* (Paris, 1942) and can be found on pp. 109–10 of the English translation: *The Early Churches of Rome*, trans. D. Buxton (London, 1960), in which a seventeenth-century copy of the fresco is reproduced as

be very few extant instances of prophets bearing apostles or evangelists on their shoulders, and at least one of these is thought to have been influenced by the Chartres window.[20] When, therefore, the scarcity of the motif is taken together with the fact that, in San Sebastiano as at Chartres, it appears together with the elders of the Apocalypse, the dependence of the window on the fresco is surely incontestable. How did the idea get from Rome to Chartres? Mâle speculated that a canon of the cathedral may have visited Rome in the early thirteenth century, but he knew no evidence of pilgrimages from Chartres to Rome.

The final step in Jeauneau's argument in favour of the view that the proverb and the window belong to two different traditions is the claim that, in the window, 'the apostles are not pygmies, nor are the prophets giants.'[21] It is exactly here, however, that the visual evidence from San Sebastiano is most telling. The apostles in the Roman painting are every bit as large as the prophets who support them, whereas the evangelists in Chartres are noticeably smaller. It beggars the imagination to suppose that this is *simply* due to the 'pressure' of the proximity of mother and child in the central light, and is not also an indication that those who designed the window had the saying in mind.

Let us review the evidence. The three principal grounds on which the indebtedness of the window to the proverb are disputed are: the date of the window, the meaning of the saying, and the iconographic evidence that the inspiration for the window is to be sought not in Chartres itself but in Rome.

I have argued that, so far as the sense of the saying is concerned, there is no good reason to suppose that it did not serve as inspiration for the window. The objection on the ground of date is very unconvincing; there was a continual stream of teachers in the schools of Chartres to keep a memorable saying alive from Bernard's death (before 1130; or Ivo's in 1116) to the construction of the window in the 1220s. That the window draws, iconographically, upon the painting in San Sebastiano seems certain

Plate 69 on p. 209. Mâle dates the painting around 970. The church has been called many things – SS. Sebastiano e Zotico, Santa Maria in Palladio, and so on – but its best-known title is also by far the best suited to this occasion!

20. This is the Princes' Gate at Bamberg cathedral, where the 12 lesser prophets carry the 12 apostles: see Mâle, art. cit.; Louis Réau, *Iconographie de l'Art Chrétien, Tome I: Introduction Générale* (Paris, Presses Universitaires de France, 1955), p. 197; *Tome II: Iconographie de la Bible* (1956), p. 324. Klibansky (art. cit.) also mentions a Saxon font at Merseberg, dating from around 1175.

21. See Jeauneau, art. cit., p. 93.

but, far from this standing as an objection against the claim that it was also inspired by the proverb, I have suggested that the visual evidence is in its favour.

In order to draw the threads a little closer together, it would be helpful to find someone who may well have known the Roman painting, who remembered and thought highly of the proverb, and who was in a position of influence in Chartres not long before the cathedral was built (work began almost immediately after the disastrous fire of 10 June 1194, which severely damaged the previous cathedral and destroyed most of the city).

There is one quite good candidate; an Englishman, born in Ivo's lifetime, who was taught by pupils of Bernard of Chartres, who served in the Roman Curia between (approximately) 1149 and 1153, and who may thus well have known the fresco in San Sebastiano; a man of vast learning and considerable public influence who was present at Becket's assassination in Canterbury in 1170 and who, from 1176 until his death in 1180, was bishop of Chartres; the man through whose writing we came to know of Bernard's saying in the first place: John of Salisbury.

The experts will, I am sure, find good reason to contest this suggestion. While awaiting their verdict, however, I remain astonished that none of the authorities to whom I have referred appears to have considered the possibility that John is a key figure in the interweaving of the two images that find such powerful expression in that transept window. It gives me great pleasure, therefore, to propose that we owe this masterpiece of theological communication, in part, to an English theologian and an ancient church dedicated to Sebastian.

Chapter 12

Fear of the Dark

The mysterium of night

Two years after Pope Pius XII's 1955 reform of the Liturgy of Holy Week in the Roman rite, Dame Aemiliana Löhr, a nun of the Benedictine convent of Herstelle, published a remarkable theological meditation on the reformed rite, entitled *The Great Week.*[1] In his Foreword to the English translation, Dom Ralph Russell of Downside Abbey (whose pupil and, later, in the Downside Symposium Group, whose colleague I had the privilege to be) wrote:

> The Benedictine nun who writes this book has seen with horror the sufferings of her Jewish countrymen under the persecution of the Nazis, has herself lived under their persecution of Christians and then has known the ravaging of her land in war. The cries of Jeremias are heard ringing out in their deepest meaning for the whole of humanity in whom Christ suffers until the end of time.[2]

Jeremiah, wrote Dame Aemiliana, 'is the prophet of Passiontide, just as Isaiah is the prophet of Advent'.[3] Here is a longer passage, from her commentary on the first nocturn for the Tenebrae of Holy Thursday:

> Our generation and our time have no difficulty in understanding the ancient songs of Sion. We have seen the late progeny of these sufferers, the Jews of our day, disappear in a cloud of destruction which choked down complaint ... At the same time we saw both the ways of suffering which others underwent and those of our own brethren ... We have seen our cities in flames and ruin, our homes bombed out, our churches desecrated and destroyed. Yet we have never had

1. Aemiliana Löhr, *The Great Week: An Explanation of the Liturgy of Holy Week*, trans. D. T. H. Bridgehouse (London, Longmans, Green, 1958), from the German *Die Heilige Woche* (Regensburg, Pustet, 1957).
2. Löhr, *The Great Week*, op. cit., p. x.
3. Ibid., p. 15.

the grace to cry out as Sion cried out. Today men have forgotten how to mourn and how to sing praises, because they have in great measure lost God ... Now it is no longer Jeremias' people alone, no longer only Jerusalem of the time of Jesus, which rise up to mourn in our dim Mattins, and to awaken the cry of sorrow. The sobs for the ruins of Sion join with the pain of all times and all places. This deserted city of ruins takes on many faces, and it is the *deserta saeculorum*, the waste of all the ages which stares out blankly at us now, age-old ruins among which we see things we can recognize ... Jerusalem still mourns, Israel still mourns; but all people and all times mourn. All mankind weeps.

God's 'assembly', 'God's true and immortal Spouse ... sits out this night's vigil in the ruins of the times and weeps for all men's guilt.'[4]

It is not, perhaps, surprising that, later in the book, we should find her insisting that 'Good Friday lasts until the world ends and its deepest darkness remains to come.'[5]

From the time that I first read her book, in 1958, one remark (which, I now realise, she makes almost in passing) left a particular impression on me. Discussing the procession of the people, on Good Friday, to venerate the cross, she comments: 'One might in fact have been satisfied with this *communio* alone without the reintroduction of the communion of the laity.'[6]

A word of background may be of help. Pope Innocent I, writing at the beginning of the fifth century, reminds the bishop of Gubbio that it is the tradition of the Church that there should be no celebration of the Eucharist on Good Friday or Holy Saturday.[7] During the seventh century, some churches in Rome introduced into their Good Friday liturgy, after the veneration of the cross, the distribution of communion with elements consecrated at the Eucharist the previous day.[8] It was, however, only in the eleventh century that this rite was included in the papal liturgy and, within 200 years, it had contracted to the point that a rubric in the Roman Pontifical stipulated: '*communicat autem solus pontifex sine*

4. Ibid., pp. 99–100.
5. Ibid., p. 143.
6. Ibid., p. 142.
7. Innocent I, Epistola xxv, cap. 4; see *PL. xx*, pp. 555–6.
8. This rite, inspired by the liturgy of the Greek community in Rome, was an adaptation of the Byzantine tradition of the 'liturgy of the presanctified', which had arisen as a result of the general Byzantine prohibition against the celebration of the Eucharist except on Saturdays and Sundays.

ministris'.[9] It was this custom which spread throughout the liturgies of the Latin rite and remained in force until the restoration of general communion in 1955. Hence, the innovation to which Dame Aemiliana refers was that of a second procession of the congregation, following that for the veneration of the cross, to receive communion.

What intrigued, and slightly shocked me, as a well-educated young Catholic of the period, was that the learned lady seemed almost to imply that a mere ritual gesture, such as the veneration of the cross, could be a satisfactory substitute for eucharistic communion. I now think that, from the standpoint of sacramental theology, her instinct was entirely sound, but what I want to emphasise is that the *grounds* on which she almost regretted the reintroduction of communion at the Good Friday liturgy were the very *antithesis* of that historicising tendency which, from time to time in Christian history, has threatened to attenuate and undermine the symbolics of Christian ritual.

To put it very crudely: the one thing she was *not* saying was that it would have been better to stay with the veneration of the cross alone because this was Good Friday, the day of the Lord's *death*, whereas eucharistic communion is always communion in the *risen* Christ. On Friday, then, think of him in his death and, on Sunday, in his resurrection. That is *not* how she was thinking.

Dame Aemiliana was a nun of Herstelle, and hence a pupil of Dom Odo Casel, one of the greatest and most influential liturgical theologians of the twentieth century. Odo Casel, monk of Maria Laach, was spiritual director of the Herstelle convent from 1922 until his death, during the Easter Vigil at the convent, in 1948. Commenting on the Palm Sunday liturgy, Dame Aemiliana quotes what became the *leitmotiv* or slogan of Odo Casel's entire life and work: that day's liturgy, she says, 'expresses what Odo Casel was never tired of repeating, "The Mysterium is always entire."'[10]

9. M. Andrieu, *Le Pontifical Romain au Moyen Âge*, 2: *Le Pontifical de la Curie Romaine au 13me Siècle*, p. 469; cited from Pierre Jounel, 'Le Vendredi Saint, ii: La Tradition de l'Eglise', *La Liturgie de Mystère Pascal: Renouveau de la Semaine Sainte, i* (*La Maison-Dieu*, 67, 1961, pp. 199–214, p. 209, from which all the historical details in this paragraph are taken. See also A. Bugnini and C. Braga, *Ordo Hebdomadae Sanctae Instauratus* [Rome, 1956]).

10. Löhr, *The Great Week*, op. cit., p. 33. See *La Maison-Dieu*, 14 (1948), pp. 1–106. As Dom Jean Gaillard said, in his contribution to *La Maison-Dieu's* rich collection of studies on the renewal of the Holy Week liturgy, to which I have already referred: '*La contribution principale à la redécouverte du sens authentique de la Pâque a été apportée par Dom Odon Casel*' ('*Le Mystère Pascal dans le Renouveau Liturgique: Esquisse d'un Bilan Historique*', *La Maison-Dieu*, 67, p. 36).

That key word recurs in two other passages which point towards the heart of the issues that I want to consider in this paper. 'From baptism until bodily death this is the life of a Christian, to act out the *Mysterium* of Christ's Passion.'[11] And again: 'the real Christian Pasch ... is and it remains the *mysterium* of night.'[12]

'The *mysterium* of night.' Is it, then, never daylight? There is, I think, an entirely proper and, indeed, necessary sense in which the Christian answer to that question always is: No, not yet. What I want to try to do in this paper is to explore the character and the contours of this suggestion.

The *mysterium* is always entire, and yet, its entirety is precisely that which we can never directly state or see. As '*mysterium* of night', the mystery is always dark, and yet the darkness of the night both falls and fades – is never, we might say, a darkness without rhythm.[13] Each night's darkness not only closes out, extinguishes, the brightness of the day before, but also contains at least the possibility of the next day's dawn. And for Christians, whose sense of temporality is far more deeply unidirectional than cyclical, this means that we must hold *together* aspects of the night, senses of the dark, which other cultures and traditions may take more sequentially – in the reiterating sequences of solar time. Christian time's relation to eternity is not controlled, but only illustrated, by the seasons.

Before leaving Dame Aemiliana's book behind, let me illustrate this with two more quotations, one from her commentary on Good Friday, the other on the Easter Vigil.

> 'And it was night', we hear John say, not for the first time this week ... It was night when Judas went out to betray his master, night when Jesus went to sacrifice for our sake. It was night, and it is still; we are in the midst of this night.[14]

And yet:

> This marvellous event belongs to the night. No other time saw it. Night embraces the beginnings of God's life in the world; into the night and the darkness of sin was this life born, to change all into light and day. In the night the child

11. Löhr, *The Great Week*, op. cit., p. 62.
12. Ibid., p. 160.
13. For putting these things a little more exactly than I had done in a previous draft, I am immensely grateful for some penetrating reflections, on that draft, by Dr Nicholas Adams of New College, Edinburgh.
14. Löhr, *The Great Week*, op. cit., p. 121.

Jesus was born from the virgin's womb; in the night the man Jesus was born again from the womb of the grave.[15]

Fear (not?)

'The real Christian Pasch ... remains the *mysterium* of night.'[16] Even our world of permanently bright-lit cities, blotting out the stars, has not quite succeeded in abolishing the animal-instinctive, body-deep association of the darkness of the night with fear: fear of the unknown, the unexpected, uncomprehended; fear of unseen danger, death and dissolution. And yet, in Christian tradition, 'fear of the Lord', '*timor Domini*', is numbered amongst the Spirit's gifts.

There is, of course, an easy way out, and that is to insist on a sharp distinction between two different kinds of fear. Thus, Xavier Léon-Dufour's *Vocabulaire de Théologie Biblique*, which I often use as a plain man's guide through the thickets of biblical allusion, says that it is important to distinguish religious fear ('*la crainte religieuse*') from the fear ('*peur*') that everyone experiences in the face of natural disaster and enemy attack. '*Seule la première*', we are told, '*a place dans la révélation biblique*.'[17] But this, surely, is just a bit too neat? Similarly, I am not entirely persuaded by the tidiness of David Parker's distinction, in his discussion of the endings of Mark's gospel (to which I shall turn in a moment), between 'fright' and 'holy fear'. The 'Gospel's first audience', he says, those who first hear the short ending read to them, are, 'like the women at the tomb ... overcome with fear, with trembling and astonishment – not fright, but holy fear at the theophany.'[18]

Aquinas, in his discussion of the Spirit's gifts, contrasts 'filial fear', the fear of being separated from the beloved, with 'servile fear', the fear of punishment. Following Augustine, he says that, whereas the former deepens with increasing love, love banishes the latter.[19] For both Aquinas and Augustine, as for the vast host of other contributors to the literature on the gifts of the Spirit, the focal text for the discussion is the eleventh chapter of Isaiah: 'And the Spirit of the Lord shall rest upon him, the spirit of wisdom

15. Ibid., p. 146.
16. Ibid., p. 160.
17. See Paul Avray and Pierre Grelot, '*Craindre*', in the *Vocabulaire de Théologie Biblique*, ed. Xavier Léon-Dufour (Paris, 1962), col. 168. There is no entry for '*peur*'.
18. D. C. Parker, *The Living Text of the Gospels* (Cambridge, Cambridge University Press, 1997), p. 144.
19. See Thomas Aquinas, *Summa Theologiae*, IIa IIae, q. 19, art. 10, c.

and understanding, the spirit of counsel and might, the spirit of knowledge and the fear of the Lord. And his delight shall be in the fear of the Lord.'[20] And if you wonder how six gifts became seven, it is because the Septuagint, followed by the Vulgate, had '... the spirit of knowledge and of reverence [or 'piety'].[21] And the spirit of the fear of the Lord shall fill him.'[22] But, however the final clause of verse 2 is taken, verse 3, in the Septuagint, has that most straightforward fear-word φοβος, *timor*. And that is the word that I now want to follow, to Mark's gospel.

(Augustine, incidentally, in a sermon, neatly brings his reading of Isaiah into line with Psalm 111: 'The fear of the Lord is the beginning of wisdom.'[23] He points out that Isaiah's list, beginning with wisdom and ending with fear, follows, as it were, the trajectory of the Spirit's outpoured gift, whereas our movement upwards towards God, borne by that gift, goes the other way: we begin from fear, and are fulfilled in wisdom; '*Nos autem ascendentes incipimus a timore, perficimur in sapientia.*'[24] But that was a digression.)

We must, as Christians, I suggested earlier, learn to hold together contrasting aspects of the night, complementary construals of the fear-engendering dark. The deepening darkness of Good Friday is, as it were, *contemporary* with the first whispers of the breeze of Easter dawn. It is all there, at the ending of the Gospel, in the *tension* between 'Fear not' and 'for they were afraid'.

A quick glance at the uses, in Mark, of φοβος and derivatives, is itself sufficient to set a question-mark against any very sharp distinction being drawn between 'fright' and 'holy fear', sheer terror and religious awe. There are, of course, passages in which it does, undoubtedly, seem to be 'awe' that is in question: thus, for example, the disciples' reaction to the stilling of the storm in chapter 4, 'καὶ ἐφοβηθησαν φοβον μεγαν', seems to be rendered adequately (if with some understatement) by the RSV's 'And they were filled with awe.'[25] Sometimes, as with Herod's fear of John the Baptist – because he knew him to be 'a righteous and holy man'[26] – the situation is not so straightforward. And, at the other end of the spectrum, the 'fear of the people' experienced by 'the chief priests and the scribes and the elders'[27] seems to have

20. Isa. 11:2–3.
21. 'εὐσεβεια', '*pietas*'.
22. 'ἐμπλησει αὐτον πνευμα φοβου θεου'; '*Et replebit eum spiritus timoris Domini*'.
23. Ps. 111:10.
24. Augustine, *Sermo 248*, PL xxxviii, col. 1161.
25. Mark 4:41.
26. Mark 6.20: 'ὁγαρ Ηερωδησ ἐφωβειτο το Ιωαννην'.
27. Mark 11:27, 32 ('ἐφοβουντο τον ὀχλον'); cf. 12:12.

been an experience familiar to most politicians, an experience owing little or nothing to awe or 'holy fear'. In other words, the general impression given by the dozen or so passages in Mark in which φοβος-words occur is of something more like a spectrum of senses between common-or-garden fright and awestruck wonder at the power of God than any neat distinction or clear contrast between the two.[28]

(Incidentally, I suspect that part of the reason why we find these fear-words in the gospels difficult to handle is that one effect of separating what we think of as 'religion' from the rest of life has been to trivialise both ends of the spectrum. Thus, on the one hand, we have no use for 'awe', no sense of what to do with 'reverence' while, on the other, 'awful' now means no more than 'frightful', and either of these words will do to describe the English weather or a disliked Ascot hat.)

'... and they said nothing to any one, for they were afraid'; 'ἐφοβουντο γαρ'.[29] On this, surely the best known of all fear-phrases in the gospels, I have three remarks to make. In the first place, this is one of five occurrences in Mark of ἐφοβουντο, the others being 9:32: the disciples did not understand Jesus' teaching that 'when he is killed, after three days he will rise, and they were *afraid* to ask him'; 10:32: 'they were on the road, going up to Jerusalem, and Jesus was walking ahead of them; and they were amazed [και ἐθαμβουντο], and those who followed were afraid' [ἐφοβουντο]; 11:18: 'the chief priests and the scribes *feared* him, because all the multitude was astonished at his teaching'; and 11:32 (which we have come across already).

In the second place, there is a small but puzzling difference between Mark and Matthew, where the relationship between the disciples' fear, and the Easter command to 'Fear not', is concerned. In Matthew, 'the angel said to the women, "Do not be afraid"' ('μη φοβεισθε', a phrase used by Jesus, in both Matthew and Mark, as he comes walking on the water, quieting the storm).[30] In Mark, whose language is usually the more rough-hewn, the young man dressed in white says 'Do not be amazed', 'μη ἐκθαμβεισθε' (the same verb as that used in the previous clause to describe the women's reaction on seeing the young man sitting in the tomb from which the heavy stone has been rolled back).[31]

What are we to make of this? I do not know, but experts whom I have consulted suggest that we should not make too much of it. In

28. Cf. Mark 5:14; 5:33; 5:36; 6:50; 9:32; 10:32; 11:18; 12:12; 16:8.
29. Mark 16:8.
30. Matt. 28:5; cf. Matt. 14:27; Mark 6:50.
31. Mark 16:6, 5 ('ἐξεθαμβηθησαν').

which case, the theologically interesting question is not whether Mark's 'Do not be amazed' means something significantly different from Matthew's 'Do not be afraid', but, rather (and this brings me to my third comment on Mark's ending): what we are to make of the fact that, in the structure of the narrative, it is those who have heard the Easter message, with its command 'Fear not', who are said, at the end, still to be afraid?

I hope that, by now, I may have given sufficient indication of why it is that, being not persuaded by David Parker's distinction between 'fright' and 'holy fear', I find C. S. Mann's concluding judgement, in his Anchor Bible commentary, more convincing: Mark wrote 'for a community overtaken by fear, a community which needed the reassurance that even those who were the first to hear of the vindication of Jesus in the Resurrection had been terrified.'[32] The next question to consider, then, concerns the kinds of context in which such reassurance might continue to be appropriate for later generations of hearers of the Easter message.

Contexts of speech

A recent issue of *Concilium* was devoted to consideration of *The Fascination of Evil*.[33] In their introduction, the editors, Hermann Häring and David Tracy, asked, rhetorically, 'can those who have once heard starving children whimper ... still be fascinated by evil?'[34] Such is our apparently endless capacity for weaving webs of evasion and false consciousness that the answer (I am afraid) is: 'Yes'. However, the reason for posing the question in that form was spelt out by Häring in his extremely interesting individual contribution to the issue. 'It seems', he said, 'that any intellectual fascination [with evil] lives on a remnant of detached observation, on the basis of an unlived life, and therefore also on the perverse hope that at least evil still conceals a secret that will enrich our horizon.'[35]

To the fascination of evil thus construed as temptation to a form of gnosticism, Häring proposed a twofold remedy. In the first place, we should resist the illusion that there is some one 'thing' that 'evil' always is: some single force, or fact, or feature of the world. 'The one word "evil"', he says, 'is overtaxed by the

---

32. C. S. Mann, *Mark*, The Anchor Bible (New York, Doubleday, 1986), p. 670.
33. Hermann Häring and David Tracy, *The Fascination of Evil* (Concilium, 1998/1).
34. Häring and Tracy, 'Introduction', *Fascination*, op. cit., p. 3.
35. Häring, 'Between Theory, Practice and Imagination', *Fascination*, op. cit., p. 34.

multiplicity of the reality which it denotes'; 'the mere fact of summarizing all destructive tendencies in the one term evil (*malum*) gives the impression of an entity which one can analyse', whereas, in fact, 'evil is an open concept and therefore one which cannot be defined'.[36]

Although the general drift of these remarks seems clearly to point towards an Augustinian doctrine of evil as '*privatio boni*', Häring is sensitive to the way in which this doctrine has too often been misread: 'Anyone who merely negates evil as a "nothing" mistakes its effectiveness and becomes an Enlightenment-type optimist.'[37] Moreover, even 'nothing' may be taken as the name of some mysterious thing (perhaps even Karl Barth did not always sufficiently guard against this danger). Hence, as I see it, Häring's version of the Augustinian doctrine takes the form of somewhat more indirect insistence on the *resistance* of 'evil' to both conceptual transparency, or definition, and to control. Which mention of 'control' brings me to the second prong of the proposed remedy against gnostic 'fascination'.

'The real Christian Pasch ... is and it remains the *mysterium* of night.'[38] There is no *banishing* of this night's darkness, either by comprehension or control. What is required of the disciples is the one thing of which they seem incapable: that they should stay *awake*. (Both despair and optimism, in other words, are to be understood as forms of daydreaming or, if you prefer, of nightmare; of visions that you see when you have closed your eyes and drifted off to sleep.) There is, in Christian and in Jewish tradition, a name for the virtue of staying awake in darkness: it is called 'patience', a kind of undergoing which, in Christian soteriology, is nonetheless understood to be a form – indeed, the fundamental form – of agency. Hence, in their introduction, Häring and Tracy say that 'The Christian tradition knows only one way: we must and can endure the experience of evil and our own disillusionment over God as our great question to God. This is the struggle which Job fought on his heap of ashes and Jesus fought on the cross. Did they win?'[39] I think it is hardly an exaggeration to say that the entire cluster of questions with which this paper is concerned, questions about the *grammar* of Easter-speech, the grammar of Christian eschatology, finds its sharpest focus in consideration of the different ways in which, in different contexts, it is appropriately announced, as *good* news, that the answer to this question may be left to God.

36. Ibid., pp. 26, 29, 39.
37. Ibid., p. 31.
38. Löhr, *The Great Week*, op. cit., p. 160.
39. Häring and Tracy, 'Introduction', *Fascination*, op. cit., p. 6.

'There is', according to Häring and Tracy, 'no great world plan of evil, with calculated destruction and deliberate annihilation. But there is a rampant, growing and ever-virulent web of recollections and goals, old calculations and new megalomanias, efforts reaching deep into the heart and utopian expectations. Evil has no centre, but is everywhere.'[40] This description corresponds quite closely to a little sketch I gave, a few years ago, in my essay on the Apostles' Creed, of the way in which, during the present century, even the forms of darkness have, as it were, merged in the process of globalisation. I will, if I may, quote the passage in full, in order to use it as a background against which to make some brief remarks about the contextuality of overarching metaphors in theology, about theological styles and what I want to call the *tone of voice* in which theology is done.

> The three concentric circles of non-moral evil, wickedness and sin are rapidly becoming coextensive as the plague of human folly tightens its grip, threatening the planet and the human race with violent, premature, slow death. One thing, at least, seems obvious: that the world's redemption is quite beyond our human capacity. I have (I must admit) more sympathy with those who say that there simply is no forgiveness strong enough to heal this darkness into daylight than with those who cheerfully insist that things are really not that bad after all. There does, at least, seem fresh scope for plausibility in the Christian doctrine that nothing less than God's own suffering is required to bring this world to birth in peace.[41]

And, of course, there is a sense in which that suffering endures. Hence Aemiliana Löhr's insistence that 'Good Friday lasts until the world ends.'[42]

The selection of what I earlier referred to as 'overarching metaphors' in Christian theology is, as I see it, controlled by two formal principles. The first of these derives from the trinitarian character of Christian doctrine, and the second from the fact that whatever is said is said by particular people in particular places at particular times.

Where the first of these principles is concerned, it is, perhaps, a limitation of Stephen Sykes's study of the identity of Christianity, in his 1978 Cadbury Lectures, that his nuanced and sensitive analysis of the dialectical or 'oscillatory' character of Christian

40. Ibid., p. 1.
41. Nicholas Lash, *Believing Three Ways in One God: A Reading of the Apostles' Creed* (London, SCM Press, 1992), p. 115.
42. Löhr, *The Great Week*, op. cit., p. 143.

orthodoxy explored no further than the edge or outer reaches of its trinitarian ground.[43] In *Believing Three Ways in One God* I attempted, although only very briefly and impressionistically, to indicate what would be entailed in following through, methodologically, the implications of the trinitarian character of Christian doctrine. We learn, as Christians (I suggested) to use the word 'God' well by learning to live, and think, and work, and suffer, within the pattern of trinitarian relations which the Creed supplies.[44] It follows that whatever we say appropriately or well, being said, as it were, 'along the grain' of one of the divine processions or relations, will also require construal *against* the grain of other utterances sprung from other points within the movement of the doctrine. Hence my suggestion that 'the very form of the Creed provides a pattern of self-correction, of restraint upon the range of its misuse'.[45]

Thus, for example, that 'Good Friday lasts until the world ends' is true (the mission of the Son endures) and its denial would, at least implicitly, entail denying that Christ's resurrection is eschatological event: that the world ends at the empty tomb. But, correlatively, from the fact that it is true that 'Good Friday lasts until the world ends', it does not follow that Easter has not dawned. The tomb *is* empty, and the Spirit sent.

So much, and far too briefly, for my first principle: that the overarching metaphors we choose (on this occasion, I have taken the darkness of the night) require, for their appropriate construal, to be contextualised by trinitarian rules of speech. But, if this first principle guides us in the *use* of such metaphors, it is the second which grounds their original selection.

'Despite the many great accomplishments of modernity', says David Tracy, in his individual contribution to the issue of *Concilium* mentioned earlier, '(accomplishments which, considering the alternatives of societal and ecclesial obfuscation, mystification, intolerance and even tyranny clearly still demand defence,

---

43. See Stephen Sykes, *The Identity of Christianity: Theologians and the Essence of Christianity from Schleiermacher to Barth* (London, SPCK, 1984). The nearest that he came, I think, was in his chapter on 'The Unity of Christianity' (pp. 239–61). He spoke warmly of 'Troeltsch's acute analysis of the internal tensions within Christianity which keep it in a state of perpetual *oscillation*', and insisted on the centrality, 'for the preservation of the identity of Christianity' of '*dialectical* interplay between external and internal elements' (pp. 101, 282, my emphases). But the language of 'oscillation' and 'dialectic', being merely bipolar, does not sufficiently evoke the richness of *trinitarian* perichoresis.

44. See Lash, *Believing Three Ways*, op. cit., pp. 32–3.

45. Ibid., p. 33.

including theological defence), modernity has ... proved impoverishing in its inability to face evil and suffering with something better than occasional outbursts of fascination.'[46] Hence, he suggests that, in order to develop a theology today, we need 'to start by facing evil and suffering'.[47] And, in order appropriately to reflect, today, on 'both evil and salvation ... we need to turn to all those peoples who have suffered throughout our history and in the massive global suffering of today. They are our truest artists and articulators of the forms of evil, suffering, fascination and hope.'[48]

Paraphrased as a proposal that 'the preferential option for the poor' be taken as a hermeneutical principle for Christian theology, Tracy's suggestion is, by now, something of a commonplace in (for example) liberation and feminist theologies. Admirable as it is, however, it does not, in my opinion, go quite far enough.

'The transcendentals', von Balthasar announced, in the first paragraph of his theological aesthetics, 'are inseparable ... neglecting one can only have a devastating effect on the others.'[49] From which it follows that no theology can express the truth or goodness of God unless it also exhibits, in appropriate measure, God's beauty. That is the first step in any discussion of the 'forms' or 'styles' appropriate to theology, and the second (according to von Balthasar) is that 'we ought never speak of God's beauty without reference to the form and manner of appearing which he exhibits in salvation-history'.[50] All forms of Christian theology, in other words, must – directly or indirectly – be *in*formed by the form of God's appearance in the crucified and risen One. Which (although von Balthasar himself might not have put it this way) I take to be a restatement, in aesthetic terms, of David Tracy's hermeneutical principle; a restatement hinted at, perhaps, by his description of the victims as 'our truest *artists* ... of the forms of evil, suffering ... and hope'.[51]

In this country (as in many others) most sermons are not preached, nor most theology written, by the poor. It is not, for the

---

46. David Tracy, 'Saving from Evil: Salvation and Evil Today', *Fascination*, op. cit., p. 116.
47. Ibid., p. 114.
48. Ibid., p. 113.
49. Hans Urs von Balthasar, *The Glory of the Lord: A Theological Aesthetics, vol. i: Seeing the Form*, trans. Erasmo Leiva-Merikakis, ed. Joseph Fessio and John Riches (Edinburgh, T. & T. Clark, 1982), p. 9. This volume was originally published as *Herrlichkeit: Eine Theologische Äesthetik, i: Schau der Gestalt* (Einsiedeln, Johannes Verlag, 1961).
50. Von Balthasar, *The Glory of the Lord*, op. cit., p. 124.
51. Tracy, 'Saving from Evil', op. cit., p. 113.

most part, the victims that have access to the libraries and seminar rooms and professorial chairs. This is not an invitation for us to indulge in an orgy of well-heeled guilt: the breast-beating of the bourgeois is a self-indulgent, ineffective and unlovely spectacle. I only want to suggest that the *tone of voice* in which our theology is done should be such that, were we to be 'overheard' by those in whose name, and from the standpoint of whose experience, we purport to seek some understanding of the mystery of God, what we say would be discernible as exhibiting something of the *patience*, made possible by Easter, which renders the world's continuing Gethsemane endurable in hope.

Tragedy, triumph, and the twofold way

'Nothing is offered', in the short ending of Mark's gospel, 'which goes beyond the experience of an audience who have heard the Gospel from eye-witnesses: they are told that he is risen, they are given the promise that they will see him, and they are fearful.'[52] Not the least of the many excellent features of David Parker's study is his sensitivity to the implications, for christology, of contrasting narrative strategies. Thus, on the one hand, he hints that a gospel-tone as relentlessly austere as Mark's, as shaped and coloured by the 'not yet' of the world's enduring night, in which Easter hope does not so much *banish* fear as give it the courage to endure, to stay awake, contains within it temptation to adoptionism, to an inability to see in Jesus, from the beginning, the shining forth of God's eternal and victorious presence in the world.[53] On the other hand, he shows how materials of more 'realised' eschatologies – such as, for example, 'Luke's view of the events in the garden (and elsewhere in the passion), which includes excising material in the tradition which show Jesus to be other than calm and confident' – are vulnerable to docetic construal.[54]

More generally, we might say that, whereas a theology that thinks along the dark grain of the world, insisting on treating with utmost seriousness the *solidity* of evil,[55] may risk being mesmerised by darkness, a more exuberant insistence on new life imperishably

---

52. Parker, *Living Text*, op. cit., p. 144.
53. See ibid., p. 145.
54. Ibid., p. 158.
55. In 1985, I was responsible for organising a series of lectures in Cambridge on 'The Legacy of Augustine', to celebrate (approximately!) the sixteenth centenary of his conversion. I was most grateful to Rowan Williams, who has thought as deeply as most people about Augustine's doctrine of evil as *'privatio boni'*, for agreeing to speak on the topic of 'The Solidity of Evil'.

sprung from womb and grave[56] may risk sitting dangerously light to the sheer *weight* of the wounds and sorrows and injustice of the world.

No theology, however, except one that restricts itself to the issuance of intolerably abstract grammatical 'reminders', can have *no* tone of voice, be written in *no* style, tell the story of the world from *no* particular perspective.

There are, of course, a handful of classic images for the patterning of the ceaselessly two-way, comprehensively *relational* movement of all serious Christian speech. Here is Karl Barth:

> The atonement as it took place in Jesus Christ is the one inclusive event of this going out of the Son of God and coming in of the Son of Man ... It was God who went into the far country, and it is man who returns home. Both took place in the one Jesus Christ. It is not, therefore, a matter of two different and successive actions, but of a single action in which each of the two elements is related to the other and can be known and understood only in this relationship.[57]

Here, as throughout the first two parts of Volume IV of the *Church Dogmatics*, Barth uses imagery from the parable of the Prodigal Son to give distinctive colouration to his version of that most ancient of theological 'overarching metaphors', the Christian reconfiguration of the neoplatonic *exitus* and *reditus*. And anyone who has studied Aquinas' successive attempts to rework the design of his theology, from his youthful recasting, in the *Commentary on the Sentences*, of Peter Lombard's use of the *exitus–reditus* schema, to his more austerely formal expression of the motif in terms of Aristotelian categories of causation – which is one (but only one) of the architectural features of the *Summa Theologiae* – knows how deeply embedded in his imagination is the imagery of the twofold journey, the *duplex via*, of Christian life and thought.

Only in recent decades, however, have theologians begun to rediscover the extent to which the *duplex via* is as richly *christological* a motif in Aquinas' theology as in that of Karl Barth. I conclude with a marvellously epigrammatic expression of this, from the beginning of the fourth book of the *Contra Gentiles*. The imagery on this occasion, however, is not primarily neoplatonic but biblical: the image, beloved to patristic and medieval thought, of Jacob's ladder. (Notice, by the way, how beautifully it echoes Augustine's use of similar imagery in the sermon that I quoted

56. See above, pp. 182–3.
57. Karl Barth, *Church Dogmatics*, IV/2, ed. G. W. Bromiley and T. F. Torrance (Edinburgh, T. & T. Clark, 1958), p. 21.

earlier in this paper.)[58] 'Human understanding', says Aquinas, 'climbs up to God from creatures, whereas faith's knowledge comes down to us by God's revealing; it is, however, the same way up and down [*est autem eadem via ascensus et descensus*].'[59] And he has told us often enough, elsewhere, the *name* of that one Way.

58. See above, p. 184.
59. '*Quia vero naturalis ratio per creaturas in Dei cognitionem ascendit, fidei vero cognitio a Deo in nos e converso divina revelatione descendit; est autem eadem via ascensus et descensus*' (Thomas Aquinas, *Summa Contra Gentiles*, book iv, ch. 1 [Proemium]).

Chapter 13

Travellers' Fare

Introduction

O happy Pyx! O happy Pyx!
Where Jesus doth his dwelling fix.
O little palace! Dear and bright,
Where He, who is the world's true light,
Spends all the day, and stays all night.[1]

The title of my paper is, of course, a rendering of *esca viatorum*. I was tempted to spell 'fayre' with a 'y', with the dreadful food available, at some railway stations, under that description, serving as a reminder of how bizarre our eucharistic habits have sometimes been. In Father Faber's poem ('imitated', he tells us, 'from St Alphonso', of whom more later on) the Prisoner in the Tabernacle seems quite contented with his lot, but the world evoked is dangerously far from that of the upper room and the garden of Gethsemane.

In this paper I want to do two things. First, drawing on P. J. FitzPatrick's *In Breaking of Bread*, I want to urge the importance of remembering that sacraments are signs and not disguises; that the kind of signs they are are gestures, ritual actions, and that actions take time. Then, in the second part, I shall take article 7 of the Constitution *Sacrosanctum Concilium* as a framework for setting our understanding of the presence of Christ in the Blessed Sacrament in the context of other modes of Christ's presence in the people God is gathering homeward.

Signs and disguises

The time it took

In the spring of 1969, Herbert McCabe, in a paper entitled 'Transubstantiation and the real presence', argued that 'a

1. Frederick William Faber, 'Holy Communion [imitated from St Alphonso]', *Hymns* (London, Burns and Oates, 1861), pp. 258–60.

Catholic view of the Eucharist' must steer a course between the view that to speak of the food and drink as the body of Christ is to speak 'merely metaphorically' and 'the view that a chemical change has come over the food and drink so that now it is food and drink no longer ... On this view, in the Eucharist the body of Christ is *disguised* as food and drink.'[2] Christ, said Herbert, 'has a better right to appear as food and drink than bread and wine have. The doctrine of transubstantiation, as I see it, is that the bread and wine suffer a revolutionary change, not that they change into something else, they become more radically food and drink, but this food and drink which is the body of Christ, appears to us still in its traditional dress, so that we will recognise it.'[3] (My interest in the paper was heightened by the fact that, a few months earlier, I had published a study of the Eucharist, entitled *His Presence in the World*.[4])

Three years later, *New Blackfriars* published two essays by P. J. FitzPatrick entitled 'Some Thoughts on the Eucharistic Presence' and 'More Thoughts on the Eucharistic Presence', interspersed by Herbert's 'Transubstantiation: A Reply to G. Egner'.[5] (When all three were reprinted in *God Matters*, in 1987, FitzPatrick added a note explaining why, at the earlier period, he had written under the pseudonym 'G. Egner' – *Gegner*, the adversary, or devil's advocate.)

'I am', said FitzPatrick, in 1972, 'nearing the end of a book, *In the Breaking of the Bread*, about the eucharistic presence', and, in the note in *God Matters*, he looks forward to the appearance 'at long last' of 'an avatar of my book'.[6] It would, however, be another

2. Herbert McCabe, 'Transubstantiation and the Real Presence', *God Matters* (London, Geoffrey Chapman, 1987), pp. 116–29. In this collection, the paper is the first of several essays in eucharistic theology which attempt 'to present "transignification" in a way that will safeguard the truths expressed in the doctrine of transubstantiation as it is found in St Thomas' (p. 115).

3. Ibid., p. 126.

4. London, Sheed and Ward, 1968 (reprinted by Wipf and Stock, 2005).

5. G. Egner, 'Some Thoughts on the Eucharistic Presence', *New Blackfriars* (August 1972), pp. 354–9; 'More Thoughts on the Eucharistic Presence', *New Blackfriars* (April 1973), pp. 171–80; 'Transubstantiation: A Reply to G. Egner', *New Blackfriars* (December 1972), pp. 546–54.

6. G. Egner, 'Some Thoughts', p. 354; P. J. FitzPatrick, *God Matters*, op. cit., p. 164.

seven years before *In Breaking of Bread* was published, in 1993.[7] For FitzPatrick, priest of the diocese of Hexham and Newcastle and for many years Reader in Philosophy at Durham University, this fresh and intelligent study of issues at the very heart of Catholic Christianity (it has, incidentally, the most hilarious footnotes of any learned work I know) was the fruit of a lifetime's labour, and I am most grateful to Dr Kate Brett and her colleagues at Cambridge University Press for making it available, in time for our conference, at a price affordable by normal human beings.

Before turning to it, however, I would like to stay with the articles in *New Blackfriars*, because what was at issue between FitzPatrick and McCabe would be central to the argument of the book.

The danger inherent in Aristotle's account of change as the actualisation of possibilities is (as Aquinas was well aware) that it may mislead us into supposing terms such as 'possibility' and 'actuality', 'form' and 'matter', 'accident' and 'substance', to be names of things.

FitzPatrick and McCabe agreed that it is no longer possible to say, with the Council of Trent, that transubstantiation 'most fittingly', *aptissime*, describes the change undergone by bread and wine (McCabe called it a 'dangerous and misleading name'),[8] but whereas he wished to argue that, however dangerous the term, the theory of transubstantiation, at least in Aquinas's hands, was coherent, FitzPatrick would have none of this.

'To make the eucharistic change substantial is tantamount to making Christ out of bread', but the damage done by calling it 'transubstantial' derives from 'the impression of content misleadingly conveyed by words that have lost their bearings'.[9] Herbert pounces: 'important theological ideas are invariably expressed through the breakdown of philosophical concepts'.[10] For the heart of his argument he drew an analogy (as Aquinas had done) between creation and transubstantiation: 'creation names an Aristotelianly impossible kind of making, just as transubstantiation names an Aristotelianly impossible kind of change'.[11] One way of putting the first point would be to say that creation is not,

7. P. J. FitzPatrick, *In Breaking of Bread: The Eucharist and Ritual* (Cambridge, Cambridge University Press, 1993). Admirably, the remote origins of the book can be traced to reflections stimulated by a request to prepare a child for her First Communion: see *Breaking*, p. 342.
8. McCabe, 'Transubstantiation: A Reply', op. cit., p. 151.
9. FitzPatrick, 'Some Thoughts', op. cit., p. 133.
10. McCabe, 'Transubstantiation: A Reply', op. cit., p. 146.
11. Ibid., p. 147.

strictly speaking, 'making': God does not, strictly speaking, 'make' the world. To express the matter thus, however, might have required Herbert to admit that, in the Eucharist, the bread and wine are not, strictly speaking, 'changed'.[12]

FitzPatrick, accordingly, questioned the appropriateness of the analogy: 'With creation, I would say, we kick away the ladder we have climbed, as good philosophers should when striving to express the transcendent; with transubstantiation, we stand firmly on its rungs and try to hoist ourselves up by our own boot-laces.'[13]

'I am suggesting', said McCabe, 'that the consecrated host exists at a level of reality at which questions of whether it is bread cannot relevantly be asked.'[14] He here falls into the trap of what FitzPatrick calls 'the Fallacy of Replacement', the fallacy of supposing that 'the introduction of a new set of questions' means that questions 'of a former set are unaskable'.[15] There are, he suggests, two questions one might ask about a bank-note:

> 'What is this?' and 'Is this a piece of paper?' ... I agree that if the first question be asked of a consecrated host, the answer must be 'the body of Christ'. But I also assert that to the question 'Is this bread?' asked of a consecrated host we must answer 'Yes', just as we should have to answer 'Yes' if we were asked of a bank-note 'Is this paper?'[16]

For FitzPatrick, the 'whole setting of the theory of transubstantiation is "physics", even if abused physics: ritual and ritual significance are only adjuncts to what it displays as the heart of the

12. I would argue that, in fact, it would only have required Herbert to admit that, in the Eucharist, bread and wine are not *physically* changed.

13. FitzPatrick, 'More Thoughts', op. cit., p. 156.

14. McCabe, 'Transubstantiation: A Reply', op. cit., p. 152.

15. FitzPatrick, 'Some thoughts', op. cit., p. 138.

16. Ibid., pp. 160–61. The title of FitzPatrick's book reminds us that St Paul did not fall for the Fallacy of Replacement: 'The bread that we break, is it not a sharing in the body of Christ?' (1 Cor. 10:16.) The second Canon of the thirteenth session of the Council of Trent (the Canon which concludes by describing the eucharistic change as '*aptissime*' called 'transubstantiation') anathematises those who say that '*in sacrosancto Eucharistiae sacramento remanere substantiam panis et vini una cum corpore et sanguine Domini nostri Jesu Christi*'. '*Una cum*', 'together with'; that is the point. With Luther in mind, the Council rejects the view that consecrated bread and wine are, as it were, a kind of *compound*. But a five pound note is not a compound of paper and currency. It is a piece of paper which has been changed into money.

matter'.[17] And the big book, when it appears, will be an argument for 'letting ritual communicate as ritual – a programme that is a good deal more arduous than it sounds'.[18]

Against the background of those early exchanges, I now propose to comment on three issues that are central to the argument of *In Breaking of Bread*: the relations between signs and disguises; the phenomenon of 'insulation'; and the recovery of ritual.

'Beneath this veil'

> O Pane del cielo,
> Che tutto il mio Dio nascondi in quel velo.
> (O Bread of Heaven, beneath this veil,
> Thou dost my very God conceal.)

Here we have 'Alphonso' himself, Doctor of the Church, treating the Blessed Sacrament as God's hiding-place. And, 500 years earlier: '*Adoro te devote, latens deitas*', made even worse in Hopkins' translation: 'Godhead here in hiding, whom I do adore'. 'In hiding' – why would God want to *lurk*?

We take for granted, these days, that sacraments are signs, and yet when Aquinas considers whether sacraments are of the order of signs: '*utrum sacramentum sit in genere signi*', while not denying that this is the case, his chief interest lies elsewhere, in sacraments as 'sacred secrets', things which have in themselves, '*in se*', a hidden holiness, '*sanctitatem occultam*'.[19]

What could God's creatures be, but deity displayed? '*Caeli enarrant gloriam Dei*': God's glory is variously shown forth in creatures and in sacraments. Signs, we might say, *disclose* – they show, announce, or indicate. Disguises, on the other hand, obscure or 'veil' the underlying reality. If we wanted a slogan, we might say that, where appearances *show* the truth, we are dealing with signs, and where they *obscure* it, we are dealing with disguises. Scholastic theology dealt in disguises.[20]

Moreover, its conceptual framework was closer to 'natural philosophy' or 'primitive natural science'[21] than to semiotics. Among the danger signals are words like 'beneath' and 'contains'.

17. FitzPatrick, 'More Thoughts', op. cit., p. 159.
18. Ibid., p. 162.
19. *Summa Theologiae*, IIIa, 60, 1, c.
20. I am not, of course, questioning the importance of the theme of God's hiddenness, of the '*Deus absconditus*'. But sacramental theology, as a theology of signs, pertains to the theme of God's appearance.
21. FitzPatrick, *Breaking*, op. cit., pp. 161, 317.

An embrace may signify affection, but the affection does not lie 'beneath' the gesture, nor does a handshake 'contain' friendship. 'Trent spoke of Christ being truly, really and substantially *contained under* the appearances.'[22] 'Is the eucharist a sacrament?' asks Aquinas. His answer is that it is, because a sacrament is that which contains something sacred ('*continet aliquid sacrum*') and the Eucharist contains Christ himself ('*continet ... ipsum Christum*').[23] Bread and wine have been transformed so that, 'beneath' their enduring appearance, Christ is contained. But why should the appearances endure? Because, says Thomas, 'it is not usual for human beings, but horrible, to eat a man's flesh and drink his blood'.[24] 'The appearances', comments FitzPatrick, 'are camouflage ... But what is being camouflaged here if it is not cannibalism?'[25]

I well remember the urgency with which, as students at Oscott in the 1950s, we were enjoined (by the Rector, who taught Scripture) to avoid, so far as possible, biting or chewing the host. Curiously, the same nervousness did not attend the drinking of the precious blood. This whole dark distortion of the sacramental maintained its grip on the imagination through the *reification* of Christ's presence.

For Aquinas, eating and drinking are not essential to the sacrament, which is 'completed' ('*perficitur*') by the consecration of the matter – and the matter is not a rite, a meal, but only *things*: bread and wine. And the form? 'This is my body. This is my blood.' The words 'Take, and eat' ('*Accipite, et comedite*') are not essential, because eating and drinking pertain to the 'use of the consecrated matter', which is not necessary: '*non est de necessitate hujus sacramenti*'.[26]

The 'primacy of transformation over distribution' which, for centuries, characterised Catholic theologies of the Eucharist was, as FitzPatrick shows, evident in every detail of the *Ritus Servandus* for the celebration of Mass before the recent Council.[27]

The theme of 'insulation' runs right through the book. We come across it early on with Carlo Colombo's removal of 'the notion of substance from anything which experience and investigation can discover about things', thereby isolating it 'from its original setting of change and continuity'. Central to FitzPatrick's

22. Ibid., p. 119 (his stress), with reference to the first Chapter and Canon of Session XIII of the Council.
23. *Summa Theologiae*, III, 73, 1, ad 1.
24. Ibid., III, 75, 5, c, cited in FitzPatrick, *Breaking*, op. cit., p. 170.
25. FitzPatrick, *Breaking*, op. cit., p. 172.
26. See *Summa Theologiae*, III, 73, 1, ad 3; 74, 7, c.; 78, 1, ad 2.
27. See FitzPatrick, *Breaking*, op. cit., pp. 167, 211–15, 218.

critique both of scholastic accounts of eucharistic presence and
those offered, in recent decades, by Dutch and Flemish phe-
nomenologists, is the extent to which they are 'far closer than
they are usually held to be', having in common 'a divorce between
appearance and reality ... prompted by a desire to preserve what
is precious'. The tragedy, however, is that the attempted insulation of the things we value from the 'rough ground' of the
familiar world of time and place and circumstance and change,
ends up, not with their protection, but with the evacuation of
their sense and content. 'Scepticism is the unwelcome destination
to which tend both the old and newer theories.'[28] Which may go
some way to explain our present predicament.

The way of ritual

'The older account', says FitzPatrick, 'interpreted eucharistic
ritual in terms of natural philosophy. The newer account interprets eucharistic ritual in terms of human relationships ... I am
trying to interpret eucharistic ritual in terms of ritual. There, in
three sentences, is the thesis of this book.'[29]

'Whatever else the Eucharist is', he says at the end of his
opening chapter 'Against transubstantiation', 'it is a *rite* of some
kind; and yet there has been no word on ritual' in the sources
he has so far examined. (He concedes that there are texts in
Aquinas which show 'an awareness of ritual and of what goes with
it',[30] and he discusses a number of them; unfortunately, those
which explicitly consider the change of bread and wine into the
body and blood of Christ are not amongst them.)

Rituals are *actions*, patterns of behaviour, and although the
rituals that we perform exhibit both our memory and our hope,
'Ritual itself is not primarily linguistic.' FitzPatrick speaks of 'the
need in eucharistic ritual for a *journey*, a journey from what is
everyday to what is not'; a journey in which the everyday is
enhanced, hallowed, but not superseded. 'Whatever else the
Eucharist is' (the phrase occurs again) 'it is a rite of immense
antiquity, with roots that go back beyond Christianity to the earliest things in human history.'[31]

And if, throughout the book, he is severely critical of those who
seek to keep the sacred safe by insulating it from time, and place,
and circumstance, attributing to it an illusory immunity, he is no
less critical of those who suppose that the past is now dispensable:

28. Ibid., pp. 24, 104, 100.
29. Ibid., p. 161; cf. p. 247.
30. Ibid., pp. 47–8, 243.
31. Ibid., pp. 175–6, 344.

'Our own age', he says, 'has taught us all too much about the willingness of autocracies to demolish the past and to reshape their present as they please.' Both to our joy and to our pain, 'The past is not only revered and unsatisfactory' (a refrain that runs right through the book), 'it is inescapable':[32] part of who and what we are.

There is 'no escaping the process by which an inheritance is modified in its transmission'. Our inheritance from the past 'is modified in retrospect by what we do in the present and by the distinctions we draw there'. And FitzPatrick has a name for this phenomenon. In the eponymous dialogue, Socrates is asked whether *he* can be said 'to have changed if the young Theaetetus ... who was previously shorter than he, should have grown up and have now become taller'. In the relations between past and present, there is no escaping 'the Theaetetus Effect'.[33]

The sharing of a meal 'is at the heart of a shared human life' and it is with 'the human activity of eating and its ritual employment' that the 'Way of Ritual', which is 'an approach towards the eucharistic presence through ritual's successive stages',[34] must begin.

During the 1972 exchange with Herbert McCabe, FitzPatrick had spoken of 'the concentric analogies of meal, ritual, and Passover', as providing the context which Christ and his friends inherited and which, at the Last Supper, he goes beyond 'in a way that only he can'.[35]

'We must accept', says FitzPatrick, that the Eucharist 'is a rite of eating and drinking, that it is bread that is eaten and wine that is drunk; and that this rite has ... been made by Christ into an eating and drinking of his body and blood.' 'We must approach the eucharistic presence, not as a concealed presence of Christ ... but as a ritually achieved sign of his presence among those with whom he already shares his risen life.'[36]

Rituals, I have emphasised, are actions. But actions, gestures we perform in time, are, by their very temporality, evanescent. The washing in baptism, exchange of promises in matrimony, imposition of hands in ordination – although in each case the action has lasting consequences, once it is performed the act is over, the ritual complete.

In the case of the Eucharist, however, the relative perdurance of bread and wine renders us vulnerable to what I earlier called

32. Ibid., pp. 271, 285.
33. Ibid., pp. 48, 42, 41.
34. Ibid., pp. 201, 199.
35. 'Some Thoughts', op. cit., p. 142; FitzPatrick, *Breaking*, op. cit., p. 202.
36. FitzPatrick, *Breaking*, op. cit., pp. 205, 204–5.

the distortion of imagination through *reification* of Christ's presence.[37]

A whole cluster of practices, grouped under the description 'devotion to the Blessed Sacrament', has become so central to Catholic spirituality that even to issue *warnings* in this area is to invite reproof. In theory some balance has been restored, in recent years, with the insistence that 'the primary purpose of reserving the Eucharist is to ensure its administration to the sick and dying'.[38] In practice, I suspect that, if a cross-section of Catholics were asked why the Blessed Sacrament is reserved in our churches, one would get a rather different answer.[39]

A final word on 'reification'. By one of those admirable quirks of inconsistency which prevents Chesterton's careering chariot of orthodoxy from falling into the ditch, it has always been insisted that Christ is not *locally* present in the Blessed Sacrament: move a host, and you do not move Christ. In practice, of course, reification dictates a rather different understanding. Let's go back to Father Faber, and the first verse of his hymn on the death of St Philip Neri. The scene is that of a procession of the Blessed Sacrament in Rome:

> Day set on Rome: its golden morn
> Had seen the world's Creator borne
> Around St Peter's square;
> Trembling and weeping all the way,

37. '*Relative* perdurance' because, of course, consecration does not render the elements immune from corruption and decay.
38. 1967 Instruction from the Congregation of Rites, *Instructio de cultu mysterii eucharistici*, cited in FitzPatrick, *Breaking*, op. cit., p. 339. In spite of which, a bizarre paragraph in the *Catechism of the Catholic Church* implies that this 'primary purpose' has been supplanted: 'The tabernacle was first intended for the reservation of the Eucharist in a worthy place so that it could be brought to the sick and those absent, outside of Mass. As faith in the real presence of Christ in his Eucharist deepened, the Church became conscious of the meaning of silent adoration of the Lord present under the Eucharistic species. It is for this reason that the tabernacle should be located in an especially worthy place in the church, and should be constructed in such a way that it emphasizes and manifests the truth of the real presence of Christ in the Blessed Sacrament' (1379). Quite apart from anything else, where are the warrants for the preposterous claim that our faith, today, is 'deeper' than the faith of the Church of Ambrose and Augustine, Anselm and Aquinas?
39. Have you ever considered how dotty it is that the verses of the *Verbum Supernum Prodiens* sung at Benediction are the only two verses of the hymn to make no mention of the Eucharist?

God's Vicar with his God that day
Made pageant brave and rare.[40]

What does the Mass look like?

Shortly after the Council, the Catholic Truth Society asked me to write a pamphlet on the Mass to replace the one then in use, which was entitled: *What is he doing at the altar?* I did so, and entitled mine: *What are we doing at Mass?* I still think that those two titles quite neatly capture the contrast between what FizPatrick calls the 'cultic pictures' of the pre- and post-conciliar liturgies.[41]

If sacraments are 'of the order of signs', '*in genere signi*', then the cultic picture that ritual presents – what Gregory Dix, in his classic study, called the 'shape' of the liturgy – is of paramount importance.[42] 'Liturgy', says FitzPatrick, 'is meant to communicate ritually, not to provide liturgists (or anthropologists, come to that) with obscured patterns of significance to decipher.'[43]

What the ritual *signifies* (the '*res sacramenti*'), what men and women are up to when they perform these rites, is quite another matter. Thus, for example, the straightforward answer to the question: 'What does the Mass look like?' is (or should be): a reading party followed by a shared meal. Casual observers will, of course, have no idea why these people read these particular texts, or why they treat them with such reverence. Nor will the uninitiated have any idea of the weight of significance which this meal bears. And yet, however baffling they find the whole affair, they should be in no doubt that they are witnessing some kind of reading party followed by some kind of meal.

With Eamon Duffy's denunciation of the misplaced 'primitivism' (as he sees it) of Jungmann and others in mind, I should perhaps emphasise that I am not privileging simplicity over complexity in matters of ritual.[44] But I am urging the indispensability, if signs are to signify, of *legibility*. There are non-trivial differences between the splendour of a Cambridge college feast and a family picnic by the river. In each case, however, there is little doubt that what is going on is that people are sharing in a meal.

40. Faber, 'St Philip's Death', *Hymns*, op. cit., p. 242.
41. See FitzPatrick, *Breaking*, op. cit., pp. 209–16, 232–4.
42. See Gregory Dix, *The Shape of the Liturgy* (London, 1945).
43. FitzPatrick, *Breaking*, op. cit., pp. 216–17.
44. See Eamon Duffy, 'Worship', *Fields of Faith: Theology and Religious Studies for the Twenty-first Century*, ed. David F. Ford, Ben Quash and Janet Martin Soskice (Cambridge, Cambridge University Press, 2005), pp. 119–34; see p. 134.

'The sharing of a meal is at the heart of a shared human life';[45] language and feasting, communication and communion, are so fundamental to human being that one might say that the 'legibility' of the sign is not merely a doctrinal, but also an anthropological requirement.

(Incidentally, in the same essay, Eamon Duffy suggested that 'the evolution of Christian worship and Christian doctrine' should be viewed 'tranquilly as a legitimate process of acculturation'. This disturbingly complacent perspective on our 'revered but unsatisfactory' past reminds me of de Lubac's assessment, at the end of *Corpus Mysticum*, of the shift of reference from Eucharist to Church, which he had charted so magisterially: '*elle était normale, donc bonne*', an assessment which FitzPatrick dismisses as a 'piece of ambiguous optimism'. It would surely be more appropriate, and more fruitful, to develop – as Eamon once urged his Cambridge colleagues in a University Sermon – 'a sense of the complexity of our own past'.)[46]

Shortly before migrating to Bologna, in March 1547 (on account of an outbreak of typhus), the Council of Trent decided 'to separate the treatment of the presence of Christ in the Eucharist from its treatment of the sacrificial character of that rite'.[47] Thus it came about that the Council saw itself as tackling, as two *different* issues, matters that would have been better understood in terms of the relations between sign and signified.

What does the Mass look like? A reading-party followed by a meal. What does the Mass mean? What is going on when people perform this ritual? Gathered into community by the Spirit of the risen Christ, we celebrate Christ's death and resurrection, share in the sacrifice on Calvary which saves the world.[48]

It took Catholic theology 400 years to re-integrate sign and signified into a single coherent account, a fact which exasperated Louis Bouyer: 'In antiquity the Eucharist was seen as the sacrifice of the Christians *because* it was the sacred meal of the Christian community. The texts of the Fathers are so clear and consistent on

---

45. FitzPatrick, *Breaking*, op. cit., p. 201.
46. Duffy, 'Worship', op. cit., p. 133; Henri de Lubac, *Corpus Mysticum* (Paris, Aubier, 1949), p. 291; Eamon Duffy, 'Let Us Now Praise Famous Men', *Walking to Emmaus* (London, Burns and Oates, 2006), p. 27.
47. FitzPatrick, *Breaking*, op. cit., p. 318; see p. 314.
48. I said something like this over 40 years ago: see Nicholas Lash, 'The Eucharist: Sacrifice or Meal?', *His Presence in the World*, pp. 42–63; this essay first appeared in *The Clergy Review* in December 1965.

this point that it can only be denied by a kind of wilful blindness.'[49]

Forms of Christ's presence

Constitution on the Liturgy, Article 7

Article 7 of the Constitution *Sacrosanctum Concilium* has been described as 'probably the most important statement in the constitution and the key to a rethinking of the liturgy'.[50] To accomplish the work of our redemption

> Christ is always present in His Church, especially [*praesertim*] in her liturgical celebrations. He is present in the sacrifice of the Mass, not only in the person of His minister, 'the same one now offering, through the ministry of priests, who formerly offered himself on the cross' [a quotation from Trent], but especially [*maxime*] under the Eucharistic species. By His power He is present in the sacraments, so that when a man baptizes it is really Christ Himself who baptizes. He is present in His word, since it is He Himself who speaks when the holy Scriptures are read in the church. He is present, finally, when the Church prays and sings, for He promised: 'Where two or three are gathered together for my sake, there am I in the midst of them' (Matt. 18:20).

I have one small regret. It is a pity that Christ's presence in the gathered people is mentioned 'finally' because, of course, as the opening clause implies, it is the precondition of the rest: without the Church, no sacraments! I rather suspect that if the Constitution, the first to be completed, had been debated later on, when the Council's ecclesiology had deepened, things might have been different.

It is, I think, worth noting that, while the sense of Christ's presence in the other sacraments is qualified as 'by His power' – and, in the case of the Blessed Sacrament, given an intensifier: '*maxime*' – for the rest it is simply said that Christ is present: in the celebrant, in the proclaimed Scriptures, in the assembly.

We do not need to dwell on the phrases referring to Christ's presence in the Blessed Sacrament or in the celebrant, because neither aspect has, shall we say, been understated in Catholic Christianity! The real breakthrough comes with the insistence on

---

49. Louis Bouyer, *Rite and Man: The Sense of the Sacral and Christian Liturgy* (London, Burns and Oates, 1963), p. 83. To my surprise, FitzPatrick seems unaware of Bouyer's study, which appeared in French in 1962.
50. Reiner Kaczynski, 'Toward the Reform of the Liturgy', *History of Vatican II*, vol. iii, ed. Giuseppe Alberigo and Joseph A. Komonchak (Leuven, Peeters, 2000), pp. 189–256; p. 223.

Christ's presence 'in His word', on which there are three points that I would like to make.

In the first place, in the Abbott and Gallagher edition, the lower-case initial letter for 'church', in the phrase 'when the holy Scriptures are read in the church',[51] might give the impression that the reference is to the building. In the Latin, the initial capital makes it clear that the reference is to the people.

In the second place, the reason why there is no mention of Christ's presence in the *preached* word is that, at this early stage in the Council's history, there was not yet a majority in favour. Two years later, however, the idea had won general acceptance, and so the Decree *Ad Gentes*, on the Church's missionary activity, says that 'by the preaching of the word and by the celebration of the sacraments ... missionary activity brings about the presence of Christ, the Author of salvation'.[52]

In the third place, the final chapter of *Dei Verbum* contains an extremely important expression of 'the sacramental conception of revelation that is at the centre of the first chapter'. The final chapter begins: 'The Church has always venerated the divine Scriptures just as she venerates the body of the Lord, since from the table of both the word of God and the body of Christ she unceasingly receives and offers to the faithful the bread of life.'[53] One table; two forms of one food.

It is not, I think, just old age which accounts for my alarm at what I see as quite widespread diminution of reverence towards the Blessed Sacrament. But, in the light of the teaching of *Sacrosanctum Concilium* (glossed by that of the other two documents which I have mentioned), surely the appropriate strategy to counteract this would be through the inculcation of appropriate reverence for *each* of the forms of Christ's presence in the liturgy. What a difference it would make, for example, if readers, on the one hand, and preachers, on the other, really believed that, through what they read and said, Christ was as truly present as he is in the consecrated bread and wine.

51. *The Documents of Vatican II*, ed. Walter Abbott and Joseph Gallagher (London, Geoffrey Chapman, 1966), p. 141.
52. '*Per verbum praedicationis et per celebrationem sacramentorum, quorum centrum et culmen est Sanctissima Eucharistia, Christum salutis auctorem praesentem reddit*', *Ad Gentes*, art. 9 (*Documents of Vatican II*, p. 595). The Decree was promulgated on 7 December 1965 after a final vote with 2394 in favour and 5 against.
53. Christophe Theobald, 'The Church under the Word of God', *History of Vatican II*, vol. v (2006), pp. 275–362; p. 345.

The strange new world of Abbot Cameron-Brown

Dom Aldhelm Cameron-Brown, sometime Abbot of Prinknash, might not agree. In a letter to *The Tablet* the Abbot said that it is 'good that nowadays we recognize' that 'Christ is indeed present in the worshipping assembly and in the celebrant at Mass' (he made no mention of the reading of Scripture). He is also present, Cameron-Brown went on, 'within my own heart, which is where I normally converse with him. But his presence in my heart, in the celebrant and in the assembly is not a presence "body, blood, soul and divinity", as in the Blessed Sacrament.'[54]

Let's pause here for a christological health check. 'Body, blood and soul' is what human beings are. Truly human and truly divine is what Christ is (forgive the baldness of expression, but the Abbot's text seems to need a nutcracker rather than a scalpel). If, in the gathered community, the celebrant, the proclaimed and the expounded word, Christ is not present 'body, blood, soul and divinity', then Christ is absent. It really is as simple as that.

'If', the Abbot goes on helpfully to explain, 'I jumped up and sat on the altar, no one would stare at me, to worship Christ present in my heart, as they stare at the monstrance.' No prizes for guessing what comes next: 'the Blessed Sacrament is a Thingly form of Christ's presence'.

Thingness is all. Reification rules! It would be difficult to imagine a more succinct expression of those clusters of confusion which *In Breaking of Bread* was written to unravel.

Nothing is said here about sacraments as signs, as ritual gestures; nothing about God coming among us as the Word, the truth that sets us free; nothing about God's self-gift as food. All that *really* matters, it seems, is the inert presence of a 'thing' – a thing to be displayed, 'stared at', and then locked away.

What this whole account cries out to say, but cannot (for that would give the game away) is that, in the Blessed Sacrament alone, Christ is *physically* present, although his presence is disguised, having the appearance of being bread and wine.

A final sentence in the Abbot's letter reinforces this suspicion. Having said that 'the Blessed Sacrament is a Thingly form of Christ's presence', the letter ended: 'In my heart, in the celebrant, his presence is real but spiritual.' Whatever 'spiritual' here

---

54. *The Tablet*, 29 April 2006, p. 22. The first of the canons to Trent's Decree on the Eucharist, of 11 October 1551, anathematises anyone who denies that '*in sanctissimae Eucharistiae sacramento contineri vere, realiter et substantialiter, corpus et sanguinem una cum anima et divinitate Domini nostri Jesu Christi ac proinde totum Christum*'.

connotes, it seems to have little or nothing to do with the doctrine of God's creative and enlivening self-gift, God's Holy Spirit. It makes better sense, I suggest, as a pious paraphrase of 'mental' – in the mind, in contradistinction from the physicality of the 'Thingly form'. At the end of the day, it seems, it is the ghost of Descartes that is presiding at the feast.

Conclusion

'The consumption of food', says FitzPatrick, 'displays the incomplete nature of our lives, which need regular replenishment, and yet which will eventually perish, despite all their replenishings.'[55] The food we need is travellers' fare, because we are *in via*, living between the times. Easter, from the memory of which, and in the light of which, we live, still lies *ahead* of us. It is no coincidence that the recovery, during the twentieth century, of a sense of contingency, of temporality, of the *bodiliness* of faith and worship,[56] went hand-in-hand with a rediscovery of the eschatological. It seems appropriate, therefore, to end with a piece of poetry more theologically distinguished than that with which I began.

> *O sacrum convivium,*
> *in quo Christus sumitur:*
> *recolitur memoria passionis ejus;*
> *mens impletur gratia*
> *et futurae gloriae nobis pignus datur.*

---

55. FitzPatrick, *Breaking*, op. cit., p. 201.
56. See J. D. Crichton, *Christian Celebration: The Mass* (London, Geoffrey Chapman, 1971), p. 5.

Chapter 14

The Subversiveness of Catholicity

In 1968, my revered Cambridge predecessor, Donald MacKinnon, delivered the annual Gore Lecture in Westminster Abbey. 'If this lecture has', he said, 'a unifying theme ... it is this. What is cushioned is likely to be invalid.' The title of his lecture was 'Kenosis and Establishment'.[1] MacKinnon, a passionately Scottish Episcopalian, had no patience with establishment. He was, however, deeply appreciative of Charles Gore's attempts, especially in his *Dissertations on Subjects Connected with the Incarnation*,[2] so to treat the 'grammar' of *kenosis* as to render the concept congruent with that of incarnation, rather than (as the standard criticisms of kenoticism charged, often with good reason) as a mythological device for evacuating the doctrine of the Cross of its sharp, actual centre.[3] 'Kenosis', as MacKinnon put it on another occasion, 'is in effect the principle that bids us measure the Logos-Christ by the *Christus-patiens*', the Word by the Cross.[4]

In the Gore Lecture, he explored the ecclesiological implications of this understanding of *kenosis*. 'It is not', he said, 'with Establishment in the narrower sense that I am concerned in this lecture, but with the cultivation of the status of invulnerability, issuing in a devotion to the structures that preserve it.'[5] With MacKinnon's example in mind, when I came to deliver the Gore

1. Donald M. MacKinnon, 'Kenosis and Establishment', *The Stripping of the Altars* (London, Collins, Fontana, 1969), pp. 13–40, 33.
2. Charles Gore, *Dissertations on Subjects Connected with the Incarnation* (London, John Murray, 1895); 'his most sustained study of the conception of *kenosis*' (MacKinnon, 'Kenosis and Establishment', op. cit., p. 13).
3. See Kenneth Surin's essay, 'Some Aspects of the "Grammar" of "Incarnation" and "Kenosis": Reflections Prompted by the Writings of Donald MacKinnon', *Christ, Ethics and Tragedy. Essays in Honour of Donald MacKinnon*, ed. Kenneth Surin (Cambridge, Cambridge University Press, 1989), pp. 93–116.
4. D. M. MacKinnon, 'Scott Holland and Contemporary Needs', *Borderlands of Theology and Other Essays*, ed. George W. Roberts and Donovan E. Smucker (London, Lutterworth Press), pp. 105–20, 114.
5. MacKinnon, 'Kenosis and Establishment', op. cit., p. 33.

Lecture in 1999, I sought to consider ways in which the catholicity of the Church may differently subvert both Anglican and Catholic propensities to 'cultivate the status of invulnerability'.

I once gave a course of lectures on the Apostles' Creed to a group of mostly Methodist students at Duke University in North Carolina. One student told me that, in the service book used in his church, there was a helpful footnote to the Creed, reassuring worshippers that 'holy Catholic Church' had nothing to do with Roman Catholicism. At the outset, then, it may be helpful if I briefly indicate my understanding of the grammar of the concept 'catholicity'. In doing so, I shall call upon Lutheran and Calvinist, as well as Catholic witnesses.

According to Wolfhart Pannenberg, the four classical 'marks' or 'attributes' of the Church – holiness, unity, catholicity and apostolicity – are not 'the characteristics of an existing and already perfected institution; they are the criteria of a missionary movement';[6] criteria, in other words, of what, as Christians, we are to proclaim and illustrate to be God's calling and God's promise for all of humankind. The Church, said Cardinal de Lubac in 1937, is 'a *convocatio* before being a *congregatio*';[7] a *convocatio* convened or called to call and convene humankind. The Church (de Lubac again) is 'the form that humanity must put on in order finally to be itself. It is the only reality which involves by its existence no opposition. It is therefore the very opposite of a "closed society".'[8] De Lubac was not dreaming. He was prophetically proclaiming, counterfactually, how and what we are, in fact, required to be.

Cardinal Congar once described the sense of the Church in the early Middle Ages as a single vision with two poles: an eschatological pole, to which corresponds the sacramentality of its life and language, and a terrestrial pole, to which correspond the dynamics of its politics, which are even now required to be the politics of the reign of God,[9] the politics of charity, and peace, and justice.

The Church that we confess in the Creed is, as I put it a few years ago, 'a people summoned, chosen, called together, for some task, some purpose. This people is, of course, the human race:

6. Wolfhart Pannenberg, *The Apostles' Creed in the Light of Today's Questions*, trans. Margaret Kohl (London, SCM Press, 1972), p. 146.
7. Henri de Lubac, *Catholicism: Christ and the Common Destiny of Man*, trans. Lancelot C. Shepherd (London, Burns and Oates, 1950), p. 22.
8. Ibid., p. 157.
9. See Yves M.-J. Congar, *L'Ecclésiologie de Haut Moyen Age: De Saint Grégoire le Grand à la Désunion entre Byzance et Rome* (Paris, Editions de Cerf, 1968), p. 19.

called, *ex nihilo*, into common life, communion, in God ... What we usually *call* "the Church" is that particular people which *thus* narrates, announces, dramatises, the origin, identity and destiny of humankind.'[10] It is this *tension* between particularity and comprehensiveness which governs the dynamics of the Church's catholicity.

'The concept of Catholicity is tainted for us', said Karl Barth, in a passage that my Methodist student would have appreciated, 'because in this connection we think of the Roman Catholics.' 'Fundamentally', however, he went on, 'the three concepts', of unity, holiness and catholicity, 'make the same assertion: *ecclesia catholica* means that through the whole of history the Church remains identical with itself';[11] a sentiment, he might have been surprised to learn, largely shared by Cardinal de Lubac: 'The Church is not Catholic because she is spread abroad over the whole of the earth and can reckon a large number of members. She was already Catholic on the morning of Pentecost, when all her members could be contained in a small room ... fundamentally Catholicity has nothing to do with geography or statistics.'[12] It is about completeness, wholeness, about the unswerving faithfulness, in every time and place, of God's self-gift.

Barth, however, went on to develop his point with that 'congregationalist' emphasis that is one of the hallmarks of Protestant theology: '*Credo ecclesiam* means that I believe that the congregation to which I belong, in which I have been called to faith and ... in which I have my service, is the one, holy, universal Church. If I do not believe this here, I do not believe it at all.'[13]

It is, however, the emphasis rather than the doctrine that is characteristically Protestant. And if, at least in modern times, Catholicism has placed the emphasis elsewhere, on the 'great church' pole of catholicity, neither in Catholicism nor in Protestantism is either pole affirmed, at least in principle, to the outright denial or exclusion of the other. Hence the insistence, in Vatican II's Dogmatic Constitution *Lumen Gentium*, that the 'Church of Christ is truly present in all legitimate local congregations of the faithful which, united with their pastors, are themselves called churches in the New Testament'.[14]

10. Nicholas Lash, *Believing Three Ways in One God: A Reading of the Apostles' Creed* (London and Notre Dame, SCM Press and the University of Notre Dame Press, 1992), p. 86.
11. Karl Barth, *Dogmatics in Outline*, trans. G. T. Thomson (London, SCM Press, 1966), p. 144.
12. De Lubac, *Catholicism*, op. cit., p. 14.
13. Barth, *Dogmatics in Outline*, op. cit., p. 144.
14. Second Vatican Council, *Lumen Gentium*, art. 26.

Each 'legitimate local congregation of the faithful' is, in that place and at that time, the Church of God, the Catholic Church. But *what*, in that time and place, it is required to be, is the 'sacrament ... of intimate union with God and of unity for the whole human race'.[15]

The catholicity of the Church, on this account, requires the simultaneous recognition of the *wholeness* of the Church in each particular place and time and of our duty of witness, as one Christian communion, one ordered people, drawn from every time and place and culture, to God's calling of the whole of humankind into his gathered peace.

That is how things are, in principle. In practice, of course, the history of the Church has been a story of unceasing struggle to achieve such simultaneous recognition in theory and in fact, in structure and imagination. And the terms in which this ceaseless labour is pursued are to a large extent dictated by social changes beyond ecclesial control.

In 1998, a Cambridge colleague, Nicholas Boyle, who is now the Schröder Professor of German, published a remarkable book entitled: *Who Are We Now? Christian Humanism and the Global Market from Hegel to Heaney* (in case you wondered, that is Seamus Heaney!).[16]

In the Foreword, he suggested that the new world order that is now emerging confronts us with a threefold challenge. The first challenge is political: 'Have economics now wholly displaced politics?'[17] Do 'market forces' now, inevitably, rule the world? The second challenge is historical. 'We have to adjust our understanding of the great conflicts of the twentieth century so that the Seventy-Five Years War, as we may call it, from 1914 to 1989, appears as a single episode in a larger story which began around 1870.' It was then that a new 'world order, which is our own, began to establish itself – an international market, with globalizing tendencies'.[18] On this account, the crumbling of the Berlin Wall was the symbol of the global market's victory over the ancient European empires.

And the third challenge is to our identity (hence the title of the book). 'The end of the empires has brought with it many new nationalisms but the concept of the nation' is increasingly unreal. 'The British, for example, are more uncertain whether they are really English ... than they were in 1923, when their United

---

15. *Lumen Gentium*, art. 1.
16. Edinburgh, T. & T. Clark, 1998.
17. Ibid., p. 4.
18. Ibid., p. 5.

Kingdom was founded. And if we are not citizens of our nation, who are we?'[19]

Nicholas Boyle's central thesis is that 'we all make up one world even if we are only gradually coming to recognize it'.[20] Taken together, his three challenges derive their urgency from the recognition that, unless a global *politics* emerges that can contain and counter the most destructive aspects of the global *market*, little but mounting pain and terror lies ahead for humankind (a lesson perhaps more easily learnt in Africa and Asia than in western Europe or the United States).

Nicholas Boyle is a Roman Catholic, and it might seem as if his argument should be music to the ears of those who applaud the massive centralisation of power that the Church has undergone this century. That would, however, be profoundly to misread him.

'Paradoxically', he suggests, 'the Church's status as an international organization is likely to be more problematic in the future than it has been for many centuries', because the new world order that is emerging 'is universal too' and 'The Church may be tempted to collaborate with worldly powers, flattered that they have at last adopted its global perspective.' To resist this temptation, he suggests

> the Church of the future will need to draw its moral strength not from its international presence but from its claim to represent people as they are locally and distinct from the worldwide ramifications of their existence as participants in the global market. Whatever currents may seem to be swirling temporarily in a contrary direction, the moral authority of the Church in future will lie, as the Second Vatican Council foresaw, with the College of bishops.[21]

The most important thing about John Cornwell's flawed and controversial biography of Pope Pius XII (with its dreadful title: *Hitler's Pope*) is that Cornwell appreciates the extent to which 'the style of papacy which Pius XII so strikingly embodied, far from being "conservative", represented a series of dramatic innovations'.[22]

It is always very difficult to persuade people of this because, on the one hand (as I will illustrate later on from Charles Gore's critique of 'Rome'), Anglican and Protestant polemic has preferred to argue that the way the papacy is now is more or less the

19. Ibid., p. 6.
20. Ibid., p. 9.
21. Ibid., pp. 90–92.
22. Nicholas Lash, 'Pius XII's Radical Moves', *The Tablet* (2 October 1999), p. 1316.

way that it has ever been – if not in fact, then in ambition, and, on the other hand, Roman Catholic apologists for neo-Ultramontane centralisation are usually referred to as 'conservatives'.

To my mind, there is still no more eloquent symbol of the radical transformation of the papal office, since the mid-nineteenth century, 'from court of last appeal to Chief Executive Officer'[23] than the historically unprecedented claim, made in the 1917 Code of Canon Law, that the Roman Pontiff nominates bishops throughout the Catholic Church 'without restriction' (Canon 329).

As Karl Rahner put it: 'Rome ought courageously and unselfishly to prove by concrete deeds that it is determined to renounce an ecclesiological monoculture in the Roman Catholic Church of the type attempted and largely realized especially during the Pian epoch of the Church of the last hundred and fifty years.'[24] (The 'Pian epoch' being the period between the pontificates of Pius IX and Pius XII.)

For much of its history, according to Rahner, the Church has seen itself as a kind of 'export firm, exporting to the whole world a European religion along with other elements of this supposedly superior culture and civilisation'.[25] (The topic of the Ramsden Sermon, one of six sermons preached each year before the University of Cambridge, is specified as: 'church extension overseas'.) Rahner saw the fundamental *theological* significance of Vatican II as that of 'the beginning of a tentative approach by the Church to the discovery and official realization of itself as *world-Church*'.[26] For Rahner, a world-Church would be a Church of all particular places, cultures, customs; a Church shaped by particular cultural memories but with no normative cultural centre. Such a Church, he insisted, 'simply cannot be ruled by that Roman centralism which was usual in the time of Pius XII'.[27]

He was, moreover, equally insistent that 'nowhere in the world will the Church of the future live in a society homogeneously Christian by nature and, as a secular society, taking for granted and supporting the Church's activity ... Everywhere in the world

23. Ibid., p. 1317.
24. Karl Rahner, 'Unity of the Church – Unity of Mankind', *Theological Investigations, Volume XX. Concern for the Church*, trans. Edward Quinn (London, Darton, Longman and Todd, 1981), pp. 154–72, 170. A lecture delivered in Hamburg in May 1977.
25. Rahner, 'Basic Theological Interpretation of the Second Vatican Council', *Investigations XX*, op. cit., pp. 77–89, 78. First published in 1979.
26. Loc. cit.
27. Ibid., p. 89.

the Church will be a Diaspora-Church.'[28] Since at least the 1960s, Rahner had been urging the importance of recognising the diaspora situation, the 'scatteredness' of faith communities in a world in which, as he put it, 'non-Christian liberal humanism, militant atheism and the atrophy of religion are everywhere apparent'. This diaspora, he went on, 'all Christians have in common, in comparison with which the differences between the various Christian confessions seem not indeed unimportant, but historically speaking secondary'.[29] Living, as he put it elsewhere, 'in a period of transition from the regional or national Church to the Church of believers',[30] we need to be alert to the danger of sectarianism entailed by this transition: the danger, as he put it, of 'becoming a "little flock" in the wrong sense of the term, with an elitist self-consciousness', insulated in lifestyle and imagination from the surrounding culture. This danger, he urged, 'must be recognized and opposed'.[31]

Some recent Anglican defences of 'establishment' (a topic on which I shall comment later on) base their case upon the argument that, if the Church of England ceases to be a 'national' Church, it will 'regress' to the status of a 'sect' (I should, perhaps, come clean and tell you that my main target here is the Dean of St Paul's' recent study, *A Broad and Living Way*).[32] The terms in which the discussion is conducted are distantly derived from Troeltsch and Weber, but the sociologists' nuanced heuristic distinctions are transformed into crude descriptive categories, the features of which are endlessly asserted without any serious attempt at conceptual rigour, historical instantiation or theological critique. 'Sects', we are told, are 'exclusive', introverted, indifferent or hostile to secular authority, 'separatist' in their attitudes towards the world.[33] 'Institutions', on the other hand, are 'inclusive' and 'comprehensive'; 'by contrast with the sect', the institution is 'universal: that is to say, it is concerned with the whole life of humanity'.[34] For 'those who believe that in a pluralist society all

---

28. Rahner, 'Structural Change in the Church of the Future', *Investigations XX*, op. cit., pp. 115–32, 128. First published in 1977.
29. Rahner, 'The Christian in his World', *Theological Investigations, Volume VII*, trans. David Bourke (London, Darton, Longman and Todd, 1971), pp. 88–99, 90.
30. Ibid., p. 92.
31. Rahner, 'Structural Change', op. cit., p. 129.
32. See, e.g., John Moses, *A Broad and Living Way: Church and State: A Continuing Establishment* (Norwich, Canterbury Press, 1995), pp. 201, 208, 213–14, 231–2. Moses draws quite heavily on Robin Gill, *Prophecy and Praxis* (London, Marshall, Morgan and Scott, 1981).
33. See Moses, *A Broad and Living Way*, op. cit., pp. 8, 208, 213–14.
34. Ibid., p. 10; cf. pp. 208, 213–14.

churches are required to function as sects', says John Moses, 'The Christian profession of faith becomes a matter of personal choice'; 'individuals are required', he says, 'to *join* a sect, whereas they are *born* into the church'.[35] (Not baptised, notice: born!)

This dire dichotomy – remain a 'national' Church, or degenerate into a 'sect' – is quite unreal. The Episcopal Church in Scotland, the Roman Catholic, Methodist or United Reformed Churches in England; none of these meet the description of a 'sect', yet none of them are, in the stipulated sense, 'national' Churches.

Rahner's very insistence on the importance of the diaspora-church's resistance to sectarian temptation itself bears witness to the fact that there is no reason whatsoever, in principle, why the 'little flock', the *pusillus grex*, should not enact and understand its relationship to the wider world in *sacramental* terms (as, following *Lumen Gentium*, I have sought to do). There is no reason why a Church which thus lived and understood its catholicity should be introverted or exclusive; no reason why it should not say (in a phrase of the Russian theologian, Paul Evdokimov): 'We know where the Church is; it is not for us to judge and say where the Church is not';[36] no reason for not concerning itself 'with the whole life of humanity' and, in solidarity with other elements of civil society, acting out its commitment to the preferential option for the poor.

I still stand by the conviction I expressed, in 1984, that: 'none of the changes which have occurred in Catholic Christianity in recent decades are of more far-reaching potential significance than ... the recovery of the "congregationalist" element in Catholicism'.[37] And the burgeoning of what are now called 'base communities', communities that have sprung up 'primarily among the poor, the oppressed, the "invisible" ', still seems to me 'the most striking single sign of the vitality of Christianity'.[38]

For the past 150 years, powerful forces in the Roman Catholic Church have, in MacKinnon's phrase, 'cultivate[d] the status of invulnerability' through establishing and strengthening, in law and structure and imagination, what Rahner called an 'ecclesiological monoculture'. It is this monoculture which is being subverted by the disappearance of the world that nurtured it and

35. Ibid., pp. 231, 9 (my stress).
36. Paul Evdokimov, *L'Orthodoxie*, p. 343; quoted from Christopher Butler, *The Theology of Vatican II* (London, Darton, Longman and Todd, 1967), p. 133.
37. Nicholas Lash, 'The Church's Responsibility for the Future of Humanity', *Theology on the Way to Emmaus* (London, SCM Press, 1986), pp. 186–201, 199. A lecture first delivered in October 1984.
38. Ibid., p. 200.

through the restoration of equilibrium in the Church's catholicity by the recovery of the 'congregationalist' dimension of Catholic Christianity: a recovery partly driven through conversion to 'the preferential option for the poor', in solidarity with whom the Church recovers the vulnerability of the *Christus-patiens.*

The massive transformation – in law, and ethos, and imagination – which this recovery requires is sometimes spoken of as the 'protestantisation' of the Catholic Church. But this description overlooks the extent to which old-fashioned, mainstream Catholics such as Karl Rahner, Nicholas Boyle and (I hope!) myself remain committed to *both* dimensions of the Church's catholicity. We should remember that the original ultramontane impulse in late eighteenth-century Europe, the renewed acknowledgement of the indispensability of papal authority to the Church's catholicity after 200 years in which the development of the modern nation state had rendered the Church increasingly exposed to political control and the myopia of nationalism, was a force for freedom, a restoration of the balance.

Paradoxical as it may seem, the more successful the recovery of 'congregationalism' in Catholic Christianity, the clearer the indispensability of the 'great church' dimension, including the office and function of the papal primacy, will be. With that observation, it is time to turn the coin and consider the subversiveness of catholicity for the Church of England.

Over 50 years ago, I sat, as a schoolboy, in Westminster Abbey, listening to my uncle, Bill Lash, then bishop of Bombay, preach at a USPG Eucharist celebrated during the 1948 Lambeth Conference, and presided over by Archbishop Geoffrey Fisher. I remember little of my uncle's sermon except the peroration, in which he expressed his vision of 'going forward to unity with a Roman on the one hand and a Syrian on the other'.

My uncle was a wise and saintly man; a friend of Gandhi's and a lifelong follower of St Francis (his last years were spent in the Friary at Cerne Abbas). His dedication to ecumenism was nowhere more apparent than in the work he did in helping to bring the Church of South India into being.

According to Bernard Reardon, 'Gore's influence upon Anglican opinion throughout the first quarter of the present century was greater than that of any other living divine.'[39] That final sentence of my uncle's, in 1948, has two features that remind me of Charles Gore. In the first place, his vision of the future seems not to include Protestants and, in the second place, who is this 'Roman' with whom he hopes to walk?

---

39. Bernard M. G. Reardon, *From Coleridge to Gore: A Century of Religious Thought in Britain* (London, Longman, 1971), p. 455.

The 'Syrian', at first sight, seems straightforward. He is what is sometimes called a 'Thomas' or 'Malabar' Christian, a member of one of the communities in Kerala that have continued, through at least 15 centuries, to use a Syrian liturgy.

That seems clear enough. Then the 'Roman', presumably, is a Roman Catholic. I am sure that that is what my uncle meant, notwithstanding the fact that the majority of 'Syrian' Christians in India are Roman Catholics, their bishops no less fully in communion with the bishop of Rome than are the archbishops of Paris and Chicago.

Anglicans, in my experience, seldom appreciate not only how offensive, to the majority of Roman Catholics, is their use of epithets such as 'Roman' or 'the Roman Church', but also the extent to which such usage trades upon a systematic imprecision shaped by the polemics of the past. To see this, we need look no further than Charles Gore's *Roman Catholic Claims*, first published in 1884.[40]

I should, perhaps, make clear that it is not the polemical character of the work that is, in itself, the problem: none of us have anything to be proud of on that score, and Catholic polemicists were quite as rude about the Church of England as Gore is about the papacy – although, for a scholar of his stature, he does, I think, from time to time go over the top: 'ambition, injustice, and dishonesty have been to a strange extent identified with the whole history of the papacy'![41] (He sounds a bit like the Chancellor of the Exchequer talking about Oxford!) *Roman Catholic Claims* was written, he tells us:

> for persons who accept, or are disposed to accept, the Catholic position; that is, who believe that Christ instituted a visible Church, and intended the apostolic succession of the Ministry to form at least one necessary link of connection in it: who accept the Catholic Creeds and the declared mind of the Church as governing their belief: and who believe in the Sacraments as celebrated by a ministry of apostolic authority.[42]

In case, perhaps, some Protestants felt marginalised by this description, he later adds a footnote: 'All baptized persons are in a *subordinate* sense inside the Church.'[43]

However, if this amounts to a reasonably clear expression of Gore's understanding of 'the Church', his criteria for distinguishing between particular traditions or (as they then said)

40. Charles Gore, *Roman Catholic Claims* (London, Longmans, 1894).
41. Ibid., p. 110.
42. Ibid., p. ix.
43. Ibid., p. 30 (my stress).

'branches' of the Church are much less clear. Here, we are given no more than vague, impressionistic references to (for example) 'the Roman, the Eastern, or the Anglican Church'.[44]

From elsewhere in his text we can infer that, here, 'the Anglican Church' refers to 'the Church of England, or Churches in communion with her'.[45] We might therefore expect that 'the Roman Church' denotes the Church of Rome or Churches in communion with her: in other words, what is usually spoken of, these days, as the Roman Catholic Church.

Surprisingly, however, the criteria to which Gore usually appeals are not criteria of communion, but of race or culture. 'Each race has had in the Catholic Church its own particular function. It was the function, for instance, of the Greek race ... to be the theologians of the Church. In theology proper the Roman Church has been by comparison weak, but her strength lay in the gift of government.'[46]

Does 'Roman Church' here denote a denomination or a diocese, a tradition or the see of Rome? Some passages point in the latter direction: 'though the Roman Church was not a great theological centre, like Antioch or Alexandria, or like the African Church among Latin-speaking peoples ... yet in proportion as she was lacking in theological power, she was endowed with a splendid capacity for "holding the tradition".'[47]

What I want to emphasise is the ambiguity that undergirds the argument. Is the 'Roman Church' the Roman Catholic Church or the diocese of Rome? Only if the latter is the case does the cultural or racial stereotype (Greeks think, Romans govern) bear even a scintilla of plausibility, and then only for a brief period of ancient history. If it is the *former* that he has in mind, then was Charles Gore seriously maintaining that, for nearly two millennia, a family, a Christian tradition, which constitutes, at present, some one-sixth of humankind, of every race and class and culture, is and always has been characterised by strong government and weak theology?

If Gore's usage had passed with the passing of Queen Victoria's diamond jubilee, then I should apologise for disinterring such old bones. But it did not. It survived, in a benign form, in my uncle's sermon of 1948 and, in my experience, it continues to infect the Anglican imagination.

I am not, nor have I ever been, a member of the Church of Rome. I am a member of the Church of East Anglia, although it is a matter of considerable importance to me that Peter Smith,

44. Ibid., p. 137.
45. Ibid., p. ix.
46. Ibid., p. 7.
47. Ibid., p. 107.

bishop of East Anglia, is in full communion with the bishop of the Church of Rome.

'I believe' said Charles Gore, 'with a conviction the strength of which I could hardly express, that it is the vocation of the English Church to realise and to offer to mankind a Catholicism which is Scriptural [and] ... historical ... [and] which is rational and constitutional in its claim of authority free at once from lawlessness and imperialism.'[48] That passage demonstrates, it seems to me, the extent to which Gore's polemic against 'Rome' was driven by his devotion to and pride in the Church of England.

The occasion of Karl Rahner's reflections on the social changes shaping and necessitating the 'transition from the regional or national Church to the Church of believers'[49] was what was called a 'Nordic' *Katholikentag* in Hamburg, in 1965, held to celebrate 'the 1100th anniversary of the death of St Ansgar',[50] the 'apostle of the North'.

His immediate audience, therefore, would have been largely Roman Catholic. From Spain to Italy, from Poland to France, 'regional or national' Catholicism was, for centuries, the rule rather than the exception. Nevertheless, even if (as I suggested earlier) the transition to a world-Church (in Rahner's sense) that is also, everywhere, a Church of the diaspora, has profound and far-reaching implications for the Churches of the Roman Catholic Communion, it cannot but pose a peculiarly daunting challenge to the Church of England, which has so proudly, consistently and comprehensively rendered its particular identity in national terms.

I would now like to offer some brief observations on that challenge under three heads: the Anglican Communion, Europe, and the 'universal primacy'. I do so, however, with considerable trepidation: I am far from being an 'expert' on things Anglican; I have never even been a member of ARCIC! I have no more to offer than the tentative musings of a friend.

The Anglican Communion

First, then, the Anglican Communion. When Charles Gore said that it was the vocation of the Church of England to offer to mankind a catholicism whose claim of authority was 'free of imperialism', it was evidently '*Roman*' imperialism that he had in mind. He was, after all, writing at the apogee of Empire, and knew

48. Ibid., p. xii.
49. Rahner, 'The Christian in his World', op. cit., p. 92.
50. Karl Rahner, *Theological Investigations, Vol. VIII*, trans. D. Bourke (London, Darton, Longman and Todd, 1971), p. 258.

quite well that the 'Churches in communion' with the Church of England were by-products of imperial expansion, for the Empire was the bearer of 'church extension overseas'.

However, the context in which most of those Churches have lived and grown has been such that now, a century later, the Anglican Communion as a whole has a great deal of experience of what it is to be, and know oneself to be, a 'diaspora Church'. Moreover, as Karl Rahner pointed out, the experience of diaspora puts things in proportion, rendering the differences between denominations 'not indeed unimportant, but historically speaking secondary'.[51] When my uncle retired from Bombay and returned to England, he felt this very deeply, becoming increasingly impatient with what seemed to him the unimaginative stuffiness of inter-church relations in this country.

The experience of travelling very widely around the world, in recent years, has deepened my conviction that the provinces of York and Canterbury are more untypical of the Anglican Communion as a whole than is appreciated by some members of the Church of England. To put it positively: it seems to me that deepening *koinonia* within the Anglican Communion may be of great help to the Church of England in making the transition from 'national Church' to 'Church of believers'.

Europe

In view of the evident incompatibility between 'Establishment' and 'Diaspora', it may seem strange that I have not yet discussed the former. The appropriate context in which to do so, I believe, is the changing relationship between Great Britain and the European Community.

On this vastly complex and contentious matter, I wish to make only three points. In the first place, England is not now, and never has been, a nation-state. Britain once was, and the United Kingdom at present is, a nation-state. These things need to be kept in mind when under bombardment from Eurosceptic rhetoric about grave threats to 'our' sovereignty. To whom, in this rhetoric, does the 'we' refer, and to whom does the speaker *suppose* it to refer?

In the second place, what Nicholas Boyle describes as the 'obsolescence' of the nation-state is a global, and by no means a merely European phenomenon.[52] What seems to be happening is that a world of nation-states, emerging initially in early modern Europe, is giving way to something more like a three-tiered world: at the top, economic and strategic needs drive the development of

51. See note 29 above.
52. See Boyle, *Who Are We Now?*, op. cit., p. 118.

confederations of interdependent nations; in the middle, nation-states endure, but with diminished state power and a more nuanced sense of sovereignty – in relation both to the larger federations of which they form a part and to often very ancient cultural and ethnic regional and local entities within their territory. From the standpoint of the nation-state, these third-level communities – from the Balkans to the Basque country, from Corsica to Scotland – have often seemed dangerously fissiparous and conflictual. The relativising of the nation-state may provide an opportunity for a more constructive vision of their place within far larger and more loosely structured political and economic organisms.

(Thirty years ago, in the referendum on Britain's entry into the European Community, I voted in favour partly because it seemed to me that entry would provide us with the context in which, eventually, the problems of Northern Ireland were most likely to be resolved.)

It will not have escaped your attention that I have used a word which makes some people in this country most uncomfortable: the word 'federation'. It is, however, 'perfectly plain', as Nicholas Boyle put it, 'that any future European system must be federal in the normal sense of that term, i.e., non-centralised'.[53] The key issue here, I think, is the one concept that Catholic social teaching has undoubtedly contributed to the development of the European Community: that of 'subsidiarity'. But, of course, the principle of subsidiarity must operate at *every* level, from the local community to the continent, and not only (as some British politicians would prefer) above the level of the state. As Andrew Marr observed a few years ago: 'Democratically-run towns and regions, as well as nations, are the best check on bullying centralizers.'[54]

The third point to be made about the relationship between Great Britain and the European Community concerns the distinction between power and sovereignty. 'Governments', says Marr, 'can choose whether to surrender power over their currency to a larger political union or to the markets; but must make that choice.'[55] In making it, they will bear in mind that transnational companies 'have power, but they do not have sovereignty'.[56] Nevertheless, a sovereignty rendered impotent by the power of the markets would be likely to prove a nursery for quite destructive nationalisms.

53. Ibid., p. 49.
54. Andrew Marr, *Ruling Britannia: The Failure and Future of British Democracy* (London, Michael Joseph, 1995), p. 213.
55. Ibid., p. 194.
56. Ibid., p. 199.

In other words, the danger that I see for the Church of England, in clinging to residual establishment, is that an arrangement which once had at least the advantage of making Anglican clergy admirably conscious of pastoral responsibility to *all* the people in their parish may now be highjacked (like the flag of St George) by those seeking, through such nationalism, fantasies of 'invulnerability' from the actual conditions in which English life, like that of other European nations, is now lived.

Universal primacy

Having now briefly considered the challenge which the transition from a national Church to a Church of the Diaspora may pose for the Church of England in relation to the Anglican Communion and to the European Community, I turn, finally, to the question of 'universal primacy'. (This is, of course, ARCIC-speak: mention of the 'universal primate' conjures up disturbing images of the Godzilla of the Vatican!)

I concluded my reflections on the ways in which a comprehensively bipolar construal of catholicity is subversive of the structure and ideology of neo-Ultramontanism by suggesting that, the more successful the recovery of the 'congregational' element in Catholic Christianity, the clearer – in the *one* world of which we now, inexorably, form part – would be the indispensability of the 'great church' dimension, including the office and function of the papal primacy.

Surprising as it may seem, I now wish to argue that something similar would be the case for a Church of England that underwent the transition from national church to church of the diaspora. Deprived of the 'invulnerability' (real or imagined) which proximity to the state has sometimes afforded it, the Church of England would surely need to find strength through ever closer relations, deepening *koinonia*, with other Churches in England and with the rest of the Anglican Communion. This much is conceded by Dr Moses, in the study that I mentioned earlier: 'The continuing evolution of the Church of England will', he says, 'require continuing awareness of the significance of ecumenism and of the place of the Anglican Communion as an international communion of faith.'[57]

But there he stops. Not so much as one sentence is devoted to the future of relations between the Church of England and the Roman Catholic Church and, therefore, to the papacy. Throughout this century, from Charles Gore to the present day, antipathy to and fear of 'Rome' runs deep.

57. Moses, *A Broad and Living Way*, op. cit., p. 244.

But that surely cannot be the last word. 'We all', said Nicholas Boyle, 'make up one world even if we are only gradually coming to recognize it.'[58] Where the 'great church' pole of catholicity is concerned, that recognition surely requires, of *all* Christian traditions and communions, that they come up with *some* account, *some* policy, *some* prospect of the future, for their relationship with the churches of the Roman Catholic communion and, therefore, with the Holy See.

And if such relationships are unlikely to grow much closer in advance of quite fundamental reform of the structures and ideology of the papacy, Pope John Paul II has acknowledged this, in taking counsel, not only with Roman Catholics but with all Christians, concerning the ways in which the papacy may be reformed. I am not so naive as to expect that the Churches of the Anglican Communion will enthusiastically and immediately endorse the ARCIC Report, *The Gift of Authority*, but it would be a tragedy, for all of us, if it were simply to gather dust upon the shelves.

The statement on *Communion in Mission*, issued last week in Toronto by the gathering of Anglican and Catholic bishops convened by Archbishop Carey and Cardinal Cassidy, is a document of astonishing far-sightedness. I wish I thought that *either* of our communions were likely speedily and enthusiastically to implement its proposals. It is not, I think, cynicism but sober realism which persuades me that enormous courage, immense imagination, profound penitence, are required, from all of us, if we are so to transform our structures, our understanding and our attitudes as to exhibit that full gift of catholicity through the exercise of which alone will authentic witness to the Gospel be, in each place and throughout the world, concretely and effectively given, for 'the healing of the nations'.[59]

58. Boyle, *Who Are We Now?*, op. cit., p. 9.
59. Rev. 22:2.

PART FOUR

The Struggle for the Council

Chapter 15

Vatican II: Of Happy Memory – and Hope?

My generation – those who have personal experience, as adults, of pre-conciliar Catholicism – have a unique responsibility. We who were brought up in the Church of Pope Pius XII know that it was a world neither of tranquil certainties and quiet obedience disrupted by dissent, nor a dark place of clerical oppression from which the Council set us free. But like others of this generation, for most of my adult life the constitutions and decrees of the Council, and the spirit which animated them, have been the benchmark by which to judge the reform of Catholic pastoral practice. And those of us who had personal experience of the context in which the Council came to birth, and of its dynamics as a historical event, still have a unique contribution to make to the assessment and evaluation of its outcome – not least because, in a few years' time, the Council will be nobody's living memory.

To what extent are we succeeding in implementing the programme of reform initiated by the Council? To answer that question, it is not primarily the period between 1962 and 1965 we should look at, but that from 1965 to the present day. Our concern, in other words, is with what biblical scholars would call the *Wirkungsgeschichte* of the Council – the history of its effects. How far have we realised, or failed to realise, the programme of reform which it initiated?

The achievements

The identity of the vast majority of Catholic Christians is formed and finds expression principally at Mass on Sunday. It is here, in the way we celebrate the Eucharist together, and relate what we are doing there to what we do and undergo elsewhere, that the doctrine of the Church expounded in the Council's Constitution *Lumen gentium*, the doctrine of God's word in *Dei verbum* and the account of Christianity's relationship to secular society in *Gaudium et spes* do or do not take shape, find flesh. In this sense, the state of the liturgy is the first and fundamental test of the extent to which the programme, not merely of the decree *Sacrosanctum concilium* but of all the Council's constitutions and decrees, is being achieved.

In 1968, the Catholic Truth Society in London invited me to produce a replacement for its standard catechetical pamphlet on the celebration of the Eucharist, *What Is He Doing at the Altar?* I entitled the new text, *What Are We Doing at Mass?* The pastoral, missionary and political implications of that shift in the identity of Christian agency are incalculable. It is the structured community that is the Church – God's gathered people – which celebrates the Eucharist, not merely the person presiding over the celebration. There are many weaknesses in liturgy today: the banality of so much that we sing, the uneven quality of translations, the poverty of so much preaching and our failure to make the liturgy what Paul VI called a 'school of prayer', among others. But to dwell on these would risk distracting our attention from what is the Council's single most profound and significant achievement.

Notwithstanding the continued nervous isolation of Russian Orthodoxy, the transformation in our relations with other Christian traditions has been hardly less comprehensive. Although full communion and common ministries with the Churches of the Reformation remain a distant dream, the depth of mutual understanding and respect, and the extent of pastoral collaboration that we have already achieved, would have seemed unthinkable a few years before the Council opened. (As recently as 1950 one of the English Catholic bishops referred, in the pages of *The Times*, to the Archbishop of Canterbury as 'a doubtfully baptised layman'.)

The third great achievement of the Council is a shift towards the preferential option for the poor. Some years ago, I was present at a lecture that the father of liberation theology Gustavo Gutiérrez gave to an enormous crowd of students at Boston College. The Peruvian spoke of the assassination of Archbishop Oscar Romero on 24 March 1980, and of his funeral a week later. 'I was at that funeral', he said, 'during which 40 other people were killed. Can you name any of them?' The students, of course, could not. 'Those', said Gustavo, 'are the poor.'

One reason why it is difficult to generalise about the extent to which the Church is becoming converted to the preferential option is that those who work with and for the poor are often as invisible as the poor themselves. But even if we cannot easily measure it, without doubt the Council's impulse in this direction has borne impressive fruit.

The phrase 'preferential option for the poor' was coined at the 1968 conference at Medellín in Colombia, where the bishops of

Latin America gathered to apply conciliar teaching to that continent. Reflecting on Medellín some 20 years later, Archbishop Michael McGrath of Panama said that the Latin-American Church was committed 'not only' to 'a preferential option for the poor in economic and political terms', but that 'this option' was to be applied 'first of all to the evangelisation of the poor, so that with them and from their point of view we can carry out the evangelisation of the entire community'.

Notwithstanding the reverses in Latin America during the present pontificate, and the Vatican's attempts to curb what it regards as the 'political' errors of liberation theology, I suspect that further historians will judge John Paul II to have been committed to the notion of evangelisation 'with and from [the] point of view of' the poor.

The Council put things in the right order in other ways, too. In 1985, one of the English bishops, shortly before leaving for Rome to take part in the Synod convened to celebrate the twentieth anniversary of the end of the Council, asked me what I thought were important clues to the quality of our remembering of what the Council sought to do. I suggested that one such clue lay in the importance which people attached to the sequence of chapters in the Council's two dogmatic constitutions, *Dei verbum* and *Lumen gentium.*

In the case of *Dei verbum*, the Council treats first, in Chapter 1, of God's being and act, God's utterance, the *Verbum Dei*; and only then, in Chapter 2, does it go on to consider what we are to do about the Word that has been spoken to us, and about the responsibility of those who teach us to 'listen' to that Word, to 'guard' and to 'expound' it. (The *Catechism*, deplorably, begins, not with God, but with our 'search' for God.)

In the case of *Lumen gentium*, Chapter 1 insists on the irreducible diversity of biblical and patristic images of the mystery of God's gathering of humankind, the mystery of the Church. Chapter 2 nevertheless privileges one such image: that of God's 'people' on the move through history. Only in Chapter 3 does the Council consider the structures and offices that this pilgrim people need.

The failures

In his 1966 Sarum Lectures, Bishop Christopher Butler gave a lengthy and careful analysis of Chapter 3 of *Lumen gentium*. It is in this chapter that the Council had struggled to incorporate the narrowly juridical teaching of Vatican I on papal primacy into its own larger view of episcopacy. 'What matters in the end', said

Bishop Butler, 'is the successful achievement of the Council's intentions.'[1]

In the distance between the theory and practice of collegiality, those intentions have, thus far, been dramatically frustrated. I do not believe that anybody, as the Council ended, foresaw the possibility that, only 37 years after the promulgation of *Lumen gentium*, the Church would be far more rigorously and monolithically controlled by Pope and Curia than at any time in its history. The Church has paid a heavy price for John Paul II's lack of interest in administration. And with hindsight, it was naive of the bishops to suppose that the Roman Curia – many of whose most senior members had been key players in that handful of bishops who had resisted the reform programme, line by line – would suddenly and easily surrender power.

To have an idea of just how new is the twentieth-century centralisation of ecclesial power, we need only go back to the early nineteenth century. In 1829 there were 646 diocesan bishops in the Latin Church. Of these, 555 owed their appointment to the State, about 67 had been elected by diocesan chapters or their equivalent, while only 24 had been appointed by the Pope. Not until 1917 (in the new Code of Canon Law) was it claimed that inherent in the papal primacy was the right to appoint bishops throughout the Catholic Church. Power swiftly taken is not as swiftly abandoned.

Until the mid-nineteenth century, such centralisation was logistically impossible to achieve even if it had been desired. It took a very long time for messages to get from Rome to Paris or Vienna – to say nothing of Cape Town or Bombay. With the coming of the railways, the world became much smaller, a process which accelerated dramatically in the century that followed with the coming of air travel, television and the Internet. Centralisation and micromanagement have grown along with technology, unimpeded by a countervailing principle.

'The most striking accomplishment of the Council', noted that shrewd commentator 'Xavier Rynne', writing in 1966, 'has unquestionably been the proclamation of episcopal collegiality, the principle that the bishops form a college and govern the Church together with the Pope who is their head.' Moreover, he went on, 'the new doctrine is bound to influence the exercise of [papal] authority in practice, particularly if Pope Paul's plans for the reform of the Roman Curia and the establishment of the Synod of Bishops are fully carried out.'[2] Which, of course, they

---

1. Christopher Butler, *The Theology of Vatican II* (London, Darton, Longman and Todd, 1967), p. 113.
2. Xavier Rynne, *The Fourth Session* (London, Faber and Faber, 1966), p. 257. Xavier Rynne was later identified as F. X. Murphy.

were not. The Curia remains unaccountable to the episcopate, and the Synods, in their present form, have become little more than further instruments of papal power.

There are areas today in which the Church is dangerously polarised, and the Council is often blamed for this. Is such blame justified? That a body of human beings comprising, at least nominally, one sixth of the human race, should display a vast diversity of temperament and attitude and opinion is both inevitable and desirable. A Church in which there were no serious disagreements would be dead. Disagreement about things that matter deeply to the disputants may create tensions but does not, of itself, do damage to the bonds of charity or threaten sacramental unity. Polarisation, in contrast – the dramatised simplification of disagreement to the point where there appear to be, for all practical purposes, two and only two approaches or opinions possible (and these two locked in mutual incomprehension and distaste) – threatens truth and charity alike.

On almost every issue considered at the Council, there was, it is true, a fairly clear division between majority and minority opinion. But for all the influence it wielded, in numerical terms the minority was very small indeed. Consider the figures: *Lumen gentium* was approved by 2151 votes to 5, *Dei verbum* by 2350 to 6, and *Gaudium et spes* by 2309 to 75. These are not the acts of a polarised episcopate, nor of a Church seriously divided.

Pope John XXIII had called the programme of reform for which the Council was convened *aggiornamento*, a bringing-up-to-date. Paul VI, in contrast, preferred to speak of *rinnovamento*, or renewal.[3] The scholars meanwhile used a French word, *ressourcement*, meaning the refreshing of Catholic thought, liberating it from the arid juridicism of late neoscholasticism, drawing once again upon the richness of its biblical and patristic sources. The journalists, for their part, unsurprisingly but unhelpfully preferring political terminology (which increasingly, in the English-speaking world, meant the language of American politics), spoke of the majority at the Council as progressive or liberal, and the minority as conservative.

The confusion resulting from all this is succinctly illustrated by the following remark from a recent biography of Cardinal Ratzinger: 'To put all this into political terms, *aggiornamento* was a liberal impulse, *ressourcement* more conservative.'[4] Yet *ressourcement* is not an alternative to *aggiornamento*, but the means of its achievement. As Yves Congar said in 1966: 'True reform implies

3. Ibid., p. 258.
4. John L. Allen, *Cardinal Ratzinger* (New York, Continuum, 2000), p. 57.

an appeal from a less perfect to a more perfect tradition, a going back to the sources.'[5] In the second place, it was misleading to describe as conservative a group of people whose principal ambitions were to sustain the thought-patterns of nineteenth-century scholasticism and the neo-ultramontane institutional innovations of the twentieth century.

The problem with open windows

On the larger issue, those who seek to hold the Council respons-ible for polarisation in the Church today underestimate the extent to which the attitudes of Catholics – bishops included – are shaped behind the Gospel's back, as it were, by the seismic shifts that there have been, in recent decades, in social and economic structures, attitudes and expectations.

Does this mean that the Council came too late? If what was needed in the 1960s was *aggiornamento*, when did the Church begin to fall behind the times? Bernard Lonergan's answer was: in the late seventeenth century: 'When modern science began, when the Enlightenment began, then the theologians began to reassure one another about their certainties.'[6]

Confronted by a western culture increasingly hostile, both institutionally and intellectually, Catholic Christianity tried to pull up the drawbridge, seeking security in disengagement from the world of which it formed a part. This stance could not last indef-initely. The pressures which began building up in the nineteenth century came to a head during the beginning of the twentieth. The Modernist crisis marked the painful and often tragic begin-ning of a rich and fruitful renaissance of Catholic life, thought and spirituality, which came near to fruition in the 1960s.[7]

But in many ways it came too late, sowing the seeds of its own dissolution. The condemnations of 'Modernism' dangerously delayed all programmes of renewal. For decades the Church remained in a state of siege, fully alerted to the danger of attacks as much from within as without. With the forces of renewal mar-ginalised and suspect for half a century, the official expression of the reform movement, when it came in the form of the pro-mulgation of conciliar documents, was greeted by many Catholics

5. See *Informations Catholiques Internationales* (1 January 1966), p. 55.
6. Bernard Lonergan, 'Theology in its New Context,' in *A Second Col-lection*, ed. William Ryan and Bernard Tyrrell (London, Darton, Longman and Todd, 1974), pp. 55–67 (55).
7. Nicholas Lash, 'Modernism, Aggiornamento and the Night Battle', in *Bishops and Writers*, ed. Adrian Hastings (Wheathampstead, Anthony Clarke, 1977), pp. 51–79 (52).

with bewilderment and incomprehension. Pointing the way, albeit hesitantly, towards an eventual transformation of structures, the documents presupposed for their understanding a transformation of consciousness which was too often lacking. Moreover, fundamental shifts of culture did not wait upon the re-engagement of Catholicism with those secular worlds which it had for so long viewed with baleful suspicion. As a result, even when the conciliar message did begin to get through to the Catholic community as a whole, it seemed not to speak to the felt concerns and expectations of increasing numbers of people.

This account goes some way, I believe, to help explain the sadness, even the bitterness, of some of those (such as Louis Bouyer and Cardinal de Lubac) who had worked tirelessly to bring about the renewal which the Council sought, only to find themselves in a situation far more anarchic and confused than anybody had expected. Culturally, ethically and politically, we live in most bewildering times; but it is not Catholicism that is, as Cardinal Ratzinger complains, collapsing, but the citadel that we erected to protect us from the tempests of a changing world.

Did the Council come too late? No, it came just in time. But it came too late for renewal to be achieved without considerable confusion, misunderstanding and distress.

The crisis of authority

To conclude these reflections on the failure of the Council, it is necessary to say something on two topics which were kept off the conciliar agenda: birth control and priestly celibacy.

Pope Paul VI will surely go down in history as one of the truly great popes of modern times. It is all the more painfully paradoxical that, if there is one event which triggered the contemporary crisis of authority in the Church, it is his rejection of the official report (not, as it is sometimes erroneously described, the 'majority report') of the Commission which he had convened to consider the question of birth regulation and his promulgation, on 25 July 1968, of the Encyclical *Humanae vitae*.

As with birth control, so with priestly celibacy. Many of the bishops wished the Council to consider the matter, but Paul VI insisted on reserving it to himself and, in 1967, issued the Encyclical *Sacerdotalis coelibatus*.

Whether or not Paul VI was well advised, in the circumstances of the time, and in view of the pressures to which he was subjected, to reserve these two questions to himself is for the historians to decide. The really striking thing to notice, however, is the disturbing frequency with which questions of sexual behaviour are decided, in the Church, not on the basis of doctrinal or ethical considerations, of what human beings should or should not do, but on account of problems of authority.

The point of crisis was probably reached for many, said Professor John Marshall, a member of the Commission, around 23 April 1965. It was now that 'the four theologians of the minority group acknowledged they could not demonstrate the intrinsic evil of contraception on the basis of natural law and so rested their case on authority'.[8]

In recent decades, the failure to tackle questions of sexual behaviour on their own terms – and in terms which honestly confront the damage done to men and women by the sexual misbehaviour of the clergy – has led, in many parts of the Church, to the scandal of widespread clerical concubinage and, most recently, to damaging revelations of the extent to which ecclesiastical authorities have covered up and condoned the sexual abuse of minors.

If ever there were a time when the Church needed to treat questions of sex and gender honestly, it is surely now – not simply for its own sake, but for the sake of the society in which the Gospel of God's friendship is to be proclaimed. In a culture increasingly corroded by destructively egocentric individualism, a culture which finds lifelong commitment not simply unsustainable but well-nigh unintelligible, the Catholic tradition of the primacy of relations, of the centrality and possibility and fruitfulness of the gift of lifelong friendship – both in the form of love given and exchanged in marriage and in the form of celibacy freely undertaken in witness to the kingdom – has so much to offer that we surely dare not squander it by preoccupation with the fear of change.

Unfinished business

Questions concerning how the Gospel of the crucified and risen one is effectively to be proclaimed, in solidarity with and from the standpoint of the poor, the weak and the disadvantaged, are vastly more important than questions of Church structure. Nevertheless, inappropriate structures frustrate appropriate evangelisation. There are, at present, few more urgent tasks facing the Church than that of realising the as yet unrealised programme of Vatican II by throwing into reverse the centralisation of power which accrued during the twentieth century, and restoring episcopal authority to the episcopate.

8. From a 1968 article in *The Times* by John Horgan, 'The History of the Debate', in *On Human Life*, ed. Peter Harris et al. (London, Burns and Oates, 1968), pp. 7–26.

The need for collegiality is crucial to the vision of the Council. When we speak of the 'universal' Church, the 'Catholic' Church, we refer, in the first place, to that gathering, by God's redeeming grace, of all the just 'from Abel, the just one, to the last of the elect'.[9] What we usually call 'the Church' subsists as a kind of sacrament or symbolic enactment of this eschatological gathering, this assembly, *congregatio* or *ecclesia*. More concretely, as *Lumen gentium* puts it: 'This Church of Christ is truly present in all legitimate local [gatherings] of the faithful ... united with their pastors.' Each celebration of the Eucharist, each parish or diocese, are not, therefore, merely fragments or small parts of some vast multinational corporation. They are the universal Church in its particular existence – in this time and at this place. Thus it is that, where episcopal office is concerned, *Lumen gentium* insists that every bishop is 'the vicar of Christ', and that bishops are not 'to be regarded as vicars of the Roman Pontiff', as branch managers of 'Church International PLC'.[10]

But, of course, the universal Church in each particular place will be a community of limited experience and resources. It can only draw on so much holiness, scholarship and wisdom. It will necessarily be a fragile group of sinful men and women in continual need of strengthening and enrichment, of education and correction, from all those – of every age and race and culture – with whom it exists in communion. In other words, the strengthening of bonds of solidarity, of *koinonia*, at every level – local and regional, national and international – is indispensable for the health and liberty of each particular instance and expression of the Catholic Church.

It is worth bearing in mind that the initial impulse behind the Ultramontane movement in early modern Europe was to strengthen the bonds of union between German and French dioceses and the See of Peter in order to ensure the freedom of the Church from state control. To the extent that, in our own day, the bishops of the Church succeed in taking back their own episcopal authority (within, and not 'above', their churches, I need hardly add) through the development, at every level, of appropriately collegial instruments, the indispensable vocation of the Holy See will become clearer: as 'sheet-anchor', 'rock' or 'court of last appeal'. This vocation of the See of Peter is (as Luke's gospel says) to 'strengthen [his] brethren' (Luke 21:32). It

9. See *Lumen gentium*, art. 2, quoting from a homily by Gregory the Great.

10. See the debate between Cardinals Kasper and Ratzinger, especially Kasper's article in *Stimmen der Zeit* (December 2000), translated as 'On the Church', *The Tablet* (23 June 2001), pp. 927–30.

is to facilitate and enable, not to control and dominate through power over all appointments and the issuing of endless streams of 'orders' and 'instructions'.

One of the most striking developments in Catholic life since the Council ended has been the flourishing of 'movements' such as Opus Dei, the Neo-Catechumenate, Communion and Liberation, and so on.[11] According to one commentator, Cardinal Ratzinger has said that these movements 'cannot be reduced to the episcopal principle, [but] represent a new justification for the Petrine ministry'.[12] In view of the enthusiasm with which Roman support for the movements, thus rationalised, is being prosecuted in the closing years of the present pontificate, it is impossible not to fear that they are being used as instruments subversive of that recovery of episcopal authority for the importance of which I have been pleading.

The ministry of women remains, quite evidently, seriously underdeveloped. If one sets aside the question of women's candidacy for the sacrament of order,[13] it is sometimes unclear whether the underdevelopment in question is specifically of women's ministry or, more generally, of the ministry of the laity. Suppose, for example, someone were to argue that there should be women nuncios or women in charge of Roman congregations. If such suggestions were resisted on the grounds that the nature of these offices is such as to require their exclusive occupancy by priests or bishops, then it would be clear that the opposition was to these offices being held by laypeople, rather than specifically by women.

For most of the Church's history, it has been maintained that women cannot hold high office in the Church because (to put it at its simplest) running things is what men do. It is instructive, in this regard, that when the Declaration *Inter insigniores* of October 1976 stated that 'the Church desires that Christian women should become fully aware of the greatness of their mission: today their role is of capital importance both for the renewal and humanisation of society and for the rediscovery by believers of the true face of the Church', the only vocations through which this mission might be exercised were specified as martyrdom, virginity and motherhood. Moreover, the evidence of the patristic and medieval authorities appealed to by recent pronouncements asserting

11. See series of reports on the movements in *The Tablet* (March–April 1997 and January 2001).
12. Gordon Urquhart, 'A Dead Man's Tale', *The Tablet* (22 March 1997), p. 367.
13. See Nicholas Lash, 'On not Inventing Doctrine', *The Tablet* (2 December 1995), p. 1544.

the impossibility of ordaining women suggests that almost the only arguments adduced against their ordination in the past were variants on two themes: we cannot do it because Our Lord did not do it, and we cannot do it because running things is what men do.

Church history tells another story. Consider Fontevraud, in whose great abbey church lie Eleanor of Aquitaine, her husband Henry II of Anjou and England, and their son Richard Coeur de Lion. Fontevraud, for centuries the largest monastic complex in the world – containing priests, lay brothers, lay sisters, contemplative nuns, invalids and social outcasts – was, from its foundation in 1101 until its dissolution at the French Revolution, uninterruptedly governed by the abbess of the community of contemplative nuns.

The question of the ordination of women – as the Pontifical Biblical Commission advised Pope Paul VI when he sought their advice on the matter – cannot be decided on the basis of New Testament exegesis. The historical evidence is if anything even more fragile. The question has never previously been raised on the assumption (now agreed on all sides) of the social equality of men and women. It is a new question, and new questions need time, attentiveness, sensitivity and careful scholarship; they cannot be foreclosed by fiat.

In 1979, Karl Rahner argued that the fundamental theological significance of the Council lay in the fact that it marked 'the beginning of a tentative approach by the Church to the discovery and realisation of itself as world-Church'.[14] He saw three great epochs in Church history, the third of which has only just begun. There was a short period when Christianity was still a form of Judaism; another period, lasting nearly 2000 years, when it was (with few exceptions) the Church of what became European culture and civilisation. The third period was now beginning, 'in which the Church's living space is from the very outset the whole world'.[15]

Rahner's argument was not about geography, but about culture. At Vatican I, there were bishops from Asia and from Africa, but these were missionary bishops of European or American origin. Vatican II, in contrast, really was a first assembly of the world-episcopate.

In order for the Church truly to be a world-Church, on this account, it has to become a Church which – while never ceasing to keep alive the memory that it grew from Jewish roots and

14. Karl Rahner, 'Basic Theological Interpretation of the Second Vatican Council', *Theological Investigations*, Vol. XX (London, Darton, Longman and Todd, 1981), pp. 77–89.
15. Ibid., pp. 82–3.

flourished, for many centuries, in European soil – will be genuinely at home in all the diverse cultures of the world.

Such genuinely pluralist inculturation of the Gospel will, of course, profoundly influence not only liturgical styles and forms of theological argument but also patterns and structures of Church order and of ministry. There will, as Rahner sees it, be no future Christendoms: he saw the Church of the future as a Diaspora-Church, a little flock, *pusillus grex*. This situation, he insisted, must not be interpreted – either in practice or in theory – in sectarian terms, in attempted insulation from the contexts in which the Gospel is to be proclaimed.[16]

At least in its broad outline, Rahner's argument seems to me persuasive, and it raises two issues of immense importance for the future of the Church. In the first place, there is the question of the relations between Christians and (for example) Jews, Muslims, Buddhists and Hindus. In western culture, since the seventeenth century, it has been customary to see these peoples as specific variants of the genus called religion. There are many reasons for believing this interpretative framework to be misleading,[17] but the question raised by Rahner's argument is this: do these other peoples now also find themselves required, on their own terms, to understand themselves as, and to live as, world-peoples? I simply raise the question, the answers to which would, I suspect, be very different in each case, with very different implications for the pattern of our quest, as Christians, for deeper mutual understanding and collaboration.

In the second place, it is clear that a Church becoming a world-Church, increasingly diverse in structure, in thought-forms, in liturgical expression, would need to sustain, with even more attentiveness and energy than has been the case thus far, the bonds of common faith, and hope, and charity. But, if the Church is truly to be a world-Church, a Church that is equally at home in every corner of the world, then the principal instrument for sustaining *koinonia*, for deepening the global bonds of faith, and hope, and charity, will be the collegiality of the worldwide episcopate (*sub et cum Petro*, by all means). Such communion of the world-Church can certainly not be sustained by structures of control from a single Roman centre, aided and abetted by movements of (for the most part) parochially Mediterranean origin and character.

In 1995, John Paul II, through the encyclical *Ut unum sint*,

16. Rahner, 'Structural Change in the Church of the Future', *Theological Investigations*, Vol. XX, pp. 115–32 (128–9).
17. See Nicholas Lash, *The Beginning and End of 'Religion'* (Cambridge, Cambridge University Press, 1996), pp. 3–25.

asked bishops to engage with him in dialogue about the reform of the papacy. One of those who responded was John Quinn, the former Archbishop of San Francisco. In the Conclusion to his study on *The Reform of the Papacy*, the archbishop said there were two great problems above others: centralisation and the need for reform of the Roman Curia.[18]

My own view is that these two problems in fact boil down to one. There is not the slightest possibility that the Roman Curia will reform itself to the extent of surrendering its control and rendering itself accountable to the episcopate. Only the world-episcopate, with the pope, can effectively instigate and supervise the necessary reforms. It would be premature to convene a general council for this purpose. A renewal of regional councils, as a regular feature of Church life, would be a great step forward. But the history of synods in Rome since Vatican II and the sustained campaign to rein in the authority of episcopal conferences demonstrate that the curial stranglehold is at present so complete that there is no serious possibility, without curial reform, for effective worldwide recovery of the ancient tradition of regional councils.

What we need, and what (in my judgement) it is not unrealistic to hope for, is the election of a pope who, broadly sharing Archbishop Quinn's diagnosis of the problem, establishes a commission, which the pope would chair, whose members would be perhaps 40 or 50 diocesan bishops, drawn from every corner of the world, and which would be advised by officials of the Roman Curia, and by historians, theologians and canon lawyers from outside Rome (many of whom, of course, might be laypeople, women as well as men). The task of this commission would be to draw up proposals for the transfer of governance in the Church from pope and Curia to pope and bishops, through the establishment of a standing synod whose members would be diocesan bishops and whose work would be assisted by the offices of a Curia so reformed as to function, not as an instrument of governance, but as a service of administration. The work of this commission, when completed, would then be submitted to the worldwide episcopate for comment and, presumably, revision, before receiving from the pope its final ratification. The centralised control from which we suffer, and which has contributed so greatly to the present crisis of authority, was built up in less than 100 years. It could be put into reverse in less than ten.

18. John R. Quinn, *The Reform of the Papacy* (New York, Herder, 1999), p. 178. See also Nicholas Lash, 'A Papacy for the Future', *The Tablet* (11 December 1999), pp. 1678–9.

Chapter 16

What Happened at Vatican II?

Remembrance

'Do this in remembrance of me.'[1] All things are born and die in time, but only in the case of human beings is an awareness of temporality constitutive of their identity. Without remembrance, we know not who we are, can make no plans and have no hope. We learn, or fail to learn, to live and speak the truth – and truthfulness takes time.

Bernard Lonergan's first words to my uncle Sebastian Moore (who had gone to work with him in Rome) were: 'Concepts have dates.' Battered by Enlightenment, Catholic Christianity pulled up the drawbridge and withdrew into a citadel of illusory time-lessness, a simulacrum of eternity in which nothing ever happened and, most importantly, nothing ever changed. If, in the 1960s, *aggiornamento* was required, when had Catholic thought begun to fall behind the times? Lonergan's answer was: around 1680, 'When modern science began, when the Enlightenment began, then the theologians began to reassure one another about their certainties.'[2]

From this point of view, Vatican II may be considered – notwithstanding the unsurprising imperfections and incompleteness of so vast an undertaking – as the high point of the Church's re-engagement with its temporality, renewed remembrance (in acknowledgement of its contingency) of the richness of its history (*ressourcement*); a re-engagement which thereby also brought it into fresh, constructive but by no means uncritical, relationship with the forces shaping the modern world in which it lived (*aggiornamento*).

1. Luke 22:19.
2. Bernard Lonergan, 'Theology in its New Context', *A Second Collection* (London, Darton, Longman and Todd, 1974), p. 55. Cf. Nicholas Lash, 'Modernism, Aggiornamento and the Night Battle', *Bishops and Writers: Aspects of the Evolution of Modern English Catholicism*, ed. Adrian Hastings (Wheathampstead, Anthony Clarke, 1977), pp. 51–79.

Telling true stories

Major historical events are not susceptible of any one, uniquely 'correct' interpretation (not for nothing do we have four gospels!). Any account of what happened at Vatican II will be told from some particular point or points of view, will select some themes and features, rather than others, for particular consideration. What we ask of historians is not that they say everything that could possibly be said, but that they be wholeheartedly committed to truthfulness and accuracy in their handling of evidence, and that the points of view from which they write be honestly and clearly indicated. Polemics makes bad history.

By these criteria, the Church has been well served by the international team of scholars, brought together by Giuseppe Alberigo of Bologna, who laboured for over ten years to produce a five-volume *History of Vatican II*.[3] With different chapters written by over two dozen different authors, an editorial board ranging from Roger Aubert and Henry Chadwick to Cardinals Dulles and Tucci, and weighing in at some 3000 pages, this is a work of daunting erudition, an invaluable aid to our remembering.

An Italian commentator has complained, in the online magazine *L'Espresso*, that 'rarely do we find critiques of this history', a judgement that I find surprising.[4] The first three volumes were reviewed, appreciatively but by no means uncritically, by John Paul II's friend and biographer, George Weigel.[5] From the first volume, he picks out Komonchak's 189-page chapter on 'The Struggle for the Council during the Preparation' as a 'masterpiece of research and exposition', and concludes that:

> the dramatic 'form' of the Council, which Professor Alberigo and his colleagues are eager to recapture, is itself the best testimony to the futility of trying to tell the history of Vatican II as a tale of political intrigue.

Weigel remarks that:

> the great challenge to any history of Vatican II is to avoid what might be called the 'Cowboys and Indians' interpretation of the Council ... Professor Alberigo's team is not

3. Edited by Alberigo, the English edition, edited by Joseph Komonchak, and published by Peeters of Leeuven, appeared in 1995, 1997, 2000, 2003 and 2006.
4. Sandro Magister, 'Vatican Council II: A Non-Neutral History' (www.chiesa.espressonline.it/english), a column issued on the publication of *History of Vatican II*, vol. v.
5. See *First Things*, 67 (1996) and 114 (2001).

altogether successful in avoiding this temptation in Volumes
II and III. But the wealth of detail assembled in each of these
books ... is such that the careful reader can make his own
interpretive judgements, and can do so in a much more
informed way.

Weigel notes:

> Pope John Paul II, who was one of the youngest Council
> fathers during the first period, has insisted for almost four
> decades that the Council can be grasped in its essence only if
> we think of it as an epic spiritual event, at which the Holy
> Spirit led the Catholic Church into a new encounter with
> modernity precisely for the sake of evangelizing the modern
> world.

With that observation in mind, I turn next to three themes that
are indispensable to our understanding of what happened at
Vatican II: the relationship between events and documents, the
extent to which the Council marked some kind of new beginning
in the Church's life, and the different relationships to the Council
of John XXIII and Paul VI.

Events and documents

Towards the end of the first session of the Council, Yves Congar
wrote in his journal: 'The episcopate has discovered itself. It has
become aware of itself. Given that, the formulas will emerge.'[6]
Already, in that first session, says Alberigo, 'the bishops and their
"experts" with them, gained an almost totally new awareness of
their concrete and common general responsibilities for the universal Church'. It is this, he says, which warrants 'the methodological choice that inspired the concept and realization of this
History of Vatican II ... That choice rested upon the view that to
equate Vatican II with the corpus of its texts not only impoverishes
the hermeneutics of those texts themselves but is also fatal to the
image of the Council.'[7]

The soundness of that judgement is borne out by my own
memories of conversations with bishops at the time, and by
everything that I have since read of their assessment of the conciliar experience. Notwithstanding the *longueurs* and exhaustion,
the confusions and the tensions, of four years of debate, the
Council was, for those who took part in it, the most profound and
transformative spiritual and educational experience of their lives.

6. *History of Vatican II*, vol. i, p. 575.
7. *History of Vatican II*, vol. ii, p. 583; cf. vol. i, p. xii; vol. iv, p. 327.

It was, said Archbishop Denis Hurley, 40 years later, 'the greatest adult education program ever'.[8]

Before the Council opened, John XXIII expressed the hope that it would be a 'new Pentecost'[9] and, after it ended, the very English voice of Christopher Butler observed: 'I am less doubtful than I once was that [the Council] was gathered for a second Pentecost.'[10]

Continuity and revolution

Between the third and fourth sessions of the Council, E. E. Y. Hales published *Pope John and his Revolution.* Insisting that the conciliar project was appropriately described as 'revolutionary', he nevertheless warned: 'We are told that the movement now started is irreversible; but it is hard to see why ... Moreover, an able and experienced civil service, such as the Curia, could circumvent it.'[11]

But may not the epithet 'revolutionary' exaggerate the difference between the Church as it was before Vatican II, and the Church as the Council fathers strove to have it be? At one level, the answer is, undoubtedly: 'No'. It is difficult for those who have grown up since the Council to appreciate how profoundly different, for better and for worse, is the *sensibility* of Catholicism today from that of the pre-conciliar Church.

Before the Council, for example, even to suggest that the Church needed to be *reformed* made one suspect of heresy, as Yves Congar discovered when, in 1956, six years after the publication of *Vraie et fausse réforme dans l'Eglise,* he was banished for a year into the wilderness – to Cambridge.[12]

In a lecture delivered in 1965, Bernard Lonergan argued that 'Classical culture has given way to a modern culture, and, I would submit, the crisis of our age is in no small measure the fact that

---

8. Cited by John Allen, *National Catholic Reporter,* 18 October 2002, reporting on a congress in Rome held to mark the fortieth anniversary of the Council's opening.

9. *History of Vatican II,* vol. i., p. 42.

10. B. C. Butler, *Searchings* (London, Geoffrey Chapman, 1974), p. 265.

11. E. E. Y. Hales, *Pope John and his Revolution* (London, Eyre and Spottiswoode, 1965), p. 205.

12. Having narrowly avoided censure simply for using the word 'reform', it seems that it was an article sympathetic to the 'priest-worker' movement which was the last straw. A decade later, Paul VI drew on *Vraie et fausse réforme* when writing his encyclical *Ecclesiam Suam* (see *History of Vatican II,* vol. ii., p. 452).

modern culture has not yet reached its maturity.'[13] So far as the Church's participation in that crisis is concerned, he insisted that 'The crisis ... that I have been attempting to depict is a crisis not of faith but of culture. There has been no new revelation from on high to replace the revelation given through Jesus Christ. There has been written no new Bible and there has been founded no new church to link us with him. But Catholic philosophy and Catholic theology are matters, not merely of revelation and faith, but also of culture. Both have been fully and deeply involved in classical culture',[14] and that culture has now, irretrievably, broken down.

The Church after Vatican II is, indeed, the same Church as the Church before, but it is required and called to be that same Church very differently.

A tale of two popes

Two men of strikingly contrasting character. There is little doubt that John XXIII's warmth and spontaneity won him a place in people's hearts more swiftly than the great respect in which Paul VI eventually was held.

During the first, 'somewhat chaotic' session of the Council, John XXIII tended to stand back and 'let things ride'. He 'wanted the bishops to find their way by themselves'.[15] Paul VI, largely 'excluded from the official preparation for the Council' by 'the Roman Curia, which was mainly in control of the preparatory phase', took a little time to find his feet, and the first few months of his pontificate, the summer of 1963, 'were marked by indecision and compromise'.[16] During the final sessions, he came increasingly 'to emphasize his role as moderator and mediator between the component parts of the assembly', his overriding concern being 'to ensure the greatest possible consensus' in the Council's decisions.[17] In this he succeeded, to an astonishing extent, and if there was a price paid – in concessions to the handful of bishops who, from start to finish, resisted the entire programme of reform – it was, almost certainly, a price worth paying.

13. B. J. F. Lonergan, *Collection* (London, Darton, Longman and Todd, 1967), p. 259. Though the terminology was not in use at the time, Lonergan's position would now, I think, be best described as 'postmodern', for the meaning of 'modernity' has changed.
14. Ibid., p. 266.
15. *History of Vatican II*, vol. ii, p. 495.
16. Ibid., pp. 504, 506.
17. *History of Vatican II*, vol. iv, p. 633; cf. vol. ii, p. 579; vol. iii, p. 443.

If only someone like John XXIII would have had the inspired courage to convene the Council, probably only someone like Paul VI could have seen the venture through.

Onslaught from the Vatican

On 17 June 2005, there was a book launch in Rome: *Il Concilio Ecumenico Vaticano II: Contrappunto per la sua storia*,[18] mostly reviews of studies of the Council, purporting (according to one news agency represented at the launch) to give 'the Holy See's point of view on that milestone event'.[19] The author: Archbishop Agostino Marchetto, an official of the Secretariat of State who seems never to have been bishop of anywhere, but is a beneficiary of the custom of ordaining senior curial officials to the episcopate as if the sacrament of holy orders were a kind of life peerage.

The focus of the launch, and the main target of the book (the account to which it seeks to supply a 'counterpoint') was Alberigo's *History* which, in *Osservatore Romano*, Marchetto had 'repeatedly ripped ... to pieces after the release of each volume, criticizing every page'.[20]

Taking part in the launch was Cardinal Ruini, Vicar General of Rome, president of the Italian bishops' conference and Grand Chancellor of the Lateran University. Comparing the *History* with the 'highly inflammatory and partisan' history of Trent by Paolo Sarpi, he challenged the 'central thesis of Alberigo and his "Bologna School", founded by Fr Giuseppe Dossetti in the 1960s ... that the documents produced by Vatican Council II are not its primary elements. The main thing is the event itself. The real council is the "spirit" of the Council.' According to Ruini, the *History of Vatican II* portrays 'The gap between John XXIII and Paul VI' as 'unbridgeable. It is almost as if the "letter" of pope Giovanni Battista Montini had suffocated and betrayed the "spirit" of pope Angelo Giuseppe Roncalli.' Another central thesis of the *History* is 'that Vatican II marked a fundamental rupture between the preceding, preconciliar period and the postconciliar period that followed. Cardinal Ruini challenged this vision at its core.'[21]

18. Libreria Editrice Vaticana, 2005.
19. ZENIT, 20 June 2005.
20. Magister, 'Vatican Council II: A Non-Neutral History', op. cit.
21. Sandro Magister, 'Vatican II: The Real Untold Story' (22 June 2005). On Dossetti, adviser to Cardinal Lercaro and, for part of the second session, secretary to the Cardinal Moderators of the Council, see Joseph A. Komonchak, 'Augustine, Aquinas or the Gospel *sine glossa*? Divisions over *Gaudium et Spes*', *Unfinished Journey: The Church 40 Years*

A few weeks later, Marchetto, interviewed by *Catholic Online*, claimed that the *History*'s 'unbalanced' and 'ideological' analysis of Vatican II 'betrays the event': the Council 'does not constitute a break, a sort of birth of a new Church'. Moreover, 'The opposition between John XXIII and Paul VI, which would separate "John's Council" from Paul VI's ... is groundless.' Asked about two other issues – collegiality and Paul VI's reservation of the question of birth regulation to himself – Marchetto said: collegiality was 'an ecclesial characteristic of the first millennium, which was rediscovered, so to speak, by Vatican II. It was placed, without contradiction, next to papal primacy, exercised personally, which developed especially in the second millennium.' As to birth regulation, Alberigo is wrong 'to speak, as he does, of a "trauma caused throughout the Christian world by the encyclical *Humanae Vitae*"'. Finally: 'from the beginning I have defined as "ideological" the interpretation made by the Bologna Group. And where ideology exists there is a lack of balance, extremism, blurred vision' (weaknesses from which, presumably, 'the Holy See's point of view' is immune).[22]

It is alarming that there should still be people in the Vatican who are unable to come to terms with the fact that the Council happened as it did, and deplorable that two such senior curial officials should distort the account given in the *History* in so misleading and unscholarly a manner.

Sacraments and power stations

'By her relationship with Christ, the Church is a kind of sacrament or sign of intimate union with God, and of the unity of the whole human race.' Commenting on this first article of *Lumen Gentium*, Christopher Butler said: 'The Council has helped me to see that this notion of the sacramentality of the Church is basic to our understanding of her.'[23]

According to Congar, the greatest shift that Catholic ecclesiology has ever undergone occurred in the pontificate of Gregory VII (1073–85). In the context of developments in canon law, Church and episcopacy, previously understood in symbolic, sacramental terms – as signs and images of God's transforming

after Vatican II, ed. Austen Ivereigh (London, Continuum, 2003), pp. 102–18.

22. 'Clearing the Record on Vatican II: Interview with Archbishop Agostino Marchetto', *Catholic Online* (14 July 2005).

23. B. C. Butler, *A Time to Speak* (Southend, Mayhew-McCrimmon, 1972), p. 147.

presence – came to be understood juridically in terms of the possession and the exercise of power.[24]

From this point of view, the debates through which the text of *Lumen Gentium* emerged – with the structuring institutions of episcopate and primacy being considered (in Chapter 3) in the light of a larger picture of a pilgrim people drawn through history towards God's kingdom (Chapter 2) which, in turn, needs to be understood in the light of our meditation on the *mystery* of God's redemptive gathering of humankind (Chapter 1) – may be considered as announcing the recovery, in Catholic Christianity, of a rich and ancient vision of the Church which had been largely overlaid, obscured from view, by the juridicism of intervening centuries.

Whatever the detailed working out of the theory and practice of episcopal collegiality, we might surely have expected, therefore, in the years after the Council, not only a diminution of the unprecedented centralised control which the Roman Congregations had acquired during the twentieth century, but a renewed attentiveness to the concerns and needs of local churches.

But this, of course, is not how things worked out. During the long pontificate of John Paul II, striding the world stage like a colossus, and largely uninterested in details of structure and administration, the Curia tightened its grip. Consider two issues: episcopal appointments and vocations to the priesthood.

Episcopal appointments

The 1917 Code of Canon Law enshrined a quite new claim: that the Pope had the right to appoint all bishops in the Catholic Church. As recently as the early nineteenth century, 'the last thing the Holy See wanted was to get involved in selecting bishops for the Universal Church'.[25] Today, far from the equivalent canon having been repealed, Rome unilaterally draws ever more narrowly its criteria for 'suitable' appointments and, again and again, rides contemptuously roughshod over nominations made by bishops' conferences.

Vocations

It is through the community of the Church that the Holy Spirit calls people to its ministries. There cannot be a 'shortage of vocations', only a failure, on our part, to invite sufficient people to

24. '*Le plus grand tournant que l'ecclésiologie catholique ait connu*' (Yves Congar, *L'Eglise de Saint Augustin a l'époque moderne* [Paris, Editions du Cerf, 1970], p. 103).
25. Garrett Sweeney, 'The "Wound in the Right Foot": Unhealed?', *Bishops and Writers*, op. cit., p. 217.

bear the burden of such service. It is intolerably paradoxical that, in 2005, the Holy See should, on the one hand, have invited us to celebrate a 'Year of the Eucharist' while, on the other, drawing the criteria of those who may be ordained so narrowly as to ensure that, in large parts of the world, the eucharistic community that is the Catholic Church is being, quite literally, starved to death.

Conclusion

What happened at Vatican II? According to some people, it would seem, the answer goes: 'Not much, really. Things looked threatening for a time but, once the bishops went away from Rome, we soon got things back on track.' Before the ice freezes on the Council's vision and programme of reform, we can be grateful for the *History of Vatican II* for keeping alive another memory of how things might yet be made to be.

Chapter 17

On Re-reading Vatican II

On 24 July 2007, Benedict XVI, before leaving his summer retreat in Auronzo di Cadore, answered questions put to him by local priests. In answer to one priest who said that he felt frustrated because so much of the Council seemed to have been lost, the Pope said, amongst other things, that what we have to do is to recover our great inheritance from the Council which is not some 'spirit' to be reconstructed 'behind' the texts, but is those great conciliar texts re-read today with the experience we have had since then, which has borne fruit in so many movements, so many new religious communities.[1]

By what criteria, then, are the 'great conciliar texts' to be 're-read today'? The complexity and the urgency of the question can easily be seen by considering the uses made of those texts by the *Catechism of the Catholic Church*. When the Catechism cites Vatican II directly, in quotation marks, the reference is given as (for example): '*LG* [for *Lumen Gentium*] 10'. But many references are given in the form (for example): 'Cf. *LG* 10'. If one does as requested, and compares catechism and Council, sometimes the version in the former is an adequate paraphrase but, on a number of occasions, the text of the Catechism appears significantly to distort that of the Council. (A thorough study of these instances might be a valuable research project.) According to what criteria, then, have the Catechism's 're-readings' been undertaken?

On 10 October 2005, Archbishop (now Cardinal) William Levada, Prefect of the Congregation for the Doctrine of Faith, gave a lecture inaugurating the academical year at the Anselmian Academy in Rome. He took as his theme: '*Dei Verbum – quarant'anni dopo*'; *Dei Verbum*, 40 years on. A significant part of the lecture (delivered in English) was devoted to criticising translations of the Dogmatic Constitution which he believes 'represent a

---

1. The key phrase is: '*E cosi dobbiamo, mi sembra, riscoprire la grande eredita del Concilio che non e uno spirito ricostruito dietro i testi, ma sono proprio i grande testi conciliari reletto adesso con le esperienze che abbiamo avuto e che hanno portato frutto in tanti movimenti, tante nuova communita religiose*' (taken from the website of the Holy See).

common mindset in favour of limiting Biblical interpretation to the "literal" sense, to the practical exclusion of the "spiritual" sense'.[2]

'Cardinal Avery Dulles', Levada tells us, 'recently gave an illustration of how this modern tendency to limit exegesis to the literal sense affected English translations of *Dei Verbum* no. 12. As Dulles notes, the opening paragraph of no. 12 implicitly, but intentionally, makes a distinction between the literal and spiritual sense of Scripture' – which distinction is, in Levada's words, 'all but bracketed out' in some of the translations.

The paragraph in question reads, in the edition edited by Walter Abbott which, as we shall see, Archbishop Levada admires: 'However, since God speaks in sacred Scripture through men in human fashion, the interpreter of sacred Scripture, in order to see clearly what God wanted to communicate to us, should carefully investigate what meaning the sacred writers really intended, and what God wanted to manifest by means of their words.' In Levada's lecture, the last two clauses appear with two glosses and a stress: 'should carefully investigate what meaning the sacred writers really intended [the literal sense], *and* what God wanted to manifest by means of their words [the spiritual sense]'.

At the time of the Council, there was a lively debate going on amongst Catholic biblical scholars as to how the notion of a *sensus plenior*, a 'fuller sense', of Scripture was to be understood. On the one hand, there were those who wished to stress that it is *through* the human authors' minds and heads, *through* the human sense of Scripture, that God expresses that deeper sense which we may discern through thoughtful, prayerful study. On the other hand, there were those who saw the two 'senses' as not only distinct but different; as if we could, as it were, have access to the mind of God by Magisterial bypass of the labour of interpretation.

In trying to understand what it means to call these books 'the Word of God', we need always to keep in mind the underlying christological considerations, to remind ourselves of what is at issue in confessing this one man, born and died in Palestine, to be God's fleshed Word. Where Christ is concerned, the *distinction* between humanity and divinity is, of course, of paramount importance. Deny it, or obscure it, and the integrity of either humanity or divinity disappears from view. But the indispensability of the distinction does not entitle us to treat it as a *separation*; as if, for example, we could say of one thing that he said, or did, or suffered, this was a *human* act, and of some other thing, this was *God's* work.

2. My citations are taken from the text of the lecture as found at 'DeiVrbm40years_eng'.

Similarly with our handling of the distinction between what we might call the 'human meaning' and the 'divine meaning' of Scripture. Once again, deny the distinction or obscure it, and the *reality* of either the divine or human authorship is called in question. But the indispensability of the distinction does not warrant the supposition that the two meanings are to be discerned by different means or, even worse, in different places.

As I remarked earlier, at the time of Vatican II a lively debate was taking place as to how the notion of a 'fuller' sense than that intended by the human authors was best understood. And, right from the outset, the Theological Commission made it clear that, in their opinion, it was not the business of a Council to decide on, or close down, a debate between Catholic exegetes. What the Commission therefore sought to do was to come up with a text which would, as it were, express the distinction between divine and human meanings, but without doing so disjunctively in a manner that would favour the view of those who saw the two dimensions of meaning as not only distinct but separate.

Here is the Latin text of what is, in Abbott's edition, the two final clauses of article 12: the interpreter of sacred Scripture '*attente investigare debet, quid hagiographi reapse significare intenderint et eorum verbis manifestare Deo placuerit*'.

The first thing to notice is that, in the Latin, we have a *single* clause (there is no comma after '*intenderint*') introduced by a *single* '*quid*'. The Abbott edition already begins to lean in the wrong direction by inserting a comma.

The handful of Council fathers who strove manfully to get the Commission to come down in favour of what we might call a 'strong' version of the '*sensus plenior*' knew that the poor little conjunction, '*et*', could not, on its own, bear the weight of a disjunctive reading of a complex clause. So, right up to the last minute, in September 1965, they sought a version which would read: '*quid hagiographi reapse significare intenderint et quid verbis manifestare Deo placuerit*'.[3] The Commission was adamant: the second '*quid*' stayed out. And, just in case anyone still tried to make the conjunction bear disjunctive weight, they added that 'the expression "and" is neutral': '*expressio et est neutralis*'. On 29 October 1965, the Council voted to approve the Commission's handling of proposed amendments with 2081 voting in favour, 27 against, and there were 7 invalid votes. Finally, on 18 November

---

3. *Commentary on the Documents of Vatican II*, ed. Herbert Vorgrimler, vol. iii (Herder and Herder, 1969), p. 219. The impressively detailed commentary on the history of *Dei Verbum* in this volume was by Joseph Ratzinger, Béda Rigaux and Alois Grillmeier (who was responsible for the material on ch. iii, with which we are concerned).

1965, in the eighth public session 'of the Council, the Constitution was approved by 2344 to 6. This was not, as is often said, merely a 'majority'. It was, as Paul VI had striven for, consensus or virtual unanimity.

So, where have we got to? A General Council of the Church votes, almost unanimously, to approve a Dogmatic Constitution which, in order to take no view on the question of the '*sensus plenior*', speaks of the importance of exegetes' seeking to invest-igate the divine and human sense of Scripture in a *single* clause, the elements of which are linked by a conjunction that is not to be read disjunctively, introduced by a *single* pronoun.

Forty years later, the Prefect of the Congregation for the Doc-trine of Faith has nothing but admiration for a translation which not only breaks up the clause with a comma but introduces the second relative pronoun which the Council had rejected. Just for good measure, he sets in bold type the poor little '*et*' which the Council had insisted must not be so overworked. On the other hand, he vigorously criticises (amongst others) the translation found in the edition edited by Austin Flannery OP which reads: 'the interpreter ... should carefully search out the meaning which the sacred writers really had in mind, that meaning which God has thought well to manifest through the medium of their words', and to show why he dislikes this surely very accurate translation, he sets 'that meaning' in bold type.

If this is what it is to 're-read', today, 'the great conciliar texts', one wonders why the Church bothered to convene a Council at all. The only possible explanation for a reading of the text so flatly contradictory of the conciliar intention would seem to be that the Prefect of the Congregation for the Doctrine of Faith thought it quite in order to deliver a lecture, trenchantly critical of two well-known editions of the Council documents, without taking the elementary precaution of acquainting himself with the history of the conciliar text.

The Cardinal rounded off this section of his lecture by saying that his experience of the 'inconsistencies in the English transla-tions' of *Dei Verbum* leads him 'to express a modest hope' that 'we might anticipate having a carefully done official translation of the principal Council documents in the major languages ready for the Council's 50th anniversary' in a few years' time.

Announcing a particular translation to be 'official' would do nothing whatsoever to guarantee its quality. The prospect of such translations being prepared under the supervision of a man who has shown himself so casually incompetent in the reading of a Dogmatic Constitution is not one that inspires confidence.

Chapter 18

In the Spirit of Vatican II?

In 2005, my wife and I were dining in Catania with a friend, a wise and experienced Sicilian theologian. For the next few decades, he said, the great struggle at the heart of the Church is the struggle for the Council. This will be, in part, a struggle about *memory*, and hence about the ways in which the event of Vatican II, and the texts it promulgated, are best interpreted, but, as the Council moves further from us in time, it will also, and more fundamentally, be a struggle to sustain the programme of reform which it initiated. Reform, however, means change, and the emphasis in high places is, increasingly, not on change but on stability. As the distinguished American historian, John O'Malley sj, noted in 2006: 'an interpretation of the council has emerged that is based on one fundamental assumption: that the council was in all important regards continuous with the Catholic past. In fact, that assumption seems to be already well along the road to achieving official and prescriptive status.'[1]

The polarisation which I lamented in Chapter 15 is at least as dangerous now as it was then, but the terms expressing it have profoundly changed. In this final chapter, I propose, firstly, to comment on these changes, and then to switch from sweeping generalisation to consideration of a handful of people in one place: Bologna. Then, after some remarks on ecclesiology and on the *Motu Proprio, Summorum Pontificum,* I shall offer some brief final reflections on reception and remembrance.

Wide-angle: a diversity of dualisms

However inappropriate it was to name contrasting groups or tendencies at the Council as 'progressive' or 'conservative' (if only because the concept of 'progress' is of exceedingly questionable value in Christian history), such terms were used, and taken, as *descriptions*. Few of the bishops of the minority – which ranged from the handful who resisted the entire programme of reform

1. John W. O'Malley sj, 'Vatican II: Did Anything Happen?', *Theological Studies*, 67 (2006), pp. 3–33, 5.

from first to last to those who were concerned that too much was happening too fast – would have objected to being described as conservative, while the bishops of the majority understood that being 'progressive' merely implied wholehearted engagement in the process of reform.[2] And, of course, 'majority' and 'minority' are merely terms of statistical description.

In recent years, however, description has been supplanted by polemic. The new dualisms are those of 'spirit' versus 'letter', of 'rupture' versus 'continuity', of 'dissent' versus 'loyalty'. And it is a striking feature of the present situation that these polemical dualisms have been constructed by the heirs of the conciliar minority.

In his Christmas address to the Roman Curia, on 22 December 2005, Pope Benedict said that the problems in the implementation of the Council

> arose from the fact that two contrary hermeneutics came face to face and quarrelled with each other. One caused confusion, the other, silently but more and more visibly, bore and is bearing fruit. On the one hand, there is an interpretation that I would call 'a hermeneutic of discontinuity and rupture' ... On the other, there is the 'hermeneutic of reform', of renewal in the continuity of the one subject-Church which the Lord has given to us. She is a subject which increases in time and develops, yet always remaining the same, the one subject of the journeying People of God. The hermeneutic of discontinuity risks ending in a split between the pre-conciliar Church and the post-conciliar Church.[3] It asserts that the

2. At least where ecclesiology is concerned, Umberto Betti drew the distinction more narrowly: those who placed the emphasis on the doctrine on the Roman Pontiff were called 'conservative' and those who placed it on the episcopal office were called 'progressive': see Umberto Betti, '*Histoire Chronologique de la Constitution*', *L'Eglise de Vatican II, vol. ii, Unam Sanctum 51b* (Paris, Editions du Cerf, 1966), pp. 57–83, 69. Incidentally, in November 2007, Betti, although now beyond the voting age (he was born in 1922), was made a cardinal.

3. On 13 July 1988, addressing the bishops of Chile in Santiago, the then Cardinal Ratzinger said that 'there are many accounts of [the Council] which give the impression that, from Vatican II onward, everything has been changed, and that what preceded it has no value or, at best, has value only in the light of Vatican II. The Second Vatican Council has not been treated as a part of the entire living Tradition of the Church, but as an end of Tradition, a new start from zero. The truth is that this particular Council defined no dogma at all, and deliberately chose to remain on a modest level, as a merely pastoral council; and yet many treat it as though it had made itself into a sort of superdogma which takes away the importance of all the

texts of the Council as such do not yet express the true spirit of the Council. It claims that they are the result of compromises in which, to reach unanimity, it was found necessary to keep and reconfirm many old things that are now pointless. However, the true spirit of the Council is not to be found in these compromises but instead in the impulses toward the new that are contained in the texts. These innovations alone were supposed to represent the true spirit of the Council, and starting from and in conformity with them, it would be possible to move ahead. Precisely because the texts would only imperfectly reflect the true spirit of the Council and its newness, it would be necessary to go courageously beyond the texts and make room for the newness in which the Council's deepest intention would be expressed, even if it were still vague. In a word: it would be necessary not to follow the texts of the Council but its spirit.[4]

I have quoted that text at some length because, although the tone is calm and dignified, the analysis is pure polemic. There are, apparently, only two parties to the debate, and one of them is right while the other is, quite simply, wrong. There is no doubt that, in the years immediately following the Council, many silly things were said and done. We are, after all, talking about the 1960s! And, the conciliar event was undoubtedly of such magnitude as unsurprisingly to generate uncertainty and some confusion. But where does the Pope find this abstract dissociation of spirit from text instantiated? Who are these people who appeal to 'the spirit' of the Council *against* the texts of its Constitutions and Decrees? To read the conciliar texts well is, surely, to read them in the context of their original production, and an element of this context is the climate, the atmosphere, the spirit, the *direction*, in which the work was done.

On 29 February 1964, the Secretary of State, Cardinal Cicognani, wrote a letter to the president of the *Consilium* established to oversee the implementation of the Constitution on the Liturgy. Amongst the tasks assigned to the *Consilium*, he said, was that of applying, 'according to the letter and the spirit of the Council, the Constitution it had approved, by responding to the proposals of the conferences of bishops'.[5]

rest' (translation from the website of *Una Voce America*, the American affiliate of the international *Una Voce* federation, a body dedicated to the preservation of the Tridentine rite). '*Modest* level' and '*merely* pastoral' are, I think, revealing.

4. Quoted from the website of the Holy See.
5. Reiner Kaczynski, 'Toward the Reform of the Liturgy', *History of Vatican II*, vol. iii (2000), p. 246.

According to Pope Benedict, those who misinterpret the Council work with a 'hermeneutic of discontinuity and rupture'. Did not the Council profoundly change the Catholic Church? Certainly, at the time, everybody seems to have supposed so, whether they approved or disapproved of what had happened. But the sweeping generalisations in the papal polemic – *either* text *or* spirit, *either* continuity *or* discontinuity – are quite unreal. We need carefully and quite concretely to specify the changes that occurred, the continuities that were sustained, and the things long forgotten that were recovered. In order to do so, abstract polemic is of much less use than the work of historians and social scientists.[6]

'There are', according to Andrew Greeley

> two major tendencies in interpretation of Vatican Council II. The first, which currently dominates the Vatican, is that the Council was an occurrence, a meeting of the bishops of the world who enacted certain reforms and clarified certain doctrines. This response and clarification were necessary but they did not drastically change the nature of the church. To find out what this occurrence meant – the 'council rightly understood' of Cardinal Joseph Ratzinger – one must go to the conciliar documents. The second interpretation holds that the council was a momentous event, indeed one of the most dramatic and important events in the history of Catholicism, a structure-shattering event which one could almost call a revolution.[7]

Perhaps Greeley's 'second interpretation' is the kind of thing against which Pope Benedict's polemic is directed. If so, however, the mature manner of proceeding would be through engagement in serious and scholarly historical debate, not by fulmination from a distance. In the article in question, drawing on the work of the social historian William Sewell, Greeley argues that

> while the council's various documents, either singly or taken together, are not of themselves the cause of the shattering of structures in the Catholic church, the council as (irrevocably) interpreted was, in addition to and beyond its decisions, a

---

6. See the fine essay by Eamon Duffy, 'Tradition and Reaction: Historical Resources for a Contemporary Renewal', *Unfinished Journey*, pp. 49–65.
7. Andrew Greeley, 'The Revolutionary Event of Vatican II', *Commonweal* (11 September 1988).

historical event of enormous importance for the church, perhaps the most momentous in its history.[8]

In a serious and closely argued paper, suggesting analogies between the Council and the French Revolution, there are characteristically playful touches:

> The occurrence which played a role something like the storming of the Bastille was the sudden opposition of two leaders of the Western European church, Cardinal Joseph Frings of Cologne and Cardinal Achille Lienart of Lille. Two elderly men with enormous prestige who had suffered through the war, they demanded that the preparatory documents be scrapped and that the council fathers themselves shape the documents on which they would vote. The pope agreed. It was clear then to at least some of the bishops that it would be their council, not the Roman curia's.

Although Greeley does not hide the direction in which his sympathies lie, he insists that it is not the business of the sociologist to *evaluate* social change, but to analyse and describe such changes as occur.

Text and spirit, continuity and revolution, or 'rupture'. For red-blooded polemic with the gloves off, I turn to Michael Novak. On 30 October 1963, the Council voted 'in favour of a renewed emphasis on the supreme authority of the entire college of bishops, united around the world with the pope'.[9] In 1963, Novak had written of that day: 'On the evening of October 30, a nearly full moon bathed St Peter's Square in such brilliance, such serenity, as was worthy of the greatest day in Roman Catholic history

8. By 'irrevocably' I take him to mean interpreted, not merely in academic texts, but in imagination, in structures and patterns of behaviour. Even if it were desirable, for example, it would simply not be *possible* to transform the imagination and self-understanding of the Church *back* into the way they were in the pontificate of Pius XII. It may also be worth pointing out that, by 'structures', Greeley means not only, or even primarily, ecclesial institutions, but structures of mind and imagination: perceptions, for example, of the possibility of change, of mortal sin, of the diffusion of authority, and so on.

9. Michael Novak, 'The "Open Church" Forty Years Later: A Reckoning', *Unfinished Journey*, op. cit., pp. 32–48, 35. The four votes were passed by majorities of 98.42%, 95.13%, 84.17% and 80.31%: see Alberto Melloni, 'The Beginning of the Second Period: The Great Debate on the Church', *History of Vatican II*, vol. iii, pp. 1–115, 105.

since 1870.'[10] 'After October 30', said Alberto Melloni, 'collegiality
and Vatican II were synonymous.'[11]

Forty years later, Novak thought that judgement stood up 'very
well'. But here, as on the previous page, is his assessment of what
he calls 'Vatican II Catholicism':

> The very pope who presided (brilliantly, by the way) over the
> final three sessions of the Council, Paul VI, said publicly
> some years afterwards that 'the smoke of Satan' had filtered
> into the work of the Council, and blown up a mirage of 'the
> spirit of Vatican II' that had subverted the letter of what the
> Holy Spirit had wrought, and blown the barque of Peter far
> off course and tossed her about on stormy seas. Many inhaled
> a spirit of self-intoxication from the air they breathed from
> 'the spirit of Vatican II'. A spirit of radical individualism and
> hatred for the way things had been swept through religious
> community after religious community, through colleges and
> universities, through the ranks of priests (and even some
> bishops, although the latter were more constrained by the
> close ties to Rome), and eventually through the educated
> laity. Thus 'Vatican II Catholicism' was born. It was much
> celebrated by its proponents.[12]

Three comments on that savage assessment. In the first place,
even from an American, this diatribe borders on fantasy, as does
the later assertion that, after the Council, 'the victorious majority
(the "progressives") acquired a vested interest both in stressing
new beginnings and in discrediting the leadership and the ways of
the past'.[13] Quite apart from the inappropriateness of speaking of
the 'victorious' majority, because it underestimates the success
with which Paul VI worked, tirelessly, for consensus, that sentence
implies that, after the Council, most of the bishops of the Catholic
Church – who, after all, constituted the 'majority' in question –
went about 'discrediting the leadership and the ways of the past'.
(I say 'even from an American' because American Catholicism is

---

10. Michael Novak, *The Open Church* (London, Darton, Longman and
    Todd, 1964), p. 210. Earlier in the same chapter, he had described
    30 October as 'the most important day of the Second Vatican
    Council' (p. 204).
11. Ibid., p. 108.
12. Michael Novak, 'The "Open Church" Forty Years Later: A Reckon-
    ing', *Unfinished Journey*, op. cit., pp. 32–48, 34.
13. Ibid., p. 44.

as dangerously polarised as American culture.[14] When the late Cardinal Bernardin sought to contribute to the healing of this gulf by establishing the Common Ground Initiative, he met with shockingly little support and encouragement from many of the senior bishops.)

In the second place, the passage gives the impression that Paul VI, on the occasion referred to, had recourse to this dualism of 'letter' and 'spirit', which he did not.

In the third place, and far more seriously, the passage gives the impression that the pope regarded these mad 'Vatican II Catholics' who went about wrecking the Church in the ways that Novak so graphically describes as being under diabolic influence.

On 29 June 1972, the feast of Saints Peter and Paul and the ninth anniversary of his coronation as pope, Paul VI preached a homily in St Peter's. In the course of it he said that, after the Council, we had believed that there would be a day of sunshine for the history of the Church. Instead, there arrived a day of clouds, of tempest, of darkness, of questioning, of uncertainty. We preach ecumenism but we constantly separate ourselves. We seek to dig abysses instead of filling them in. How has this come about? He then confided to the congregation his belief that 'through some fissure the smoke of Satan has entered the temple of God'; 'something preternatural has come into the world to disturb, to suffocate the fruits of the Ecumenical Council, and to prevent the Church from breaking into a hymn of joy at having renewed in fullness its awareness of itself'.[15]

It is an extraordinary homily, but what it is *not* is what Novak presents it as: an attack on some destructive and fanatical horde of devotees of a fictional 'spirit' of the Council, contemptuous of its letter. As I read it, Paul VI was conducting something more like an agonised examination of conscience of the Church as whole, and finding himself forced to the conclusion that the emergence of so much darkness and confusion where we had hoped there would

---

14. Those who doubt this should spend an hour or so trawling American Catholic 'blogs': I never cease to be repelled by their violent and vituperative language.

15. '*Si credeva che dopo il Concilio sarebbe venuta una giornata di sole per la storia della Chiesa. E venuta invece una giornata di nuvole, di tempesta, di buio, di ricerca, di incertezza. Predichiamo l'ecumenismo e ci distacchiamo sempre ti piu dagli altri. Cerchiamo di scavare abissi invece de colmarli ... de qualche fessura sia entrato il fumo di Satana nel tempio di Dio ... Crediamo in qualcosa di preternaturale venuto nel mondo proprio per turbare, per soffocare I frutti del Concilio Ecumenico, e per impedire che la Chiesa prorompesse nell'inno della gioia di aver riavuto in pienezza la coscienza di sé*' (from the website of the Holy See).

be daylight and delight can only be attributed to a diabolic effort to frustrate the fruitfulness of the Spirit's work.

Polarisation can have unexpected outcomes. Here is one American blogger, writing in February 2007:

> The Traditional documents of the Church in councils, and from Popes are considered beautiful precisely because they are concise, and teach in a beautiful manner what the Church has always and everywhere believed. In my opinion, while rejecting the proposition that Vatican II is heretical, or that its documents contain heresy, the documents are horrible and need to more or less be forgotten ... I really think we need something akin to a Pope saying forget about it, this happened but it's in the past, the way Pope St Gregory the Great acted concerning the very unpopular 2nd Council of Constantinople.[16]

It is my impression that such voices are becoming increasingly frequent, as we move further in time from the Council. But to which of the two 'tendencies' beloved by those whose polemics trade upon dualisms of 'letter' and 'spirit', of 'rupture' and 'continuity', should such voices be allotted?

There is one final dualism to be considered: that which sees the Church polarised between 'loyalists' and 'dissenters'. I have long believed 'the subordination of *education* to *governance*', the collapsing of all authority into governance and, as a result, the substitution, for teaching, of proclamation construed as command, to be 'at the very heart of the crisis of contemporary Catholicism'.[17] *The Tablet* recently reported a striking example of this disease, in the form of an interview given, on 5 November 2007, on the Vatican website, *Petrus*.

Asked by Bruno Volpe: 'Your excellency, what kind of reception has Benedict XVI's *Motu Proprio* which liberalized the Holy Mass according to the Tridentine Rite had? Some, in the very bosom of the Church, have got their noses bent out of shape', Archbishop Malcolm Ranjith, the Sri Lankan Secretary of the Congregation for Divine Worship, replied:

> There have been positive reactions and, it's pointless to deny it, criticisms and opposing positions, also on the part of theologians, liturgists, priests, bishops, and even cardinals. Frankly, I don't understand this distancing from and, let's

16. Blog, 'The American Inquisition', 17 February 2007.
17. Nicholas Lash, 'Authors, Authority and Authorization', *Authority in the Roman Catholic Church: Theory and Practice*, ed. Bernard Hoose (Aldershot, Ashgate, 2002), pp. 59–71, p. 59.

just say it, rebellion against the Pope. I invite all, above all shepherds, to obey the Pope, who is the successor of Peter. Bishops, in particular, swore loyalty to the Pontiff ... You know that there have been, on the part of some dioceses, even interpretive documents which inexplicably aim at putting limits on the Pope's *Motu Proprio*. Behind these actions there are hidden, on the one hand, prejudices of an ideological kind and, on the other hand, pride, one of the gravest sins.[18]

The recent *Motu Proprio* (to which we shall return) was issued notwithstanding the fact that a considerable number of bishops, including several bishops' conferences, had implored the Pope not to do so. In view of the strenuous and successful attempt, in the drafting of *Lumen Gentium*, to keep the conciliar minority on board by holding in tension 'papalist' and what we might call 'conciliar' views of the relationship between the college of bishops and its head, there is no doubt that, in issuing the *Motu Proprio*, the Pope was acting in accordance with the *letter* of the Dogmatic Constitution. But it would not be difficult to make a case for saying that he acted against its *spirit*. On the other hand, in view of *Lumen Gentium*'s insistence that 'Bishops govern the particular churches entrusted to them as vicars and ambassadors of Christ' and that they are *not* to be regarded 'as vicars of the Roman Pontiff' (article 27), Archbishop Ranjith might be thought to come close to collision with not only the spirit but the letter of the text.

I find it difficult to believe that Benedict XVI was surprised to discover that he had stirred up a hornets' nest, nor to learn that many bishops sought to minimise the pastoral damage they thought likely to ensue. The discussion will, undoubtedly, continue, but there is something vaguely preposterous about the picture of a middle-ranking curial official deeming it his business to declare an unstated number of 'priests, bishops and even cardinals' to be in peril of damnation for disagreeing with their elder brother.

18. Translated by John Zuhlsdorf, an American priest ordained by John Paul II for the Italian diocese of Velletri-Segni, and published on his website WFFH – 'Wanderer Forum Foundation History'. Fr Zuhlsdorf writes a weekly column on liturgical translation in *The Wanderer*, a vigorously conservative American paper, which has been going since 1867. I am grateful to Robert Mickens for pointing me in this direction.

Close focus: Bologna

On 27 February 2006, the Italian journalist Sandro Magister reported that, three days previously, Benedict XVI had received in private audience 'brother Enzo Bianchi, prior of Bose'.[19] (Bianchi, who is not only prior but also founder of that community had, in 1982, taken over the presidency of the Institute of Religious Studies in Bologna from its founder, Giuseppe Dossetti.) Rightly or wrongly, Magister saw the occasion as marking a rift between Bianchi and the historian Alberto Melloni, because whereas the latter had been very critical of the encyclical *Deus Caritas Est*, the former had warmly welcomed it.

> Until a few months ago, Bianchi and Melloni were like the two gods of progressivism: they proceeded united and stuck together. Both were important members of the 'school of Bologna' founded by Don Giuseppe Dossetti and directed by Giuseppe Alberigo, author of an interpretation of Vatican II – which Benedict XVI has criticized harshly, both before and after he became Pope.[20]

One is reminded of the policeman at the end of *Casablanca*: 'round up the usual suspects'.

In Chapter 16, I briefly defended the *History of Vatican II*, edited by Alberigo, from savage criticisms it had received from Cardinal Ruini and Archbishop Marchetto.[21] Archbishop Marchetto has not, it seems, given up the fight. In a lecture which he gave in Ancona, on 10 November 2007, entitled 'For a correct interpretation of Vatican Council II', and constituting the most sustained and personal attack that I have seen, not simply on the Bologna school, but on Alberigo himself (who, of course, can no long answer back), the archbishop said that it is time to bring to an end the Bologna group's ideological manipulation of the history of the Council. 'The focus on discontinuity', he said:

> is also the result of the current general historiographical tendency that (after and against Braudel and the Annales) privileges, in historical interpretation, 'the event', understood as discontinuity and a traumatic transformation. So then, in the Church, if this 'event' is not so much an

19. Sandro Magister (www.chiesa.espressonline.it/English). Magister, born in 1943, has been on the staff of the weekly magazine *L'Espresso* since 1974.
20. Ibid.
21. Alberigo died in June 2007. The last communication I received from him, 18 months earlier, was a letter warmly thanking me for that small essay.

important fact, but a rupture, an absolute novelty, the emergence *in casu* of a new Church, a Copernican revolution, in short the transition to a different form of Catholicism[22] – losing its unmistakable characteristics – this perspective cannot and must not be accepted, precisely because of the uniqueness of Catholic identity ... It thus emerges that what was an extreme, radical position (opposed to 'consensus') in the heart of the conciliar majority (there was also extremism in the minority, which would later be manifested with the schism of Archbishop Lefebvre), succeeded, after the Council, almost in monopolizing the interpretation until now, rejecting any alternative approach, sometimes with the barbed accusation that these are anti-conciliar (see G. Dossetti, '*Il Vaticano II. Frammenti di una riflessione* [Vatican II: Fragments of a Reflection]').[23]

It would be hard to imagine that any account of Vatican II could be more resolutely 'ideological' than Archbishop Marchetto's insistence that the question of which interpretations are to be accepted, and which rejected, is to be decided on the basis of a disjunction between purely formal historiographical generalisations – couched in extravagantly polemical terms which disgracefully misrepresent the approach taken by the *History of Vatican II* – regardless of what actually *happened* (and was recorded, in massively rich and particular detail, as *having* happened) in and to the Catholic Church between 1962 and 1965.

It may be worth reminding those who have not closely studied the *History of Vatican II* of the sheer scale of the operation. The five volumes, which appeared in English between 1995 and 2006, run to just over 3000 pages. Assisting the 27 authors was a 51-strong editorial board, drawn from 18 countries, and including many of the most distinguished scholars in the field, such as: Roger Aubert, Henry Chadwick, Cardinal Avery Dulles, Gerald Fogarty, Hermann Pottmeyer, Roberto Tucci and, editing the English edition, Joseph Komonchak. An unlikely group of people to be up to the kind of heretical skulduggery ascribed to them.

The reviews in the learned journals have been, for the most part, extremely complimentary. Here is John O'Malley's verdict:

22. '*Ad un altro cattolicesimo*'. A detailed report of Marchetto's lecture appeared on the Vatican website 'Petrus' (www.papanews.it): '*Monsignor Marchetto: "Errata l'interpretazione del Concilio da parte del gruppo di Bologna"*'.

23. The full text of an English translation of the lecture is available on www.chiesa.espressonline.it/English (15 November 2007), from which I quote.

I have studied the five Alberigo volumes. I consider them a remarkable achievement of historical scholarship, and in print I have compared them ... to the authoritative history of Trent published in the last century by Hubert Jedin. This is of course not to say that the work is perfect. It has, for instance, all the advantages and disadvantages of a collaborative history in which subjects have been parceled out to different authors. Yes, between the lines and sometimes in the lines, one can detect sympathy for 'the progressives'. But I am generally impressed with the authors' efforts to be fair to the so-called conservatives or minority and especially to be fair to Pope Paul VI, whom they recognized as being in an extraordinarily difficult and delicate situation ... Nowhere in the Alberigo volumes is there the slightest suggestion that the 'new beginning' meant in any way a rupture in the faith of the Church or a diminution of any dogma.[24]

Nowhere. It almost begins to look as if powerful forces in the Vatican, unable to make a scholarly case for their Orwellian reinvention of what went on between 1962 and 1965, are reduced to having recourse to abuse and misinterpretation. There is something in this but there is also, I have come to believe, something else going on. We need to go back to the foundation of the Bologna Institute by Giuseppe Dossetti.

In this excellent 2003 Annual Lecture of the Common Ground Initiative, Joseph Komonchak said: 'To try to locate Dossetti, who is largely unknown to Americans, I suggest trying to imagine what Vatican II might have done if Dorothy Day had set the agenda.'[25] In other words, throughout his life, he was passionately committed to what would in due time be called the 'preferential option for the poor'.

Born near Bologna in 1913, at the end of World War II de Gasperi made him deputy secretary of the newly founded Christian Democrat Party. He left parliament in 1947 and, returning to Bologna, sowed the seeds of what, a few years later, became the

24. O'Malley, 'Vatican II: Did Anything Happen?', op. cit., p. 6. For readers lacking the time or energy to work through these five large volumes, I warmly recommend Giuseppe Alberigo, *A Brief History of Vatican II* (New York, Orbis Books, 2006), an attractively autobiographical account, with a Foreword by John O'Malley.

25. Joseph A. Komonchak, 'Dealing with Diversity and Disagreement: Vatican II and Beyond', cited from the website of the Common Ground Initiative (www.nplc.org/commonground.hym). As an indication of *how* unknown Dossetti is, throughout the English-speaking world, there is no reference to him in any of Xavier Rynne's four volumes on Vatican II.

Institute of Religious Studies. He was considering becoming a priest but, in 1956, Cardinal Lercaro of Bologna asked him to run for mayor of the city against the Communist candidate. He did become a councillor but, two years later, was ordained priest by Lercaro. He was advisor to Lercaro throughout the Council and was also, for a time, secretary of the four cardinal moderators of the Council, of whom Lercaro was one. His political influence was as lasting as his religious, and the Italian Prime Minister, Romano Prodi, regards him as his mentor.[26] After Lercaro's retirement, Dossetti founded a religious community near Bologna and later extended its activities to the Holy Land, establishing communities of monks and nuns who, in collaboration with Jews and Muslims, study and pray for peace in the Middle East. He died on 15 December 1996.[27]

In August 1978, he drafted a memorandum 'For the Renewal of the Pope's Service. The First "Hundred Days" ', which was sent to all the cardinals participating in the conclaves that elected John Paul I and John Paul II.

> The initial acts of a new pontificate carry a decisive import-ance for all successive developments, [the memorandum began] because they constitute a public indication of the orientation of the pope and the Church, and above all because during the first weeks the newly elected pope's internal energies are intact and his prestige is not yet dead-ened by routine. It is thus fundamental that the guiding principles emerge clearly and vigorously during the first 'hundred days', indicating courageously the dominant phys-iognomy of the new period of Petrine service underway.

Of the proposals that follow, I will quote a handful. On 'collegial governance', Dossetti wrote:

> As the patriarch of the Western Church and head of the Roman Catholic Church, some of these first acts cannot help but pertain to the nerve centre of the bodies dedicated to communion, solidarity, and the unity of the Churches. This especially brings up the problem of the creation of a true and proper body which, together with the bishop of Rome, would

26. I am not sufficiently informed to know, but it seems to me quite possible that the sustained attempt, on the part of people in the Roman Curia, to discredit the Bologna School, may be rooted as much in Italian politics as in historical or doctrinal disagreement.

27. See Desmond O'Grady's obituary in the *National Catholic Reporter* (31 January 1997). See also the editorial in the journal *Thirty Days* (November 2006), commemorating the tenth anniversary of his death.

preside over the common aspects of Church life ... One can
think, that is, of a collegial body that, under the personal and
effective presidency of the pope, would consider on at least a
biweekly basis the problems facing the Church as a whole, and
would make the related decisions. The formation of such a
body could be, initially, nothing more than an 'ad experi-
mentum', on the condition that it be composed exclusively of
members of the Episcopal college chosen freely by the pope.
Some of these could later be designated by the synod of
bishops ... It would need to be clear that this is not an
instrument for coordinating the congregations of the Roman
Curia, but rather a new body situated at the highest leadership level of the Catholic Church, expressing and putting into
effect the shared responsibility of the universal episcopal
college with its head, the bishop of Rome.

Then, after a paragraph on the importance of recognising 'the
true and proper legislative capacity of the synod of bishops', which
should meet annually or perhaps twice a year, came a paragraph
on the Curia:

It is easy to see that the Roman Curia – possibly scaled down,
and in some case with its offices merged – would need to
carry out a subordinate function of preparation and,
respectively, of the execution of the decisions of the synod of
bishops and of the collegial governance body.

Other proposals concerned 'Rome's early acceptance of and
promotion of different and experimental ways of selecting bishops, in order to prepare a progressive, effective re-appropriation
of this responsibility by the interested ecclesial communities', and
the abolition of papal nuncios, the task of managing relations
between governments and particular churches being handed to
the presidents of bishops' conferences.[28]

One can well understand why Father Dossetti would not have
been the favourite priest in the corridors of the Vatican. But that
was 1978. Why are the attacks on the *History* and on the 'Bologna
School' in general continuing so vigorously today? Perhaps one
clue lies in the fact that, in 2004, Alberigo published a small
volume celebrating the golden jubilee of the Institute's

---

28. Sandro Magister, 'For the Renewal of the Pope's Service to the
    Church: The First Hundred Days' (www.chiesa.expressonline.it/
    english for 15 November 2007). For the Italian text, see the volume
    mentioned in the next footnote.

establishment, which includes the full text of Dossetti's memorandum, which might still prove useful at a future conclave.[29]

Subsistit in and a new Novatianism

In the run-up to the first Vatican Council, John Henry Newman deplored the spirit of nervous and narrowing papalism emanating from Rome:

> I view with equanimity [he wrote to a friend in November 1866] the prospect of a thorough routing out of things at Rome – not till some great convulsions take place (which may go on for years and years, and where I can do neither good nor harm) and religion is felt to be in the midst of trials, red-tapism will go out of Rome, and a better spirit come in, and Cardinals and Archbishops will have some of the reality they had, amid many abuses, in the middle ages.[30]

'We are', he went on, 'sinking into a sort of Novationism [*sic*], the heresy which the early Popes so strenuously resisted ... we are shrinking into ourselves, narrowing the lines of communion, trembling at freedom of thought'.[31] There is something perceptive to the point of the prophetic in Newman's connection of nervous Roman 'red-tapism' with the diminishing 'reality' of episcopal office.

Thus, in our own day, the pope and senior members of the Curia, while they fulminate against those who appeal to the 'spirit' of the Council to the neglect of its texts, set to work narrowing the construal of those texts. 'What often emerged', from the process of debate at the Council, Joseph Komonchak reminds us, was 'a decision not to resolve a disputed issue, but to leave it for further theological or canonical clarification. This happened, for example, with the disputed question about Scripture and Tradition and with the relation, both in theory and in practice, between papal primacy and episcopal collegiality. This choice disappointed

---

29. See Giuseppe Alberigo (ed.), *L'Officina Bolognese, 1953–2003: Giuseppe Dossetti* (Bologna, EDB, 2004).
30. John Henry Newman, *The Letters and Diaries of John Henry Newman*, vol. xxii, ed. Charles Stephen Dessain (London, Nelson, 1972), p. 314.
31. Loc. cit. In the same letter he spoke, with strikingly outspoken imagery, of 'the gratuitous shriekings' which surround the papal throne. Novatian was condemned as a heretic in the third century because, although doctrinally quite orthodox, he refused re-admission to communion of those who had performed pagan rituals under persecution by the Emperor Decius.

some people on both sides, but there was large agreement that it was a wise policy.'[32]

Cardinal Levada's misreading of *Dei Verbum*, documented in Chapter 17, would be an example of such premature foreclosure, where the *sensus plenior* of Scripture is concerned (although, admittedly, apparently due to incompetence rather than deliberate strategic decision).

Where the tension between papalism and collegiality is concerned, we have hardly yet even *begun* to develop either the institutions or the habits of episcopal self-understanding which would enable some slackening of tension to occur through a deeper, more constructively integrative sense of the relations between the primacy and episcopacy in general: a sense and style of governance in the Catholic Church which would banish, for ever, the impression that bishops are 'vicars of the Roman Pontiff'. In this context, the issuing of the *Motu Proprio, Summorum Pontificum* would seem, as I indicated earlier, to be a quite uncalled-for act of what one might call one-sided papalism.

There are two other examples of this tendency towards narrowing or foreclosure of conciliar teaching that I wish to consider. The first concerns the sense of 'Church' in recent Roman pronouncements, and the second the attempt narrowly to interpret the statement in article 8 of *Lumen Gentium* that the Church of Christ 'subsists in' (*subsistit in*) the Catholic Church.

In September 2000, the Congregation for the Doctrine of the Faith issued a document, entitled *Dominus Jesus*, on the role of Christ and his Church in the salvation of people. Especially coming only three months after another document issued by the same Congregation, 'Note on the expression "sister churches"', *Dominus Jesus* thoroughly alarmed members of other Christian Churches, who saw it as 'ignor[ing] or even negat[ing] the progress towards reconciliation that had been made in over 30 years of ecumenical dialogue'.[33]

---

32. Komonchak, 'Dealing with Diversity and Disagreement', op. cit.
33. Francis A. Sullivan SJ, 'The Impact of Dominus Jesus on Ecumenism', *America* (28 October 2000). I cite the article from the website www.americamagazine.org. For an interestingly different account, not of the text of *Dominus Jesus*, but of reactions to it on the part of many bishops, see Peter Chirico, '*Dominus Jesus* as an Event', *America* (26 March 2001), which I cite from *America*'s website. Chirico, according to whom 'until the middle of the 1980s, bishops almost never raised their public voices in criticism of the Holy See', says of the increasing tendency of bishops, singly and in groups, to voice 'respectful but still genuine criticisms', a tendency he sees instantiated 'in the critical responses, however gentle, by bishops to *Dominus Jesus*', that 'if this trend continues, bishops will more and more

Dominus Jesus followed Vatican II in distinguishing between 'Churches' and 'ecclesial communities' (to which distinction I shall shortly turn). It then, however, went on to assert, as the Council had not done, that the ecclesial communities are 'not churches in the proper sense'.

This contention was reasserted by the Congregation in a document published in *L'Osservatore Romano* on 10 July 2007, entitled 'Responses to some Questions Regarding Certain Aspects of the Doctrine on the Church'.[34] I have no idea why this document was produced nor where the 'questions' came from. The fifth and last question reads: 'Why do the texts of the Council and those of the Magisterium since the Council not use the title of "Church" with regard to those Christian communities born out of the Reformation of the sixteenth century?'

The answer given is that, 'according to Catholic doctrine, these communities do not enjoy apostolic succession in the sacrament of orders, and are, therefore, deprived of a constitutive element of the Church'. Accordingly, these ecclesial communities 'cannot, according to Catholic doctrine, be called "Churches" in the proper sense' (the authority for the final clause being given as *Dominus Jesus*). The curious expression 'in the proper sense' does not occur in the documents of Vatican II. If a community may 'properly' be called 'ecclesial', it would seem to follow that it must, in some sense, properly be called 'Church'.

The distinction between 'Churches' and 'ecclesial communities' occurs in article 15 of *Lumen Gentium* and in the title of the third chapter of the Council's Decree on Ecumenism, *Unitatis Redintegratio*: 'Churches and Ecclesial Communities Separated from the Roman Apostolic See'. The distinction is intended, as a note on Abbott's edition of the conciliar documents puts it, to convey 'the idea that the more a Church has of the essential structures of the Catholic Church, the more it approaches the ideal of the Church'.[35]

One of the achievements of *ressourcement* at Vatican II was to create an intellectual climate in which the narrow juridicism of

act not as vicars or simple repeaters of the pope but as vicars of Christ, who collaborate in the formulation of papal teaching or in the improvement of what has already been formulated by the Vatican'. It would be a nice idea, but, on the evidence of the 2007 'Responses', there seems little evidence that the CDF is susceptible to episcopal 'improvement' of its publications.

34. The following paragraphs are adapted from my article, 'Churches Proper and Otherwise', *The Tablet* (21 July 2007), pp. 13–14.
35. *The Documents of Vatican II*, ed. Walter M. Abbott SJ (London, Geoffrey Chapman, 1966), p. 355.

neoscholastic ecclesiology was replaced by a much richer, more genuinely *theological* account of what we mean by 'Church'. It is at the heart of traditional Catholic doctrine, as recovered and expressed in the conciliar documents, that concepts central to our attempts to give expression to the mystery of God, and of God's relationships with humankind, are not reducible to the kind of tight and tidy definition with which the officials of the Congregation for the Doctrine of Faith seem most at ease.

I have long insisted that the central doctrinal achievements of Vatican II are to be found in the sequence of chapters of its two Dogmatic Constitutions, on Revelation and on the Church.

Where the latter is concerned, the subject of the first chapter is 'The Mystery of the Church'. It is a marvellous biblically and patristically rich meditation on the irreducibility of the mystery of the Church, the mystery of God's gathering of sinful scattered humankind into communion with him, to any single model, image or description.

The second chapter does, nevertheless, relatively privilege one such image or description in treating of 'the People of God'. The selection of this theme ensures that the Council's teaching on the Church is both historical and eschatological: we are a people on the way, on pilgrimage, a people whose finishing began at Calvary and at the empty tomb, but which still lies ahead of us in the consummation of the kingdom. Of central importance is the Council's treatment, in articles 13 to 16, of the theme that all of humankind is called by God to be his people, to be that gathering, that *ecclesia*, of which that which we usually call the Church is the already symbolically realised expression or (as article 1 had put it) 'sacrament'.

The account of the ways in which different kinds and conditions of people already live within this 'People's' scope runs all the way from those, 'fully incorporated into the society of the Church who, possessing the Spirit of Christ, accept her entire system and all the means of salvation given to her, and through union with her visible structure are joined to Christ' (article 14), through other Christians, 'consecrated by baptism, through which they are united to Christ', and who 'recognise and receive other sacraments within their own Churches or ecclesial communities' (article 15), and so on to Jews, Muslims, and those 'who have not yet arrived at an explicit knowledge of God, but who strive to live a good life, thanks to His grace' (article 16).

Notice especially the expressions 'possessing the Spirit of Christ' and 'thanks to His grace'. This is a description of humankind's relationship with God according to which the holy atheist is closer to being part of God's People, closer to being

'Church', than a wicked pope. The point may be obvious, but may still be worth making.

Against the sweep of these articles, it is easy to see why the late Bishop Christopher Butler was never tired of insisting that the heart of the Council's teaching on the Church was well captured in an expression of the Russian theologian Paul Evdokimov: 'We can say where the Church is, but not where she is not.'

Only in the third place, after these two doctrinally rich chapters, did the Council treat, in Chapter Three, of 'The Hierarchical Structure of the Church, with Special Reference to the Episcopate'. Structures matter. Structures, in an incarnational and sacramental dispensation, are indispensable. From the standpoint of Catholic doctrine, other Christian traditions are, in widely varying ways, structurally defective. But, according to Catholic doctrine, as represented by the Dogmatic Constitution *Lumen Gentium,* structures do not come first, or even second, but third. The Congregation claims that, with its answers to its own questions, it is 'clarifying the authentic meaning of some ecclesiological expressions', such as what it is to be, or not be, 'Church'. But to treat, for example, the distinction between 'Churches' and 'ecclesial communities' in complete abstraction from the context in which that distinction is shaped and figured by the rich teaching of the first two chapters, and to deem, without further authority than *Dominus Jesus,* that ecclesial communities cannot be called Churches 'in the proper sense', is to misrepresent the Council's teaching by narrowing the sense of 'Church' in a juridical direction.

The third of the questions to which the CDF responded on 10 July 2007 ran: 'Why was the expression "*subsists in*" adopted instead of the simple word "*is*"?' The reply was:

> The use of the expression, which indicates the full identity of the Church of Christ with the Catholic Church, does not change the doctrine on the Church. Rather, it comes from and brings out more clearly the fact that there are 'numerous elements of sanctification and of truth' which are found outside her structure, but which 'as gifts properly belonging to the Church of Christ, impel towards Catholic unity'.[36]

'Full' identity would seem to indicate *complete* identity. Read this way, the Response would seem to be saying that the boundaries of the Church of Christ are the boundaries of the Roman Catholic Church, albeit outside her there are bits and pieces, 'elements of sanctification and of truth' to be found.

In the light of the 'Responses', the same question was put, on

36. The two phrases quoted are from *Lumen Gentium,* art. 8.

9 November 2007, by Sandro Magister, to Archbishop Amato, the Secretary of the CDF. He responded:

> This change of terms is not, and cannot be interpreted as, a rupture with the past. In Latin, '*subsistit in*' is a stronger form of '*est*'. The continuity of subsistence entails a substantial identity of essence between the Church of Christ and the Catholic Church ... But at the same time, the phrase '*subsistit in*' also expresses the fact that outside the Catholic Church there is not an absolute ecclesiastical void.[37]

Even before we reach the churches of the Reformation, one can imagine how reassured the Patriarchs of Constantinople and Moscow will be to learn that they do not inhabit an 'absolute ecclesiastical void'!

'Is not, and cannot be interpreted as, a rupture with the past.' We have been here before. One almost has the impression that Archbishop Amato is less interested in expounding what the Council taught than in insisting that it did *not* teach anything different from what had been taught before. It is as if the teaching of Vatican II is either *identical* with what was taught before or there has been a 'rupture'. It does not appear to have occurred to him that the Church might have *learnt* something – about itself, and about other Christian churches and communities. It does not, in other words, appear to have occurred to him that, guided by the Spirit, doctrine might have, shall we say, developed?

Amato's language is somewhat vaguer than that of the Response: what precisely does 'substantial identity of essence' mean? And ' "*subsistit in*" is a stronger form of "*est*" ' certainly seems to suggest that *Lumen Gentium* sought to reinforce, rather than in any way qualify, the claim that (as I put it just now) the boundaries of the Church of Christ are the boundaries of the Roman Catholic Church.

This is certainly the view of Karl Becker sj, professor emeritus at the Pontifical Gregorian University and, for 20 years, a consultor to the Congregation for the Doctrine of Faith. In the Conclusion of a lengthy, richly documented article published in *Osservatore Romano* in December 2005, he insists:

> [1] The Church of Christ in all its fullness is and remains for ever the Catholic Church. Before, during and after the Council this was, is and will remain the teaching of the Catholic Church. [2] There are present in other Christian communities elements of truth and sanctification that are

37. Sandro Magister, www.chiesa, 9 November 2007.

proper to the Catholic Church and which impel towards unity with it.[38]

The 1963 draft of the Constitution on the Church said (as had the first draft the previous year) that 'The Church of Christ is [*est*] the Catholic Church' whereas the text approved in 1964 had, not '*est*' but '*subsistit in*'. Becker's thesis is that 'the change from *est* to *subsistit in* does not mean that Vatican II ever abandoned or even weakened its original assertion of total identity between the Church of Christ and the Catholic Church'.[39]

Francis Sullivan SJ, a long-time colleague of Becker's at the Gregorian, does not agree. He agrees with Becker that, out of three possible meanings of the phrase, as used in *Lumen Gentium* the phrase '*subsistit in*' means 'remains', 'is perpetuated'.[40] Becker had noticed that it was the formidable secretary of the Doctrine Commission, Sebastian Tromp SJ, who had 'suggested using *subsistit in* to express the relationship between the Church of Christ and the Catholic Church', on which Sullivan comments:

> I am sure that anyone who knew Tromp as a colleague, as I myself did, would agree that he would not have changed his mind about the total identity between the Church of Christ and the Catholic Church. The question, however, is whether the doctrinal commission that accepted his suggestion, and the council that approved the change from *est* to *subsistit in*, understood it to mean what Tromp insisted it had to mean.[41]

38. *L'Osservatore Romano* (5–6 December 2005), pp. 5–7. The English translation, originally published in the weekly English edition of *L'Osservatore Romano* of 14 December 2005, was printed in *Origins* 35.31 (19 January 2006), pp. 514–22. I have taken it from the version of that translation provided by the Eternal Word Television Network at www.ewtn.com.

39. Francis A. Sullivan SJ, 'Quaestio Disputata: A Response to Karl Becker SJ on the Meaning of *Subsistit in*', *Theological Studies*, 67 (2006), pp. 395–409, 397.

40. The excluded senses are 'is realised in' and 'subsists ontologically' because, as the scholastics used the term, what subsists must exist in itself, not in another (see Sullivan, 'Quaestio Disputata', op. cit., p. 396).

41. Sullivan, 'Quaestio Disputata', op. cit., p. 399. According to notes made at the time by Yves Congar and Otto Semmelroth, it was the formidable Father Tromp who, without any authorisation, and to the fury of the doctrine commission, removed the word 'dogmatic' from the title of *Lumen Gentium*. It was soon replaced. See Joseph Komonchak, 'Towards an Ecclesiology of Communion', *History of Vatican II*, vol. iv, pp. 1–93, 42.

That the Doctrine Commission did not agree with Tromp is suggested by the fact that the draft which incorporated the change also spoke, for the first time in conciliar history, of ' "Churches" and "ecclesiastical communities" that are found outside the Catholic Church'.[42] Becker maintains that no reason for the change was ever given but, as Sullivan points out, the Doctrine Commission explained that the change was made 'so that the expression might be in better accord with the statement about the ecclesial elements that are present elsewhere', and he suggests that the key word here is 'ecclesial'.[43]

Noting that 'Vatican II nowhere said that outside the Catholic Church there are *only* elements of the church', Sullivan also points out that, in the discussion of proposed amendments, 'The commission said that to return to *est* would give the text a restrictive meaning. Therefore they understood *subsistit in* to be less restrictive.' He therefore suggests that 'what motivated the approval of the change from *est* to *subsistit in* was that it would make it possible for the council to acknowledge the fact that outside the Catholic Church there are not only elements of the Church, but that there are churches and ecclesial communities.'[44]

These may seem distant details and yet on them depends the very heart of the doctrinal achievement of Vatican II, where the self-understanding of Catholic Christianity is concerned, a self-understanding which the Congregation for the Doctrine of Faith seems set to erode or undermine. Father Tromp seems to be having his finest hour 30 years after his death in 1975.

The most depressing feature of the present stage in the 'struggle' for the Council is the extent to which the 'non-historical orthodoxy' – the view, to put it polemically, that doctrine *has* no history, because nothing ever changes; there is only either repetition or error – from which we thought that Vatican II had set us free, is now presented, especially in Rome, as Catholic orthodoxy, while accounts of what actually *happened* at a General Council and of the impact of what happened on the Church at large are regarded as dangerously subversive.

The return of the Unreformed Missal

Peter Chirico recalls

> being astounded at an event that occurred in the fall of 1984, when representatives of the English-speaking countries of the

---

42. Sullivan, 'Quaestio Disputata', op. cit., p. 400.
43. Ibid., p. 401; Komonchak, on the other hand, stresses 'are present'.
44. Ibid., pp. 408, 402.

world were assembled in Rome for a meeting. During that meeting, one of the Roman congregations issued a decree that permitted residential bishops to authorize the celebration of the Tridentine Mass. The representatives of the English-speaking countries promptly issued a document objecting to the congregation's decree, since it opposed the will of 98 percent of the bishops of the world.[45]

The decree in question was the Indult, *Quattuor Abhinc Annos*, sent from the Congregation for Divine Worship to the presidents of all episcopal conferences, on 3 October 1984. In 1980, 'the bishops of the whole Church' had been asked to report on the way in which the Missal of 1970 was being received and 'concerning possible resistance that may have arisen'. On the basis of their replies, 'it appeared that the problem of priests and faithful holding to the so-called "Tridentine" rite was almost completely solved'. However, since then, the Congregation went on, 'the same problem continues', and John Paul II has therefore decided to allow bishops to permit the use of the 1962 Missal, under certain conditions.[46]

It would seem that 'the problem' consisted mostly in Archbishop Lefebvre and his followers, for on 2 July 1988 Pope John Paul II issued a *Motu Proprio, Ecclesia Dei*, which declares the archbishop and four of his colleagues to be excommunicate, and establishes a Commission

> whose task it will be to collaborate with the bishops, with the Departments of the Roman Curia and with the circles concerned, for the purpose of facilitating full ecclesial communion of priests, seminarians, religious communities or individuals until now linked in various ways to the Fraternity founded by Mons. Lefebvre, who may wish to remain united to the Successor of Peter in the Catholic Church, while preserving their spiritual and liturgical traditions, in the light of the Protocol signed on 5 May last by Cardinal Ratzinger and Mons. Lefebvre.[47]

Whatever the prudence and propriety of issuing the 1984 Indult in the teeth, it would seem, of the advice of most of the world's bishops, the steps taken then and in 1988 were clearly intended to deal with a serious practical problem. With the *Motu Proprio, Summorum Pontificum*, of 7 July 2007, the situation is entirely

45. Chirico, '*Dominus Jesus* as an Event', op. cit.
46. See the English translation of the Indult, published in the English edition of *L'Osservatore Romano* for 22 October 1984.
47. From the website of the Holy See.

different. According to Benedict XVI's letter accompanying the *Motu Proprio*, the desire for more widespread use of the Missal of 1962 'occurred above all because in many places celebrations were not faithful to the prescriptions of the new Missal'.

'Look', says Archbishop Ranjith:

> I don't want to criticize the Novus Ordo. But I have to laugh when I hear it said, even by friends, that in some parish, a priest is a 'saint' because of his homily or how well he speaks. Holy Mass is sacrifice, gift, mystery, independently of the priest celebrating it. It is important, nay rather, fundamental that the priest step aside: the protagonist of the Mass is Christ. So I really don't understand these Eucharistic celebrations turned into shows with dances, songs or applause, as frequently happens with the Novus Ordo.[48]

On this helpful gloss on the papal letter, some comments are in order. In the first place, it is increasingly said that use of the unreformed Missal of 1962 is a remedy for abuses of the Missal of 1970. Not only do I fail to understand why the appropriate remedy for misuses of the Novus Ordo should not be its better use, I see no reason whatsoever for supposing the unreformed Missal to be more conducive to reverence than that of 1970. In another interview, Archbishop Ranjith associates the Novus Ordo with 'banalisation' and the unreformed missal with 'mysticism'.[49]

In late 1944, I used regularly to serve Mass celebrated by the parish priest of Fleet, in Hampshire. It was his invariable custom, during the recitation of the Canon, to hoick up his alb, remove a silver snuff-box, noisily inhale a pinch, replace the box and resume the Eucharistic Prayer. So much for mysticism. I have seen strange things happen liturgically since the Council, but have never yet come across a priest smoking a cigarette during the Canon.

During my life, I have taken part in celebrations, using both Missals, of great reverence, dignity and beauty. I have also endured some casualness and many dreadful hymns, although the behaviour which Archbishop Ranjith deplores does not seem any *more* irreverent than the 'twenty-minute mutters' which were by no means unusual in my youth.

It is, perhaps, the question of what counts as reverence which

---

48. For the source of this translation of the archbishop's remarks, see note 18 above.
49. Interview given on 15 September 2007 to Alessandro Gnocchi and Mario Palmaro in *Il Foglio*. I cite it from the translation on the website of the New Liturgical Movement (thenewliturgicalmovement. blogspot.com).

needs to be considered. Before doing so, however, I return to the Archbishop's remarks. 'It is important, nay rather, fundamental that the priest step aside: the protagonist of the Mass is Christ.' There was a strand in post-Tridentine spirituality which suggested that the more a priest, as it were, 'evacuated' his humanity, the better he represented Christ. But this, with its whiff of Docetism, is very bad theology. It is through their humanity and not through its evacuation, that the saints display the love of Christ. As Cardinal Montini, the future Paul VI, said during the debate on the liturgy in the first session of the Council, 'The Liturgy was instituted for people and not people for the Liturgy.'[50]

'What is probably the most important statement in the Constitution [*Sacrosanctum Concilium*] and the key to a rethinking of the liturgy is to be found in Article 7',[51] in the statement that, in the liturgy, 'public worship is performed by the Mystical Body of Jesus Christ, that is, by the Head and his members'. As I argued in Chapter 15, one of the most momentous achievements of the Council was the shift of eucharistic *agency* from the priest alone to the whole assembly. With the Missal of 1962, in which the congregation had no role, it did not matter in the least if nobody paid any attention to anybody else. Now it does (consider, in this context, the introduction of the sign of peace).

In deploring abuses, Archbishop Ranjith seems to have underestimated the significance of this seismic shift in agency. Before the Council, it seemed more reverent for each member of the congregation to ignore all the others, and for the priest, when he turned to face the people, to keep his eyes fixed on the carpet. Now, this is just bad manners.

In the rubrics of the 1962 Missal, the people have nothing to do, because they are not celebrating Mass, but simply 'attending' it. According to the ethos which this rite fostered, reverence came to be construed as the solitary concentration of each individual – priest or person in the pew – on the mystery of God. The Missal of 1970 requires reverence to have, as it were, a horizontal as well as a vertical dimension. We do not attend to God in *spite* of each other, but with and in each other. Belloc had it about right:

> Of Courtesy, it is much less
> Than Courage of Heart or Holiness,
> Yet in my Walks it seems to me
> That the Grace of God is in Courtesy.

50. Matthijs Lamberigts, 'The Liturgy Debate', *History of Vatican II*, vol. ii, pp. 107–66, 114. The translation has 'men', but I presume that Montini said '*homines*' and not '*viri*'.
51. Kaczynski, 'Toward the Reform of the Liturgy', op. cit., p. 223.

It is time to return to Pope Benedict's letter. The 1962 Missal, he insists, 'was never juridically abrogated and, consequently, in principle, was always permitted'. I am no canon lawyer but, if this is the case, one wonders why *Quattuor Abhinc Annos* was ever issued. 'There is no contradiction', the Pope insists, 'between the two editions of the Roman Missal. In the history of the liturgy there is growth and progress, but no rupture.[52] What earlier generations held as sacred, remains sacred and great for us too, and it cannot be all of a sudden entirely forbidden or even considered harmful.'

We are now, it seems to me, near the heart of the issues raised by the publication of *Summorum Pontificum*. A General Council of the Church decided that a major reform of the liturgy was needed. The ground had been prepared, during the previous decades, by the excellent historical, theological and pastoral work done in the liturgical movement, especially in Europe. The debate in the first session of the Council gave a good idea of the enthusiasm that there was for such reform but, even so, the vote on the draft schema, on 14 November 1962, came as a surprise: 2162 votes in favour and 46 against.[53]

It is certainly possible to argue, as many have done, that some of the work done, after the Council, to implement *Sacrosanctum Concilium*, was not well done; that the Missal of 1970 made changes far more radical than anything envisaged by the Council, and made them far too rapidly. But the passage in the Pope's letter seems to imply that no reform was needed: what else can he mean by 'What earlier generations held as sacred, remains great and sacred for us too'? It begins to seem as if the logic behind *Summorum Pontificum* is that the Latin Church has two versions of the Mass, one 'Ordinary', the other 'Extraordinary', but both of them equally good and equally splendid.

'In conclusion, dear Brothers', says Pope Benedict, 'I very much wish to stress that these new norms do not in any way lessen your own authority and responsibility, either for the liturgy or for the pastoral care of your faithful. Each Bishop, in fact, is the moderator of the liturgy in his own Diocese.' A reassurance rather hard to square with article 2 of the *Motu Proprio*, according to which, if a priest wishes to celebrate *sine populo* (what used to be called, bizarrely, saying a 'private' Mass) using the Missal of 1962, 'he does not require any permission, neither from the Apostolic See, nor his own Ordinary'. Stranger still, article 4 says that 'even

---

52. Here we go again!
53. See Lamberigts, 'The Liturgy Debate', op. cit., p. 149. The following year, on 4 December 1963, the Constitution *Sacrosanctum Concilium*, was approved with 2147 voting in favour and 4 against.

Christ's faithful who spontaneously request it', may be admitted to such celebrations. In which case, they surely cease to be celebrations *sine populo.*

> Great is the confusion! Who can still see clearly in this darkness? Where in our church are the leaders who can show us the right path? Where are the bishops courageous enough to cut out the cancerous growth of modernist theology that has implanted itself and is festering within the celebration of even the most sacred mysteries before the cancer spreads and causes even greater damage? ... We can only hope and pray that the Roman Church will return to Tradition and allow once more that liturgy of the Mass which is well over 1,000 years old.[54]

That is the voice of Klaus Gamber, a very learned liturgical historian, passionately opposed to the Missal of 1970 in general and to Mass celebrated facing the people (which he believed entirely lacking in historical warrants) in particular.[55] His study *The Reform of the Roman Liturgy* was published in 1981, the French translation appearing in 1992 and the English in 1993.[56] A 'Testimonial' by Mgr Wilhelm Nyssen tells us that 'Recently, Cardinal Ratzinger described Klaus Gamber as "the one scholar who, among the army of pseudo-liturgists, truly represents the liturgical thinking of the center of the Church".'[57]

54. Klaus Gamber, *The Reform of the Roman Liturgy. Its Problems and Background* (San Juan Capistrano, Una Voce Press, 1993), pp. 113–14.
55. Although the ground of his opposition to Mass facing the people is ostensibly historical (discussion of the matter takes up 56 out of 193 pages in his book), it is also rooted in poor theology and suspicion of Protestantism: 'Most significant, however, is the shifting of emphasis in the new Mass to that of being a communal meal (celebration of the Eucharist) in the Protestant sense, the deliberate de-emphasizing of the purpose and function of the Mass as a sacrifice' (pp. 66–7). As I argued in Chapter 13, this kind of thinking confuses what we are doing at Mass with the way that, in obedience to Christ's command, we do it (see above, pp. 204–5). Gamber takes it for granted that the arrangement of people and furnishings in a Catholic Church must be such that any casual observer, dropping in while Mass is going on, can see that a priest is offering a sacrifice. What would the casual observer have made of Calvary?
56. Klaus Gamber, *Die Reform der Römischen Liturgie* (Regensburg, 1981); *Le Réforme Liturgique en Question* (Le Barroux, Monastère Ste Madeleine, 1992).
57. Nyssen in Gamber, *The Reform*, op. cit., p. xiii. This statement is frequently quoted, but Nyssen gives no reference and I have not be able to find one. If Gamber is at the centre, it must be chilly at the edges!

Gamber did not advocate the abolition of the Missal of 1970, but its toleration as an experimental form (an 'extraordinary' form we might say) until it died out, which he was confident it would. He is dismissive of the much wider provision of Scripture readings in the *Novus Ordo*: 'most among the faithful do not have the necessary background and knowledge to understand, let alone appreciate, certain passages from Scripture ... they know little about salvation history prior to Christ ... therefore, there is little in the Pentateuch or in the Books of Kings that would have any real meaning to them.'[58] It comes as no surprise to him 'when "progressive" pastors carry "liturgical renewal" yet a step further, substituting for the texts taken from Scripture passages from the writings of Karl Marx and Mao Tse-Tung'.[59] He is in no doubt as to the gravity of the situation: 'Today, we are standing before the ruins of almost 2,000 years of Church tradition ... The real destruction of the traditional Roman rite with a history of more than a thousand years, is the wholesale destruction of the faith on which it was based.'[60]

'A young priest said to me recently', began the Preface to the French edition of Gamber's book, ' "What we need today is a new liturgical movement." ' Why? Because the reform of the liturgy, as it has actually occurred

> has been not a reanimation but a devastation. On the one hand, we have a liturgy degenerated into a 'show', in which people try to render religion interesting with the help of fashionable stupidities and seductive moral maxims ... One cannot 'fabricate' a liturgical movement [of the kind we need] any more than one can fabricate any living thing, but one can contribute to its development.

Such a new liturgical movement needs ' "fathers" who would serve as models ... Those in search of such "fathers" today will undoubtedly encounter Mgr Klaus Gamber, who, unhappily, was taken from us too soon.'[61] 'What happened after the Council' was not the 'liturgy which is fruit of development' advocated by Jungmann:

> one of the truly great liturgists of our century ... but something else entirely: instead of liturgy the fruit of continuous development came a fabricated liturgy ... We abandoned the growth and organic maturation of a living thing over

58. Gamber, *The Reform*, op. cit., p. 71.
59. Ibid., p. 75.
60. Ibid., pp. 95, 102.
61. Gamber died in 1989.

centuries, and replaced it – as in a manufacturing process – with a fabrication, a banal on-the-spot product.[62]

The author of this Preface was Cardinal Joseph Ratzinger.

The distinction between the 'organic' and the 'manufactured' is rhetorically very effective, but is, for two reasons, nonetheless misleading. In the first place, it gives the impression that the process of liturgical reform took place in abstraction from the sea-changes of social attitude and expectation which were, for better and for worse, occurring at the time. In the second place, the liturgy is *not* an organism, but a set of arrangements made by human beings for the public ordering of the worship of almighty God, arrangements which may be well or badly undertaken.

The 'positive reason' which 'motivated my decision to issue this *Motu Proprio*', says Pope Benedict in the letter

> is a matter of coming to an interior reconciliation in the heart of the Church. Looking back over the past, to the divisions which in the course of the centuries have rent the Body of Christ, one continually has the impression that, at critical moments when divisions were coming about, not enough was done by the Church's leaders to maintain or regain reconciliation and unity.

But *is* the Church divided? I have had the good fortune, in recent decades, to travel widely in Europe, America, Asia and Africa. I am confident that I have participated in ordinary parish Masses in a far wider variety of countries and cultures than either the Pope or

---

62. '*Un jeune prêtre me disait récemment: 'Il nous faudrait aujourd'hui un nouveau mouvement liturgique'. . . . n'a pas été une reanimation mais une devastation. D'une côté, on a une liturgie dégénérée en* show, *où l'on essaie de render la religion intéressante à l'aide de bêtises à la mode et de maxims morales aguichantes . . . On ne peut pas 'fabriquer' un mouvement liturgique de cettte sorte – pas plus qu'on ne peut 'fabriquer' quelque chose de vivant – mais on peut contribuer à son développement . . . Ce nouveau depart a besoin de 'pères' qui soient des modèles . . . Qui cherche aujourd'hui de tels 'pères' rencontrera immanquablement la personne de Mgr Klaus Gamber, qui nous a malheureusement été enlevé trop tôt . . . Ce qui s'est passé après le Concile . . . 'liturgie fruit d'un développement' . . . l'un des vraiment grands liturgists de notre siècle . . . signifie tout autre chose: à la place de la liturgy fruit d'un développement continu, on a mis une liturgy fabriquée . . . On n'a plus voulu continuer le devenir et la maturation organiques du vivant à travers les siècles, et l'on les a remplacés – à la manière de la production technique – par une fabrication, produit banal de l'instant'.* When Archbishop Ranjith speaks of 'banalisation', and of Mass celebrated with the new Missal as a 'show', he speaks, it seems, with his master's voice.

the late Mgr Gamber.[63] The nightmare vision expressed by Archbishop Ranjith, Mgr Gamber and Cardinal Ratzinger (and Benedict XVI?) of a Church divided between those desperate for the return of the unreformed Missal and those who interrupt their weekly knees-up to listen to readings from *Das Kapital* leaves out of account the experience of (at a rough guess) 95 per cent of the Catholic Church, in which the *Novus Ordo* is regularly used with reverence, dignity and gratitude.

Reception and remembering

Stephen Dessain, Newman's tireless archivist, died in 1976, a week before he was due to preach a retreat to the Oratory of France. Here is an extract from the materials for that retreat:

> at the Second Vatican Council the tides of clericalism, over-centralisation, creeping infallibility, narrow unhistorical theology and exaggerated mariology were thrown back, while the things Newman stood for were brought forward – freedom, the supremacy of conscience, the Church as a communion, a return to Scripture and the fathers, the rightful place of the laity, work for unity, and all the efforts to meet the needs of the age, and for the Church to take its place in the modern world. Any disarray or confusion there may now be in the Church is the measure of how necessary this renewal was.[64]

Thirty years later, many of the boxes ticked by Dessain may stay that way, but some cannot: 'over-centralisation' and 'creeping infallibility' pose, if anything, an even greater threat now than they did then (anyone doubting this should remember Cardinal Ratzinger's attempt, in 1995, to attach the label of infallibility to John Paul II's announcement that the Church had no authority to ordain women). Not only does the coagulation of power at the centre frustrate the ability of the episcopate to recover a proper sense of episcopal authority and the development of appropriate structures and instruments of collegial governance, but it has greatly weakened the recognition of the indispensability of the *sensus fidelium*.

On 24 July 1870, Newman wrote to a friend:

63. The Pope became a Cardinal in 1978. Masses with a Cardinal are not ordinary.
64. C. S. Dessain, *Newman's Spiritual Themes* (Dublin, 1977), p. 30. See Nicholas Lash, 'Tides and Twilight: Newman since Vatican II', *Newman after a Hundred Years*, ed. Ian Ker and Alan G. Hill (Oxford, Clarendon Press, 1990), pp. 447–64, 460.

I saw the new Definition yesterday, and am pleased at its moderation, if the doctrine in question is to be defined at all ... And further, if the definition is eventually received by the whole body of the faithful, as valid or as the expression of a truth, then too it will claim our assent by the force of the great dictum, '*Securus judicat orbis terrarum.*'[65]

Saint Augustine's motto against the Donatists: 'the verdict of the whole world is conclusive', was central to Newman's understanding of the doctrine of the *reception* of Church teaching by the people of God.[66] 'Some power', he wrote in 1875, 'is needed to determine the general sense of authoritative words – to determine their direction, drift, limits, and comprehension, to hinder gross perversions. This power is virtually the *passive infallibility* of the whole body of the Catholic people.'[67]

I suggested, at the end of Chapter 15, the kind of institutional steps that are necessary if the massive redistribution of power in the Church which we so urgently need is to get under way. It has been the argument of this chapter that, central to the struggle for the Council, is the struggle for the *memory* of what happened in and to the Catholic Church between 1962 and 1965. It seems appropriate to give the final word to Giuseppe Alberigo:

the most striking innovation of Vatican II lies not in any of its *formulations* but rather in the very fact that it was convoked and held. From this point of view the Council was a point of no return; the conciliar age has begun again and has found a very important place in the consciousness of the Church. It is impossible to imagine a politically more skilful and more effective 'normalization' of the Council and of the impulse it has given to the Church than *through a refusal to admit the epoch-making significance of its occurrence.* That would be a way of emptying out its meaning, which, while avoiding its brusk rejection by the traditionalists, would bury it in the normality of the post-Tridentine period.[68]

65. John Henry Newman, *Letters and Diaries of John Henry Newman*, vol. xxv, ed. Charles Stephen Dessain and Thomas Gornall SJ (Oxford, Clarendon Press, 1973), pp. 164–5.

66. For brief discussion of reception as a criterion of authentic doctrinal development, see Nicholas Lash, *Newman on Development: The Search for an Explanation in History* (London, Sheed and Ward, 1975), pp. 134–7.

67. Newman, *Letters and Diaries*, vol. xxvii, ed. Charles Stephen Dessain and Thomas Gornall SJ (Oxford, Clarendon Press, 1975), p. 338; his stress.

68. Giuseppe Alberigo, 'Transition to a New Age', *History of Vatican II*, vol. v (Leuven, Peeters, 2006), pp. 573–652, 643. For the two phrases

He went on:

> The frequent emphasis here on the importance of Vatican II
> as a total event and not solely for its formal decisions may
> have led some readers to suspect the intention of playing
> down the documents approved by the Council. It would seem
> hardly necessary to remove such a suspicion ... It would be
> paradoxical to imagine or fear that recognition of the
> importance of Vatican II as a global event could reduce or
> lessen the importance of the Council's documents.[69]

that I have italicised, Matthew O'Connell's translation has: 'And yet
the most important novelty of Vatican II did not consist in its new
formulations ... than to deny its epochal significance'. The Italian
has: '*Eppure la novita piu significativa del Vaticano II non e costituita da
queste formulazioni ... che negarne il significato epocale*' (*Storia del Concilio
Vaticano II*, Vol. 5 [Bologna, 2001], p. 646). 'Novelty' seems to me too
trivial a term, in English, for the point that is being made. I am most
grateful to Professor Robin Kirkpatrick for his help.
69. Loc. cit.

Index